CINDERELLA
SOLDIERS

CINDERELLA SOLDIERS

THE IRISH IN LIVERPOOL
IN THE GREAT WAR

COLIN COUSINS

First published 2019

The History Press
The Mill, Brimscombe Port
Stroud, Gloucestershire, GL5 2QG
www.thehistorypress.co.uk

British Library Cataloguing in Publication Data.
A catalogue record for this book is available from the British Library.

ISBN 978 0 7509 9124 7

Typesetting and origination by The History Press
Printed and bound in Great Britain by TJ International Ltd.

CONTENTS

Acknowledgements 7

List of tables 9

List of maps 10

List of abbreviations 11

Preface 12

Introduction 15

1 Liverpool 1914: Division, Recruitment and Unity 27

2 Trench Life, Patrols and Raids 51

3 Officers, Men and Morale 72

4 Discipline and Leadership 104

5 Battlefronts: Givenchy, the Somme and Passchendaele 133

6 Kultur and Captivity 168

7 Homefront 195

Appendix 1 215

Appendix 2 217

Appendix 3 224

Bibliography 231

Endnotes 241

Index 269

ACKNOWLEDGEMENTS

My first debt is to Mr George Wilson whose interest in the battalion precedes my own by more than twenty years. Throughout that period, George amassed a vast dossier on the battalion, comprising details of individual soldiers of the Liverpool (Irish) Battalion stretching from the Boer War to beyond the end of the Great War. I met George by way of a highly speculative enquiry to a London auction house. Since then he has been extremely generous in sharing his research material and invaluable expertise on the battalion. George had intended to write his own account of the battalion, and the fact that he was willing to share his research with someone he did not know is a remarkable testimony of his trust and generosity. I am indebted to George for his kind permission to use many of the sources from his research and to reproduce many of the images within his private collection.

I am grateful to the staff of the following institutions for their help and kind permission to use the sources and to reproduce many of the images contained in this book. In London: The National Archives, for permission to reproduce Haig's Routine Order, the Imperial War Museum and for their kind permission to reproduce the images of the Western Front contained in this book. To the National Portrait Gallery, for their kind permission to reproduce the photograph of Brigadier-General Fagan; The Institution of Engineering and Technology Archives for permission to use the image of Lieutenant H.L. Downes and Aberdeen University Museums and Special Collections for permission to use the image of Captain J.E. Milne. I am also grateful to the staff of Liverpool Central Library and to St Helens Library, for their kind permission to reproduce the recruiting poster of the Liverpool Irish; the Wellcome Archives, Army Medical Museum, Aldershot, and the Wolfson Centre at Birmingham Library. My thanks are also due to the staff at the National Library of Ireland, University College Dublin and the Bureau of Military History, Dublin. Further afield, I am indebted to the Australian War Museum for their permission to reproduce the image of

Private Lambert and to the International Committee Red Cross, Prisoners of the First World War Archives.

I am much indebted and grateful to the following copyright holders for their kind permission to use photographs, letters and diaries: Tom Fisher for his kind permission to quote from the George Tomlinson papers and to reproduce George's photograph; Mr Ian McIntosh, for his permission to use the James Green papers; Patricia Normanly, Dublin, for permission to use Private James Jenkins' photograph and background information. I am also very grateful to Mrs Anne Hayton, for the Moynihan papers and photograph of Lieutenant Moynihan; M. Geerhard Joos, Brent Whittam and Terry Heard, at https://www.ww1cemeteries.com, for their assistance concerning war graves and for Geerhard's kind permission to use his photograph of Private Joseph Brennan's grave; to the Headmaster of Stonyhurst College for his kind permission to use the photograph of Captain H.M. Finegan. I am also grateful to Joe Devereux and Kath Donaldson, Liverpool, for their comments and knowledge of Liverpool soldiers during the Great War. I had some help in preparing this book for publication and I am very grateful to Nicola Guy at The History Press, and Averill Buchanan in Belfast for her advice and for compiling the index. My gratitude is also due to Sandra Mather, formerly of Liverpool University, for her cartographic skills in producing the maps contained in this book. All maps in this book are the copyright of Sandra Mather.

My final debt is to my wife Linda for her long-suffering indulgence of my fascination with the Great War. Hopefully, the fact that this book relates to her native city is of some minor consolation.

LIST OF TABLES

Table 1 Irish-born residents of Liverpool 1841–91 17

Table 1.1 Home districts of 100 men enlisted in the 8th (Irish) Battalion, King's Liverpool Regiment 39

Table 1.2 Occupations of 100 men of the 8th Liverpool (Irish) Battalion, King's Liverpool Regiment 40

Table 1.3 Home districts of 100 men enlisted in the 8th (Irish) Battalion, King's Liverpool Regiment 41

Table 1.4 Occupations of 100 men of the 8th Liverpool (Irish) Battalion, King's Liverpool Regiment 42

Table 3.1 Summary of accidental and self-inflicted casualties, 55th (West Lancashire) Division, February–July 1916 99

Table 4.1 Death sentences passed on soldiers of the 8th (Irish), Battalion, King's Liverpool Regiment, 1914–1918 110

Table 4.2 Disciplinary record Private Joseph Brennan 111

Table 4.3 Total number of death sentences passed and number of executions in all battalions of the King's Liverpool Regiment 1914–18 126

Table 4.4 Total number of offences tried by Field General Courts Martial for all battalions of the King's Liverpool Regiment 19 May 1915–21 September 1916 128

Table 5.1 Somme battle casualties for three battalions of 55th (West Lancashire) Division, 27 July–29 September 1916 152

Table 6.1 Strength of British Army and total numbers of British soldiers killed in action and prisoners of war, 1914,1916 and 1918 173

LIST OF MAPS

Map 1   Electoral Districts of Liverpool *c.*1900   14

Map 2   The dispositions of the 55th Division at Blaireville
prior to the trench raid by the Liverpool Irish on
17/18th April 1916   65

Map 3   The objective of the Liverpool Irish at Rue D'Ouvert,
16 June 1915   137

Map 4   Artillery map of Guillemont on the Somme indicating
the dispositions of 164th and 165th Infantry Brigades on
8 August 1916   149

Map 5   Battle of Pilckhem Ridge. Map showing the objectives
of the 55th Division 31 July–2 August 1917   159

Map 6   Compiled from hand-drawn sketch detailing the
topography and events around the areas of Schuler
and Wurst Farms 31 July–2 August 1917   165

LIST OF ABBREVIATIONS

ASC	Army Service Corps
BEF	British Expeditionary Force
BMH	Bureau of Military History
Capt.	Captain
CCS	Casualty Clearing Station
CO	Commanding Officer
Col.	Colonel
Coy	Company
Cpl.	Corporal
CPWHC	Central Prisoners of War Help Committee
CSM	Company Sergeant Major
CQMS	Company Quartermaster Sergeant
CYMS	Catholic Young Men's Society
DCM	Distinguished Conduct Medal
DCM	District Court Martial
DSO	Distinguished Service Order
DOW	Died of Wounds
FGCM	Field General Court Martial
FP	Field Punishment
GCM	General Court Martial
GHQ	General Headquarters
GOC	General Officer Commanding
GSW	Gun Shot Wound
INV	Irish National Volunteers
IPP	Irish Parliamentary Party
IRB	Irish Republican Brotherhood
IWM	Imperial War Museum
KIA	Killed in Action
Lt.	Lieutenant
Lt. Col.	Lieutenant Colonel
MC	Military Cross
MIA	Missing in Action
MM	Military Medal
MO	Medical Officer
NBSP	National Brotherhood of St Patrick
NCO	Non-Commissioned Officer
OCB	Officer Cadet Battalions
OTC	Officer Training Corps
POW	Prisoner of War
PWHC	Prisoners of War Help Committee
Pte	Private
RAMC	Royal Army Medical Corps
RASC	Royal Army Service Corps
RCM	Regimental Court Martial
Sgt.	Sergeant
TNA	The National Archives
UVF	Ulster Volunteer Force
VC	Victoria Cross
VD	Venereal Disease

PREFACE

The 'national amnesia' surrounding Ireland's participation in the Great War has undergone an extensive period of rehabilitation throughout the last decades of the twentieth century. Sadly, the wartime experiences of Irish exiles in Britain have been ignored and neglected. This is certainly true in respect of Liverpool's massive Irish population.

The Irish contribution to military life in Liverpool emerged in 1860 with the creation of the Volunteer movement in the city. Originally designated as the 64th Liverpool Irish Volunteer Corps, their creation came about just thirteen years after the great influx from famine-stricken Ireland. Between its creation and the Great War, the popularity of Liverpool's part-time Irish soldiers endured a series of peaks and troughs which were closely aligned to events in Ireland or related to the sectarianism of their host city. While most British Army regiments or battalions enjoyed close relationships with their native towns and cities, the Liverpool Irish part-time soldiers had an inextricable ethnic affinity with the north end of Liverpool and Ireland itself. In attempting to recover the narrative of the 8th (Irish) Battalion during the Great War, it has been impossible to sever the ethnic and social bonds which attached the battalion to its Celtic enclaves and Ireland.

Occupying 'a curious middle place', the Irish in nineteenth-century Liverpool were at once exiled from their native country and ostracised within their host city. Located in the north end of Liverpool, they constituted an isolated Celtic residuum whereby they could live in the city and yet remained apart from it. They inhabited the courts and cellars of Scotland Road and its environs which prior to their arrival had been deemed as unfit even for the city's slum dwellers. The Irish propensity for drinking and fighting invited newspapers and journals to portray them as filthy, drunken and violent. Second and third generations of Liverpool Irish, reared within the city's Irish enclaves, still identified themselves as Irish despite never having visited their ancestral island. The fact that they had been born in Liverpool was immaterial, as

Liverpool's Irish children were immersed in a patriotic Celtic culture and became 'sternly Irishised'. During the virulent 'No Popery' campaign, their Catholic faith became synonymous with their Irishness. Nationalist uprisings in Ireland in 1798 and 1848 and the Fenian scares of the 1860s tainted the Liverpool Irish with suspicions of disloyalty. Sectarian clashes and political tensions surrounding the Home Rule crisis in the years leading up to the Great War meant that Liverpool, like Belfast, was a divided city.

Following the declaration of war in August 1914, as a territorial unit, the 8th (Irish) Battalion, King's Liverpool Regiment could have opted for Home Service; instead, they volunteered to fight abroad. When the good people of Liverpool rallied to supply the city's fighting men with comforts, the local press reminded them that many of the Liverpool Irishmen came from impoverished backgrounds and therefore did not receive as many comforts as those serving in middle-class units; the papers declared that there should be no 'Cinderella battalion' in Liverpool.

This book is an attempt to recover the story of how the Liverpool Irish and their Cinderella soldiers endured the Great War.

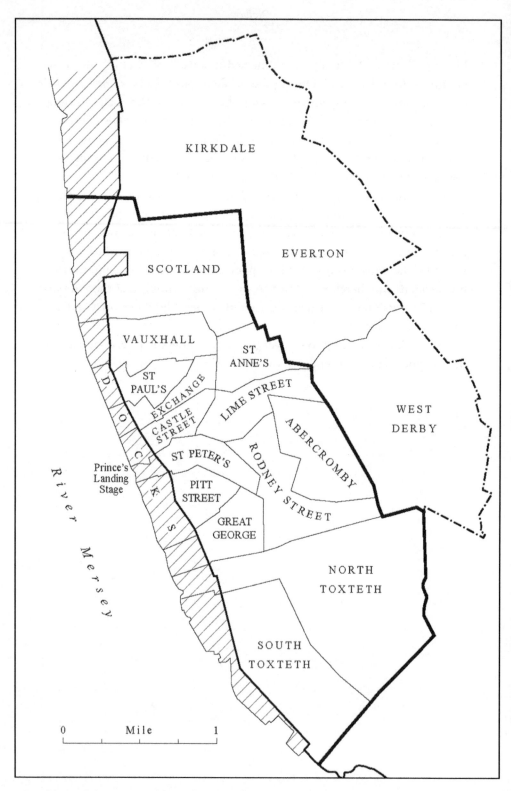

KIRKDALE

EVERTON

SCOTLAND

VAUXHALL

ST ANNE'S

ST PAUL'S

EXCHANGE

CASTLE STREET

LIME STREET

ABERCROMBY

WEST DERBY

River Mersey

D O C K S

Prince's Landing Stage

ST PETER'S

PITT STREET

RODNEY STREET

GREAT GEORGE

NORTH TOXTETH

SOUTH TOXTETH

0   Mile   1

Map 1: Electoral Districts of Liverpool *c.*1900.

INTRODUCTION

The Irish in Liverpool: The Social and Political Background

The popularity of Liverpool as the location of choice among Irish migrants is evident even in the years prior to the famine influx of 1847. In 1841, the city had an Irish-born population of nearly 50,000. It was during the following decade, with the devastation caused by the Irish potato blight and resultant hunger and destitution, that the numbers of Irish-born inhabitants in Liverpool escalated to nearly a quarter of the total population. Wealthy nineteenth-century-Liverpool justifiably wallowed in civic pride; it was, after all, a thriving port and a centre of trade and commerce where the sweat, clamour and commotion of the docks contrasted with the halcyon atmosphere of the nearby business districts. Liverpool was also a city of contrasting sobriquets; it was known as 'the Second City of the Empire',[1] and the 'gateway to America'.[2] It was also, rather less obsequiously, described as 'the black spot on the Mersey'[3] and 'the cemetery of Ireland'.[4] A more recent and unflattering depiction of the city has been provided by the historian Don Akenson in *An Irish History of Civilization: Volume two*.[5] Akenson, an eminent scholar on the history of the Irish diaspora, described mid-nineteenth century Liverpool as a 'machine'. Akenson's description (written, one suspects, with his tongue firmly in his cheek), stresses the important and significant role played by Liverpool in processing the multitudes of migrant Irish: 'Liverpool in 1851 is second only to Dublin and Belfast in the number of Irish-born inhabitants. Some machine. Necessary. No one loved Liverpool, but if the devil had not invented it, some god would have had to.' Many of the poorest migrants who left Ireland during the nineteenth century brought very little with them. They did, however, bring their poverty, their Irishness, their religion and politics. It was these characteristics which would unwittingly lead to conflict and half a century of tension and discord in their host city.

The geographical convenience of Liverpool across the Irish Sea, the expansion of its port, the growth of commercialism within the city and the development of steam-powered ships during the first quarter of the nineteenth century combined to make Liverpool an attractive destination for the disenchanted Irish.[6] Whether reluctant migratory agricultural workers, labourers in search of work, or willing professional 'micks on the make',[7] the Irish made their way to Britain to remain, or to board other ships bound for America or Australia. While economic necessity may well have been a significant factor compelling some to leave Ireland, hunger and destitution did not induce the Irish to cross the Irish Sea in the years before the famine. For the starving thousands of 1847 who had survived the trek from their rural homesteads to the Irish ports and endured the cramped conditions on their voyage across the Irish Sea, further challenges awaited them in Liverpool.

Many of those arriving at Liverpool had been weakened by malnutrition and the journey. Once ashore, an ethnic compass led them to the north end of the city where some 30,000 were packed into filthy overcrowded cellars in the densely overpopulated districts of Scotland Road, Vauxhall Road and Great Crosshall Street. In their desperation for accommodation, the homeless Irish smashed down the doors of cellars which had been condemned as uninhabitable and sealed by the council.[8] These congested and unsanitary conditions were all that was available to the starving Irish in the 1840s. Slum housing also provided ideal conditions for the spread of diseases such as typhus, dysentery and measles. Statistics of the rates of infection were overwhelming and the city of Liverpool struggled to cope with the disaster. During 1847, some 60,000 people had been treated for typhus, while a further 40,000 suffered from dysentery and diarrhoea.[9] Around 8,500 of those 100,000 died, and Frank Neal has estimated that 5,500 of those who had died were Irish famine refugees.[10] Given the scale of the influx of famine refugees and the resulting epidemics during 1847, it is morbidly fitting that the Register General of Births Deaths and Marriages described Liverpool as 'the cemetery of Ireland'.[11]

The Irish who chose to remain in Britain began their search for employment, self-fulfilment or mere survival, have been described as 'a restless, transient people.'[12] Some educated Irish immigrants moved south from Liverpool to London, or to wherever their talents were in demand. Other, unskilled workers, travelled inland through Lancashire to the manufacturing centres such as Manchester and its environs.[13] Protestant Irish migrants of the mercantile class appear to have discovered Liverpool early in the nineteenth century, unlike their less fortunate Catholic countrymen, and they possessed not only the means but the will to integrate themselves within Liverpolitan society.[14] While

Liverpool was undoubtedly a thriving port and an important centre for commerce, it lacked the major manufacturing industries of other northern English cities. Predictably, many of the low-skilled Irish settled in those areas close to the employment opportunities provided in the docks of Liverpool.[15] Thus, the Irish established themselves in the north end of Liverpool which comprised the political wards of Scotland, Vauxhall, Exchange and St Paul's.[16]

Table 1: *Irish-born residents of Liverpool 1841–91*

Year	Population	No. of Irish-born	Irish as % of the population
1841	286,656	49,639	17.3
1851	375,955	83,813	22.3
1861	443,938	83,949	18.9
1871	493,405	76,761	15.5
1891	517,980	66,071	12.6

Source: Census reports, England, 1841–91.

Once established in the north end of the city, it was inevitable that a substantial second generation of Liverpool Irish would inflate the ethno-Celtic character of the city. Frank Neal has suggested that the number of Irish-born inhabitants of Liverpool in 1833 was 24,156 and that given the census total of almost 84,000 in 1851, the number of English children born to Irish parents was 'relatively large'.[17] To many native Liverpolitans and the local press, there was no distinction between native-born Irish and their offspring who were born in the city; they were all 'Irish'.[18] Table 1 reveals that there was a total of 49,639 Irish-born residents in 1841 in Liverpool representing 17.3 per cent of the city's population. Ten years later, in 1851, the numbers of Irish-born residents rose to 83,813, representing 22.3% of the population of Liverpool. By 1891, the numbers of Irish-born inhabitants fell to 66,071. However, these figures fail to include the offspring of the Irish-born residents of the city.

When the ships unloaded their vast malnourished human cargoes at the port of Liverpool throughout 1847, it was the city rather than the government which bore the financial burden of providing relief. This meant that the costs would fall on the businessmen and rate payers of Liverpool who were far from satisfied with this arrangement.[19] In the years following the great influx, the Irish were put under a moral and social microscope where their appearance, behaviour, faith and habits were examined. Comments and reports were made in the local and national press, opinions were offered, and racial comparisons were made. Even the liberal *Liverpool Mercury* opined that the government could not 'convert a slothful, improvident and reckless race' except by means of 'indirect action' and 'gradual process'.[20] The article argued that responsibility for the famine and the cause of Irish misery lay with the Irish themselves due to their racial inadequacy: 'There is a taint of inferiority in the character of the pure Celt which has more to do with his present degradation than Saxon domination.' Racial stereotyping of the Irish continued throughout the nineteenth century. 'Paddy,' the reckless buffoon performing in the guise of a peasant or soldier, became the stock character on the London stage; he also appeared, more menacingly in cartoons as an ape. Steven Fielding concluded that, 'The fully-fledged "simianisation" of the Irish occurred during the 1860's.'[21] The physical appearance and behaviour of the Irish inhabitants of the north end of the city attracted the attention of their fellow citizens and the local press in Liverpool. In one particularly venomous attack on the Irish populace of the north end, the *Liverpool Herald* claimed that the filth, drunkenness and criminal behaviour of the Irish was due to their nationality and their 'papish' faith:

> The numberless whiskey shops crowded with drunken half-clad women, some with infants in their arms, from early dawn till midnight – thousands of children in rags, with their features scarcely to be distinguished in consequence of the cakes of dirt upon them ... And who are these wretches? Not English but Irish papists. It is remarkable and no less remarkable than true, that the lower order of Irish papists are the filthiest beings in the habitable globe, they abound in dirt and vermin and have no care for anything but self-gratification that would degrade the brute creation ... Look at our police reports, three fourths of the crime perpetrated in this large town is by Irish papists.[22]

Protestant anxieties had been heightened since the 1829 Catholic Emancipation Act. The Act, which was drafted with the intention of preventing civil war in Ireland by signalling an end of hostility towards the Catholic Church, ironically contributed to Protestant fears about Catholic influence and aggression.[23]

Few would have predicted that events in County Armagh during the late eighteenth century would influence the socio-political landscape of Liverpool up to, and beyond, the Great War. In 1795, the Orange Order emerged from a series of violent agrarian disputes which had plagued north Armagh during the last decades of the eighteenth century.[24] The two opposing factions, the Protestant Peep O'Day Boys, who supposedly derived their title from their proclivity for making early morning raids on the homes of their adversaries, and the exclusively Catholic 'Defenders', had clashed in a series of brief yet bloody encounters prior to a defining battle which took place close to the Diamond at Dan Winter's cottage near Loughgall in 1795. Having routed the Defenders, the victorious Peep O'Day boys resolved to form an organised body to protect themselves in the event of any further attacks. Thus, the Orange Order was born. Their erstwhile opponents did not disappear, rather they transformed into a secretive oath-bound society known as the Ribbonmen. Orangeism spread rapidly from its fountainhead in north Armagh to England and beyond. Donald MacRaild has suggested that the pace and distribution of the Orange Order throughout Britain was due to the migration of Ulster Protestants and militiamen returning from Ireland after the failed rebellion of 1798. Many militia units brought Orange warrants with them, which enabled them to establish lodges in their native districts.[25] The first Orange lodge in England was formed in Lancashire in 1798.[26] Five years later, the first public Orange procession took place at Oldham near Manchester in 1803.[27] By 1819, Liverpool had a grand total of three lodges which held their first procession in the city on 12 July that year.[28] The Orangemen carried the lamb, the ark and bibles on poles; they also brought Catholic insignia which they burnt. Predictably, the local Irish Catholic inhabitants of the city took offence and violence followed, arrests were made, and several ringleaders were imprisoned for their role in the disturbance.[29] Frank Neal has suggested that it was this first Orange parade in 1819 when sectarianism among the working class in Liverpool became institutionalised.[30] In 1834, an Ulster-born Protestant cleric, the Reverend Mr Hugh McNeile, arrived at St Jude's church in Liverpool.[31] Controversial and eloquent, McNeile played a significant role in the No Popery agitation in mid-Victorian Liverpool. For McNeile, Popery was 'religious heresy' and a 'political conspiracy'. McNeile went on to form the Liverpool Protestant Association which harnessed the city's burgeoning sectarian culture.[32] Liverpool Conservatives were quick to harness the concerns of the city's Protestant working class and cultivate its support.[33] Widely held perceptions that the Irish had driven down wages in the unskilled labour market contributed to sectarian tensions, and the associational Tory–Orange bonds served to protect the marginal privilege of the Protestant working class in Liverpool.[34] The evolution of rabid sectarianism in nineteenth-century Liverpool had arrived at a juncture whereby 'Catholic' became interchangeable with Irish, and that any activity of an overtly Protestant nature became synonymous with Orangeism.[35] If the Irish were maligned and treated with hostility, the feeling was mutual. The Jesuit poet-priest, Gerard Manley Hopkins, who had served at St Francis Xavier's church in the city, recalled that in comparison with the Irish in Glasgow, the Liverpool Irish possessed an undying hostility towards their host city.[36]

The Irish in Liverpool enjoyed a drink. Whether it was for refreshment, conviviality or as a means to escape the miserable gloom of their slums, the Irish crowded into the pubs and beer houses of the north end. Given the sheer weight of their numbers, demand for alcoholic beverages among the Liverpool Irish was high, and the market duly responded by providing the means of supply. In 1874 there were 1,929 pubs and 383 beer houses in Liverpool.[37] According to John Belchem, 'Competition for custom was intense, particularly in Irish areas where publicans encouraged various forms of convivial and bibulous associational culture'.[38] While many of the Irish tended to be unskilled labourers, Irish navvies possessed a talent for illicit distillation.[39] Drunkenness and violence within the Irish enclaves was a problem for the police in the year preceding the famine, the triangle between Vauxhall Road, Great Crosshall Street and Scotland Road being a particularly dangerous one to police.[40] Old enmities originating from long-standing family and territorial disputes had been transplanted from the villages and provinces of Ireland. Ultimately, these led to 'Irish' or 'faction fights' in the courts and streets of the north end and were often extremely violent.[41] Throughout the nineteenth century the Liverpool Irish provided work for the police and kept the city's courts and hospitals busy. Parades such as 12 July, when Liverpool's Orangemen commemorated the Battle of the Boyne, or 17 March when the Irish celebrated their national saint, provided a physical representation of the religious and sectarian divide within the city where they frequently descended into riots.

Concerns about Louis-Napoleon Bonaparte's *coup d'état* in France, and his expansion of the French Navy, led to a series of panics in the British press throughout the 1850s. Various military and political debates ensued as to how the French threat should be dealt with. It was agitation by the press and public opinion rather than any demands from politicians or senior military figures which led to the creation of the Volunteer movement in 1859.[42] In the end it came down to cost. An increase in taxation would have been required to maintain the militia, whereas the establishment of Volunteers would cost nothing. Volunteers were raised under the Yeomanry and Volunteer Consolidation Act of 1804. The conditions of service were uncomplicated; prospective volunteers were required to take an oath of allegiance, and to attend eight drills within four months, or twenty-four drills within one year.[43] The movement proved popular throughout the country and recruiting commenced in Liverpool. On 7 December 1859, a meeting was held at the London Hotel in the city to discuss the formation of 'an Irish Volunteer Rifle Brigade'.[44] Fifty men attended the event which was addressed by Captain Faulkner. He expressed the view that if a body of Irish Volunteers could be raised in the city, that it would be 'the finest in the country and one upon which her Majesty might place the utmost dependence'. He then proposed the following resolution:

> That in the presence of the armed demonstration now being made through-out this country, and to which our Scotch and Welsh fellow-subjects have respectively attached a distinctively national character, we, on the part of the Irish inhabitants of Liverpool, consider it our duty to form, after the model of our countrymen in London, a Liverpool Irish Volunteer Rifle Corps.[45]

The Volunteer movement served to provide prospective officers from Liverpool's *petite bourgeois* Catholic community with an opportunity to enhance their personal profile within the city. More importantly, the establishment of an Irish contingent in the city demonstrated the willingness of the 'low Irish' to play an active role within their host city by representing their own community. Provisionally known as the Irish Volunteer Rifles, by April 1860 they were designated as the 64th (Irish) Volunteers and their numbers grew to 100 men. In September that year, they attended a review at Lord Derby's estate at Knowsley Park. The 64th continued to recruit and by 1863 they had six companies comprising 600 men.[46] These are very impressive figures. Just four-teen years earlier, Sir Arnold Knight, MD, addressed a meeting of the Health of Towns Association at South Chester Street in Liverpool. Commenting on the physical condition of prospective army recruits, Knight informed his audience that, 'Out of every hundred young men who enlisted at Liverpool, for the army, three-fourths were rejected at Headquarters as unfit to be shot at'.[47] If Knight's statistics were correct, then either the diet of Liverpool's Irish recruits had improved markedly during the intervening years, or the required physical standards for prospective recruits to the Volunteers were very low. After some initial changes in leadership, the 64th (Irish) Volunteers were eventually led by Captain P.S. Bidwell, a middle-class Roman Catholic corn importer. Bidwell was also a Liberal councillor for the Vauxhall Ward and therefore well known to his men. However, unlike many of his subordinates, Bidwell was opposed to Home Rule for Ireland.[48]

Within a few years, the 64th (Irish) Volunteers grew in respectability. Dressed in their rifle-green uniforms, the Volunteers were known within the Irish enclaves of Liverpool as the 'Irish Brigade'.[49] This peak of respectability within the city for the Liverpool Irish was to be short-lived. While many in the Liverpool Irish enclaves remained committed to their nationalist aspirations and constitutional politics, others were convinced proponents of physical force.[50] The Irish Republican Brotherhood (IRB), a secret, oath-bound organisation, had its origins among the Irish exiles in America. Formed in 1858, Michael Doheny and John O'Mahoney wanted to explore the feasibility of organising a rebellion in Ireland and to organise an Irish-American invasion.[51] The organisation, which came to be known as the 'Fenians', was organised in Dublin by James Stephens, a veteran of the 1848 rebellion.[52] Liverpool, with its large Irish population and busy port, provided an ideal 'halfway-house' for Fenians or their sympathisers to smuggle men and munitions to and from Ireland or America.[53] Launched in Liverpool in 1861, the National Brotherhood of St Patrick (NBSP), offered more sober and intellectual facilities to the Liverpool Irish away from the pubs and beer houses.[54] However, the NBSP had among its membership a number of men with nationalist militant tendencies. It was these physical force nationalists who used the organisation as a cover for the Fenians in Liverpool.[55] In September 1865, the *Mercury* reported that Fenians had managed to infiltrate the Volunteers:

> It has been ascertained that numbers of Fenians, not only resident in Liverpool, but coming from Ireland and other places, have joined Volunteer corps in this town for the purposes obtaining knowledge of military drill, and that they have subsequently left and gone to Ireland for the purpose, it is supposed, of tutoring in military tactics the 'boys' who are to form the nucleus of the army of independence.[56]

While the report failed to identify any specific units, suspicion inevitably fell on the 64th (Irish) Volunteers. Research by Simon Jones into claims that the 64th (Irish) Volunteers had been infiltrated by large numbers of Fenians concluded that the allegations were without merit. Jones concedes that while many Liverpool Irish Volunteers might have harboured Fenian sympathies, the intelligence surrounding Fenian infiltration had been garnered from informants within the Irish drinking dens and they were eager to provide their police handlers with exaggerated accounts to ensure a good pay day.[57] The reputation of the 64th (Irish) Volunteers was damaged further following clashes with the 12th Liverpool Artillery Volunteers (12th LAV), a neighbouring unit with a distinctly Orange hue. In July 1868, both units were on duty at an inspection of the 4th Liverpool Artillery Volunteers.[58] When a member of the 64th attempted to cross the parade ground, he was prevented from doing so by men of the 12th LAV. The Liverpool Irishman was 'bodily seized' by men of the 12th LAV and pushed back. When the man eventually returned to his unit he told them what had occurred. Later, when both units approached the junction of Low Hill and Prescott Street, around thirty men from both units fell out of the ranks and a fight ensued. The *Mercury* reported that during the fight 'the butt end of some of the rifles was used with telling effect upon the combatants of the opposing side'. Order was eventually restored when the police arrived. While the paper failed to provide any precise explanation of why the violence had erupted, it stated that one of the rumours circulating was that it had been initiated 'from the exhibition of an orange-coloured handkerchief, which was regarded as an insult to the Catholic feeling of the Irish Brigade'.[59] The status and reputation of the 64th Liverpool Volunteers suffered throughout the 1860s. Allegations that the unit had been infiltrated by Fenians and public exhibitions of indiscipline did nothing to improve their standing in the city. By 1873, Fenianism had faded and the IRB suspended its revolutionary activities. Later, the Brotherhood passed a motion when they agreed to 'wait the decision of the Irish nation, as expressed by the majority of the Irish people, as to the fit hour of inaugurating a war against England'.[60]

By 1871, the numbers of Irish migrants had fallen to 76,761, although the figures for second and third generations of Liverpool Irish increased.[61] The rise in numbers of Liverpool-born Irish impacted on municipal politics within the city. In 1875, the Scotland electoral division was won by Lawrence Connolly, who had campaigned on an Irish nationalist ticket. The influence of the Liverpool Irish within Liverpool's council chamber grew between 1875 and 1922.[62] After Connolly's victory in 1875, a total of forty-eight Irish nationalists served on the city council. In 1885, another nationalist, T.P. O'Connor, was elected as MP for the Scotland Ward. Thomas Power O'Connor, also known as Tay Pay, 'who, at a little distance looked like a Jap', was urbane, eloquent and a prolific journalist. Although more at home in cosmopolitan London, O'Connor was regarded as a hero among his Irish constituents in Liverpool's Scotland Road.[63] O'Connor's reign was to be a long one, lasting until 1929. In case any prospective Liverpool Irish voters were in doubt as to where their loyalties lay, George Lynskey, an Irish nationalist councillor, urged them to remember that they 'were Irish first and Liverpudlian after'.[64] Harry Sefton reminisced about his childhood on Scotland Road, recalling the local atmosphere and blatant irregularities on polling day:

Elections were carnivals. There were the larks of the 'Bhoys' eminently practical; their slogan was: Vote Early and Vote Often! Wherefore on polling days
scores of long-dead voters came dutifully from their graves to exercise their
franchise.[65]

This period also saw changes to the 64th Liverpool Irish Volunteers.
Inexplicably, the battalion moved its headquarters to 206 Netherfield Road
in 1876. This was an interface area which marked the dividing line between
the orange and green populations in the north of the city. Unsurprisingly,
several clashes occurred between members of the battalion and local 'Orange
roughs'.[66] In 1880, their title changed when they became the 18th Lancashire
Volunteers (Liverpool Irish). Just eight years later, under the reforms instigated
by Lord Cardwell, the Secretary of State for War, they were renamed the 5th
(Irish) Battalion, King's (Liverpool) Regiment.[67] Frank Forde asserts that the
organisational changes made no impact on the battalion; they still dressed
in the black-buttoned, rifle-green uniforms modelled on those of the Royal
Irish Rifles. Their regimental march also remained unchanged. Long before
the Hollywood era of Lieutenant Colonel George Armstrong Custer and the
7th US Cavalry, the Liverpool Irish continued marching past to the strains of
Garryowen.[68]

The battalion continued to thrive during the final decades of the nineteenth century. On Sunday 20 June 1897, they attended Queen Victoria's
Jubilee celebrations at Wavertree Playground where 7,000 men paraded in
front of a crowd of 60,000 spectators.[69] High Mass was celebrated and the
5th (Irish) Battalion's chaplain, Monsignor Nugent, officiated while the
battalion's band played throughout the service. Three years later, the peacetime routine of drill nights and occasional musketry practice was about to
be interrupted by the war in South Africa. The Boer War was not popular
with Irish nationalists, who set about voicing their support for the Boers
and discouraging recruitment for the British army. In Dublin, 1,500 posters
adorned lampposts and billboards proclaiming, 'Enlisting in the English Army
is Treason to Ireland'.[70] Nationalist Ireland was in the grip of 'Boer fever' and
the Irish Transvaal Committee was formed in Dublin where prominent figures
such as Ireland's own Joan of Arc, Maud Gonne (actress, activist and soldier's
daughter), the poet W.B. Yeats, founder of Sinn Fein Arthur Griffith, and James
Connolly, a revolutionary socialist and former soldier.[71] Pro-Boer sympathisers
were delighted to receive the news of the British army's 'Black week', when
the Boers achieved success in a series of battles at Stormberg, Magersfontein
and Colenso. British losses increased the demand for replacements to bring

regiments up to strength and the 5th (Irish) Battalion, King's Liverpool Regiment were asked to supply a service company to reinforce the 1st Battalion of the Royal Irish Regiment in South Africa.[72]

On 20 January 1900, the men who had volunteered for South Africa attended a farewell banquet hosted by the Lord Mayor at the Town Hall.[73] Two days later the company mustered and paraded to Lime Street accompanied by their band. Cheering crowds lined the streets waving green handkerchiefs, and green flags and banners flew from houses. The parade's progress was hampered by the crowds and 'Women relatives of the men forced their way into the ranks and proudly marched alongside their sons, brothers, or sweethearts'.[74] At Lime Street the band played popular songs, including; *The Girl I Left Behind Me, Steer My Bark to Erin's Isle,* as well as the 'inspiring' *St Patrick's Day* and *Garryowen.* The men entrained for Warrington for four months' training after which they departed from Southampton on board the SS *Gascon* on 17 February.[75] Liverpool's Celtic purists and pro-Boer sympathisers despaired at the spectacle of their countrymen's neglect of 'Ireland and Irish ideals' by allowing themselves to be influenced by 'Saxon ways' and jingoistic khaki fever.[76] The Liverpool Celtic Literary Society, rather than politicians, took the lead in voicing the city's Irish nationalist dismay against the Anglicisation of the Irish in Liverpool. In line with their nationalist counterparts in Ireland, many of Liverpool's Irish nationalist councillors supported the Boers; however, their support was largely muted. More overt expressions of nationalist pro-Boer sentiments in Liverpool came from the Liverpool Irish Transvaal Committee who provided a green silk flag adorned with a golden harp, bearing the words 'God bless the South African Republics'; 'From the Irishmen of Liverpool to the Transvaal Irish Brigade'.[77]

The 5th (Irish) returned home in November 1900 to a tumultuous welcome from the people of Liverpool. Thousands lined the footpaths to watch the 5th Irish marching past, while flags, banners and streamers were hung from buildings.[78] By volunteering to serve in a foreign war the battalion ensured that the status of the Irish within Liverpool would rise. The *Mercury* led the praise, seizing the opportunity to take a swipe at those politicians who had previously questioned the loyalty of the Irish in the city:

> Such a spectacle as that which was witnessed in Liverpool yesterday afternoon afforded another attestation of the communal feeling that surges up when the Empire needs and has the service of those who, by the wily tricks of passing politicians, are fraudulently suggested as its enemies.[79]

After receiving an official welcome home from the Lord Mayor at the Town Hall, the men were invited to a banquet at St George's Hall where an Irish flag had been hoisted above the building.[80] At the banquet, the Mayor praised the Special Service Company of the 5th Irish and outlined their exploits during their time in South Africa. He went on to mention that the company had endured offensive and defensive actions at Senegal and at Bethlehem, where Captain Warwick William and eight members of the company had been wounded.[81] Highlighting their defence of the town of Belfast, the Mayor asked his audience, 'What better place could an Irishman be in to defend? (Laughter and applause)'.

The Boer War had exposed tactical and manpower difficulties within the British army. Senior British military figures looked enviously and warily across the Channel at the large conscript armies of continental Europe and began a debate on National Service. In 1902, the National Service League was established to educate the nation to appreciate military questions.[82] In 1905, Lord Roberts, a Boer War hero, voiced the concerns of many Edwardian soldiers of the threat posed by Germany and the necessity for National Service. He was, however, also aware of the fact that conscription was contrary to British notions of consent and the volunteer spirit. The army reforms instigated by W.B. Haldane, Secretary of State for War, reorganised the Volunteer units into a second-line army to be known as the Territorial Force. Used primarily for home defence, Haldane's reforms also included an Imperial Service Option, which meant that units could volunteer for foreign service in time of war.[83] The organisational restructuring led to the renaming of the Liverpool Volunteer Battalions. The 5th (Irish) Battalion now became the 8th (Irish) Battalion, King's Liverpool Regiment. The battalion would form part of the Liverpool Infantry Brigade of the West Lancashire Division of the Territorial Force. The division was organised and administered by the West Lancashire Territorial Association, and Lord Derby, a local aristocrat and future Minister for War, became its chairman.[84] Apart from the change in their title, nothing else was altered by Haldane's reforms. In 1912, Haldane visited the battalion in Liverpool to open their new drill hall in Shaw Street.

1

LIVERPOOL 1914: DIVISION, RECRUITMENT AND UNITY

While some in Britain retained a healthy suspicion of German intentions in the years leading up to 1914, Germanophobia had become less obvious. World politics, including events leading up to the crisis in the Balkans in the summer of 1914, certainly featured in the British press, but were much over-shadowed by the Home Rule crisis and the possibility of civil war in Ireland.[1] The political and sectarian tensions surrounding the Home Rule crisis in Ireland were easily transported across the Irish Sea where they resonated, and were readily cultivated within the fertile Irish enclaves of Glasgow and Liverpool.

In the years leading to the introduction of the Third Home Rule Bill, a trio of nationalist grandees, John Redmond, John Dillon and T.P. O'Connor, visited various nationalist enclaves throughout Britain preaching to the converted and extolling the virtues of Home Rule.[2] In Liverpool, the Orange and Tory faithful were praised and flattered by the fiery anti-Home Rule rhetoric of Archibald Salvidge, Sir Edward Carson and his 'galloper', F.E. Smith, the MP for Walton. If required, Pastor George Wise, the ultra-Protestant and anti-Romanist cleric, could be relied upon to inflame an already volatile situation.[3] When Sir Edward Carson visited Liverpool in September 1912, he was greeted by thousands of cheering anti-Home Rule sympathisers including members of the Liverpool Orange Order and bands playing patriotic airs.[4] Archibald Salvidge, Tory 'boss' and chairman of the Liverpool Workingmen's Conservative Association, was the principle organiser for Carson's visit, and accompanied the unionist leader throughout his stay in the city.[5] The following day, he addressed a crowd estimated at 100,000 which had gathered to hear him speak at Sheil Park in the city. The event received national coverage and *The Times* described the scenes as 'the orderly brigades of working men' arrived at Sheil Park to the strains of *The Red, White and Blue* and *Derry's Walls* along with other loyalist favourites of the day.[6] Acknowledging the support of the Liverpool loyalists, Carson told them, 'if there is to be a row I'd like to be in it with the Belfast men, and I'd like to have you with them. And I will (loud cheers)'.[7] Shortly afterwards, F.E. Smith took to the podium where he made an extraordinary claim. Smith informed the audience that he had been speaking to three important ship owners in the city who had promised him that in the event of violence erupting between nationalist and unionists in Ulster, that they had agreed to supply ships to transport 10,000 Liverpool men across the Irish Sea to help their unionist allies.[8] Carson was unable to attend Pastor George Wise's lecture on 'The Covenant' held at the Protestant Reformers' Memorial Church; however, he did send his apologies. In any event, several senior unionist notables including Col. Kyffin Taylor, MP for Kirkdale, and Lord Templeton, an Irish landowner, managed to attend where they heard Wise's 'characteristic' address on the Ulster Covenant.[9] Wise pledged his support for the unionist cause assuring his audience that by 'relying on the God of their fathers, the God of Luther, John Knox, Ridley and Latimer' that they would never surrender to Home Rule. In a somewhat optimistic yet witty conclusion, Wise stated that when Home Rule was dead, he might be asked to officiate at the funeral.

The crisis surrounding the Home Rule Bill did not die; on the contrary, in the two years preceding the outbreak of war in 1914, Ireland witnessed what David Fitzpatrick described as 'an extraordinary outburst of mimetic militarism'.[10] In 1913, unionist determination to resist the implementation of Home Rule in Ulster led to the formation of the Ulster Volunteer Force (UVF).[11] After initially dismissing Carson's bellicose rhetoric as mere 'bluster' and pouring ridicule on the UVF, Irish nationalists responded by raising their own organisation and the inaugural meeting of the Irish National Volunteers (INV) was held at the Rotunda in Dublin on 25 November 1913.[12] Around the same time, Frank Thornton, a member of the Irish Republican Brotherhood (IRB), became a founder member of the Irish Volunteers in Liverpool.[13] Thornton stated that the movement in Liverpool had its origins at a meeting at St Martin's Hall in the city and that members of the IRB used their influence to urge members of the United Irish League (UIL) and the Ancient Order of Hibernians (AOH) to enlist. The Liverpool contingent grew to a membership of 1,200 and later paraded at Greenwich Park near Aintree racecourse.

The seemingly imminent achievement of Home Rule gave the Irish inhabitants of Liverpool cause to celebrate St Patrick's Day in 1914 with additional enthusiasm and patriotic fervour. Lorcan Sherlock, Lord Mayor of Dublin, was the honoured guest at a banquet held by Liverpool nationalists to celebrate their national Saint. T.P. O'Connor, who was unable to attend having been summoned to Westminster by the Whip, sent a letter which was read to the guests by Austin Harford:'I would have been glad of the opportunity of giving to my countrymen the most joyous message it was ever my privilege to deliver. Home Rule is won.'[14] A few days later, O'Connor managed to visit Liverpool where he attended a demonstration organised in his honour. The nationalist and Catholic press, including the *Freeman's Journal* and the *Liverpool Catholic Herald,* produced lengthy accounts of the parade which was estimated to have stretched for five miles as it made its way through the nationalist streets of Scotland Road, Kirkdale and Exchange districts in the north of the city.[15] Participants in the parade included several Catholic confraternities, including the Irish National Foresters, the Ancient Order of Hibernians and the Gaelic Athletic League. The *Freeman's Journal* was keen to reveal that the parade also included many Irishmen who had served in the army and that 'a body of three thousand men who were observed by everybody for the regularity of their marching and their military bearing'.[16]

The militaristic posturing of the Irish and Ulster Volunteers persisted throughout the first seven months of 1914 on both sides of the Irish Sea. Sympathetic editors of nationalist and unionist papers in Belfast, Dublin and Liverpool regaled their respective readerships with boastful accounts of men of 'military bearing' drilling and marching in Liverpool. The unionist *Belfast Weekly News* kept its readership informed of the development of the Ulster Volunteers in Liverpool.[17] A 'representative' acting on behalf of the paper reported that Liverpool claimed to have 'upwards of 15,000 Ulster Volunteers' and that they were 'fully determined to take an active part in any serious troubles that might ensue in Ulster'. According to the report, the Liverpool UVF comprised two sections which were split between Liverpool and Birkenhead. Led by a retired general 'who was also an MP', the reporter emphasised that the men were armed and well drilled. During his research on the UVF, Timothy Bowman asserts that membership of the UVF was largely connected with the British League for the Support of Ulster and the Union and that the UVF hierarchy in Belfast were reluctant to accept semi-trained or untrained and unarmed men into their ranks.[18] Conversely, it seems that the contribution made by the Irish National Volunteers in the Liverpool was accepted by the leadership. The Liverpool INV attended drill sessions at various locations throughout the city including the Foresters Hall in Seaforth, Bootle Gaelic League Club and the Catholic Defence Association in Burlington Street.[19]

Unionist determination to resist Home Rule manifested itself the following month at Larne where the UVF landed a consignment of 25,000 rifles and 3 million rounds of ammunition.[20] In late July 1914, the police in Liverpool raided a building close to the Exchange area in the city where they seized a considerable quantity of arms. The weapons were taken to Dale Street police station and officers from the Royal Irish Constabulary stationed in Liverpool were summoned to examine the weapons. The *Liverpool Echo* was unable to state whether the rifles were intended for the INV or the UVF 'as the authorities preserve much reticence over the affair'.[21]

The expansion of civilian armies in Ireland during 1914 did much to enhance the bank balances of private arms dealers in Germany and Belgium. They must have been delighted when Professor Tom Kettle, barrister, poet and former MP, accompanied by John O'Connor MP arrived in Belgium to purchase rifles for the INV. The dealers were to enjoy an additional bonus. Unknown to Kettle and O'Connor, Sir Roger Casement had dispatched another group of men on a similar mission. Casement's group succeeded in purchasing 1,100 rifles and had landed them by means of a private yacht at Howth on 26 July 1914.[22] Unlike the UVF night-time operation to unload and disperse their haul of firearms, the INV landing was completed in daylight. As the volunteers made their way back to Dublin, they were confronted by police and later by a company of the King's Own Scottish Borderers. The volunteers refused to surrender their rifles and after a few scuffles the volunteers managed to dispose of the rifles. As the Scottish Borderers were returning to the centre of Dublin, they were confronted by a hostile crowd which pelted them with stones and missiles. Without receiving any further orders, the soldiers loaded their weapons and fired on the crowd, killing three people and wounding more than thirty others.[23]

The incident caused great indignation among nationalists in Ireland and Britain, not least due to the disparity in the British government's attitude towards the UVF and the INV.[24] At the end of July 1914, Austin Harford chaired a meeting of the United Irish Societies of Liverpool where the shootings were discussed. The decision was taken to send a telegram offering their sympathies and pledging their support to the Lord Mayor of Dublin:

> The United Irish Societies, Liverpool and District, meeting last night, asked me to express their abhorrence of the cowardly and savage attack on defenceless Dublin citizens, and to tender deepest sympathy with the relatives. And we assure our fellow-countrymen that 100,00 Liverpool Nationalists stand staunch with them in their fight to sweep murderous Dublin Castle completely away.[25]

Three days after the publication of Harford's telegram, Britain declared war on Germany.

The declaration of war against Germany on 4 August 1914 did not inspire any jingoistic displays or anti-German excitement among the citizens of Liverpool. The *Liverpool Courier* reported 'Large but sombre crowds in Liverpool', adding that the usual Bank Holiday atmosphere was absent in the city and that this was 'entirely due to the ominous and imminent possibility of this country being plunged into war'.[26] Lime Street, however, remained a hub of activity where large crowds had gathered to await the return of the Liverpool Territorials from their camps, or to witness the departure of army and naval reservists to their regiments and ships. Pat O'Mara noticed a change in the slums of the north end of Liverpool, which went from being enveloped in 'deadness and dullness', to places of 'lights and gaiety'. Scotland Road and the streets surrounding it were filled with 'exceedingly happy soldiers, young and mature'.[27] When his errands for Sneddon's fishmongers led him to Lime Street or Bold Street, O'Mara stopped to watch the soldiers departing from the railway stations. 'I would forget all about the fish and listen to the loudly blaring bands at the heads of the various contingents. There were all kinds of soldiers, with many of the faces well known to me and from my neighbourhood: Connaught Rangers, Scotch soldiers – very hilarious in their kilts, Liverpool's own pride, the Eighth Irish, and many others all happy and in a distinctly holiday mood.' A day later, the same paper bemoaned the fact that the Territorial Army required some 50,000 men and 5,000 officers to bring it up to strength.[28] The paper urged men of military age to enlist, hinting that the war would bring unemployment and that the only way to avoid it was to serve with the colours. Additional military training for the Territorials would, the paper argued, 'make them finer fighting material even than our regiments, certainly better than the machine-made fighting automatons of Germany.' During the August Bank Holiday, men of the Liverpool Territorial Battalions had been attending a series of annual training camps. The Liverpool Irish along with the 5th and 7th Battalions of the King's Liverpool Rifles had been based at Farleton, Westmoreland, while the Liverpool Scottish, the 9th Kings and the 4th and 5th South Lancashire Regiment were camped at nearby Hornby. Some men had anticipated being moved to Aldershot or some other military centre; however, they were surprised when the order came to strike their tents and they were told to return home and await further orders.[29]

During the first months of the war, Liverpool Irishmen were faced with the decision as to whether to make their way to the recruiting office or wait for guidance from their political and religious leaders. Confirmation that John Redmond had managed to deliver Home Rule came on 18 September 1914 when the Home Rule Act received Royal Assent. Redmond had already committed the INV to home defence during the war, but in an apparently extempore address at Woodenbridge, County Wicklow, on 20 September, he went further:

> The war is undertaken in defence of the highest principles of religion and morality and right, and it would be a disgrace forever for our country, and a reproach to her manhood, and a denial of the lessons of her history, if young Ireland confined her efforts to remaining at home to defend the shores of Ireland from an unlikely invasion, and shrunk from the duty of proving on the field of battle that gallantry and courage which has distinguished our race all through its history. They should first make themselves efficient, and then acquit themselves as men, not only in Ireland itself, but wherever the firing line extended, in defence of right, freedom and religion in this war.[30]

Liverpool Irishmen who were regular soldiers or reservists were obliged to mobilise. Like every other territorial battalion, the Liverpool (Irish) Battalion of the King's Liverpool Regiment complied with Haldane's intention that the primary purpose of the Territorial Force was home defence.[31] Territorial battalions could, of course, volunteer for foreign service, and every territorial battalion in Liverpool volunteered to serve abroad. Having volunteered, the Liverpool Irish began a recruiting drive to bring the battalion up to strength. In September 1914, recruiting adverts for the Liverpool Irish appeared in the local press: 'This battalion has volunteered for foreign service and requires a few picked men to complete. Also, men for home defence battalion now form-ing.'[32] The advert invited potential recruits to call at the battalion's headquarters at 75 Shaw Street and carried the banner heading of 'ERIN GO BRAGH' (Ireland forever) ending with 'GOD SAVE THE KING'. The phraseology of this appeal is noteworthy; it manages to assure prospective Irish recruits of the battalion's ethnic origins and to reassure English recruits of its allegiance to the crown. Moreover, it informed the populace of Liverpool of the 8th (Irish) bat-talion's commitment to the war effort as a fighting battalion as opposed to one on home service, thereby enhancing its reputation in the city. T.P. O'Connor telegraphed Colonel Myles Emmet Byrne, commanding the Liverpool Irish, congratulating him on his efforts and expressing his satisfaction at the numbers coming forward to enlist. 'I am delighted to hear Irishmen are acting up to Mr Redmond's manifesto and speeches by going to the front in defence of liberty, justice and the sacred principle of nationality and that they are joining distinctly Irish [sic] so once more an Irish Brigade may play an historic part in defending free Europe against a military despotism.'[33]

Just two days after Redmond's Woodenbridge speech, T.P. O'Connor spoke at a mass recruiting meeting at the Tournament Hall in Liverpool where he shared the platform with another pro-Home Ruler and First Lord of the Admiralty, Winston Churchill, and his old adversary and anti-Home Ruler, F.E. Smith.[34] The *Echo* stressed the fact that this was a 'non-party demonstration'. An audience estimated at between 12,000 and 15,000 listened to O'Connor's peroration which began with a 'stirring indictment of Prussian militarism' after which he told the crowd that the nations and faiths of the world were praying for the success of Britain in its war with Germany. He went on to claim that prayers could also be heard 'from the Catholic altars of every chapel in Ireland.' Placing Ireland firmly within the British Empire, O'Connor went on to extol its virtues; 'Our Empire is founded on freedom,' he declared, before assuring the assembly that he would encourage the Irish to fight for the empire, 'I will call with all the energy I can command from the very depths of my soul and conscience that every Irishman who can go to the front should range himself in this fight for freedom against despotism.' Thus, O'Connor assumed the role of Recruiter General and dedicated himself to the task of encouraging recruitment among the Irish throughout Britain.

As early as 7 August 1914, the *Liverpool Courier* reports on the war boasted of 'More Patriotic Sons' in Liverpool, as a rush of men made their way to recruiting offices in Liverpool, and that 'Busy scenes are being witnessed the various Territorial headquarters throughout the district'.[35] While the decision to enlist was ultimately an individual one, other factors including patriotism, duty, unemployment, boredom, an urge for adventure and familial or peer pressure may have influenced whether a man made his way to the recruiting office. Not long after German troops had stormed into Belgium, press reports appeared describing the bombardment of the University of Louvain (which housed an Irish seminary), and early accounts of German atrocities. In September 1914, the *Liverpool Echo* reported on the establishment of a Committee of Inquiry into alleged atrocities in Belgium, where farmers and civilians had been shot, men had been locked up while the women were raped.[36] The report claimed that German soldiers had pillaged the local treasuries, taken hostages and used local women and children as human shields against the French. Such reports caused outrage among the Irish population of Britain who drew parallels with Ireland. For some Irish nationalists, the plight of 'Poor Catholic Belgium' mirrored historical events in Ireland; a small Catholic nation under the rule of a foreign oppressor.[37] In October 1914, the *Xaverian* reported that Father Schul and Father Krufthorft, two priests from the Belgian port of Antwerp, were staying at St Francis Xavier church.[38] Referring to the alleged atrocities in Belgium, 'Both agree in saying that the barbarities perpetrated in Belgium have not been exaggerated in our newspaper accounts; on the contrary, no newspaper would dare to publish the crude facts in their columns.' The arrival of Belgian refugees in Liverpool in 1914 also provided a gruesome and highly visible corollary of the impact and devastation of war. On 11 October 1914, Ada McGuire from Wallasey wrote to her sister describing the condition of some refugees who had arrived at Waterloo and Birkenhead, 'Two little Belgian girls whose parents were dead, and their nurse had been found bayoneted at their side but both children had had their arms chopped off from above the elbows!!'[39]

The declaration of war and the subsequent confirmation of Home Rule had caused Irishmen, both native and exile, to examine their national identity, their loyalties and their relationship with Britain and its empire. Since the seventeenth century, Irish regiments had been at the forefront in defending the British Empire, where they encountered their fellow Irishmen on battlefields in Ireland, Europe and in South Africa. The Irish, it seems, developed an ambivalent attitude towards the empire. As Keith Jeffery observed, the paradox of Ireland's status meant that it was both 'imperial *and* colonial'.[40] Constitutional nationalist politicians like Liverpool's own T.P. O'Connor had no difficulty in placing an independent, self-governing Ireland within the empire. Further down the social scale, Pat O'Mara, a self-styled Liverpool Irish slummy, struggled with the competing nationalistic demands for his allegiance prescribed by his school and his home. Patriotism, it seems, was a very complex concept for Catholic Irish children in Liverpool. O'Mara attempted to summarise his own, personal dilemma: 'The best I can say is that what I derived from my elementary English-Irish schooling was an intense love for the British empire and an equally intense hatred for England as opposed to Ireland.'[41] O'Mara was educated within the Catholic tradition in Liverpool where he was 'rather patriotised and "Britishised"'. Conversely, on returning home to his English-hating parents he was 'sternly Irishised'. O'Mara described this rather obfuscated perspective of the British Empire as being a personal 'paradox'. He went on to claim that he was a 'ferocious, sacrificial Irish-Catholic first; ferocious, sacrificial patriotic Britisher second', and a wondering dreamer third. This convoluted and contradictory view of the empire was, he alleged, shared by 'most slummy Irish-Catholic "Britishers"'.

For the British working classes of Victorian and Edwardian Britain, economic pressures rather than any high-blown patriotism had long been a major incentive for enlistment in the army. The appeal of a regular wage, food and clothing provided the army with a regular supply of recruits throughout the nineteenth century.[42] In 1914, the attraction of a regular income and the payment of separation allowances for married men would have been inviting to working-class Liverpudlian Irishmen, perhaps more so to those employed in casual labour. In March 1915, the Jesuit preacher and patriot Father Bernard Vaughan appealed to the Irish Catholic workers of Liverpool, by merging the 'Empire of Christ and the Empire of Great Britain'.[43] Vaughan went on to pledge that he 'would carry that cry down to the Merseyside, and to shout with all the vehemence of his soul – he would shout it out loud, to his brothers, the dockers – "Do your duty, and do it now"'. Despite the decline in Irish immigration to Liverpool towards the end of the nineteenth century, the Irish in the city retained their identity, politics and their faith. The *Liverpool Catholic Herald*, owned by Charles Diamond, kept the Liverpool Irish populace of the city well informed on municipal matters and religious events from an unashamedly nationalist perspective. Diamond was a newspaper entrepreneur and native of Maghera, County Londonderry. As an exile he recognised and exploited the opportunity of providing the well-established Irish Catholic readership throughout Britain with local and national religious and political news.[44] Having endorsed Redmond's support for the war, Diamond laid the blame for the war squarely on the anti-Home Rulers with the headlines, 'ULSTERS PRO GERMANS' and 'HOW WILD CARSONITES BROUGHT ON THE WAR'.[45]

Poetry was summoned to the recruiting platform as an encouragement for Irishmen to enlist. On 12 September 1914, the *Liverpool Catholic Herald* published a Kiplingesque parody entitled *Paddy*, written by Tom Kettle. The last two verses mock the perceived British ambivalence towards the Irish, while eulogising the supposedly superior fighting qualities of the Irish soldier over his English counterpart.

> Yes! Sneerin' round at Irishmen and Irish speech and ways
> Is cheaper – much than snatchin' guns from the battle's red amaze;
> And when the Deaths Head Dragoons roll up the ruddy tide
> The "Times" won't spare a Smith to tell how Dan O'Connell died.
> For it's Paddy this and Paddy that, and "The Fifth'll prate and prance!"
> But it's "Corks and Inniskillings Front!" when the Hell is loose in France.
> When Clare and Kerry take the call that crowns the shrapnel-dance,
> O, its "Find the Dublin Fusiliers!" when Hell is loose in France.
>
> We ain't no saints nor scholars much but fightin' men and clean.
> We've paid the price, and three times thrice, for Wearin' o' the Green,
> We held our hand out frank and fair, we half forgot Parnell,
> For Ireland's hope and England's too – and it's yours to save or sell!

For it's Paddy this and Paddy that, "Who'll stop the Uhlan blade?"
But Tommy Fitz from Malahide, and Monaghan's McGlade.
When the ranks are set for judgement, lads, and the roses droop and fade,
It's "Ireland in the firin' line!" when the price of God is paid.[46]

A few months later in November 1914, the nationalist MP Stephen Gwynne penned a more romanticised account of Irish soldiery in his poem *The Irish Brigade, 1914*, which invoked memories of the deeds of the Irish Brigade at Fontenoy. Similar sentiments were echoed by Colonel Miles Emmet Byrne, of the Liverpool Irish, who went on to command a battalion of the Northumberland Fusiliers of the Tyneside Irish, and urged his men to recall the actions of the Irish Brigade on mainland Europe during the War of the Austrian Succession, where they fought on the side of the French against the British.[47]

From Fontenoy, from Landen, the message runs again
Once more the fields of Flanders are strewn with Irish slain
And once again, oh once again, the herald thrills to tell
How gloriously an Irish charge avenged the brave who fell.

And we who sit at home and read – the tale rings in our ears,
We know our part; we claim our right, in those victorious cheers
We boast our splendid heritage in the old fighting race
Yet have we marked the cry that comes from each dead soldier's face?[48]

Since making his declaration in support of the war, John Redmond had envisaged the creation of an Irish 'Brigade'; one with its own distinct identity, colours and emblems. This brought him into conflict with the War Office and Lord Kitchener, who, despite being Irish himself, retained an unhealthy suspicion of Irish nationalists. Redmond was not a military man and had no understanding of the hierarchical divisional structure of the British army. General Parsons, commander of the 16th (Irish) Division, informed Redmond that 'three essentially Irish Brigades form the 16th Irish Division, a much finer and larger unit than a brigade'.[49] In Liverpool, Colonel Miles Emmet Byrne's attempt to raise an Irish battalion for Kitchener's army resulted in failure.[50] The *Liverpool Catholic Herald* advised any recruits which the battalion had managed to obtain to transfer to the Dublin Fusiliers if they so wished.[51] This suggestion was not as straightforward as it might appear. General Sir Lawrence Parsons, commanding the 16th (Irish) Division, had a penchant for native, rural, sporty Irish lads and he dismissed a suggestion by Mr Crilly, leader of the United Irish

League in Great Britain, that Irish recruits for the 16th Irish Division could be obtained from Britain:

> I told him that they can enlist at any recruiting office and make it known that they want to come to my Division, stating battalion. To establish special recruiting centres where Mr Crilly suggests, would mean filling us with Liverpool, and Glasgow, and Cardiff Irish, who are slum-birds that we don't want. I want to see the clean, fine, strong, temperate, hurley-playing country fellows such as we used to get in the Munsters, Royal Irish, Connaught Rangers.[52]

By December 1914, slow recruiting in Ireland and the reluctance of 'strong, temperate, hurley-playing country fellows' to enlist, compelled Sir Lawrence to set aside his prejudiced attitude to 'slum birds'. T.P. O'Connor wrote to Maurice Bonham Carter, Asquith's Principle Private Secretary, complaining that Parsons was writing frequent letters to him, 'begging me to help him fill up some of the Irish battalions of the 16th Division'.[53] During the first months of the war, the Irish Parliamentary Party had an acrimonious and fractious relationship with Kitchener and the War Office. O'Connor became disillusioned by the lack of full press coverage for his recruiting campaign and by the pessimism expressed by 'all officials' as to the likelihood of running a successful campaign.[54] He also had scant regard for Kitchener, who he described as being an 'Irish Orangeman'.[55] O'Connor faced further discouragement in February 1915, when he was informed that he was not to hold any recruiting meetings in Liverpool or Newcastle.[56]

Following the Battle of Festubert in June 1915, the 8th (Irish) Battalion had their own dispute with the War Office. The *Liverpool Catholic Herald* announced that 'Liverpool Irish Get Tardy Justice from the War Office'. The paper explained:

> One of the many matters in connection with the differentiation between the 8th Irish and other Liverpool battalions at the front which have been productive of much dissatisfaction has been the omission from the casualty lists – in which the 8th figured largely and with honour – of the title "Irish" of which they are jealously and justly proud. This has now been remedied, Mr T.P. O'Connor, MP, having induced the War Office to recognise them as the Liverpool Irish in all future lists.[57]

Following the Liverpool (Irish) Battalion's exploits at Festubert, some of the decorated and wounded war heroes from the battalion returned home. In

September 1915, the *Echo* reported that 'corporal Cuddy, the wounded DCM, of the local Irish battalion, made it his business to visit all the recruiting offices and helped materially to swell Liverpool's gift to the allies'.[58]

Economic necessity, appeals from the pulpit, poetry (of whatever genre) and the pages of the Redmondite press may well have induced Liverpool Irishmen to call at the recruiting office. However, as David Fitzpatrick has suggested, more secular factors including membership of fraternities, youth organisations, workplaces, clubs and Catholic Young Men's Societies could also have influenced recruitment.[59] In Liverpool, for example, a correspondent to the *Liverpool Catholic Herald* claimed that 40 per cent of the National Volunteers had enlisted as opposed to just 2 per cent of the Carsonites.[60] Frank Thornton, a prominent member of the IRB who had infiltrated the INV in Liverpool, stated that Redmond's support for the war and T.P. O'Connor's pleas to the Liverpool INV members had 'a very serious effect' on the INV in the city.[61] When the volunteers 'split', all members of the United Irish League and the Ancient Order of Hibernians withdrew from the National Executive of the INV. Most of the constitutional nationalists in Liverpool abandoned the INV in the city and the organisation went from having a total pre-war strength of 3,000 members, to just twenty-five members in Duke Street and the same number in Bootle. Catholic youth organisations also supplied recruits; fifty members and former members of St Francis Xavier Boys Brigade had enlisted up to September 1914. By December 1914, the school had provided 143 former pupils for the ranks of the 8th (Irish) Battalion of the King's Liverpool Regiment.[62] Following the Battle of Festubert in June 1915, one soldier who survived the battle stated that 'Many of the St Mary's CYMS (Catholic Young Men's Society) have gone down.'[63] In August 1914, prior to the arrival of recruits from outside the city of Liverpool, the core of the Liverpool (Irish) Battalion was quintessentially Catholic. The *Xaverian* reported that on 15 August 1914, while the battalion continued their mobilisation and preparations for war at St Francis Xavier school, they availed themselves of the opportunity to attend Mass at the Feast of the Assumption: 'In the morning they attended the six o'clock Mass (some six-hundred Catholics are in the battalion), and a special Mass at 7.15 on Sunday saw them again in force in the church.'[64]

In March 1915, Austin Harford addressed a reunion of the Irishmen of Liverpool where he stated that 'recruiting had been so heavy in some streets in the Scotland Division, that almost every house had a soldier from it fighting at the front'.[65] Harford was keen to emphasise the contribution and sacrifice made by the Catholics of the city and claimed that the Catholic parishes of Liverpool and its suburbs had provided an estimated 14,000 men. Given his audience, he singled out the 'Irish Parishes' for particular praise: 'Out of what might be fairly called seventeen Irish parishes of Liverpool a total of 7,800 fighting men were forthcoming.' According to Harford, since the declaration of war, Irishmen from Liverpool and elsewhere had rushed to the colours and 'when the Home Rule Bill was placed on the Statute Book they trooped into the ranks in still larger numbers'. Harford went on to contend that more Irishmen had enlisted in Liverpool than any other nationality in proportion to the population. Not all Liverpool 'Irish' recruits favoured distinctly Irish regiments, or indeed the 8th Liverpool (Irish) Battalion. Harford's collection of recruiting statistics had revealed that 'Not the least remarkable feature about the figures was that scarcely ten per cent of the men had joined Irish regiments.' If so, then choices made by those Liverpudlian Irishmen may have been determined by factors other than their nationality. Perhaps friendships made during their employment, familial connections, or preference for a regular army battalion might have proved influential in their choice of regiment, other than serving in a territorial battalion. Pat O'Mara and his friends discussed their wartime service options and preferences: 'My cousin Benny and Jonny Ford wanted very much to be seen in the uniform of the Eighth Irish. Henry Roche, still a paradoxical Irishman, wanted the plaid kilts of the Liverpool Scottish, no less.'[66]

Table 1.1: *Recruiting figures for parishes in the Scotland Division of Liverpool.*[67]

Parish	Population	Serving
St Alban's	5,696	310
All Souls'	2,820	158
St Anthony's	8,136	484
St Augustine's	3,025	235
St Bridget's	3,013	222
Our Lady's	5,333	375
St Joseph's	6,347	415
St Sylvester's	7,922	592

Table 1.2: *Recruiting figures for those parishes outside the Scotland Division.*

Parish	Population	Serving
St Alphonsus's	8,165	402
St Alexander's	8,012	419
St Francis Xavier's	10,220	1,069
The Friary	5,069	691
Holy Cross	3,380	371
St John's	6,721	379
St Mary's	2,867	219
St Patrick's	8,245	424
St Vincent's	4,329	492

Writing in 1916, T.R. Threlfall claimed that the Liverpool Irish was one of the strongest and most popular battalions in Liverpool, and that 'It speaks volumes for the esprit de corps of the battalion that between the order for mobilisation on the August 1914 and February 1916, 3,300 men were recruited for it under the voluntary system.'[68]

Given the paucity of personal accounts of individual service, in an attempt to discover who some the men of the 8th Liverpool (Irish) Battalion were, what they did, and where they came from, it was necessary to examine their original attestation papers and service records. Constraints of time and space required that the number involved was limited to 100, which equates to around one-tenth of a battalion.[69] Table 1.1 provides the number of recruits in the Liverpool Irish obtained from the various districts in the city. Unsurprisingly, many of the recruits originated in the north of the city; twenty-two men came from Everton close to the Liverpool (Irish) Battalion Headquarters at Shaw Street and a further four from neighbouring Anfield. Eleven men joined from Scotland Road, six from nearby Kirkdale, four each from Vauxhall and Islington districts. These districts had a high proportion of Irish residents. While some men enlisted from areas like Old Swan and Bottle, the battalion appears to have attracted fewer recruits from the more affluent suburbs of Mossley Hill and Fairfield.

Table 1.3: *Home districts of 100 men enlisted in the 8th (Irish) Battalion, King's Liverpool Regiment.*

District	Number
Abercromby	2
Anfield	4
Baltic	9
Bootle	4
City Centre	3
Docks	1
Edge Hill	3
Everton	22
Fairfield	1
Islington	4
Kensington	3
Kirkdale	6
Mossley Hill	1
Old Swan	4
Ropeworks	2
Scotland	11
Seaforth	2
Sefton	1
Stoneycroft	1
Toxteth	3
Vauxhall	4
Walton	1

Waterloo	1
Wavertree	5
Canada	1
Not known	1

Source: Compiled from the service records of 100 men of the 8th (Irish) Battalion, King's Liverpool Regiment. See Appendix 1.

The working-class Liverpool Irish tended to live near their places of employment and for many that meant the docks, mills and warehouses in the city. As revealed in Table 1.2, almost one-third of the men classed themselves as labourers, six were marine workers and four stated that they were dockers. Five of the soldiers were carters, which were much in demand to ferry goods to and from the docks. Only five of those included were tradesmen (monumental sculptor, painter, plumber, etc.) and there was only one apprentice. The remainder were employed in a disparate variety of occupations including bottle washer, tanner, hairdresser and groom.

Table 1.4: *Occupations of 100 men of the 8th Liverpool (Irish) Battalion, King's Liverpool Regiment.*

Employment	Number
Apprentice	1
Blacksmith/ Striker	2
Bottle washer	1
Brass finisher	1
Bricklayer	1
Carter	5
Chair maker	1
Clerk	2
Dock worker	4
Dripping maker	1
Driver	3

Engine driver	1
Fireman	2
Fishmonger	1
Groom	1
Hairdresser	2
Ironmonger	1
Labourer	27
Locomotive fireman	1
Marine worker	6
Mill worker	1
Monumental sculptor	1
Painter	2
Plumber	1
Point cleaner	1
Porter	2
Printer	1
Railway worker	2
Sawyer	1
Shop assistant	1
Soda water bottler	1
Tanner	1
Waiter	1
Warehouseman	1
Wheelwright	1
Not known	16
Total	100

Source: Compiled from the service records of 100 men of the 8th (Irish) Battalion, King's Liverpool Regiment. Unfortunately, some of the records regarding employment are missing and some were not recorded depending on the type of attestation form which was used.

Prospective recruits who could meet the age, height and medical require-ments were undoubtedly sought out and welcomed at the recruiting offices throughout Liverpool. There were, however, some men who despite meeting these requirements were certainly not wanted; more than that, they were ille-gal. In January 1916, the courts heard a series of cases involving attempts by Americans to enlist in the Liverpool Irish. On 7 January 1916, Stanley Watkins, a private in the Liverpool Irish, appeared before Blackpool Court charged with failing to register as an alien, being found in a restricted area and with making a false statement on enlistment.[70] Captain Duder, prosecuting, told the court that Watkins had registered as an alien at Liverpool in August 1914 but that he had subsequently enlisted in November of that year claiming to be a British subject. Watkins had been arrested the previous day on a charge of causing injury to himself by opening the sole of his foot with a razor. Captain Duder stated that Watkins had also threatened to kill the doctor who had been called to treat him. Duder stated that the Head Constable of Liverpool had written to him informing him that there were seven similar cases involving Americans who had joined the Liverpool Irish. 'They caused a considerable amount of trouble and were not subject to discipline,' Duder explained. 'After occupying the time of officers for some months, when the time came for them to be sent out, they become insubordinate, declaring that they were American citizens and refused to be dealt with.' Watkins told the court that when he arrived in Liverpool he was 'not in his senses when he joined' and that he might have been drugged when he came off his ship. This held no sway with the court and he was sentenced to six months' imprisonment with hard labour.

A week later, another two Americans, Newton W. Logan and James E. Daley, appeared at Blackpool Court. They were dressed in khaki, and the pair were charged with failing to register as aliens.[71] James Daley, who had claimed to be a Canadian, told the court that he had registered at Liverpool where he had joined the army. Logan stated that he was told in Liverpool that there was 'no need to register in Blackpool City'. He had been arrested the day prior to the court case and brought to the battalion Orderly Room for obtaining money by false pretences by pretending to have been a wounded soldier; it then 'leaked out' that he was an American. They both admitted making false attestations. Captain Duder of the Liverpool Irish told the court that 'these were two more of a long series of similar cases which had occurred in the 8th Liverpool Irish'. Both men were sentenced to six months' imprisonment.

American soldiers who evaded registering as aliens and managed to join the British army became aware of the significance of the penalty under Kings' Regulations for desertion in the field. In January 1916, an army censor intercepted a letter written by Charles Joseph Kaudy, to his mother in the United States.[72] Kaudy, who had fraudulently enlisted in the Liverpool Irish in April 1915, was completing his training prior to being posted and he was homesick and regretting his decision. He had been made aware of the fact that he would be leaving for France in three weeks and was undergoing a final rifle training course when he decided to leave. 'I am a disgrace to this country and I will go mad if I do not get out of Europe,' he wrote. Kaudy then asked his mother to send him some money to assist him with his plan to avoid service in France. 'I am registering this letter to you so that you can send me 30 dollars to flee with. I will be asked why I don't want to fight. A man refusing to fight shall be shot like a dog and do you want me to be put to death?' Having employed some emotional blackmail, he urged his mother not to delay in sending the funds; 'I might as well tell you now I will never see home. I will close now, and for God's sake rush the money to your son.' Kaudy appeared at Blackpool Court, where he was charged with failing to register as an alien and with entering a prohibited area. Captain Duder of the Liverpool Irish prosecuted the case and he told the court that he had reluctantly withdrawn a charge of false attestation since Kaudy had enlisted more than six months previous. Duder stated that Kaudy had been in the army 'enjoying the hospitality of the country' and that he had 'lived as a parasite upon our resources'. Kaudy would not be going to France; instead, he was sentenced to prison with hard labour for four months.

Mobilisation and Home Defence

The battalion's base at Shaw Street in the city was inadequate for a large-scale wartime mobilisation and the Liverpool Irish were given permission to use the grounds and buildings of St Francis Xavier school. The school magazine described the sights and sounds of a battalion as they mustered and made their preparations for war:

> August 10th, 1914 brought a sudden and startling change on our deserted col-lege: the porter and cleaners were unceremoniously bidden to depart, and all their work of the previous three weeks was quickly undone. That night saw six hundred and sixty-two soldiers the 8th Irish, all but two companies occupying the building and sleeping on the premises. The college playground was the scene of military parade; the cycle shed ground reverberated with the heavy tread of hundreds of men passing to and fro, and bugle-calls from before six in the morning until after ten at night pierced through every nook and corner

of the Presbytery. We needed nothing more to remind us that war had begun, even though we were hundreds of miles from the fighting lines.[73]

The arrival of the soldiers caused a great deal of excitement among the pupils and according to the *Xaverian*, 'the children were in clover' as they watched the commandeering of horses, drill and the arrival of Maxim guns. The school also provided the 600 Roman Catholics of the battalion with the opportunity to attend Mass on Sunday morning and again in the evening. As they left the church, the Rector presented each man with a badge of the Sacred Heart.[74] Their stay at St Francis Xavier was all too brief, and on Thursday, 20 August the battalion departed for Knowsley where they would remain under canvas awaiting deployment.

George Tomlinson, an 18-year-old bank employee from Clifton near Preston, was critical of the standard of some of his fellow recruits from Preston when he described his introduction to life in the Liverpool Irish.[75] 'They were rather a rough crush that went from Preston but it's not so bad now as about thirty of the Blackpool nuts have joined our company.' On arriving at Exchange Station in the centre of Liverpool, the men were formed up and marched to the battalion Drill Hall at Shaw Street. 'Just after we landed, we saw about 600 of our Regiment going on parade, grand sight it was; band too.' The recruits were then marched back into the city for dinner at the Cunard Hotel where they enjoyed 'soup first, then meat potatoes and gravy galore after that tapioca pudding'. After marching back to Shaw Street and the drawn-out process of completing paperwork, George wrote that 'some of the rough gang have been sent back'. The men were then put up in boarding houses where they had to be in by ten o'clock in the evening, with lights out at 10.15 p.m. The routine in Liverpool was repetitive: 'reveille 6 a.m., breakfast 7 a.m., march to the Drill Hall 9 a.m'. For young men, unaccustomed to being away from home, this strange new military existence was too much, and George Tomlinson agreed to comfort a youngster from Preston who, after just a few days away from his family, was already feeling homesick.

Following mobilisation, the Liverpool Irish were ordered to carry out a series of home defence duties which included periods of guarding various locations around the Mersey coast. They were then sent to guard 58 miles of railway lines before being sent to the Thanet coast in Kent.[76] During their time in Kent, the 8th Liverpool Irish were billeted in Canterbury and Whitstable. Private James Green, along with several others, spent his first night in Canterbury sleeping in the tap room of a pub called the Three Cups.[77] The following morning, his Sergeant arrived and asked the men to draw lots for the chance to stay with a local family. Green noted in his diary:

'John Thompson won it for us, so Dixon, Clough, Thompson and me went as a billet to the Edney family of 106 Broad Street. We had a good time and they were very homely people. Mr Edney worked on a tractor engine in the hop fields, he used to take us down to the hop fields to watch them tying up the hops.'

Some less fortunate Liverpool men from the 1/6th King's, another Liverpool territorial unit, were made to feel unwelcome in a house in Canterbury. One of the men, Norman Ellison, suspected that the woman of the house had made her displeasure at having soldiers billeted in her home known by smearing jam in and around the bolts of their rifles.[78] The people of Whitstable seemed to warm to the Liverpool Irishmen and began to organise a series of entertainments for the men. On 5 December 1914, the second house at the Palace Theatre in the town hosted a talent competition performed by the Liverpool Irish. The competition was judged by Captain Smith, who commanded the Whitstable contingent of the battalion.[79] The local paper reported that Smith received a warm reception from his men and commented that Smith had 'studied their welfare, not only in comfort but amusement also'. Many prizes had been given by the townspeople which included: Private Murphy, a silver cigarette case; Bugler Devaney, a pipe and tin of tobacco; Sergeant Donnelly, a compass; and Private Butler received a silver medal. The paper also announced that the Liverpool Irish would be hosting a boxing tournament in the town, 'which would be a red-letter night to lovers of the noble art'.[80] Later in December, an 'Irish Night' was held at the Oxford Picture Hall in the town, where the 'picked talent of the 8th Irish Liverpool Regiment' performed in front of two packed houses.[81]

Having been a pre-war territorial, Private James Green was selected to join a company of trained men and was moved from Canterbury to Whitstable where he became a member of a machine gun team.[82] Unlike many others in his battalion, Green was not billeted with a local family; instead, he and his team found themselves 'in a big hotel on the front, it was our headquarters there were no civilians in it. We were on army rations and then there were not enough of them.' This did not alter his impression of the town and its people, 'It's a nice place Whitstable, and we made a lot of new friends, we even got an invitation to go with the local fishermen to catch oysters.' Entertainments and excursions notwithstanding, the local Wesleyan church opened its doors every evening at six o'clock to provide the men of the Liverpool Irish with a 'large and comfortable' room for their personal use. They also provided the men with writing materials, games and refreshments.[83] James Green wrote that the battalion did a lot of intensive drilling and training while they were at Canterbury and Whitstable. Winter days filled with hard training and physical exertion did not appear to have had any adverse effect on the Liverpool Irishmen's night-time activities. Green (who was neither Liverpudlian, nor Irish) was soon enjoying their company and their nocturnal musical efforts; 'it was right lively being in an Irish regiment, there was always a lot of jigging and Irish reels, some of the lads could keep it up for hours. I sent my concertina home; I did not need it now.'[84]

With Christmas approaching, and having been away from home for some four months, no doubt many of the men had been looking forward to returning to Liverpool on leave. James Green was one of the unfortunate ones who remained on duty over the Christmas period manning a machine gun post on the coast.[85] Those men who remained in Whitstable over the Christmas period were not forgotten by the people in the town. The local paper commented that: 'Christmas away from home would be very dull to many of the Tommies, but for the kind acts of a large number of our townspeople.'[86] On Christmas Day and Boxing Day, the people of Whitstable gave up part of their own celebrations to entertain the Liverpool Irish. The Seasalter Parish Hall, the Foresters' Hall and the Wesleyan Schoolroom were opened to feed and entertain the soldiers. The Christmas Day festivities began at the Wesleyan Schoolroom which had been decorated in a 'Christmassy fashion'; and the men were treated to a 'sumptuous tea' and a 'plentiful supply of fruit and nuts'. Later, Captain Smith joined his men who greeted him with a chorus of 'For he's a jolly good fellow'. Smith addressed the gathering on the subject of drink; he stated that while he was a strict disciplinarian and had to mete out punishment, nevertheless, he had a 'warm corner in his heart for his men'. Smith laid the blame for excessive bibulous indulgence on those civilians who had treated his men to drink, and when a soldier appeared before him on a charge, he 'always took into consideration the fact that it was not always the man's fault'. Captain Smith was then presented with a pair of green boxing gloves, which had been donated to the battalion by the editor of *Boxing* magazine. The men of the battalion cheered as Smith thanked everyone concerned with the gift and said that the donors 'could not have picked a more appropriate colour'.[87]

The amusements continued into Boxing Day when the battalion was entertained at the local Parish Hall and the Foresters' Hall.[88] Here the men enjoyed a meal followed by smoking concerts. Following a series of toasts, Father Ryan, a local priest, rose to address the men. He received loud cheers when he revealed that he had been speaking to some of the men who had told him that since being mobilised, that they had been posted to seventeen various locations, and that they had never been happier than at Whitstable. Striking a political note, Ryan stated that some of his Conservative friends had noticed a change since John Redmond, leader of the Irish Parliamentary Party, had spoken in the House of Commons. They were surprised, he said, that Irishmen were laying down their lives for England. Invoking the historical rhetoric of the exploits of the Irish Brigade, Ryan asked his Tory friends to 'remember that they were not only fighting for their faith, for this was a Christian war, but for dear old Ireland because this would be remembered later on. They were fighting for that which their forefathers had fought so well.' The men of the Liverpool Irish had, he said, 'the glorious traditions of their regiment before them and surely, if Irishmen fought well in those days, they would fight well now for gallant little Belgium'. In proposing a toast, Father Ryan said that the Liverpool Irish would 'fight as British soldiers, as men of Lancashire, as the sons of Irishmen or as Irishmen themselves'.[89]

The pleasantries and distractions of Whitstable failed to console one member of the battalion who voiced his dissatisfaction in the *Liverpool Echo* with the fact that the Liverpool Irish had been refused any home leave.[90] 'Why do the 8th get no leave while the others get five days?' he asked. He stressed that he was not complaining about Colonel Neale, 'who is a trump and the right man for our lot' but since as they were not yet in France, the soldier failed to see why they could not get any leave. 'If we were at the front, we could not expect to get it, but we are not there, and I hope it won't be long before we are, as I think we are pretty well trained.'

On Wednesday, 27 January 1915, as the battalion's time in Whitstable was coming to an end, the people of the town crowded into the Assembly Rooms to watch a performance of *Little Red Riding Hood* and to watch the presentation of a trophy to the officers and men of the Liverpool Irish.[91] Following the performance, Mr Morris told the audience that 'the people of Whitstable were not backward in coming forward to show their appreciation for the gallant soldiers in their midst'. A collection had been held in the town to purchase a memento for the soldiers in appreciation of their time in Whitstable. After discussing the matter with Captain Smith, it was decided to present the battalion with a silver cup. Morris told the audience that the cup was solid silver, weighed 115 ounces, 18 inches tall and 15.5 inches wide. Morris said that he mentioned these details 'because they might be valuable someday to a detective. (Laughter)'. The impressively named Lieutenant Colonel Algernon Hastings Campbell Neale, Commanding Officer of the Liverpool Irish, received the cup on behalf of the battalion. It was inscribed with the words:

Presented by the people of Whitstable to Lt. Col. A.H.C. Neale the officers & men of the 8th Irish Batt. The King's Liverpool Regt. In appreciation of the good conduct of the men of the detachment quartered at Whitstable under the command of Major J.J. Smith. Jan. 27, 1915.[92]

Neale joked that since Major Smith had been promoted he had refused to move to the battalion's headquarters at Canterbury and had insisted on remaining at Whitstable. He added that this was not an isolated instance, as forty or fifty men who had gone into Whitstable from Canterbury at the weekends had taken 'French leave', and when they were brought before him at Canterbury every Monday they always offered the same excuse, that they 'had missed the last train'. Neale told the audience that since mobilisation, most of the public had been unaware that the battalion had been guarding railway lines and coastal defences, but since they had been at Whitstable the people in the town knew what the soldiers were doing. He went on to say that the cup would become a 'regimental heirloom' and that 'for generations to come, men would be proud of it'. Private James Green, who had been at the presentation, wrote that it 'was a good send off'.[93]

Given late Victorian ambivalent attitudes towards soldiering in general and a mistrust of the Irish, it may be surprising that relations between the northern, urban, city-dwelling Liverpudlian Irish and the populace of the southern coastal towns of Canterbury and Whitstable were excellent. The Liverpool Irish had entertained and had been entertained by the people of Whitstable and an atmosphere of mutual hospitality and appreciation prevailed during the winter of 1914. Except for a few minor disciplinary offences involving drink, or those who returned late to camp after spending an unofficial extended weekend in Whitstable, the Liverpool Irish and the people of Canterbury and Whitstable more than managed to coexist during the first months of the war. This was obvious when the time came for the battalion to leave the area. There were emotional scenes when the Edney family from Canterbury, who had billeted James Green and his friends, came to the railway station to wave them off; 'they were all crying,' he wrote, 'but the best of friends must part.'[94]

TRENCH LIFE, PATROLS AND RAIDS

While the officers and men who experienced the war on the Western Front came from separate classes within British society, they undoubtedly endured and shared the same wretched conditions, climate, sights, smells and dangers. It is difficult to reach any precise conclusions about how well prepared the different classes were in 1914 to withstand the horrors of the industrialised war zones in France and Belgium. Moreover, it is equally problematic to demonstrate with any real certainty how the shared experiences of trench warfare impacted on these classes. Historians have offered differing explanations. John Bourne has asserted that, 'The British soldier of the Great War was essentially the British working man in uniform', but that nothing which he had experienced in civilian life could have prepared him for what he might encounter at the front.[1] Others have argued that British perceptions of how the war was experienced had been shaped by the literature of middle-class veterans and rural poets who were more susceptible to the shock of warfare than their working-class, urban subordinates.[2] Like their Glaswegian counterparts, some of those who served in the ranks of the Liverpool Irish and had the misfortune to inhabit the slums of Scotland Road or Vauxhall might well have been accustomed to squalor, cold, rain, meagre meals and sectarian violence. The undoubted hardships of slum conditions and occasional sectarian clashes, however violent, could not have prepared them for the onslaught of machine guns, mortars, high explosive shells and flamethrowers which awaited them on the Western Front.[3] On 3 May 1915, both officers and men of the Liverpool Irish arrived in France where they had their first experiences of trench warfare.

On a personal level, Captain Harold Mahon was relieved to be in France and free from puerile military bureaucratic requests such as, 'Will the large chestnut mare kindly condescend to be inoculated twice before going abroad?' Or, mundane directives; 'The battalion being the battalion for duty, all ranks will sleep in their boots.' More importantly perhaps, Mahon was unimpressed by the quality of the local beer being sold in the estaminets which 'tastes like dandelion beer mixed with vinegar and water, plenty of water'. He was, however, even less enamoured with the inhabitants of the villages behind the lines. 'Taking the people of these villages all through, they seem to be a money grubbing lot and don't appear to appreciate a bit that it is very much to their benefit to have English soldiers over here. Maybe they are very ignorant.'[4] An army censors report confirms that Mahon's views of the French were widespread:

> Of the French civilian population – 'A dirty lot' is a common phrase – they have the poorest opinion; and complaints as to the exorbitant charges made by the French are very frequent and widespread. The opinion is in general that Tommy is simply 'fleeced'.[5]

The battalion stayed at Locon for a brief time where the men had their first encounter with an estaminet. Bad beer notwithstanding, the challenge for the thirstier men among the Liverpool Irish, was that a canal ran through the village and, as Private Green noted, the estaminet was on the opposite bank; 'if you wanted a drink you had to get into a small boat and pull yourself across with a rope'.[6]

The Irish had very little time to familiarise themselves with trench life. Having arrived in France on 4 May 1915, they began their first tour in the trenches in a redoubt just south of Rue du Bois near Le Casan some three weeks later. Writing home, Private George Tomlinson described the excitement and danger of his first experiences in the line:

> We are not allowed to sleep at all during the night, we have to get a bit of a nap in the day time if possible. The 8th Irish are doing great things now. You must watch the papers, especially the Liverpool ones. Our Colonel is fine. He is simply delighted with us especially last night. We had some very dangerous work to do then. B Company had to set off about 9 o'clock last night and go 200 yards in front of trench. It was half exciting. The Germans send up flares at night which burst over our lines. I've never seen such great lights before. I don't know whatever they are made of. We had about 3 or 4 hours in which we had to dig ourselves in. We filled 3,500 sand bags and made quite a decent cover. Snipers bullets and shrapnel was flying all round, but in the dark, they couldn't get the correct range, so we never lost a man. It was a marvellous piece of work for Terriers. The Colonel was just quivering with delight, 'You see, the British have now advanced 200 yards. Well done B.'[7]

The Germans shelled the party, killing two men and injuring three others. Later that night, the Gurkhas sent some men to lie out in No Man's Land where they captured two German snipers and were obviously delighted, creating some noise in celebration. Casualties, shellfire, flares and screaming Gurkhas combined to create an unnerving debut for the inexperienced Liverpool Irish. 'What with their yells and the heavy firing they brought on us, I am afraid our boys got somewhat panicky. It was a very nasty experience and we got well out of it.' Although nerve-wracking, Captain Mahon believed that such events made the men 'much steadier'.[8] The men had to deal with the impact of one of the more obnoxious weapons of trench warfare: gas. The antidote to the German gas, as described by Private James Green, was nevertheless primitive and disgusting. When the gas alarm sounded, the men would get their respirators out: 'it was a piece of muslin and inside was a piece of cotton wool rolled tight, you then had to soak it in a bucket of urine in the corner of the trench and put it over your nose and mouth. That was the only protection we had against the gas.'[9]

In a letter home, Private George Tomlinson wrote of the stark contrast between the ghastly landscapes of the battlefield and the beauty of the surrounding countryside. 'There must have been thousands of lives lost around that place. In the shell holes, sticking out of the trench walls you can see perhaps a man's head, or a leg or an arm sticking out. They can't have been buried – just covered with earth and left.' Realising that he was dwelling on the morbid reality of trench life, changing the subject he asked, 'Are the flowers out in England? The roses are in full bloom here and the gardens are quite brilliant with colour. It seems a shame that men are killing each other on a day like this.'[10] Corporal Percival wrote that he preferred the trenches to his billet behind the line.[11] 'We have just come out and are "resting" in a battered old barn. I was more comfy in the trenches, because when the rain did come on we had good shelter; but going in and coming out we had to come through a communication trench half-full of water.' In a few short weeks, the Irish had experienced the harsh realities of trench warfare.

Private James Green was disgruntled when supposedly at 'rest' behind the lines. 'The rest we get when we come out of the line consists of going back up the line carrying sandbags, barbed wire and mortar shells to the engineers and sappers also duck boards to put down in the trenches, so you are not walking in water. You get them kind of jobs nearly every night all for 1/- a day and I allow half of that home to my father. He gets 7/6d a week.'[12] Being an officer, Captain Harold Mahon was not required to participate in digging, repairing, sentry duty, or indeed hauling trench supplies up to the lines. He witnessed his men performing these tasks and was filled with admiration for them:

After being in the trenches two weeks, we were relieved by another brigade of ours and my battalion marched right through to Millencourt, where we billeted. Seven miles, after standing about for two weeks and carrying a load fit for a pack mule – blanket, oil sheet, woolly coat, a wet great coat mud-died up and weighing any old figure, rifle gear and equipment etc. This told somewhat on the men, but then Thomas is perfectly wonderful. I admire him more every day. Nothing is too good for him.[13]

British imagery of soldiers of the Great War has been dominated by press reports, photographs and films of enthusiastic young men rushing to join the colours in 1914. Clearly, those images do not lie; the age limit for recruits in 1914 was for men from 19 to 30 years of age. The upper age limit for the army was extended in October 1914, to 38 years for initial recruits and to 45 years of age for former soldiers. Some less discerning recruiting Sergeants may well have turned a blind eye to potential recruits who were obviously under age. One much older recruit managed not only to dupe the recruiting Sergeant and the MO to enlist in the Liverpool Irish in 1914, and he went on to serve in the firing line alongside his friends in France. Private O'Rourke, who was more than twenty years older than the upper age limit, was in the trenches at Aveluy in August 1915. Captain Harold Mahon was impressed. 'Whilst here we lost a character who went to the base. This was O'Rourke, 67 years of age, he had managed to leave the band of which he was a member and by giving a wrong age, he had actually come out with us and stuck it as well as the best.'[14] Mahon went on to write that that O'Rourke had not finished his service but had been employed at the base doing odd jobs at the base: 'anyway he has done his share'. Private O'Rourke's notoriety spread, and in October 1915, he was interviewed at his home in the north of the city by a reporter from the *Liverpool Echo*.[15] The paper reported that O'Rourke had managed to enlist through being persistent and demanding to be sent to France 'with the "Irish bhoys" [*sic*] for he was one of them "entirely"'. O'Rourke was evidently proud of his service and his battalion: 'I've done night and day marches without ever falling out and those have done me not the slightest of harm.' Praising his comrades in the Liverpool Irish (in a linguistic turn which modern day readers might find amusing), he said, 'All the Irish out there are gay and frisky and panting for the fray and when they get the chance they are off to the Germans like greyhounds slipped from the leash.'

More nauseating than the sights of war, perhaps, was the stench which accompanies it. At Festubert, Captain Mahon noticed a cart full of bodies 'supposed to be Germans' and although chloride of lime had been used to cover the bodies, 'the whole place reeked like a shambles and one hurried past'.[16] Life at the front with all the inherent dangers and monotony led some soldiers among the Liverpool Irish to discuss (in an ironic fashion) the difficulties involved in attempting to get back home. While a severe wound guaranteed a berth on the boat to 'Blighty', according to Captain Harold Mahon, the favoured and less drastic alternative was 'shell concussion', or 'to turn looney'. Mahon wrote that one wag in the Liverpool Irish suggested, 'painting a duck on the Orderly Room door and then going to feed it every morning. He thought this would soon "work a ticket" as they call being sent home.'[17]

To alleviate the monotony and routine of trench life, some men resorted to taunting the enemy. Private Green had a lucky escape, 'At Festubert, me and Thompson had a narrow escape, we were looking over the top kidding Fritz, we just got back down in time as he sent a lot of whiz-bangs over; they are deadly things you don't hear them coming till they burst among you and they do a lot of damage.'[18] In August 1915, Signaller Nichols, of the Liverpool Irish wrote, 'The Huns seem pretty well informed as to the occupants of our trenches for on several occasions they shouted across to us "Come out and fight us Irish".'[19] Sergeant Britt struggled to restrain one of his men who was continually yelling abuse at the German trenches.[20] Britt thought the man had a 'charmed life' because he had made himself a target for the German snipers. As he had failed to prevent the man from continuing his crusade, he 'got a megaphone for him and he is not half enjoying himself'. In November 1915, the *Liverpool Daily Post* provided an account of 'a reckless, hot-blooded Irish soldier' who, being disgruntled with his confinement in the narrow trenches, suddenly leapt onto the parapet to alleviate his frustrations on the Germans, shouting, 'Shoot ye larger swillin' sausage guzzlers.'[21] The Germans obliged and promptly shot his cap off, leading him to retort, 'Too high, yer blind, fat pigs, too high.' Recklessness was not just the preserve of the ranks. Captain Bodel acquired a reputation for risk-taking among his men; on a moonlit night around Christmas time in 1915, he crawled across No Man's Land to steal a German flag which he sent home to Bootle. On another occasion he went out on his own to rescue a wounded man who turned out to be one of his Sergeants. According to his local paper Captain Bodel was 'universally' admired and 'with the Irish section he was an especial favourite'.[22]

Not all Germans reacted angrily to the insults hurled by the Irish. Corporal Percival witnessed their humorous side when he fired at the German lines. 'I've had a few shots at a periscope, but the Germans just waved me a "wash out".'[23] Conversely, the marksmanship of some of the German soldiers was excellent. According to Percival, 'They smashed three of our periscopes yesterday and the size of them is 2in by 1in at 350 yards. Not bad shooting we must admit.' Signaller Nichols also commented on the prowess and accuracy of the German snipers who had just killed two men from the Irish. According to Nichols, another two men had been fortunate when each had been shot in the head. They had 'their hair parted', he wrote, fortunately both escaped with grazes.[24] On 28 August 1915, Captain Mahon celebrated his birthday by performing watch duty in the trenches, when the Germans fired a few whiz-bangs at the Liverpool Irish lines:

> When I tried to get their direction from our parapet, a sniper nearly put paid to my account. Right past my ear, I was deaf for hours after, shaved my cap and right through a corporal's cap alongside me. For a moment, each of us thought the other had been playing the fool and given him a crack on the ear. Might have been a case for the Doc or the firing squad. Nuff said.[25]

Locating the enemy's snipers was difficult and dangerous. On 20 March 1916, at Bretincourt, Private Edgar Sandell, a battalion sniper was shot dead while attempting to establish the location of his sniping counterpart in the German lines.[26] All soldiers in the front line needed to exercise vigilance when moving around the trenches. To emphasise the point, a 'humourist' in the Liverpool Irish managed to procure and place a French railway sign in the trench to warn of the hazards in looking over the top of the trench: '*Il est dangereuse se pencher dehors*'.[27] The question as to whether the linguistic competencies of the Liverpool Irishmen and their Lancastrian comrades in the ranks allowed them to understand or appreciate the joke remains unanswered. The high water table in some areas meant that the trenches could not be excavated to the required depth to provide cover from enemy fire. This meant that breastworks had to be constructed by stacking sandbags on the parapet to provide cover from view and the attentions of German snipers. However, the historian of the 51st Highland Division noted when the division arrived in France that the German machine gunners, usually famed for their expertise in defence, were equally proficient in demolishing the British breastworks:

> German machine gunners were also expert at firing a series of bursts into a particular position of breastworks until it became non-bullet-proof. They would continue firing bursts at irregular intervals at the same spot, with the result that the bullets penetrated the parapet and came through into the trench. Casualties were often caused in this manner.[28]

Not all deaths and injuries were due to enemy action in the firing line, and accidents did occur. On 29 May 1915, just weeks after their arrival, one man was killed and another injured whilst 'playing with old hand grenades'.[29] Even when relaxing, accidents happened. In July 1915, a man from 'A' Company drowned while bathing in a nearby river. The man had been a strong swimmer but had become entangled in weeds. He was buried by his comrades close to the river bank where he had died.[30]

For the fortunate few who were carrying injuries or were for whatever reason deemed unsuitable for the rigours of trench life, opportunities for alternative duties materialised in January 1916 when the battalion moved to join the 55th Division. Captain Mahon noted that the division now required men from the battalion for employment behind the lines; 'everything from flying pigeons to looking after baths. Here is where we get rid of the "stiff", which includes the aged, the halt, the maimed and the blind. Many men find a cushy or nice soft job, such as they and the officers also, dream about when under heavy fire or knee deep in mud.'[31] When Mahon was dispatched to carry out a survey to check the suitability of all the barns and buildings behind the lines for potential billets, he began to feel isolated and detached.[32] 'Of course, this makes things rather lonesome as I am detached from my regiment, but then I have a good billet, my servant to look after me and there are always other officers' messes to visit.' Mahon commented that 'most people would jump at the job'. Lance-Corporal Long, of the Liverpool Irish, who had been a trap driver for the *Liverpool Echo* before the war, summarised the rigours, trials and tribulations of trench life and soldiering in this piece of doggerel:

When your billet's in a cowshed and the bloomin' roof all leaks.
When you're only paid five franks for pretty near twelve weeks.
When if sick the doctor gives you 'M' and 'D' and sends you back.
When you've lost your iron rations, your smoke helmet and your pack.
When your rifle's choked with mud and got 'F.P.' number two.
When your pals all go to Blighty, every bloomin' one but you.
When you've got to hop the parapet and courage is at zero.
Just remember who you are my boy, a bloomin' British hero.[33]

Gripes about pay and squalid billets notwithstanding, complaints about food, either the quantity of their meals or the lack of variety in their diet, often occupied soldiers' minds. The censor noted from soldiers' correspondence that complaints about army food usually preceded a request for treats from home: '"such delicacies as pieces of pork with plenty of crackling" being undoubtedly a welcome variety to bully beef a la mode as the unceasing plat du jour'.[34] Unsurprisingly, the monotony of the army menu encouraged some of the more resourceful gourmands among the Liverpool Irish to procure some locally raised livestock. Put crudely, they pilfered any animal which presented itself. It did not take long before complaints were received from local farmers about their missing animals. Captain Harold Mahon had scant sympathy for the victims and was amused by the antics of his men:

> An old French Dame said that English soldiers had stolen a prize rabbit; it is always a prize thing if it is stolen. Captain Meadows told his company what would happen if it didn't turn up at once, dead or alive. Shortly afterwards the rabbit walked back into its hutch.[35]

According to Harold Mahon, Captain Meadows continued his quest to find any poachers in his company. One evening he encountered Private Powell 'stewing something in a dixie'; when he checked the contents he discovered some old bones. However, returning an hour later across a nearby field, he kicked an old biscuit tin and discovered a 'steaming duck' inside the tin. No one claimed ownership of the duck. A month later, Captain Mahon spoke to Powell about the incident and he admitted that the duck was his. Powell's questionable explanation amused Mahon; Powell stated that he met the duck on the road and that it said, 'quack and was generally insolent'. Powell warned it that if it continued he would 'put it on the roll of honour'; the duck quacked again, and Powell hit it on the head and its name was duly entered.[36]

Patrolling and Raiding

> So long as men who took part in the war are alive, the subject of raids is likely to crop up whenever two or three are met together.[37]

In his discussion of battle tactics during the First World War, Paddy Griffith states that the tactical benefits of raiding on the Western Front have been 'buried under a mountain of ill feeling'.[38] Griffith argues that some soldiers believed that raiding was carried out at a disproportionate ratio in terms of the insignificant ground and intelligence obtained against the excessive number of casualties. With some justification, many believed that for senior commanders on the Western Front, raiding was merely an instrument for instilling an 'offensive spirit' in their troops.

One of the first trench raids to occur on the Western Front took place in November 1915. The Indian Division carried out several raids in the Neuve Chapelle sector. The first raid was carried out without artillery support, relying solely on the element of surprise. The second raid was covered by an artillery barrage which alerted the Germans and the raiders were forced to withdraw. A third raid was organised due to necessity rather than a planned display of aggression since the Germans were digging saps dangerously close to the Indian lines.[39] Soon afterwards, Canadian troops mounted a well-researched 'butcher and bolt' raid at Petite Douve Farm near Ypres.[40] Prior to the raid, reconnaissance patrols had scouted the area and the artillery had bombarded the German lines to clear the enemy wire. Detailed plans of the area had taken up to two weeks to prepare before a raiding party of ten officers and 170 men raided the German lines. The raid was a success, resulting in the capture of twelve prisoners and an estimated thirty to forty Germans being killed. The Canadian raid had impressed the British hierarchy and it set the standard for British raiding on the Western Front.

In 1914, previous military experience within the ranks of the Liverpool Irish men was confined to drill, the occasional route march and basic musketry. These men were essentially civilians, inculcated with civilian values. Joanna Bourke has argued that no amount of military training could prepare men who lacked the 'elusive offensive spirit'.[41] Irish soldiers had gained a reputation as aggressive combatants. One commentator explained, 'there is in the Irish soldier a particular quality of electric zeal and dash. "Missile troops" they have been called and the phrase is eloquent of much.'[42] In 1914, the egotistical and self-serving Percy Crozier briefed the officers of the 9th Royal Irish Rifles on the subject of the offensive spirit, telling them, 'I can teach you the offensive spirit to a certain extent – I have it myself – but it is largely born in a man, not made.'[43]

For military commanders in 1914, the bayonet charge epitomised the supposed innate aggression and physical courage of the British soldier. Instructions on infantry training documented the importance of firepower; however, they stressed that it was close-quarter fighting that secured victory. 'The object of fire is to prepare the way for the charge with the bayonet, and that success can only be achieved by closing with the enemy.'[44] Surprisingly, this view was shared by the other ranks but for different reasons. Soldiers became frustrated and disillusioned at being mutilated by an enemy they never saw and longed for hand-to-hand combat.[45]

Death was an omnipresent hazard on the Western Front. The risk of injury or death could be mitigated if both sides desisted from any aggressive action 'whereby antagonists maximised life chances and minimised death chances', creating an unspoken agreement to 'live and let live'.[46] Some front-line battalions sought to dominate No Man's Land, the contested space between the British and German lines, by constant patrolling to acquire intelligence or to seek out and to engage enemy patrols. While some soldiers felt that they were 'doing their bit' by the fact that they were in the front line, others – for whatever reason: revenge, excitement or out of the sheer monotony of trench life – volunteered as scouts, patrol men or raiders. Tony Ashworth postulates the view that most of the historiography of the war has concentrated on large battles. However, between major offensives, it was junior officers and soldiers who often made choices as to whether offensive operations should take place. When small-scale operations did occur, specialist scouts and patrol men armed with a variety of trench fighting weaponry were deployed.

In early 1915, trench raids were largely localised affairs, planned and organised at battalion level. By 1916, raids became more centralised, with GHQ directing raids in accordance with Haig's policy of attrition.[47] The supposed belligerence and fighting qualities of the two Irish Divisions on the Western Front were harnessed by their respective commanders. General William Hickie of the 16th Irish Division and Major-General Oliver Nugent of the 36th Ulster Division could arguably be described as 'thrusters' and both expected an elevated level of aggression from their men. From the opening of the Somme offensive on 1 July 1916 to the Battle of Messines on 7 June 1917, the 36th Ulster Division carried out more than a dozen raids against the German trenches.[48] The 16th Irish Division commanded by General William Hickie, and Brigadier-General George Pereira, commanding 47th Infantry Brigade, were convinced advocates of the British high command's raiding policy. The cost to the division collectively, and to the 6th Connaught Rangers specifically, was high. In the three 'raiding months' prior to their attacks on the Somme in September 1916, the division sustained a total of 2,670 casualties: 380 killed, 2,268 wounded and 22 missing. By the end of September 1916, the 6th Connaught Rangers required drafts of 15 officers and 328 other ranks to bring the battalion back up to strength.[49] General Oliver Nugent commanding the 36th Ulster Division was an aggressive commander who did not believe in the 'live and let live' system of trench warfare.[50] Yet Nugent's belligerence was tempered by a careful appreciation of the risks and benefits of a raid. He was not prepared to sacrifice men needlessly on trench raids in the face of a well-prepared enemy defending an impregnable trench line. Writing home after two unsuccessful raids against well-defended German positions, Nugent told his wife that 'it is never the policy to lose men if it can be helped', he wrote, 'so if the Boche is prepared we don't try to do anything'.[51]

Before the war, Captain Harold Mahon had been a Sergeant in the 6th Liverpool Rifles, another Territorial Army battalion in the city. During this peacetime service, Mahon trained as a battalion scout when he acquired a variety of skills including patrolling, map reading, signalling and military sketching. In November 1915, while the Liverpool Irish were still attached to the 51st Division, the battalion found themselves at Authuille where Mahon could exercise his previous military scouting expertise. By the winter of 1915, the British were utilising aerial photographs of the front, which Mahon found invaluable in preparing for 'these little affairs'. Accompanied by a 'stout corporal and two men' he carried out a reconnaissance patrol of a wood which lay between the British and German lines. The battalion occupying the trenches prior to the Irish believed that the Germans were in the woods; however, Mahon's patrol confirmed that the wood was clear and showed no signs of enemy activity. The patrol impressed Mahon's superiors at Brigade Headquarters and he commented that some men were keen to carry out patrols into No Man's Land. 'Of course this work goes on at every trench we occupy [and], you could always get a party to bring in a sample of German wire.' Apart from receiving plaudits from the staff officers at Brigade, Mahon believed that the patrols also had a positive impact on morale within the battalion; 'Brigade have taken to publishing the men's names who form the patrols and it bucks them up wonderfully.'[52] The army recognised that some patrols involved face-to-face encounters and that while the hierarchy continued to extol the virtues of the bayonet, a shorter, less cumbersome weapon would be useful. In October 1915, while the Irish were in the trenches, the battalion was issued with a new patrol weapon. It was, wrote Captain Mahon, 'a weapon such as the ancient Saxon would think his great, great grandfather had left him as a trophy. A piece of timber some two feet long, rounded off, heavily leaded at the thick end and with horseshoe nails heads sprouting from it. "A thing of beauty is a joy forever".'[53]

With the onset of Christmas in December 1915, the hierarchy of the 51st Highland Division was keen to ensure that there would be no repetition of the 1914 yuletide pleasantries in No Man's Land. According to the historian of the 51st Highland Division, any seasonal fraternal overtures on the part of the enemy were swiftly discouraged:

On Christmas Day a curious exchange of compliments took place with the enemy. On Christmas Eve he sang carols; this was at once stopped by the Divisional artillery. He then came out of his trenches to fraternise; this was also stopped by the divisional artillery. He retaliated by shelling Albert; the

Division on the right immediately shelled Courcelette. The enemy then shelled Aveluy; the gunners replied by shelling Pozieres. The enemy had the last word, for he then shelled Martinsart, where he hit a horse, a mule, and a limber loaded with grenades, which fortunately did not burst.[54]

The belligerent attitude continued when the Liverpool Irish left their comrades in the Highland Division and returned to the 55th West Lancashire Division in January 1916. J.O. Coop, the division's official historian, noted that having relieved the French south of Arras, the division immediately assumed an aggressive stance towards the enemy. 'To harass the enemy as much as possible; to keep him ever on the alert; to lose no opportunity of inflicting casualties upon him – these were from the first the methods drilled into the division and the enemy was not slow in learning to appreciate them.'[55] In May 1916, the battalion instigated a system of 'standing patrols', were each company supplied a group of men to lurk in No Man's Land immediately in front of their wire where they would engage any German patrols.[56]

By 1916, the General Staff had become aware of the fact that tacit truces existed in certain sectors of the Western Front. To counter any such scheme of peaceful co-existence, they issued instructions in the form of a booklet entitled *Notes for Infantry Officers on Trench Warfare*.[57] The General Staff stated that there was 'an insidious tendency' for troops to become 'passive' and 'lethargic' when in the front lines, and they urged officers to display leadership and to guard against these attitudes. The booklet called on all officers of all ranks to foster 'the offensive spirit'.[58]

Defence-minded Germans were alert to the possibility of British raids and reconnaissance patrols and took the precaution of fitting small warning devices to the wire entanglements in front of their trenches. During a patrol by 'A' Company of the Liverpool Irish, Private Boyes 'brought in a nice little brass bell from the enemy wire, this was on a stick and attached to a trip wire, which he cut and brought the stick and bell back as a souvenir'.[59] Captain Mahon had a well-known character among his patrol men who he referred to as 'The famous Powell'. Private Powell was also the battalion's mimic, who provided some of the entertainment at the Liverpool Irish concert parties. Unfortunately, for his comrades, he did not confine his talents to the stage:

On one occasion, he took off a cow when out on patrol between the lines. The rest of the patrol had to stand this, but when he called out loudly 'Look out I'm a bomber', they thought it high time to come back. As our boys put it, he's a skin and doesn't know what fear is. So much for one of our characters.[60]

The act of crawling across No Man's Land up to the German trenches in pursuit of a piece of wire, even if the patrol was uneventful and successful, was also strenuous. On 20 March 1916, at Bretencourt, Captain Meadows led a patrol towards the enemy lines and returned with some German wire. Harold Mahon noted that, 'Meadows rather overworked himself the last time we were in the trenches and had a day or two in hospital.'[61] By 1916, the 55th Division began to monitor and register any aggressive and offensive actions carried out by individual battalions.[62] The Liverpool Irish were obliged to record any such actions on forms which were then dispatched to the divisional head-quarters. Details of the nature of the patrols, the officer who led them and the names of individual soldiers who participated in the patrols were also recorded. The requirement to provide details of the amount of small arms ammunition expended by the battalion also provided an indication of the level of aggression displayed by the battalion. Whether Captain Harold Mahon could be described as a 'thruster' is questionable. While he was certainly dedicated to the welfare of his men, he maintained a healthy belligerence and was keen to engage the enemy. Even when 'resting' behind the lines in the relative luxury of a chateau, he was unable to forget the war: 'The CO, Captain Leech and I were billeted in a small chateau and we were very comfortable. Leech and I had long chats on the best means of strafing the Boche and carrying the war home to him in a practical manner.'[63]

Arguably the most famous raid carried out by the Liverpool Irish took place in April 1916. The battalion was in the lines at Blaireville, south-west of Arras, when Captain Harold Mahon conceived the idea for a raid on the enemy trenches. In the weeks prior to the raid, Mahon trained his men and practised for the main event. On the night of 16 April 1916, a party of wire cutters comprising Captain Mahon, Captain Limrick and Second Lieutenant Baxter approached the German wire where they managed to cut through thirteen rows of the enemy's barbed wire in preparation for the raid. At 3.30 a.m., due to the approach of dawn, the party returned, leaving their work unfinished. On the evening of 17 April, a patrol was sent out to ascertain whether the German wire which had been cut the previous night had been repaired; they found it untouched. Another wire cutting patrol went out at midnight to continue cutting the enemy wire. A pre-arranged artillery bombardment of the enemy trenches accompanied by machine gun fire covered the raiders. By 2.10 a.m. the cutting was complete and an NCO returned to the Irish lines to fetch the trench-storming party of one officer and twenty-three men. The storming party entered the German trenches at 2.25 a.m. when they cut a wire cable and proceeded to bomb the dugouts and 'cries and groans were heard from all the dugouts'. On returning to their own trench, it was discovered that Lieutenant Baxter was missing, and a further patrol was sent out into No Man's Land in attempt to find him, but they were unsuccessful. The raiding party returned with two German helmets as trophies, but they took no prisoners.[64] Just over a month later, the battalion War Diary noted that a German prisoner who had deserted to the battalion on the left of the Irish trenches claimed that the Germans had sustained fifty-seven casualties during the raid.[65]

If the battalion War Diary lacked the space for a full account of the raid, the Liverpool *Evening Express* had no such restrictions and published an account from an unnamed member of the battalion.[66] Given wartime censorship and the need for secrecy, it is somewhat surprising that the paper not only named Harold Mahon as having overseen the raid, it also named Captain Limrick, Lieutenant Baxter and Sgt. McClelland as his fellow participants. While detailed, the account provides an enthusiastic, if rather dramatic depiction of the raid and is worth quoting at length:

When the signal came through the field guns opened rapid fire all along the German trench, the howitzers crashed in and our party returned, wonderfully calm and filed along the communication trench to their dug out in the support line. And now for an account of the operations in the front. Our men had got into their positions in good time. There was a shallow, disused trench running between the two German saps, and it was there that the main body waited while the wire cutters continued their work of the night before. They were already half way through, but there was still much thick wire to be cut, and, of course, the nearer the Hun the greater the chance of discovery. A flare would have given the game away in a second, but mercifully none went up. Baxter was in charge of this part of the business and he and his small party worked away with extraordinary skill and silence, helped by the noise of the machine guns which fired continually over their heads to drown the occasional and inevitable click. It was when they were nearly though, and could hear the movements of a sentry a few feet away, that Baxter dropped a Mills bomb he was carrying. He had previously removed the split pin, and of course the lever flew out and commenced to fizz. He had only five seconds before it would have exploded, shattered the wire party and given away the whole show, but he picked it up, unscrewed the base plug, and threw away the detonator, which went off unnoticed. I have not heard of any action during the war showing a more extraordinary combination of nerve, skill and strength. Then they rapidly cut through the remaining wire and jumped into the trench. They went in single file, turning alternately

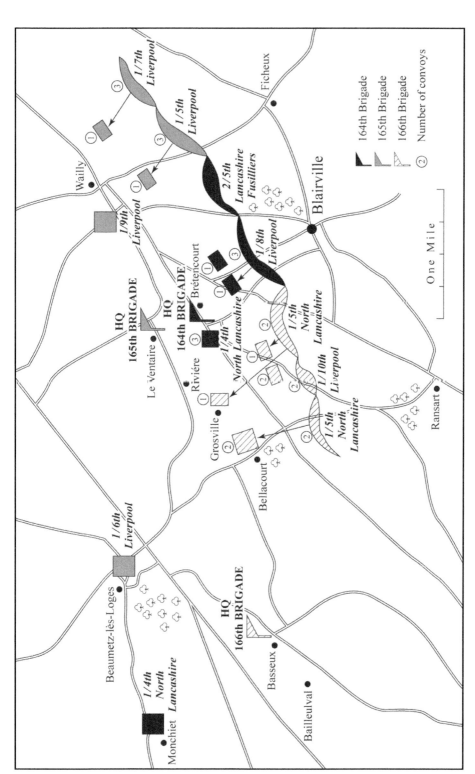

Map 2: The dispositions of the 55th Division at Blaireville prior to the trench raid by the Liverpool Irish on 17/18th April 1916.

right, led by Sergeant McClelland, and left, led by Baxter. The trench was very deep, about 12 to 15 feet, and it was immediately obvious that there would be trouble in hauling a fat and unwilling Hun, much as we wanted a souvenir in the shape of a prisoner. The sentry they had heard was promptly shot. Another, who came running out a dug out was promptly bayoneted, and as he fell back a bomb was thrown out, which exploded at the entrance and did our men no harm. So, they threw down six in exchange and passed on. More sentries were met and ('screaming like a lot of old women', one of our men said) dispatched. Three more dug outs were attended to by our bombers, and then on the signal all withdrew without noise or confusion. It was only when we reached our own lines that it was discovered Baxter was not with them. Search parties at once went back to the German wire, but no sign of him could be found. It is certain that he climbed out of the German trench, for he helped to pull up the last man of his party. Evidently, he had gone back for some purpose, perhaps to try to secure a German rifle and bayonet and had been killed or captured before he could again get out.[67]

In the battalion Orders the next day: 'It was largely owing to this officer's pluck, determination, coolness and resource that the raid was successful. Dead or missing, he is a great loss to the battalion.' While tributes poured in from the military hierarchy, the correspondent to the *Evening Express* stated that the praise of their battalion commander that pleased the men of the Liverpool Irish more than any other plaudits: 'The Commanding Officer is intensely proud of the battalion's exploit, though it was no more than he expected.' The paper went on to report that some 4,000 men were serving with the various units of the Liverpool Irish, which represented 'a splendid object lesson of the loyalty and courage of the Irish in Liverpool'.[68]

With the tragic exception of Lieutenant Baxter's loss, the raid had been a total success and the battalion justifiably basked in the flurry of congratulations emanating from their brigade, divisional headquarters and the Liverpool newspapers. The fact that Edward Felix Baxter was neither from Liverpool nor Irish mattered little after the event. Edward Felix Baxter was born in 1885 at Oldswinford near Stourbridge in Worcester and attended Queen Elizabeth's Grammar School Hartlebury and later moved to Christ's Hospital School at Horsham. After leaving school he found employment at the United Counties Bank and later became a tutor at Skerry's College in Liverpool. He married his wife Leonora in 1906 and their daughter, Leonora Frances Baxter, was born the following year. Baxter was a keen motorcyclist, and he took part in the Isle of Man TT races in 1910.[69] Shortly after the war broke out, he enlisted in the Royal Engineers in September 1914 as a sapper and was immediately promoted to the rank of Sergeant.[70] He was subsequently posted as a dispatch rider at the headquarters of the Mersey Defences at Rodney Street in Liverpool under the command of Brigadier-General Edwards and Colonel von Stomm. Given his educational background, the rapid expansion of the army and the urgent need for officers, it is perhaps unsurprising that Baxter applied for a commission. He did so the following year and having been successful he was commissioned into the 3/8th (Irish) Battalion, King's Liverpool Regiment in September 1915. Arguably, Baxter had a 'cushy' job, he was far removed from the privations, vermin, squalor and dangers of the trenches and the risks of negotiating the wartime traffic in the city notwithstanding, he was close to his home and family at 5 Blantyre Road. Perhaps he longed for something more adventurous, or he believed that he had more to offer his country than riding around Liverpool on a motorbike. Or, possibly, he may have been more pragmatic in that he would have received a better wage as an officer and certainly a higher status than that of an NCO.

There is no doubting Baxter's courage and leadership in crossing No Man's Land, cutting the enemy wire, his quick thinking and dexterity in dealing with a grenade which was about to explode, and his ruthlessness in dealing with the German sentry once he had entered the enemy trench. He led his men throughout their attack and organised their safe withdrawal. At this point, no one except Baxter himself knows why, after achieving their objective and without having sustained any casualties, he chose to go back into the German trench alone. He may have heard some enemy activity and wanted to deal with it to ensure that his men escaped safely to their own lines. Another plausible reason for re-entering the German trench was that he might have returned to obtain a trophy or souvenir of the raid. Whatever his motivations, his actions cost him his life and earned him a recommendation for the Victoria Cross, which was awarded posthumously.[71]

It was Captain Harold Mahon who had conceived the idea of the raid; he also planned, trained the men and rehearsed it. He also took an active part in the raid by cutting the wire in front of the enemy trenches prior to the storming party launching their attack. The raid had been a very personal achievement for Mahon and he was proud of his men and for the battalion. He was, however, much less comfortable with the events immediately afterwards. He confided in his journal: 'For a day or two after, we were inspected by Generals from the Corps Commander (General Snow) downwards: GHQ sent us congratulations and the official photographer snapped us. I preferred the deed to what followed as I dislike peacock parades and know full well that this is a mere incident to what is yet to come.'[72] He repeated the same sentiments in a letter home to his mother when he told her that he had overseen the raid. He praised his men: 'of course it was the boys who carried the operation through', but he informed his mother that he was 'pretty well sick' of being interviewed by generals and that he would 'almost sooner do the thing again' than be interviewed to by senior officers.[73]

Having read various accounts of the raid in the local Liverpool newspapers, Mahon's friends wrote to him congratulating him on his achievement. A few noted erroneously that he had been recommended for the DSO, given that it was essentially Mahon's operation, the only award he received for his endeavours was a Divisional Commendation. Occasionally when surveying historical sources, historians, whether part-time or academic, are unable to uncover any reference to an event or episode which happened. The omission of any important event inevitably begs questions. Throughout Harold Mahon's journal and his private correspondence, no mention is made by Mahon of the death of Lieutenant Baxter, nor is there any mention of the award of his Victoria Cross. Baxter's death was the sole casualty of the raid and his Victoria Cross was the only one awarded to the battalion during the war, yet Mahon mentions neither event. Mahon had previously recorded details of casualties in his journal, of both officers and men. He also mentioned the fact that a Distinguished Conduct Medal and three Military Medals had been awarded to four soldiers from the battalion for their part in the raid. It might be reasonable to assume that Mahon was displeased with the fact that having planned, practised and organised the raid with the intention of inflicting damage on the enemy, while attempting to keep his own men as safe as possible in the circumstances, that Baxter had needlessly put his life in danger. Baxter's actions in returning to the enemy's trench had marred what would have been a flawless operation and might have secured a medal for Mahon rather than a slip of paper from the Divisional Commander. For whatever reason, Harold Mahon's journal stops in April 1916 after he had written his feelings about the raid.

On 5 October 1916, the *Liverpool Daily Post* reported that plans were being made to construct a commemorative memorial in the city as recognition of Edward Baxter's exploits in winning the Victoria Cross: 'Active steps are being taken to promote a permanent memorial to Lieutenant Felix Baxter, V.C., of the 8th Liverpool (Irish). In a sense, it might be said that Lieutenant Baxter was the first Liverpool man to win the VC inasmuch as the deed for which he was awarded the coveted honour was performed some months before the gallant act which secured the Cross for Rifleman Proctor.'[74] The proposed memorial never materialised.[75]

Aggressive operations mounted by individual battalions of the 55th Division since its formation in January 1916 had demonstrated the existence of an offensive spirit within the division. The number of raids and patrols had impressed their Divisional Commander, and in July 1916, Major General Jeudwine issued a 'Special Order of the Day' to communicate his admiration.:

> The Major General has watched with particular pride the gradual develop-ment of a system of patrolling, the persistence with which the enemy has been observed and thwarted, the many plucky acts performed in the course of this development, and the skill and resource which have been displayed by all ranks. It is thanks to the thoroughness with which patrolling has been carried out that we are now – as we ought to be – undisputed masters of all ground up to the German wire.[76]

Not all raids were entirely successful, and inevitably there were costs to be met when the raiders encountered German resistance. On 5 and 6 June 1917, the Liverpool Irish carried out a successful raid on the German trenches at Potijze, northeast of Ypres.[77] The War Diary states that the raid had been led by Lieutenant Whitehead and was preceded by a rapid bombardment, after which some men from the 'left' raiding party stormed the German trenches. The remaining group from this party came under a counterattack and were unable to enter the enemy trenches. The 'right' raiding party also met with resist-ance, but was more successful. A German was captured and taken prisoner, but he was 'too big and heavy' to be dragged from his trench. The prisoner was resisting, so the decision was made to knock him over the head with the butt of a pistol to prevent him from firing at the raiders as they withdrew. This seems to have been an uncharacteristically chivalrous action by the Irish, given that the purpose of a raid was to kill and or capture the enemy. Private Murphy received a special mention: 'Private Murphy accounted for at least five Germans himself and acted throughout with great dash and gallantry and at the end remained behind to carry back a wounded comrade.' Lieutenant Whitehead and seven men were wounded during the raid and one man was missing. The battalion carried out a similar raid two months later, on 20 July 1917.[78] On this occasion, one half of the raiding party were held up by enemy fire, although the other raiders managed to enter the enemy trenches; they found that the trenches had been evacuated.

The decision as to whether a raid should be preceded by an artillery bom-bardment was a difficult matter. A bombardment had two very useful purposes: it kept the enemy under cover and made sufficient noise to cover any movement or sounds made by the raiders such as wire cutting close to the enemy trenches. The major disadvantage of a sudden bombardment was that soldiers on both sides of No Man's Land became alert to the possibility that the artillery barrage signalled that a raid was imminent. Raiding, like patrolling, was not a one-sided affair, and the Germans ensured that the British did not have a monopoly on belligerence, aggression and the offensive spirit.

At 6 a.m. on the morning of 18 May 1917, near Wieltje, the Germans opened a bombardment of the Liverpool Irish trenches on a broad front.[79] The bombardment of 77mm, 4.25 howitzer shells as well as medium and heavy *minenwerfer* mortars continued throughout the day. At 9.20 p.m. that evening, the barrage intensified and, using this as cover, the Germans launched a raid into the Liverpool Irishmen's lines at Warwick Farm in the Wieltje sector. The battalion War Diary reported that the raiders were 'quickly driven out' and that the battalion had suffered five casualties and that two men were missing. Within a week of the raid having taken place, a more detailed account of the event was provided by Captain Riley of the Liverpool Irish in a letter to the wife of Private John Fletcher.[80] Private Fletcher from Preston, a machine gunner with the battalion, had enlisted in November 1914 and had acted as Captain Riley's servant at Blackpool, Fleetwood and at Canterbury before being transferred to the front line as a machine gunner. Captain Riley informed Mrs Fletcher that he had always taken a keen interest in her husband as he was 'such a good fellow and also an excellent soldier'. On the night of the German raid, Private Fletcher was manning his machine gun when the enemy entered the Liverpool Irish trenches. According to Captain Riley, they made straight for Private Fletcher's position to seize his machine gun. 'The first German was tackled by one of our boys who got him down; your husband shot him dead with his revolver.' A few minutes later, more Germans arrived, and Private Fletcher shot every one of them as they rounded the corner of his trench. Captain Riley was justifiably proud of Fletcher's 'clever and level headed' actions and the 'presence of mind and quick action' which had saved the lives of his comrades. Riley stated that his purpose in writing the letter was to inform Mrs Fletcher that her husband was unscathed during the raid. Praising his bravery, he stated that Private Fletcher had been recommended for the award of the DCM. The raid had not been carried out by novices; one of the attackers was a decorated German officer, and Riley had taken the trouble to remove the dead officer's medal ribbons and enclose them in the envelope with his letter. He explained: 'The medal ribbons accompanying this letter are – The black and white ribbon of the Iron Cross of the first class; The black and blue ribbon of the Iron Cross of the second class; A white, black and blue ribbon, representing a Bavarian decoration not exactly identified.' It seems that May 1917 had been a busy month for Private Fletcher. On 7 May, he received a 'Commendation Card for his "gallant conduct and devotion to duty" from General Broadwood'. The recommendation for the award of a DCM to Private Fletcher was successful and he received his DCM the following January in his home town of Preston. Local worthies turned out to honour their townsman's bravery.[81] The medal was presented by the Mayor, Alderman Cartmell, while standing on top of a tank named 'Egbert' which sat in Preston's Market Square. During the ceremony, Cartmell told the crowd that while Private Fletcher was serving with the Liverpool Irish, he hoped that he would be pleased to call himself a Prestonian, after which the crowd gave Fletcher a rousing three cheers.

By and large, aggressive and offensive actions undertaken at battalion level were pre-planned and proactive. However, there were occasions when enemy activity along the front lines demanded a more extempore response. On 2 August 1916, near Guillemont, Lieutenant Colonel Fagan observed that the Germans had adopted a more belligerent posture and that they were moving to install posts on the crest overlooking the Liverpool Irish lines.[82] He ordered a platoon comprising twenty men and led by Captain Ward and Lieutenant Duncan to establish a post of their own. At 6 p.m. the men were to make their way along a sunken road towards their objective. As they emerged from their trenches, about twenty Germans bolted along the sunken road in the direction of Guillemont and were 'disposed of' by a machine gun which was sited at Arrow Head Copse. As the Liverpool Irish made their way further along the road, Fagan was informed that sixty or seventy Germans emerged from trenches in front of the battalion to his right. Lieutenant Fisher, the machine gun officer, informed Fagan that at the same time Germans began to emerge from shell holes and other cover on both sides of the crest. The platoon then halted and formed up on the bank of road where they 'took a good toll of the advancing Germans'. At the same time, the Liverpool Irish trench mortar battery 'opened fire most opportunely'. The Germans then broke and ran and were harried by machine gun and Lewis gunfire. The Germans then sent up SOS flares after which they bombarded Trones Wood for about an hour.

OFFICERS, MEN AND MORALE

Across the ages, soldiers and historians have attempted to define exactly what constitutes morale. According to the nineteenth-century military philosopher Clausewitz, morale comprised 'mood' and 'spirit'.[1] Ian Beckett has suggested that battlefield morale and 'fighting spirit' could be enhanced by ensuring that a number of traditional military components were present, including 'the appeal to patriotism, religion, regiment, or honour; good leadership; discipline; rewards such as medals; accurate information; good medical arrangements; adequate leave arrangements; efficient administration; realistic training; rest; and palliatives like alcohol or cigarettes in appropriate measure'.[2] In his study of how British and German soldiers managed to endure the war, Alexander Watson stressed the importance of factors such as training and the inculcation of primary group solidarity, as well as regimental *esprit de corps* and good leadership.[3] For all the British army's power to control, coerce and discipline men, the privilege to tell them where to fight and when became negligible if soldiers felt that their physical and psychological needs were being neglected and their fighting spirit had been eroded. The responsibility for ensuring soldiers' needs were met and that their fighting spirit was retained rested with their officers.

The relationship between officers and their men was based on an informal and unwritten exchange of paternalism and deference. John Bourne has suggested that this relationship had its foundation in contemporary social and working relationships and that the working classes brought 'the tried and tested survival strategies' of the workplace into the army.[4] There are, however, some important caveats; as Ian Beckett has argued, deference did not mean subservience, rather it was extended to superiors by the working classes in return for paternalism.[5] Moreover, unlike the army, a working man was entirely free to ignore this arrangement, disobey the rules of his workplace, refuse to work and hurl abuse at his employer. He might well have lost his job and been escorted from the premises; however, his employer could not have him imprisoned, chained to the wheel of a gun carriage or brought before a firing squad. Some working-class recruits retained what they considered as perfectly acceptable workplace–employee behaviour only to discover that their actions were deemed to be 'crimes' in the army.[6] Officers held the King's commission and therefore their rank *demanded* respect which was (and still is) acknowledged physically by means of a salute. In April 1916, the topic of saluting was being taken quite seriously by staff at the 55th Divisional Headquarters who issued a memorandum on the subject.[7] It stated that the 55th Division had been complimented on the 'smartness' of soldiers paying the necessary compliments, but that Major-General Jeudwine had noticed that men had failed to do so 'especially in the forward villages'. Stressing the importance of saluting, it continued 'it is invariably the case that units which are slack in paying the regulated compliments are also slack in other ways'. If discipline was a constantly crucial factor in maintaining order and cohesion within a battalion, conversely there should have been a time and a place for the 'bullshit' of army life, especially at the front. Unfortunately for the rank and file, senior military officers had a penchant for bullshit, which seemed to emanate from the top down. Soldiers from the 16th (Irish) Division incurred Haig's displeasure when they were too slow in saluting his car while he was being chauffeured around the front.[8] Presumably the Irishmen had more important things on their minds than indulging in brass-hat car spotting while they trudged around the Western Front.

Nevertheless, it is important to recognise that formalities were based firmly on rank and not on class. It is also disingenuous to suggest that the composition of the hierarchal structure of the British army, which changed during the Great War, was wholly class-based.[9] If deference had its roots in contemporary British society, paternalism was a well-established principle within the upper echelons of British society and one which was fostered in the public-school ethos. There was a tacit acknowledgement among the officer class of the British army that along with rank and privilege, there was an onus on officers to behave in certain ways and to take care of the men who were in their charge. Writing in 1920, a former officer claimed that the success of the British army during the war was due largely to the inherent characteristics displayed by its officers: 'Very much of the success of the British army has been due to the qualities of courage, coolness and *noblesse oblige*.'[10]

Historians have suggested that some of the supposed characteristics and qualities necessary to become a competent officer – manliness, sportsmanship, selflessness, leadership and paternalism – had been formulated and inculcated within the public-school ethos.[11] During the first months of the war, prospective officers from the major public schools managed to obtain commissions with relative ease, while men from grammar schools were unsuccessful. Yet, as Gary Sheffield has observed, the criteria changed when the army came to value the previous military experience of potential grammar school applicants.[12] Thus, having shed some of its pre-war prejudices and snobbishness, the army began to accept officer candidates from grammar schools which had an Officer Training Corps (OTC). The prestigious Liverpool College, the local public school of choice for the sons of middle-class professional men, shunned militarism in the wake of the Boer War. When the school's cadet corps was re-founded amidst a flurry of short-term interest in 1901, it promptly disbanded shortly afterwards.[13] In 1908, following the establishment of the Territorial Force, several sixth formers at the college began to agitate for the formation of a cadet corps. The principal, the Reverend Mr J.B. Lancelot, despite his distaste for militarism, allowed the matter to be debated and 180 boys filed into the school hall to listen to the motion 'that in the opinion of this House it is a matter of the utmost importance that the College Cadet Corps should be revived forthwith'. The motion was successful due to the determination of a pupil who had written to Field Marshal, the Earl Roberts, whose reply in support of the motion was read out at the start of the debate.[14]

Life as an officer in the pre-war army could prove expensive. Most entrants to the officer training centres at Sandhurst and Woolwich had to contribute £100 per year towards their training.[15] Officers lacking any additional private income found it difficult to manage on their army salary; uniform, equipment, mess bills and paying for the necessities of life created a financial struggle for some junior regular army officers. Newly commissioned temporary officers were expected to conform and adhere to the standards of etiquette, behaviour and dress of their regular counterparts. Officers were set apart from the other ranks by their social status, income, education and, more visibly, by their uniform. Once commissioned, the army provided an allowance of £50 to enable the new subaltern to purchase his uniform and equipment.[16] Liverpolitan officers could call at Albert Henderson's Military Tailors in Brunswick Street, where they could purchase 'The New Trench Cap', regulation Burberry coats and camp kits.[17] In December 1914, Moss Bros. offered greatcoats at 63 shillings (no mention of 'trench' coats just yet), tunics at 50 shillings, breeches at 21 shillings and a Sam Brown belt for 30 shillings.[18] Other accoutrements such as washing kits, valises, field binoculars and swords were additional requirements. Having been commissioned into the Liverpool Irish in December 1914, Lieutenant John Sutton Sharpe's uncle offered to purchase a sword for him. Sharpe wrote thanking him and suggested that one could be obtained for 5 pounds and 10 shillings. A few days later the sword arrived; an elated Sharpe wrote: 'I am very delighted with my sword, it is exactly right in every detail and has been much admired and perhaps a little envied as it is no easy task to procure a really good one just now.'[19]

The initial clutch of officers listed for service with the 8th Liverpool (Irish) battalion in the opening months of the war comprised a few of their pre-war officers; the majority, however, were men who had been newly commissioned into the battalion. Lieutenants John Smitham, Robert Keating, George Brown and Herbert Marion Finegan were among those officers already serving with the battalion when war was declared. Lieutenant Smitham had been a colour Sergeant with the 5th Battalion of the Liverpool territorials when he applied for and was successful in obtaining a commission with the 8th (Irish) Battalion in 1910.[20] Lieutenant Keating was educated at Liverpool Catholic Institute; like Smitham, he had been with the battalion since 1910.[21] Lieutenant George Brown, educated at Liverpool Institute, had served as a cadet and an officer with the 1st Cadet Battalion of the King's Liverpool Regiment and was commissioned into the Liverpool Irish in 1912.[22] Arguably, Lieutenant Herbert Marion Finegan possessed many of the qualifications and characteristics demanded by the military hierarchy. Being an Irish battalion, other less formal characteristics might prove beneficial. Apart from his middle-class origins and education, Finegan was a Catholic, a second-generation Irishman and a convinced Home Ruler. Like many of his 'Irish' subordinates, he was born in Liverpool, credentials which must have enhanced his standing among the rank and file of the battalion. He also had strong familial connections to the battalion, his father, Dr J.H. Finegan and his maternal grandfather, Dr Daniel Parsons, had both served as Surgeon-Colonels of the Liverpool Irish during the battalion's previous incarnations as the 18th Liverpool Rifle Volunteers and 64th Liverpool Rifle Volunteers, respectively.[23] Finegan attended Stonyhurst College, a leading Catholic public school, where he excelled academically.[24] A gifted scholar, he went on to study history at Liverpool University where he won an array of prizes; having shunned sports at Stonyhurst, Finegan developed a keen interest in athletics and shooting throughout his time at university and won distinctions in both.[25] Herbert Finegan then transferred to studying law, where even more prizes followed before he passed the Bar Examination with first-class honours. The son of an Irishman, Finegan was a devout Catholic and Irish nationalist, and while at university he became President of the Catholic Society of Liverpool and the Liverpool Irish Society.[26]

The need to bring the battalion up to fighting strength in 1914 inevitably led to a search for prospective officers. Between August and December 1914, an assortment of educated middle-class men, having been employed in various occupations, joined the Liverpool Irish not just from Liverpool, but from areas throughout England and Scotland, including some from more exotic climes such as Australia, New Zealand and Rhodesia. Helen McCartney's study of the 'collar and cuff' 6th Rifles and 10th (Scottish) territorial battalions in Liverpool revealed an exclusive, middle-class disposition which set them apart from their more proletarian neighbours within the territorial force in the city.[27] While some rankers of the 6th Rifles rejected the opportunity to apply for commissions, the social status and educational background of the men made the battalion a particularly fertile unit for providing prospective officers. Sergeant Harold Mahon and Corporal William David Heatherington Lilley, as well as Privates Robert Noel Mountfield and Gerald Fisher from the 6th Rifles, were successful in obtaining commissions in the Liverpool Irish.[28] The legal profession was well represented among the officers of the Liverpool Irish. Lieutenants Harvey Duder, Walter Duncan and George Brighten were all qualified solicitors.[29] In addition to Lieutenant Herbert Finegan, Lieutenants Frederick Ernest Bodel and Algernon Kenneth Hastings Neale, son of the Commanding Officer, Lieutenant Colonel A.H.C. Neale, were admitted barristers.[30] If Captain Finegan's political and religious credentials made him an ideal match for the Liverpool Irish, then Lieutenant Bodel's religious background and political beliefs were at odds with the Catholic and nationalist character of the battalion. Bodel was the son of a Northern Irish Presbyterian minister and an anti-Home Ruler. A friend recalled that 'his enthusiasm and eloquence had over a large area of the North of England advanced the political principals which were part of his birthright as a Protestant native of the North of Ireland'.[31] Lieutenant Henry Mackey Drake was born in New South Wales, Australia, as was Major (later Lieutenant Colonel and battalion CO) James Alexander Campbell Johnson.[32] Henry Drake had been privately educated before finishing his education at Lausanne in Switzerland. Major Campbell Johnson had seen action during the Boer War, where he had served as a Sergeant with an irregular outfit known as Kitchener's Horse. After his time in South Africa, he came to London where he worked as a journalist and newspaper manager. When the war was declared he became an intelligence officer working in the London District prior to making an application for a commission.[33] Laurence Hutchison, a mining specialist from New Zealand, who had been on a golfing holiday in Scotland before the war, met Harry Leech, a mill owner from Liverpool and his sister Ede.[34] The families had been introduced by a mutual friend, David Murray-Thompson. Laurence Hutchison became romantically involved with Leech's sister Ede, while Harry began a relationship with Murray-Thompson's sister. When war was declared, Hutchison and

Leech made their way to Blackpool to offer their services at the camp. Initially, both men applied to serve in the New Zealand contingent; however, they withdrew their nominations and received commissions in the Liverpool Irish.[35] Sometimes, family acquaintances and social connections proved influential for prospective officers. The magnificently named Donal Stuart Champion D'Espinassy O'Connell O'Riordan had been a Gentleman Cadet at Sandhurst in 1914.[36] O'Riordan was born in Dublin, where his father, Captain Daniel Stanislaus O'Connell O'Riordan, served with the Antrim Artillery, an Irish Militia unit. His father was killed in action during a tribal uprising in Nigeria in 1903.[37] While 18-year-old O'Riordan had passed the entrance examination to Sandhurst, he failed the medical examination because his chest measurement was one and a half inches below the required standard. Nevertheless, he was permitted to enter Sandhurst on condition that he managed to attain the required physical standards on completion of his training. On 20 September 1914, the Director of Military Training at Sandhurst wrote to O'Riordan's guardian informing her that her ward would not be granted a commission as he 'did not possess the necessary aptitude to justify his being entrusted with the powers of command in the field'.[38] Undaunted, O'Riordan enlisted as a private soldier in the 18th Battalion, Royal Fusiliers, on 21 October 1914, which had been formed at Epsom by the Public Schools and University Men's Force. He was remarkably honest on his enlistment form, where he stated that he had been dismissed from Sandhurst for 'slackness'. Thus, having enlisted in the Royal Fusiliers in October 1914, the following month O'Riordan travelled to Canterbury where he applied for a commission with the Liverpool Irish. Following a bout of 'string-pulling', Lieutenant Colonel A.H.C. Neale, CO of the Liverpool Irish, endorsed O'Riordan's application form by emblazoning the front page in red ink: 'ADDITIONAL – I strongly recommend this boy for a commission. I have known him practically all his life. His father, a "gunner" officer was killed in action. I can pass him on to a regular unit after completing his training.'[39]

At least three Irishmen were commissioned from the ranks: Lieutenants Daniel McCabe, an insurance clerk, and James Allison Free, an elementary school teacher, both originally from Londonderry, had enlisted as private soldiers in the Liverpool Irish.[40] Lieutenant Michael Moynihan, from Tralee in County Kerry had no connections with the city of Liverpool, or the Liverpool (Irish) Battalion. Moynihan came from a well-known Irish nationalist family in Tralee; educated at University College Dublin, he was undoubtedly committed to the prospect of a united Ireland.[41] Intelligent and erudite, Moynihan was successful in passing the civil service examination and was initially employed in the Inland Revenue department in Dublin before moving to London where, much to the chagrin of some of his relatives, he joined the Civil Service Rifles.[42] Always restless, his pre-war political sympathies shifted from socialism to conservatism; however, his distaste for Orangeism and anti-Home Rule countrymen in the north remained constant.[43] The Civil Service Rifles, more properly known as the 15th (County of London) Battalion (Prince of Wales' Own, Civil Service Rifles), was a territorial battalion designated as a home service battalion at the beginning of the war. With the introduction of conscription in 1916, the battalion undertook the Imperial Service obligation and Michael Moynihan went to France with the battalion in June 1916.[44] Moynihan served on the Western Front through the winter of 1916 until he received his commission in February 1917 and was later posted to the 8th (Irish) Battalion, King's Liverpool Regiment.

Pre-war territorial officers in the battalion had some experience in musketry, drill, scouting, signalling; they would also have attended a series of annual camps. Their counterparts who had arrived from the various OTCs would also have been familiar with the rudiments of soldiering. During the early months of the war, the training of newly commissioned officers was provided within the battalion. On 4 December 1914, junior officers of the Liverpool Irish at Canterbury attended a lecture delivered by their CO, Lieutenant Colonel Neale.[45] Neale asserted that 'war is a game but played with bullets and bayonets'. He went on to stress that winning could only be achieved by adopting an offensive stance; continuing with the sporting motif, he told his audience that 'a team playing on the defensive can hope at the best to make a draw'. Neale's lecture seems to have been based on open, or mobile, warfare and his notes which accompanied the lecture contained illustrations of how to attack and defend a village. In January 1915, officer training became a more formalised affair with the establishment of four-week courses organised by OTCs. Those who had passed the course then progressed to a Young Officers' Company attached to a reserve brigade prior to joining their battalion. By 1916, a number of Officer Cadet Battalions (OCB) were established, the course lasted four months and the majority of those temporary officers who underwent training at an OCB and had received commissions were men who had previously served in the ranks.[46] Inevitably, the numbers of officer casualties increased during the conflict and in December 1917, the battalion War Diarist recorded that regimental courses had commenced for 'junior officers, NCOs and senior privates (who were likely to become NCOs)'.[47] The quality and intensity of the training provided by OCBs and Reserve battalions varied. Prior to joining the Liverpool Irish, Lieutenant Willie Spargo wrote to his brother and sister in Cape Town from Park Hall Camp in Oswestry where he was attached to the reserve battalion of the Liverpool

Irish. 'I am dead beat, I am studying for a Captaincy, but I don't expect to get it as I am junior to quite a lot of officers. I expect you heard I passed 1st class as an instructor of musketry, I worked hard for that course and thought I had finished but this one is even worse than the last.'[48] Unlike Willie Spargo, Lieutenant Michael Moynihan had seen active service with the Civil Service Rifles and he was unimpressed with the training and his instructors at No. 13 OCB at Newmarket. Moynihan complained that 'it was more like school life than army life' and that much of his time was devoted to cleaning equipment and rifles:

> The business of the officers and NCOs here is simply to impart knowledge, as best they can. They are not perfect at their job indeed, very far from it. Most, if not all, are here simply because having been wounded at the front they are unfit for further service. Some are veterans from Mons and the Marne. The captain of B Coy, for example, went out with the Lincolns in the original expeditionary force, was wounded and has never smelt powder since, scarcely the ideal way of selecting teachers, and the methods in vogue betray the hand of the amateur.[49]

Circumstances improved for Moynihan in September 1917 when he joined the reserve battalion at Oswestry, where he was relieved to feel free from 'petty restrictions and bossing'.[50]

While officers undoubtedly enjoyed more privileges than the NCOs and men under their command, they also assumed responsibility for their performance and welfare. Junior officers had to ensure that men adhered to the standard operating procedures while in the trenches, that they were in possession of the proper equipment and weapons, and were adequately trained in its use. In October 1915, Brigadier-General Edwards, 154th Infantry Brigade, decided to carry out an inspection of the battalions under his command. After inspecting the Liverpool Irish, he found, 'trench discipline was faulty. Many rifles with uncharged magazines. Officers had not instructed men.'[51] This was inexcusable. By October 1915, the battalion had been through the Battle of Festubert and had five months in which to acclimatise and perfect their trench discipline. The fact that soldiers were standing in front line trenches without having rounds in the magazines of their weapons reflected badly on the level of training and supervision within the battalion. Matters improved when the battalion moved from the 51st Highland Division to their own 55th (West Lancashire) Division in 1916. Whenever the battalion was undergoing training sessions behind the lines, the 55th Divisional Hierarchy demanded to know the precise location of the individual training areas. Details of the training schedule were then forwarded to the division's headquarters, which included a map reference for each training discipline. Captain Harold Mahon was unimpressed by the intrusion and noted wryly, 'Thus, on Tuesday morning A company will practice bayonet fighting at a point 300 yds. N. of the A in Airaines. The General knows this, turns up, strafes and departs.'[52]

Officers were also expected to display leadership, competence and courage; any signs of nerves or 'windiness' on the part of an officer were met with derision and disapproval by the men under his command.[53] Bravery, it seems, was a *sine qua non* for officers. Private James Green of the Liverpool Irish was uninspired by the actions of Lieutenant Colonel Neale, CO of the Liverpool Irish, and another officer just before the battalion went into action at Festubert in June 1915. According to Green, both men 'got the wind up when we came out of the trenches at Richebourg and went home to England, we did not see them again'.[54] Shortly afterwards, as the battalion was making its way along the road to commence their attack, Green was wounded in the knee by a shell fragment. He again voiced his criticisms when another officer from the Irish arrived at the scene: 'my two chums, Thompson and Clough, were bandaging me up but the officer came up and sent them up the line. He was a windy officer. I believe he went back to England shell shocked.' Conversely, soldiers' acknowledgement and praise for the bravery of individual officers became apparent when an officer was killed. After the Battle of Festubert in June 1915, Private Baker wrote, 'Lieutenant Drake, the bravest man whom I have ever met, was hit right through the neck and died soon after. He died the noblest death possible to any man.'[55] Sergeant McCabe wrote to a friend in Liverpool describing how Captain Herbert Finegan had died at Festubert: 'He was a hero if ever there was one, and you ought to hear the fellows talk about him. He told me once that he would either go home with a Victoria Cross or a wooden one and he kept his word'.[56] Some men, such as personal servants, were unavoidably closer to their officers than others in the battalion. When Captain Harold Mahon, who had planned and executed the famous trench raid of the Liverpool Irish at Blaireville in April 1916, was killed by shellfire in September of that year, his personal servant, Private William McCleary, felt compelled to offer his condolences to Harold Mahon's father in Wallasey. William McCleary was obviously affected by Captain Mahon's death and considered him a 'friend':

> No doubt you will have received official notification, but I take it as my duty to write to you considering I had been his servant since we first came to France. I beg to offer you and your family my deepest sympathy I feel his loss greatly he being my best friend. He was a friend of everyone. Loved by all. He was always happy. His main concern was for the welfare of his men and to make everyone happy. He was hit by a shell about midnight on the 12th. He lived for a few

hours but was unconscious all the time. Finally, he passed away on September 13th in hospital. I was with him until he was taken away to the hospital.[57]

Early in 1917, Captain Ellis Milne, the MO of the Liverpool Irish, took the time to write to Lieutenant John Sutton Sharpe's father in Edgbaston.[58] Lieutenant Sharpe had been missing since the battalion went into action on the Somme on 8 August 1916. Milne wanted to make Lieutenant Sharpe's father aware of 'one fine and plucky piece of work' his son had carried out during an incident which had occurred in the trenches to the east of Trones Wood on 1 August 1916, just one week prior to his son's disappearance near Guillemont. Battalions from the 16th and 18th Manchester Regiment had been in action in that sector in the days prior to the arrival of the Liverpool Irish. A soldier from the Manchester Regiment managed to get into the Liverpool Irish lines, where he informed them that he had been sheltering for a couple of days in a German dugout about 50 yards from the German position. He then made his way back to the British lines under the cover of darkness. He told Lieutenant Sharpe that half a dozen men wounded, exhausted men were still in the dugout. Milne described the events which followed:

> It was arranged a reserve party should go out as soon as darkness arrived with this man as a guide and bring in the cases. Accordingly, that night a party of stretcher bearers, the guide and a covering party of bombers under the command of Lieutenant Sharpe went forward to find the dugout. After a difficult search under dangerous circumstances, they at last discovered the place and found 11 British and one dying, also one dead German in the dugout and all the British were rescued and safely conveyed to the British lines. During the time, the stretcher bearers were engaged in bringing out these cases, Lieut. Sharpe with his men were in the open, not more than a score of yards from the German positions.[59]

The stretcher bearers managed to retrieve the wounded from the dugout while Sharpe and his party waited in the open. He asked if all the men had been removed and was informed that they had left one man who was in great pain and making a lot of noise. The stretcher bearers explained that if they tried to remove him he might make enough noise to rouse the enemy; nevertheless, Sharpe ordered them back to get the man. According to Milne, the rescue had been due to Sharpe's courage and his insistence that every one of the isolated men, including a severely wounded soldier, should be recovered. The battalion War Diary mentions this event in the briefest terms: 'Several wounded and unwounded men of the 16th and 18th Manchester Regiment brought in.'[60]

As a non-combatant officer, Captain Milne was not obliged to write to the families of the missing or the dead. However, this was an exception. Milne had known 19-year-old Sharpe as a patient in October 1915 when he reported sick and was subsequently diagnosed as suffering from 'neurasthenia' (shell shock). He was then sent home to England to recuperate.[61] Lieutenant Sharpe's youth, his resilience in overcoming the understandable mental stresses of trench warfare, or a perceived lack of recognition of his actions in rescuing the stranded men may have influenced Milne's decision to write to the young officer's family.

Officers had an obligation to instil a sense of *esprit de corps*, whether it was directed at divisional, regimental or battalion level. At Airaines on 30 January 1916, all officers and platoon commanders from the 164th Infantry Brigade were ordered to attend a lecture delivered by the commandant of the 3rd Army Training School on '*Esprit de Corps* etc'.[62] Local identity, pride and cohesion were key factors cultivating *esprit de corps* thereby maintaining and improving morale.[63] The fact that the Liverpool Irish was serving in a Lancastrian-English Division, did not prohibit Irishmen (and others) celebrating their identity. If the British Army failed to appreciate or recognise the significance of their patron saint's day, the Liverpool Irishmen made their own arrangements to 'drown their shamrocks'. In the spring of 1915, the battalion was stationed at Kent, when Private George Tomlinson wrote home to his family: 'It's St Patrick's Day tomorrow, so there's only a church parade at 10. I'm afraid there'll only be a poor congregation. The 8th mean making a day of it I can tell you. They're getting a bit merry tonight.'[64] Some soldiers in the battalion who could not be identified as Irish or Liverpudlian remained justifiably proud of the exploits on their battalion on the battlefield. Private A.C.M. Harvey, a Blackpool man, composed the lyrics of a song entitled *The Song of the Liverpool Irish* while recovering from his wounds at Heaton Park in Manchester.[65] Adopted to be sung to the tune of the Irish ballad *A little bit of heaven*, his 'song' was published in the *Blackpool Gazette;* it recalls the actions of the Liverpool Irish at Festubert. Whatever its quality, his humble offering exudes unit and county pride:

Have you ever heard the story how the 8th Irish got their name?
Have you ever heard the story how they won undying fame?
T'was at Festubert and Rue De Ouvert they made the Germans run
And they captured lines of trenches, prisoners and maxim gun.
Sure, twelve hundred lads from Lancashire went o'er to France one day
And they nicknamed them the 'Ghurkhas' for the part that they did play
At Festubert and Rue De Ouvert, each man gave up his all,
For Home, for King, for Country, to conquer or to fall.[66]

1914 Recruiting poster for the 8th (Irish) Battalion, King's Liverpool Regiment. *Thanks to St Helens Libraries and Archives Services for their kind permission to reproduce this image.*

Left: Photograph of the cup which was presented to the Liverpool Irish Battalion on behalf of the people of Whitstable on 27 January 1915. The inscription reads, 'Presented by the people of Whitstable to Lieut. Col. A.H.C. Neale and the officers and men of the 8th (Irish) Batt, The King's Liverpool Regt in appreciation of the good conduct of the men of the detachment quartered at Whitstable under the command of Major J.J. Smith during the Great War'. *Author's collection*

Below: 'F' Company, of the Liverpool Irish. *Author's Collection*

above: The band of the Liverpool Irish *Author's Collection*

right: Private George Tomlinson, a dapper looking 18-year-old bank employee from Clifton near Preston. George would not live to see his 19th birthday; he was killed during the Battle of Festubert in 1915. *Thanks to Mr Tom Fisher and his family for their kind permission to reproduce this image.*

Above left: Captain Herbert Marion Finegan, a pre-war officer in the Liverpool Irish. The son of an Irish doctor, he was also a gifted scholar and athlete. Educated at Stonyhurst College and Liverpool University, Finegan was an active supporter of Home Rule for Ireland and was active in local Irish groups in the city. He was killed in action at Festubert. *Thanks to the Headmaster of Stonyhurst College for his kind permission to reproduce this image.*

Above right: Lieutenant Herbert Laidlaw Downes who was killed during the Battle of Festubert. Lt. Downes was commended by Brig. Gen. Hibbert for his bravery in supplying grenades and ammunition to the battalion during their assault on the German lines. *Thanks to the Institution of Engineering and Technology Archives for their kind permission to reproduce this image.*

Left: Lieutenant Henry Mackey Drake was born in New South Wales, Australia. According to his friend, Capt. Harold Mahon, Drake was just 20 years old '6 feet 3 inches high and a man every inch of him'. He was mortally wounded within the first few minutes of the attack at Festubert. *Author's Collection*

Above: Wounded survivors of the Liverpool Irish from the Battle of Festubert photographed outside their battalion headquarters at Shaw Street, Liverpool in 1915. Among the wounded is Lance-Corporal Cuddy, a hospital porter from Claudia Street, Walton, who was awarded the Distinguished Conduct Medal for bravery while rescuing wounded men during the battle. Included in the photograph are, in the back row, left to right: Privates R. Sanderson, T. Williams, G. Davis, W. Kerr, J. Forsythe, G. McKinley, and J. Jones. Sitting: Corporal E. Jones, Private F. Simmons, Sergeant T. Slater, Lance-Corporal E. J. Cuddy DCM, Sergeant L. Kelly, Privates C. Coldrick and A. Davies. Front row: Privates D. Singer and C. Kavanagh. *Wilson Collection. Great thanks to Mr George Wilson for sharing his research and for granting permission to reproduce images from his collection.*

Below: Sergeants of the Liverpool Irish. *Author's Collection*

Captain Harold Mahon from Wallasey was a pre-war territorial who had served in the ranks of the 6th Liverpool Rifles. He received his commission into the Liverpool Irish in1914. He admired the men under his command, writing that 'nothing was too good for them'. He planned and partially executed the famous raid by the Liverpool Irish at Blaireville in April 1916. His diary and letters provide a valuable insight into the experiences of the battalion until September 1916 when he was fatally wounded by a German shell. *Wilson Collection*

Lieutenant Paul Osborne Limrick, who had been with the battalion from the beginning, was killed by the same shell which had wounded Captain Mahon. *Author's Collection*

Above: Hard men. A famous photograph of the Liverpool Irish raiding party taken after they had carried out a successful and bloody raid on the German lines at Blaireville in April 1916. *IWM Q510. Thanks to the Imperial War Museum for granting permission to reproduce this image.*

Left: Second Lieutenant Edward Felix Baxter VC, who was killed in action during the raid at Blaireville in April 1916. Originally from Oldswinford near Stourbridge, he was a keen motorcyclist and took part in the Isle of Man TT races. Later, he moved with his wife to Liverpool where he was a tutor at Skerry's College. *Wilson Collection*

A la mémoire du Lieutenant Edward Felix BAXTER
Du l/8ème Bataillon Irlandais du KING'S LIVERPOOL Régiment
à qui fut décernée la VICTORIA CROSS pour sa bravoure et sa conduite héroïque
lors de l'attaque des tranchées et des positions ennemies situées devant le village
de BLAIRVILLE entre les 16 et 18 Avril 1916

PASSANT ! SOUVIENS-TOI

To the memory of Lieutenant Edward Felix BAXTER
1/8th (Irish) Battalion KING'S (LIVERPOOL REGIMENT)
This officer was awarded the VICTORIA CROSS for conspicuous gallantry and
expert leadership while attacking German trenches and dugouts in front of
BLAIRVILLE 16th/18th April 1916

REST IN PEACE

SF Arras 2016

bove: The memorial to Second Lieutenant
Baxter at Blaireville. There are no memorials
to the memory of Second Lieutenant
Baxter or to the Liverpool Irish Battalion
in Liverpool. This memorial was organised
and erected by Mr David Moore who now
resides near Arras. *Thanks to David Moore
for this photograph and his kind permission to
reproduce this image.*

right: Commanding Officers: Lieutenant
Colonel Edward Arthur Fagan (later Sir E.A.
Fagan), who commanded the battalion from
December 1915 until 26 August 1916. He
left on promotion to Brigadier. *Reproduced by
and permission of the National Portrait Gallery*

Lieutenant Colonel Edward Charles Heath commanded the battalion from 16 November 1916 until the end of the war. After the war, Heath was instrumental in adopting the poppy as the symbol of remembrance. He later became Secretary of the British Legion from 1921 until 1940. *Wilson Collection*

On 17 March 1916, the Liverpool Irish were in the trenches at Bretencourt, where every member of the battalion was issued with shamrocks which had been provided by John Redmond MP, leader of the Irish Party.[67] Later in the evening, the officers refused to allow their circumstances or the war to deny their obligation to celebrate Ireland's patron saint. According to Captain Harold Mahon, the question of nationality was immaterial: 'Now we like calling ourselves the Liverpool Irish and that being so, whatever sentiments we may have, or whether we are real Irish or not, we always try to do our best by the name.' Captain Chamberlin, based in the support line, issued invitations to any officer who could be spared from the firing line to visit him in his 'palatial quarters in the supports'. Harold Mahon described it as a large cellar beneath two demolished houses. 'As the evening wore on, officer after another [*sic*] popped down from the front line, had refreshments and a sing song and the last men didn't leave until close on midnight It was a topping night and will be long remembered by those who were there.'[68]

The soldiers of the 8th (Irish) Battalion of the King's Liverpool Regiment, as well as their relatives and neighbours, cherished the 'Irish' prefix of their title. Any perceived slight, omission or lack of acknowledgement of the battalion's Irish character, origins and contribution to the conflict was seized and dealt with. The significance of the Irish title became apparent when it was omitted from casualty lists after the Battle of Festubert which were published in the Liverpool press. Charles Diamond's *Liverpool Catholic Herald* castigated the War Office for the omission with the headline 'LIVERPOOL IRISH – Get Tardy Justice from War Office.'[69] In Dublin, Colonel D. Edgar Flynn complained to the *Freeman's Journal* that a territorial force battalion bearing the Scottish prefix had received their full title in casualty lists and Rolls of Honour, whereas the Irish prefix had been removed from the lists of the Liverpool Irish.[70] 'The Irish territorial regiments are doing splendid work,' he wrote, 'and their nationality should be given in the casualty lists in the same manner as the Scottish regiments.' In the House of Commons, T.P. O'Connor, the Irish Party's MP for Liverpool's Scotland Division, sought an assurance from Harold Tennant, the Under Secretary of State for War, that this 'unconscious slight of Irish soldiers in the regiment will be removed'.[71] Any recognition and acknowledgement of the actions of Liverpool Irishmen at the front enhanced morale and the men enjoyed reading about themselves in the local press. Captain Harold Mahon asked his mother to cut out and send him any references to the battalion in the Liverpool newspapers.[72] In October 1915, a disgruntled, unnamed soldier from the Liverpool Irish wrote to the *Liverpool Catholic Herald* criticising the Liverpool papers for their failure to report the exploits of his battalion.[73] After praising the *Herald* for always 'doing justice' to the battalion, he voiced his displeasure at the other papers in the city. 'But as you may surmise, we are surprised by the absolute silence of the Liverpool press.'[74]

While the Liverpool (Irish) Battalion prized and maintained their Irish identity, it was, however, just one of the many battalions which constituted the West Lancashire Division. By August 1916, the voluntary recruiting system had failed to provide sufficient manpower to replace casualties at the front. In order to address the problem, Bertram Cubitt, Assistant Under Secretary of State at the War Office, wrote to Haig informing him that it was no longer possible to send replacements from specific territorial areas to their respective battalions.[75] Cubitt wrote that he understood the 'special regard' that was given under the voluntary recruitment system for sending men to their local battalions 'not only on account of local feeling, influence and interests, but above all to keep up esprit de corps to which the regimental system owes so much'. He went on to state that, in any event, the National Service Act would remove the necessity to send men to their local battalions. In short, replacements would be sent to where they were needed rather than to their local territorial battalions, or to battalions of their choice. Symbols and identity were important for *esprit de corps*, and General H.S. Jeudwine, commander of the 55th (West Lancashire) Division, was keen to exploit his division's association with its eponymous title and adopted the historic rose of Lancashire as the divisional badge.[76] This was a shrewd response by Jeudwine to the changes made by the War Office. It was an attempt to unite individual battalions and regiments under a solitary symbol of their native county rather than individual towns and localities. It is difficult to evaluate whether the Irishmen serving with the division evinced any homage or loyalty towards the county symbol.

As well as fostering *esprit de corps*, officers were obliged to see to the welfare of the men under their command. The morale of a battalion plummeted under the command of a bad officer and peaked when he was replaced by a good one.[77] In February 1916, the Liverpool Irish endured a hard march in the wind and rain from Amplier to Saulty, a distance of 9 miles. According to Captain Harold Mahon, due to the conditions it felt more like they had done 20. Mahon praised the swift actions of Lieutenant Colonel Fagan, CO of the Liverpool Irish: 'Luckily, the CO turned up trumps by making the ASC (Army Service Corps) produce coal, straw, and an issue of rum in quick time.'[78] Conversely, soldiers of all ranks became frustrated and aggrieved by poor leadership and organisation. On 30 August 1916, Brigadier-General G.T.G. Edwards of the 164th Infantry Brigade was having a difficult day. Having been woken late by his servant, matters took a turn for the worse.

Reached Merricourt at 10 a.m. No one to meet us there. Got the men out of the train & got the best shelter we could in the pouring rain. McCready turned up after about an hour & told us our bivouac area. Marched there in the pouring rain and camped in a corn field. Only 26 tents for the brigade. Transport did not arrive till 7 p.m. and motor lorries with kits at 6 p.m. Gen. Jeudwine came around at 5.30 & was full of complaints that the officers were not looking after their men. Told him the best thing for them would be an issue of rum & he agreed but it never arrived.[79]

Evidently disgusted by his experience, the following day Edwards summoned the officers of the 164th Brigade and outlined their responsibilities and obligations: 'Had all officers up and gave them a good talking to in care of men & horses – coping with emergency – discipline etc.' Away from the front, on leave, the welfare of his men remained Captain Harold Mahon's primary concern. On 31 October 1915, Mahon arrived at Waterloo station in London with about a dozen men from the Liverpool Irish. It was the middle of the night and Mahon ensured that his men were 'settled in' for the night before making his own sleeping arrangements at the Euston Hotel.[80] When they eventually reached Liverpool, they 'caused quite a sensation at Lime Street, my boys all having their furry coats on'.

The twelve men from the Liverpool Irish who accompanied Mahon on leave were extremely fortunate. Leave, or the prospect of leave, dominated the thoughts of men in the trenches and had a powerful effect on their morale. The supposed reason for censoring letters sent by soldiers to their families and friends was to ensure that they did not contain any sensitive military information. However, the letters also provided military censors with a wealth of genuine first-hand accounts of soldiers' thoughts and opinions, thereby enabling censors to gauge morale. Captain M. Hardie of the British Army's Censors Staff wrote, 'judging by the letters, it is impossible to emphasise too strongly the importance of leave as a factor in the moral [*sic*] of the army'.[81] Unsurprisingly, anything which interfered with leave, or caused leave to be stopped or postponed, was greeted with contempt. On 13 April 1916, Captain Mahon noted in his diary: '13th!!! LEAVE – all leave stopped. Easter traffic. Did you ever hear the like?'[82] Some officers thought that the disparity between leave for officers and their men was unfair. Officers were permitted leave once every six or seven months, while ordinary soldiers had to endure between fifteen and eighteen months of warfare before getting home on leave.[83] Leave, while highly prized, could turn out to be something of an anticlimax for unmarried men. Private James Green of the Liverpool Irish was granted leave while recuperating from the wound he had received at Festubert. Arriving home, he found that Preston had changed: 'Quiet time at home, all my pals and friends were in the services and Queen St. was deserted. I was pretty fed up with wandering about. I was really glad when it was time to go back and join my regiment.'[84]

During the fifteen- or eighteen-month phases between leave, life for the vast majority of soldiers was punctuated by periods in the frontline trenches, marching, resting and training. Officers and men used whatever spare time available to enjoy themselves, by organised activities such as sport or by making their own arrangements. Football was extremely popular throughout the BEF and the Liverpool (Irish) Battalion was no exception.[85] In January 1916, football matches seem to have become more frequent and better organised affairs. Captain Harold Mahon wrote: 'Most afternoons the men get a game or the chance of watching one. Inter-company or in inter-regimental. On the 21 January, we beat the 1/4th Loyal North Lancs by 6 goals to nil. I played outside right for the battalion.'[86] Details of football matches acquired sufficient prestige to be entered into the battalion's War Diary: 'In a football match, the battalion beat the 4th West Lancashire (Howitzer) Brigade, RFA by 6 goals to 1.'[87] Other sporting events, such as boxing, were also popular. On 31 January 1916, Captain Harold Mahon wrote that 'at Airaines, we were treated to as fine a night's sport as I have witnessed'.[88] The 1/4th Battalion of the Loyal North Lancashire Regiment challenged the Liverpool Irishmen to put up seven men from various boxing weights to fight men from their own battalion. The Liverpool Irish won six out of the seven contests. Harold Mahon was clearly impressed by the event and the standard of boxing despite the lack of preparation and training; he recorded a detailed account in his diary. 'Sgts. Little and Tighe, Pts McNamara, Seddon, Skelland and Cook and Cpl. Valante kept our colour (green) flying … may we have another such night again soon, we have many such men to put up'.[89] This demonstration of the 'noble art' of pugilism not only boosted morale but did no harm whatsoever to the Liverpool (Irish) Battalion's reputation for fighting.

Concerts also raised morale and provided a welcome (if brief) diversion from the realities of war. The 55th Division had its own divisional concert troupe, appropriately named the Red Roses.[90] At Saulty, on 24 February 1916, the Liverpool Irish held a 'jolly good concert' of their own in the regimental canteen.[91] Captain Harold Mahon wrote that an unnamed Major had put up 'a prize or two, which added additional interest'. Mahon went on to describe the variety of acts performing: 'you get every kind of entertainment, from a pair of humorous boxers to a mouth organ recital. A step-dance generally helps a man well on towards a prize should there be one.' Lieutenant Colonel Fagan acknowledged the importance of music within the ranks of the Irish. In the absence of a band, Fagan purchased a flute for Lance-Corporal Ellis to amuse his comrades and lead them to and from the trenches. Before the war, Lance-Corporal Ellis had been a member of Garston Irish National Foresters' Band.[92]

While the army attempted to maintain and improve morale, their ability to do so was affected by something over which they had no control. Soldiers on both sides of No Man's Land were at the mercy of the weather and belligerents of all ranks dreaded the arrival of winter on the Western Front.[93] By 1917, British soldiers were much more apprehensive about leave and the prospect of having to endure winter in the trenches than they were about actual combat. According to the Army Censor, 'References to winter privations and to the lack of leave outnumber references to the horror of fighting in the ratio of 5 to 1.'[94] Marches along winter roads followed by prolonged periods of standing in cold, wet trenches resulted in cases of frostbite and trench foot. However, these were not the only causes; boots which were laced too tightly and putties which were tightly bound restricted circulation to the feet and aggravated the problem.[95] Research by Stephen Bull confirms that the British army identified the dangers of frostbite early in the war and had produced 250,000 copies of a pamphlet entitled *Prevention of Frostbite or Chilled Feet*.[96] However, just 103 copies were distributed. On 7 March 1916, three men from the Liverpool Irish were reported as suffering from trench foot.[97] Trench foot was a preventable ailment and improvements in medical care and advice from MOs, regular foot inspections carried out by officers, and individual soldiers taking care of their feet led to an improvement.[98] Men were encouraged to dry their feet at the earliest opportunity, to carry a clean, dry pair of socks, and to apply Vaseline or whale oil to their feet as a preventative measure.[99] Unsurprisingly, the British army's hierarchy was concerned by the number of incidences of trench foot within the ranks and regarded them as an indicator of the discipline and morale within a battalion. Any rise in the weekly number of cases of trench foot within a battalion was regarded with suspicion by senior officers who demanded a report explaining the increase.[100]

Winter also interfered with the necessities of life in the trenches. In November 1915, while the Liverpool Irish were in the trenches at Authuille, a water pipe had been laid on for the men; the water was then 'tanked'. When the temperature fell below freezing, the pipe and the tank froze. To rectify the situation, a water cart was organised to carry water up to the battalion, but it too suffered the same fate.[101] Undoubtedly, winter and all that it brought conspired to sap the morale of soldiers on the Western Front. Yet even in the harshest conditions it was possible to boost morale. In February 1916, while they were out of the line, the battalion made appropriate use of the adverse weather conditions created by a heavy snowfall. Captain Harold Mahon described the battalion's non-lethal battle at Saulty:

> All available ranks including the CO and the Major organised a snowball fight on the bombing trench field. It was great fun holding trenches against bombers with snowballs. Ammunition was brought up on oilsheets and it was attackers versus defenders. There were no casualties, which made it a perfect melee. You never knew where the next one was coming from or where you would be hit. Of course, the attackers had the best of it. [102]

Winter was somewhat less appealing a few days later when the battalion marched to Bavincourt in a blizzard, and 'the men looked like old Father Xmas with his bundles'.[103]

Enemy action, the weather, illness, accidents and downright bad luck caused the most casualties on the Western Front. For some, the hostile environment, filth, lice, rats and the constant fear of death or mutilation became unbearable. It was described as a world where 'the brittle cracked and the solid crumbled'.[104] For those soldiers desperate to escape from the privations and dangers of trench warfare, the options were limited. A wound, sickness or disease 'honourably obtained' might entitle a soldier to a period in hospital, a transfer to England for further treatment or to convalesce until he became fit for duty or discharged from the service. Some more disconsolate men were unable or unwilling to wait for providence to deliver their escape and resolved to inflict the wound themselves. Official statistics regarding self-inflicted injuries are suspiciously low and therefore invite questions as to the extent of self-mutilation in the British army during the war.[105] Any attempt to interpret the official statistics for self-inflicted wounds is hampered by how they had been recorded. The medical statistics for the number of self-inflicted wounds for infantry soldiers treated during the war is just 197, whereas the total number of infantrymen treated for 'accidental or undefined wounds' is 18,411.[106] Self-mutilation was also a disciplinary offence, and men who had committed the offence were treated in France and sent before a FGCM once they had recovered.[107] During the war, a total of 12 officers and 2,882 men were court-martialled for this offence.[108] Helen McCartney offers a convincing theory that the actual numbers of those men who were prosecuted for the offence had been charged under the 'catch-all' Section 40 of the Army Act – conduct to the prejudice of good order and military discipline.[109]

Some statistics from the 55th (West Lancashire) provide a summary of the numbers of casualties due to accidental and self-inflicted wounds from February to July 1916.[110]

Table 3.1: *Summary of Accidental and self-inflicted casualties, 55th (West Lancashire) Division, February–July 1916.*

Battalion	Accidental	Self-Inflicted	Total
4th King's Own Royal Lancaster Rgt.	7	2	9
8th Liverpool (Irish) King's Liverpool Rgt.	1	4	5
4th Loyal North Lancs. Rgt.	5	6	11
5th King's Liverpool King's Liverpool Rgt.	8	1	9
6th King's Liverpool King's Liverpool Rgt.	3	1	4
7th King's Liverpool King's Liverpool Rgt	6	2	8
9th King's Liverpool King's Liverpool Rgt.	3	2	5
5th King's Own Royal Lancs. Rgt.	3	3	6
10th Liverpool Scottish	7	1	8
5th South Lancashire Rgt.	8	1	9
2/5th Lancashire Fus.	8	0	8
1/5th Loyal North Lancs. Rgt.	2	0	2
Totals	61	23	84

Source: LRO, 356 FIF 1/2/3, Records of the 55th (West Lancashire) Division, 1914–19, 'Summary of accidental and self-inflicted casualties since the division has been in the line, February to July 1916'.

As seen in Table 3.1, the 55th Division sustained a total of eighty-four casualties due to accidents and self-inflicted wounds. Accidental wounds accounted for 72.69 per cent of the total, while the figure for self-inflicted wounds was just 27.38 per cent. During this five-month period, the 4th Loyal North Lancashire

Battalion sustained the highest number of self-inflicted casualties, with six men deliberately wounding themselves. The Liverpool Irish had four self-inflicted casualties but just one soldier had been accidently wounded. Three battalions: 5th Kings, 5th South Lancashire's and 2/5th Lancashire Fusiliers – all had eight men accidentally wounded, yet just one or no cases of self-inflicted wounds. In the case of the Liverpool Irish, the battalion War Diary recorded three cases of self-inflicted wounds during June–July 1916.[111] Another difficulty in attempting to determine the extent of self-inflicted wounds was the rather obvious question faced by the army commanders of whether the wound occur by accident or was it deliberate?

On Tuesday, 26 October 1915, Captain Mahon sat on a Court of Enquiry into an alleged accidental shooting incident. It occurred while a private soldier was cleaning his rifle and the rag he was using caught on the trigger and fired the weapon causing an injury to the soldier's little finger. The purpose of the enquiry was to determine whether the injury was self-inflicted, wilful, negligent or accidental. Mahon gives a whimsical account of the proceedings:

> Now poor Private Blank shall we call him, was cleaning his rifle at 1 a.m. (A.M. note) as he wished to fire his rifle and the mud loves to prevent this. There was a deadly bullet in the breech, but he did not know until his rag caught in the trigger guard and pulled the trigger and proved beyond all doubt that the rifle was loaded and cocked. Damage very slight to little finger of left hand. Now Private Blank as he 'had drawn blood' should have reported to the MO, or on sick parade next morning.[112]

The wound was bandaged, and the man's injury was noticed by a corporal who in turn reported the matter to the company Sergeant Major, who insisted that Private Blank should see the MO. The MO in turn placed the matter before the CO who convened a Court of Enquiry. The matter was dealt with very swiftly: 'The man is a good soldier, gives his evidence well, explains why he didn't report sick. CSM and Cpl. give evidence. Captain Jackson DSO says to Lieutenant Fisher and self "Well gentlemen, we concur – Accidental". Nuff sed. As Tommy says "Napoo – Finey".' Proper military procedures and reporting through the chain of command notwithstanding, why was the soldier cleaning his weapon at one o'clock in the morning? Why was the weapon loaded when he intended to clean it? Why was there a round in the breech if he intended to use a pull-through on the barrel? What was the man doing with his little finger on the muzzle of the rifle? On this occasion, it seems that Captain Mahon and his fellow officers on the Court of Enquiry did the decent thing by not asking too many obvious questions. Unfortunately, suicide was the only option available to an irredeemably depressed soldier on the Western Front. On 26 June 1917, while the Liverpool Irish were in the trenches at Quercamps, the battalion's War Diarist noted that there had been one casualty that day: '1 Killed <u>(Shot himself)</u>'. The diarist seemed keen emphasise the cause of death by underlining and bracketing the fact that the unnamed soldier had taken his own life.[113] The anonymous soldier was 22-year-old Private Harold Potter from Blackburn; his entry in *Soldiers Died in the Great War* lists him as having 'died'. He was mourned by his widowed mother, who had the words 'Gone but not forgotten' inscribed on his gravestone.[114]

The frostbitten, the sick, the wounded and the undeniably exhausted could all derive some comfort and confidence if they knew that they would be looked after. Skilled medical expertise was provided by doctors of the RAMC, who had applied for their commissions through a sense of patriotism and humanitarianism as well as a professional obligation to treat the sick and wounded.[115] Life for Medical Officers (MOs) attached to battalions at the front could be uncomfortable, dangerous and, during offensives, extremely busy. Doctors who had joined the RAMC from general practice had undoubt-edly spent years gaining experience and developing an ability to empathise and sympathise with their patients. Once at the front, the MO's primary concern shifted away from the patient; his primary role was to maintain the fighting strength of the battalion.[116] This military obligation presented doctors with an unpalatable dilemma: if they were too sympathetic and excused men from duty they experienced the wrath of the battalion CO. Conversely, if they refused to acknowledge a soldier's alleged symptoms and returned him to duty they were reviled by the men. Given the physical hardships of trench life and the emotional stresses and strains of warfare, it is understandable that soldiers might attempt to dupe their MO. Some MOs were hard-hearted and were viewed as nothing more than 'red caps with stethoscopes'.[117] Humorous stories of uncaring medics were circulating as early as 1915. Captain Harold Mahon recorded that when a soldier attended his MO complaining of his inability to sleep, the MO stated that his insomnia meant that he was just the man for night sentry duty. Another soldier complained that he was alright but could not run; again the man was assured that this was an asset as he would 'not be able to run away from the Boshes'.[118] Not all MOs were callous and unsympathetic. A doctor who was firm but fair and could discriminate between malingerers and those who were in genuine need of medical help enhanced morale within a battalion.[119] Medical expertise notwithstanding, doctors on the Western Front required qualities of guile, diplomacy, sympathy and assertiveness.

The Liverpool Irish were fortunate to have Captain Joseph Ellis Milne as their MO. Before the war, Ellis Milne had a large practice in Aberdeen. Although he was 47 years of age he applied to join the RAMC and was posted to the 51st Highland Division.[120] Not content with being at a Casualty Clearing Station behind the lines, Milne wrote informing a friend and fellow medic, 'I am still on its strength but have at last managed to get where I have hoped to land ever since I came out here – viz, right up in the firing line.'[121] Milne had somehow managed to persuade the Director of Medical Services to make an exception to his rule that no doctor over the age of 40 was to serve on the front line. 'I suppose the old chap thought that three months of it would cure me or sicken me, but now that I have at last got up here I shall be able to stick in the front until the curtain drops and the show is over.' The winter weather failed to curtail Milne's enthusiasm, while the old hands were 'bewailing their cold feet and strafing the trenches', Milne declared himself 'as warm as toast'. He concluded his letter with praise for the Liverpool Irish. 'The crowd up here really are a wonderful, cheery plucky lot and the Tommies, poor chaps are a perpetual marvel to me, they are so patient and light hearted.'[122] A friend of Milne's wrote that it was with 'particular gratification' that Milne received the news of his posting to the Liverpool Irish, as the men came from the same districts of Liverpool where Milne began his medical career.[123]

In April 1916, Captain Mahon witnessed Milne's dentistry skills when he removed one of Sgt. Bamber's back teeth. 'I remember this because it was done so quickly that neither he nor I thought the Doc had touched it before it was out.'[124] Milne's courage earned him the respect of the officers and men of the Liverpool Irish. He was also a shrewd judge of character which enabled him to 'sum up the constitution and guess the idiosyncrasy of each man. Very soon these Irish Lads knew that in the grey-haired Scotch [sic] doctor they had a man with a warm heart and a ready skill.'[125] Captain Chamberlin of the Liverpool Irish recalled, 'I remember one night when we were shelled heavily in billets and instead of waiting in the safety of his dressing station for the wounded to be brought to him, he went out to the house that had been struck and amidst the ruins and amputated the leg of a man, under heavy shellfire all the while.'[126] Milne's bravery during the Somme offensive and throughout 1916 was rewarded with a DSO on 20 October 1916.[127] If he was brave in the field, he was equally spirited in his defence of exhausted soldiers. According to a friend, 'If a company returned from the trenches dead to the world, and needing a rest – Milne was adamant, no more fatigues till these men are rested.'[128] Behind the lines, Milne organised football matches for the men and, despite his age, pulled on his kit and participated.

Captain Ellis Milne, like many other MOs on the Western Front, took risks to rescue men and to treat their wounds and like many doctors he paid the price. He was killed by a sniper at Potijze near Ypres on 22 February 1917.[129] Captain Chamberlin, who had been wounded at Festubert and the Somme, wrote to Milne's brother in March 1917: 'I am certain that no doctor did finer work at the war than your brother, or was more admired and esteemed by the officers and men under his charge, and the news of his death was a heavy blow to all of us.'[130] Mr A.J.A. Wilson from Liverpool was keen to express his sympathy and gratitude to Captain Milne's family. The fact that Wilson did not know the Milne family's address did not prevent him from writing to an Aberdeen merchant in the hope that his condolences could be forwarded to Ellis Milne's family:

> My son is in the Liverpool Regiment and has been in France 22 months. The doctor attached to his battalion was your fellow citizen Captain J. Ellis Milne, and as the brave man has made the great sacrifice, I am sending you a line to express my regret. My son had many kindnesses from Captain Milne, and he writes me that he and the other few remaining officers with the battalion feel their loss greatly and will ever remember him and respect the example he was to those who shared with him the hardships and dangers on the Western Front.[131]

Captain Milne was also remembered by his Alma Mater, Aberdeen University: 'Joseph Ellis Milne had a dynamic personality. An iron will endowed him with great powers of physical and mental endurance. A high conception of duty was united to a complete indifference to personal danger; a heart in sympathy with each Irish lad brought him the love of all in the Battalion'.[132]

4

DISCIPLINE AND LEADERSHIP

Regimental pride, local identity, comradeship and discipline combined to act as the glue which bonded and maintained a battalion. While the first three elements were largely down to the distinctiveness of individual units, the army as whole was subject to military law. The *Manual of Military Law* stated that 'the object of military law is to maintain discipline'.[1] Like other part-time soldiers, the pre-war territorial soldiers of the Liverpool Irish attended drill and musketry courses and their annual camp. The men, NCOs and their officers knew each other personally: their status, where they came from and their occupations. Such familiarity attracted criticism from Territorial Force Inspectors and regular soldiers who suggested that territorial NCOs lacked the ability to order their men to perform a task, preferring instead to ask them.[2] While subject to the same military laws as their counterparts serving in regular battalions, territorial soldiers did not experience the same rigid disciplinary regime. They were, after all, part-time volunteers and as such they experienced a more liberal interpretation of how and when those laws were enforced. Unlike a regular soldier, a territorial volunteer who became disgruntled with his unit could resign after giving fourteen days' notice. There were also difficulties regarding the sanctions an officer could impose, with the only options being a fine or dismissal.[3] With pre-war territorial recruiting at a low ebb, the hierarchy of territorial battalions were loath to impose a sterner or 'regular army' form of discipline on their men which might well have led to a further depletion of the ranks.

The Liverpool Irish, like most other territorial units, required additional recruits to bring them up to fighting strength and to provide reserves which would be vital to replace the inevitable casualties, promotions and transfers. While the established pre-war core of the Liverpool Irish had been accustomed to the basic infantry skills – dressing appropriately, marching, weapon handling and obeying orders – new recruits to the battalion needed time to assimilate and learn basic infantry skills. Apart from training days, ceremonial parades and annual camps, the men who formed the core of battalion could forget about the army and carry on with their domestic existence. Everything changed in August 1914. Military training and discipline made no distinction in how the army treated the pre-war territorial and the recruit; they were all subjected to both. The army ensured that soldiers dressed the same, marched in step together, ate and slept together and did exactly as they were told. Individuality was removed, they were virtually identical, differentiated only by their regimental badges and buttons, and the chevrons which denoted their rank; every volunteer was expected to conform to military discipline. Ian Beckett has argued that the willingness of British working-class recruits to accept and expect the imposition of military discipline was due to the prominence of deference towards social superiors in British society. According to Beckett, deference did not mean subservience; rather, it was a mechanism whereby deference itself was exchanged in return for paternalism.[4] Gary Sheffield has highlighted the 'striking' parallels between the pre-war strict elementary school discipline where children were first broken by severity and constraint and subjected to mechanical obedience and basic wartime infantry training.[5]

Apart from knowing that discipline involved doing what you were told as well as dressing and acting according to the rules, no precise definition existed of what discipline actually meant. After the Battle of Pilckem Ridge in August 1917, General Stockwell of the 164th Infantry Brigade addressed his men. Congratulating them on their achievements, he also stressed the importance of discipline and gave them his own definition of what discipline meant:

> It was a great example of determination and discipline and by discipline you know what I mean. It isn't bright buttons and clean boots – that is a sign of it, but it means a great deal more than that. Discipline means confidence in oneself and in each other. It means the confidence which each man has in himself and his weapon. It means the confidence that these officers have in you.[6]

Rank, of course, came with a rise in pay and certain responsibilities, not least the requirement to carry out orders and to ensure that others complied with those orders. The parade ground was certainly not the place to have an informed and reasoned debate about the legitimacy of an order. The archetypal, profanity-screaming British NCO of 1914 was unlikely to countenance any refusal or hesitation to obey an order.[7] A NCO might rebuke an offender with a verbal reprimand or by detailing him to perform a variety of unpleasant tasks in the cookhouse or the latrines. However, a more aggressive NCO could make his point by means of a well-directed kick or punch.[8] During the hectic mobili-sation process at St Francis Xavier school, the editor of the *Xaverian* witnessed some men from the battalion undergoing punishment. 'The weather was ideal for the soldiers all the time they were with us except perhaps for those who, with full kit, had to do drill as a punishment for some misdemeanour for a couple of hours at a time.'[9] The author claimed that these were isolated incidents and that the battalion was 'extremely well-behaved and caused the minimum of trouble'. The hidden nature of military law and its application attracted little public atten-tion during peacetime and remained so throughout the war. Meanwhile, soldiers underwent punishment or detention in guardrooms and cells behind the walls of the numerous army establishments throughout the British Isles.

Minor infringements against military discipline could be resolved by informal and ad hoc punishments; more serious breaches resulted in a soldier being for-mally charged and brought before his company commander. Depending on the seriousness of the offence, the company commander could hear the case himself or, if necessary, pass it up the chain of command to the Commanding Officer (CO). Company commanders could issue fines, have a man confined to bar-racks or placed on fatigues. The names of those charged appeared on Company Orders. A perception existed that the summary nature of such cases was indeed 'rough justice', whereby the normal legal presumption of innocence prior to conviction was replaced by an unspoken belief that the soldier in question would not have been charged had he not been guilty in the first place.[10]

Essentially, this legal military authority provided company commanders and commanding officers with the power to deal with less serious military 'crimes', and meant that minor offences committed by the rank and file could be dealt with relatively quickly. More importantly, perhaps, it kept minor disciplinary transgressions within the battalion.[11] Commanding Officers were relatively autonomous in their power to dispense 'justice' within their respective battalions and could try a total of twenty-three offences and impose a variety of punish-ments.[12] An important distinction between the powers of a company commander and the CO was that the latter had the power to have a man detained.[13] More serious crimes involving capital offences were dealt with by court martial. Four types of court martial were available to the army in 1914: Regimental (RCM), District (DCM), General (GCM) and Field General Courts Martial (FGCM).[14] Only two of these, the General Court Martial and the Field General Court Martial, had the jurisdiction to deal with capital offences.

One of the first men of the Liverpool Irish to face a District Court Martial was Francis Egerton Rodden, a 31-year-old brass finisher from Everton. Private Rodden had been charged with striking an NCO on 6 May 1915 while the battalion was stationed in Kent.[15] A District Court Martial was convened at Canterbury, where Private Rodden was found guilty and sentenced to seventy-two days' detention with hard labour. The sentence was subsequently reduced to fifty days. War enhanced the necessity to impose a strict disciplinary regime throughout the army. Provisions made by the Army Act 1914 ensured that several offences were liable to attract a more severe punishment if they were committed while on active service.[16] On 15 November 1915, while the Liverpool Irish were at Millencourt on the Western Front, Private Sumner, No. 1974, was sentenced to two years' detention with hard labour for disobeying an order and using violence against a superior officer.[17] Although Sumner's offence was aggravated because he had also disobeyed an order, the severity of the penalty he had received was due to the fact that it was committed 'in the field'.

Flogging as a military punishment had been abolished in peacetime in 1881. The British army in the field required an alternative form of punishment which would be both visible and severe, whereby it would punish the offender and act as a deterrent to others. Thus, the much reviled and controversial Field Punishment Number 1 (F.P. No.1) was introduced and was available as a penalty to Commanding Officers and FGCM.[18] A FGCM could award F.P. No.1 for a period not exceeding three months and a battalion CO could sentence a man to twenty-eight days. An offender sentenced to F.P. No.1 was fastened to a fixed object by means of irons, ropes or straps. Regulations stipulated that an offender was only to be attached to a fixed object for periods of up to two hours a day and that he must not be attached during more than three out of four consecutive days.[19] Between 4 August 1914 and 31 March 1920, F.P. No. 1 was awarded on 60,085 occasions, this figure not including those men sentenced to F.P. No.1 by their respective Commanding Officers.[20] When a Commanding Officer believed an offence merited a greater sentence than he was entitled to award, he could have the offender sent for trial by FGCM. This was the case on 25 November 1915, when the Liverpool Irish was at Authuille. Private O'Connor, No. 2691, was sentenced to a gruelling fifty-six days No.1 field punishment by an FGCM for disobeying a lawful command.[21] Except for the daily rum issue, men on the front lines had no access to alcohol, unless they had procured and stashed it prior to leaving for the trenches. Conversely, when in billets to rear, soldiers could visit the many estaminets where they could drink and enjoy themselves. While the Liverpool Irish were at rest behind the lines on 27 April 1916, Private James Jenkins' overindulgence resulted in a conviction for being drunk and hesitating to obey an order at Monchiet where he was sentenced to fourteen days' F.P. No. 1.[22] Soldiers could be strung up on F.P. No. 1 for any number of offences, including drunkenness, refusing or hesitating to obey an order, losing equipment and falling out on the march without permission.[23] The humiliation, discomfort and embarrassment of the victim notwithstanding, it was a repulsive sight to those who witnessed it being performed.[24] In France and Belgium, the 'witnesses' sometimes included civilians, who were not only offended by the plight of the offender, but felt that in tying the outstretched offender in a cruciform fashion, the British were mocking their Catholic faith.[25] By 1916, letters and anecdotes about the barbaric treatment being meted out to the volunteer citizen soldiers reached England and caused outrage among disgusted friends and relatives of those serving as well as politicians and commentators.[26] In October 1916, Robert Blatchford, a former soldier, journalist and author, wrote an article which appeared in the *Illustrated Sunday Herald*; the title asked: 'Why "Crucify" Tommy?'[27] In his article, Blatchford praised the volunteer army and alleged that the nation had not done enough to honour them and treat them as well as it should. He went on to relate the contents of a letter which he had received in August 1916. The letter informed Blatchford that six men from a battalion of the Liverpool Pals had been sentenced to Field Punishment No. 1 for having lost their gas masks in a marsh. The letter also alleged that during the punishment one of the men had died. Blatchford denounced the inventor of such a 'barbarous and Boche-like penalty' and that he had deliberately withheld publishing details of the letter until parliament had assembled. He voiced his hopes that this 'Hun-like' torture would be eradicated along with the 'doltish martinets' who inflict it. A day later, the *Liverpool Echo* carried a report describing the public spectacle of F.P. No. 1 having been carried out in Egypt.[28] The report stated that the punishment known as 'Crucifixion' persisted, despite attempts to have it abolished. A soldier who had witnessed the punishment said that he thought that it was bad for the prestige of the British army 'that soldiers should be so degraded in front of "blacks"'.. Towards the end of 1916, the paper printed a statement on Field Punishment made in the House of Commons which said that opinions on the matter were being sought from every General Officer currently in the field.[29] It also revealed the views of the Commander-in-Chief, Sir Douglas Haig, who argued that the abolition of F.P. No. 1 would 'lead to more frequent resort to the death penalty'.

Public consciousness and the historiographic debate surrounding the subject of FGCM and the execution of British soldiers during the Great War remains an emotive and controversial aspect of how the British Army enforced discipline on its soldiers. Supposed first-hand accounts of executions appeared in some sections of the press in the aftermath of the war.[30] Given the public sensitivity surrounding the issue, in 1919 the government took the decision to restrict access to the files under the 'hundred-year rule', which meant that relatives of those executed (or anyone else for that matter), were unable to establish the facts surrounding the trials and executions which occurred during the conflict. Unsurprisingly, this led to assumptions that successive governments had conspired to conceal the truth of the incidents which led to the FGCM and hence to the firing squad. Since the 1970s, historians, scholars and commentators have attempted to address concerns about the lack of legal expertise of those officers who participated in the FGCM, the ability of the accused to defend himself and the severity of the sentences which they passed.[31] There is certainly evidence that the hierarchy of the 55th Division sought to influence the 'type' of officers selected to act as Presidents and Members of FGCM; they 'should always be officers known to have a true sense of military discipline'. The instructions issued by 55th Divisional Headquarters also indicated that the officers sitting at FGCM should always demonstrate an inclination for severe sentences.[32] The official memo advised that it was possible that a severe sentence could always be reduced on 'review', whereas a lenient sentence could not be increased.

However well intentioned, it is impossible to right the wrongs (real or imagined) of the application of the 1914 version of the Army Act 1881 and what passed for justice at the various FGCM on the Western Front between 1914 and 1918. It is also futile to attempt to foist any liberal modern attitudes and laws, however rational, onto the function of the British military justice system a century ago. Ian Beckett has criticised the fascination of some historians with the 'relatively minor matter of wartime executions' and the decision made in 2006 to pardon (except for those convicted of murder) all of those who had been executed.[33] Beckett is absolutely right in postulating the view that the total number of men executed, which represented just 0.006 of the wartime whole, is lost in the obscene necrology of British war dead. However, the attention paid by historians and others to the subject of British military executions was due in part to the reluctance of various British governments to relax the hundred-year rule, thereby inviting interest, intrigue and suspicion. That, coupled with the public perception that the men who were executed had been suffering from shell shock, bestowed impetus on the public campaign to pardon those who had been executed.

During the war, the British Army passed a total of 3,077 death sentences for capital offences; however, the total number of men who were executed was 351.[34] The majority of cases (2,004) were awarded for desertion; of these, 272 men were executed.[35] While records of the proceedings of the FGCM exist for those men who were executed, the files of men whose sentences were commuted have been destroyed. Unfortunately, this restricts any meaningful comparison as to how or why some men, having been found guilty, were then spared from the death penalty. As shown in Table 4.1, nine men from the

Liverpool Irish were tried by FGCM for the offence of desertion. The first trial involved two men from the battalion, Privates J. Roberts and J. Russell, who appeared before an FGCM, charged with desertion on 29 June 1916, just two days prior to the commencement of the Somme campaign.[36] Both men were found guilty of desertion and both were sentenced to ten year's penal servitude. This did not mean that they were led off to prison, thereby escaping the war. Instead, both were returned to the battalion, where along with all the dangers and miseries of trench life the gloomy prospect of a prison awaited them. This 'sword of Damocles' hung over them as they had the additional and unpleasant expectation that they would be going to jail for ten years when hostilities ended. But why were these men spared while others were executed?

Table 4.1 *Death Sentences passed on soldiers of the 8th (Irish) Battalion, the King's Liverpool Regiment, 1914–1918.*

Name	Rank	Date	Offence	Final Sentence
J. Roberts	Pte.	29.6.16	Desertion	10 years P.S.
J. Russell	Pte.	29.6.16	Desertion	10 years P.S.
J. Brennan	Pte.	30.6.16	Desertion	*Executed* 16.7.16.
T. Perrin	Pte.	1.7.16	Desertion	10 years P.S.
S. Larginson	Pte.	17.10.16	Desertion	15 years P.S.
B. McGeehan	Pte.	21.10.16	Desertion	*Executed* 2.11.16.
M. Flynn	Pte.	22.5.17	Desertion	10 years P.S.
E.E. Jackson	Pte.	22.5.17	Desertion	10 years P.S.
A.A.J. Cole	Pte.	19.7.17	Desertion	10 years P.S.

Source: Compiled from Gerard Oram, *Death Sentences passed by military courts of the British Army 1914–1924*. (P.S. Penal Servitude).

While records of their FGCM were destroyed, the War Service record for Private Russell survives.[37] John Russell, a chair maker, from Hughes Street, West Derby Road in Liverpool, was a pre-war territorial having enlisted on

12 March 1914, aged 17. After training, he went to France with the battalion in May 1915 and he had no entries in his disciplinary record until 25 June 1916, when he was charged with being late on parade and 'continued inattention on parade'. He was awarded seven days' Field Punishment No.1 for these charges. Russell and Roberts must have deserted very shortly after Russell had received his sentence, since he would have to have been missing for a sufficient period to support a charge of desertion, given that his FGCM was heard just four days later at Dainville on 29 June 1916. Although he was found guilty of desertion and sentenced to death, his personal service record notes that the verdict and sentence were forwarded 'with a strong recommendation to mercy'. There are several factors which might have influenced the decision to commute Russell's sentence. Private Russell had been a pre-war territorial, and therefore a member of the 'core' of the battalion. He was also native of Liverpool and the fact that he had an unblemished record prior to the incident on parade on 25 June might well have swayed the FGCM officers to recommend mercy. Although the record of his FGCM has been destroyed, it is also possible to speculate that the post-sentencing reports from his commanding officer and others may have added sufficient weight to the appeal for leniency.

Just one day after Private Russell's FGCM, another soldier from the Liverpool Irish was on trial for his life, having been charged with desertion. Private Joseph Brennan, a 32-year-old driver from Coaticook in Canada, appeared before an FGCM charged with having deserted on 4 June 1916 while the battalion was at Simencourt.[38] Brennan had enlisted in Liverpool on 9 July 1915, he was 5ft 9in tall and was in good health except for a slight varicose vein in his left leg.[39] Brennan would not make a good soldier. Table 4.2, which has been compiled from Brennan's conduct sheet, reveals a litany of disciplinary offences which contain varying degrees of gravity. He committed his first offence just fifteen days following his enlistment.

Table 4.2: *Disciplinary record Private Joseph Brennan.*

Enlisted on 9 July 1915.

24 July 1915 at Weeton:
    i. Absent from camp from 10 p.m. 24/7/15 to 8.15 a.m. 25/7/15.
    ii. Absent from church Parade.
    iii. Not complying with an order.

iv. Using obscene language.

v. Sleeping in his clothes.

29 July 1915 at Weeton: Gross irregularity on parade 6.45 a.m.

2 August 1915 at Weeton: Absent from camp from 8 a.m. 2/8/15 until 6 p.m. 3/8/15. Wandering about at 10.30 p.m. on 3.8.15.

7 August 1915 at Weeton: (i). Absent from camp from 10 p.m. 7/8/15 until 12 noon 8/8/15; (ii) Absent from camp from 10pm 6/8/15 till 9 a.m. 9/8/15.

16 August 1915 at Weeton: Absent from camp from 10 p.m. 8/8/15 until 11.30 a.m.; ii. Disobedience of B.O.

17 August 1915 at Weeton: (i) Absent without leave from 1 p.m. 17/8/15 until return at 8 a.m. on 20/8/15; (ii) Breaking out of camp while a prisoner.

22 August 1915 at Weeton: Disobeying an order and wearing a bright cap badge.

23 August 1915 at Weeton: Breaking away from camp while under detention 23/8/15 about 6 p.m. Absent until apprehended by GMP Blackpool. 3 a.m. 4/9/15.

12 September 1915 at Weeton: Escaping from custody on 12/9/15 at 2.30 p.m. (2) Absent without leave from 2.30 p.m. 12/9/15 to 7.00 p.m. 2/10/15.

7 January 1916 at Blackpool: Striking an NCO while in the discharge of his duty.

On 16 January 1916, Joseph Brennan embarked at Southampton and arrived at Rouen in France the following day. Nine days later on 26 January 1916, he was admitted to hospital at Le Havre suffering from venereal disease and was discharged several weeks later on 1 March 1916. He eventually joined the battalion on 11 March 1916. Brennan's stay in hospital did little to improve his attitude towards military discipline; unsurprisingly, he found himself in front of his CO at the end of May 1916.

29 May 1916 in the Field: Hesitating to comply with an order. Awarded 7 days No.1 Field Punishment.

4 June 1916 at Simencourt: When on Active Service deserting His Majesty's Service in that he at Simencourt on 4 June 1916 when under orders for the trenches absented himself without leave from 1/8 Liverpool Regiment until apprehended by Military Police at Abbeville on 8 June 1916 with intent to avoid duty in the trenches.

13 June 1916 Arrived as a prisoner.

17 June 1916 to the Front as a prisoner.

18 June 1916 rejoined the battalion.

26 June 1916 Tried by FGCM on the charge of desertion.

30 June 1916 At his Court Martial he was awarded twenty-one days' Field Punishment No. 1 by Major Bridgewater, President of the FGCM for the offence of Contempt of Court.

16 July 1916 Executed by firing squad at 3.50 a.m.

Brennan's real name was William E. Clark of Pawtucket; he was the son of Mrs Josephine Clark, 29 Whipple Street, Pawtucket, Rhode Island, USA.

His mother wrote to the army in October 1917:

'Regarding my son William E. Clark alias No. 4547, Private Joe Brennan of the 8th King's Liverpool Regt. Being shot in July 1916, I would like to know if he had nothing to say or nothing that belonged to him as he was sick in the hospital there for two months previous to that. I would also like to know if there is not pension [*sic*] due me as he was my support.'

The Infantry Records Office in Preston replied to Mrs Clark's letter on 24 October 1917 stating:

I regret to inform you that you are not entitled to same insomuch as your son made no allotment and you would not therefore appear to be dependent on him.

Source: *Service Record, Pte. Joseph Brennan, No. 4567, 8th (Irish) battalion, King's Liverpool Regiment.*

Brennan's behaviour throughout his basic training would have challenged the mildest NCOs in the battalion. Having arrived in France, Brennan eventually joined the battalion having spent a few weeks recovering from venereal disease. Trench life and the war seem to have suited Brennan even less than training with the battalion in Blackpool. Given his disciplinary record, it is unsurprising that Brennan deserted on 4 June 1916. On 4 June 1916, while the battalion was behind the lines at Simencourt, Sergeant Done instructed his platoon, which included Brennan, that they were to stand fast in preparation for a move to the trenches. When the platoon paraded later that evening at seven o'clock, Brennan went missing. The battalion moved off to the trenches where they spent the next sixteen days. Four days later, Lance-Corporal Gavin was on duty at Abbeville, where he was acting as the triage at a first-aid post, when Brennan and another soldier appeared. They informed Lance-Corporal Gavin that they were deserters and that they had boarded a train, 15km from Rouen. Lance-Corporal Gavin stated that the men did not have rifles or equipment with them. Gavin then took both men to the guardroom. Joseph Brennan was then charged with desertion and he remained a prisoner pending his FGCM.[40] He appeared before an FGCM on 30 June 1916, where Major Bridgewater of 2/5th Lancashire Fusiliers acted as president. He was assisted by Captain Widdows, 1/4th Loyal North Lancashire Regiment, and Captain Hall, 2/5th Lancashire Fusiliers, and 2nd Lieutenant. Courthorpe, 1st Battalion Bedfordshire Regiment. Having heard the evidence from Sergeant Done and Lance-Corporal Gavin, Brennan declined the invitation to cross-examine the witnesses and he offered no defence or any other testimony in mitigation.[41] Even while he was on trial for his life, Brennan failed to observe the authority of the FGCM. It is impossible to know what Brennan did, or did not do, during his trial. Nevertheless, he was found to be in contempt of court by Major Bridgewater and sentenced to twenty-one days' Field Punishment No.1. Surprisingly, this incident is not recorded among the papers of Brennan's FGCM, but is contained as an additional comment on the conduct sheet of his service record.[42]

Brennan was found guilty of desertion and sentenced to death. Predictably, neither his company commander, Major Harry Leech, nor the CO, Lt. Col. Fagan, had anything to say in Brennan's favour. Major Leech wrote, 'In the trenches he is slack and neglectful. Never displayed any keenness for aggressive work such as patrolling.' Leech went on to say that his comments were based on 'good knowledge' of Brennan's character that he had deliberately planned to desert. Brigadier-General Edwards, 164th Infantry Brigade, recommended that the sentence of death should be carried out: 'As there have recently been a number of cases of absence and desertion from this unit, an example is needed.'[43] Joseph Brennan played a dangerous game with the British military justice system. In July 1916, he informed the army that he was in fact an American citizen. On 11 July 1916, General Allenby sent a note to the Adjutant General informing him of this latest development, adding that he was not making any recommendation in Brennan's favour. If Brennan believed that his eleventh-hour revelation about his citizenship was going to stop the British Army's disciplinary machine, thereby removing the death threat, he was mistaken. Joseph Brennan was executed at 3.50 a.m. on 16 July 1916. Joseph Brennan was indeed an American citizen; his identity was confirmed in a letter from his mother to the War Office in October 1917. Mrs Josephine Clark, of Whipple Street, Pawtucket, Rhode Island, stated that the man known as Joseph Brennan was her son, William E. Clark.[44]

The second soldier from the Liverpool Irish to have been executed for desertion was Private Bernard McGeehan, a 27-year-old originally from Raphoe in County Donegal.[45] His father was a horse dealer and his family moved to Londonderry and then to Dublin.[46] When war was declared, Bernard McGeehan was living in Daulby Street in Liverpool where he enlisted in the Liverpool Irish on 11 November 1914.[47] McGeehan listed his profession as being a groom. The medical officer who examined him found him to be in good health, but commented that his teeth were very bad and would need to be corrected before he went on foreign service. After his initial training, Bernard McGeehan went to France with the battalion in May 1915, where he was attached to the battalion's transport section working with horses behind the lines. The only offence on his conduct sheet for 1915 was for being absent from his place of duty in July 1915. Private McGeehan's demise began on 23 March 1916, when he was charged with neglecting to obey an order and with 'losing by negligence' several items of horse tack, including pack saddles, cropper and breast-plates. Incensed by the loss, Major Smith awarded him fourteen days' Field Punishment No.1, and he would also be required to pay for the missing equipment. Smith also ensured that Private McGeehan's time behind the lines was over. McGeehan was dispatched to a refilling point on fatigues on 4 May 1916, and was then ordered to join the battalion in the front line on 20 July 1916. The precise circumstances surrounding the missing equipment are unknown. Whether it was stolen by men from another battalion was immaterial as far as the army was concerned: Private McGeehan had been entrusted with taking care of it and had failed to do so. Precisely how long it would take the unfortunate McGeehan to repay the cost, based on his 1 shilling per day pay, is a matter of conjecture.

Inexperienced and unaccustomed to the routines of trench life and the concussive effects of enduring enemy bombardments, Private McGeehan joined a battalion of relative strangers. These were seasoned veterans, schooled in trench craft; they knew how the battalion functioned, the omnipresent dangers from enemy snipers as well as the personalities and idiosyncrasies of each NCO and officer. The unfortunate McGeehan did not. Friendless, bullied, disillusioned and financially much poorer, McGeehan deserted on 20 September 1916. Having walked for five days, he approached a Sergeant from the Royal Engineers to ask where he could find something to eat.

Suspecting that something was amiss, the Sergeant brought him to the APMs office where he was arrested. Private McGeehan was then kept in confinement pending an FGCM which was convened on 21 October 1916 at Ypres.[48]

Major Wolf of the Royal Artillery acted as president for Private McGeehan's FGCM, assisted by Captain Benterick, 13 Rifle Brigade, Captain Hathwaite, 1/4th Royal Lancashire Regiment, and Captain Cockrill, 1/4th Loyal North Lancashire Regiment. The court heard from Private Canning, a member of the Liverpool (Irish) Battalion's regimental police. Private Canning stated that on 17 September 1916 he had brought McGeehan from the guardroom to his company for duty. He also informed McGeehan that the battalion was due to move closer to the front line. McGeehan's conduct sheet does not contain an entry explaining why he was in the guardroom under the supervision of the battalion's regimental police. One possibility is that he had managed to incur the wrath of an NCO who had placed him on fatigues or pack drill. Sergeant Jones stated that he had received McGeehan into his platoon on 17 September and that he last saw him on 19 September at a bivouac near Mametz. He stated that he noticed that McGeehan was missing on 20 September when he called the roll before the battalion moved up the line to Clairmont trench. Private McGeehan reappeared near Montreuil on 25 September. Sergeant Law, of the Royal Engineers, testified that he was approached by Private McGeehan near Montreuil at about 5 p.m. on 25 September 1916. He asked Sergeant Law for something to eat and drink as he had had nothing for three days. When he asked Private McGeehan where he had come from, McGeehan told him that he had come from the Somme and that he was on his way to join his regiment at Boulogne. Sergeant Law then brought McGeehan to the APMs office in Montreuil. Sergeant Law noticed that Private McGeehan did not have his rifle or any equipment with him at that time. Sergeant Waldron, who was on duty at the APMs office at Montreuil, stated that McGeehan had told him that he had got lost coming out of the trenches at Ginchy. When Sergeant Waldron asked him how he had managed to get past the posts, Private McGeehan said that he had 'dodged them'. Private McGeehan was returned to the battalion on 28 September 1916.

Unlike Private Brennan (alias Clark), McGeehan gave evidence in his own defence under oath:

> Ever since I joined, all the men have made fun of me and I didn't know what I was doing when I went away. Every time I was in the trenches they throw stones at me and pretend it is shrapnel and they call me all sorts of names. I have been out here 18 months and had no leave.[49]

'B' Company, Liverpool Irish near Arras 1916. *Wilson Collection*

Some pugilists of the Liverpool Irish honing their skills while under canvas. *Author's Collection*

Left: Old Soldiers: CQMS Carr enlisted in the Liverpool Irish in the 1890s and served with them in South Africa. A wheelwright by trade, he re-enlisted in October 1914 when he joined 'D' Company as a Sergeant. CQMS Carr had a good war; he was promoted to CQMS in 1916 and was later mentioned in dispatches. He was awarded the DCM in 1919. He was a popular man among the soldiers of 'D' Company and after the war he was presented with a rose bowl by the officers and men of the company who brought it to his home. *Wilson Collection. Thanks to George Wilson for this source.*

Below: The oldest man in the battalion. This photo was taken at Bedford in 1915 just before the battalion went to France. It includes Private Jim O'Rourke (seated on the left of the middle row) who was 67 years of age. He had been a member of the band of the Liverpool Irish, lied about his age and went off to France with the battalion. O'Rourke endured life at the front and never fell out on the march or reported sick. He survived the Battle of Festubert, he was much admired among the officers who found him a job behind the lines. *Author's Collection*

above left: Sergeant Samuel Fraser an employee of the British American tobacco company in Liverpool. Sergeant Fraser received a stern reprimand from Lt. Col. Heath for permitting a man to fall out while on the march without the permission from an officer. He later went on to win the DCM. *Wilson Collection*

above right: Through the ranks. Lieutenant James Alison Free was born in Londonderry but moved to Liverpool where he became an elementary school teacher. He was taken prisoner and was later awarded the Military Cross. *Wilson Collection*

right: Somme casualty: Private James Jenkins, a docker from Northumberland Street in Liverpool. His family originated in Warrenpoint, County Down, and he died from wounds received at Guillemont on the Somme on 8 August 1916. *Thanks to Mrs Patricia Normanly for this source and for her kind permission to reproduce this image.*

The Doctor: Captain Joseph Ellis Milne DSO, RAMC attached to the Liverpool Irish. Ellis Milne had a large practice near Aberdeen and, despite his age, he applied for a commission with the RAMC. Not content with serving behind the lines, he demanded to serve at the front. Well loved by the officers and men of the Liverpool Irish, Milne thought nothing of pulling on his boots for a game of football with the men. He was personally brave and was awarded the DSO. A non-combatant, he was killed by a German sniper in February 1917. *Thanks to the University of Aberdeen for their kind permission to reproduce this image.*

Lieutenant Michael Moynihan came from a staunch nationalist family in Tralee, County Kerry. Having enlisted in the Civil Service Rifles, he was commissioned into the Liverpool Irish. He was accidently shot and killed during a German bombardment. *Thanks to Mrs Ann Hayden for her kind permission to reproduce this image.*

Captain Richard Pears Keating with his wife and child. Captain Keating was a pre-war Liverpool Irish officer from Danehurst Road in Wallasey. He was wounded at Festubert in 1915 after which he returned home to convalesce. He returned to active service and was killed in action in Belgium on 18 July 1917. *Author's Collection*

Sketch prepared by the War Office depicting Field Punishment No.1. The unpleasant reality was that men undergoing FP No.1 often found themselves tied to wheels and barn doors. *TNA, WO32/5460, Thanks to The National Archives for their kind permission reproduce this image.*

The wrong name. The grave of Private Joseph Brennan, Liverpool Irish who was executed for desertion at 3.50 a.m. on 16 July 1916. Shortly before his execution Brennan claimed to be an American citizen; the authorities disregarded his claims and shot him anyway. He was indeed an American named William E. Clark, of Whipple Street, Pawtucket, Rhode Island, USA. *Picture © Mr Geerhard Joos, of ww1cemeteries.com. Thanks to Mr Joos for his kind permission to reproduce his image.*

GENERAL ROUTINE ORDERS

BY

GENERAL SIR DOUGLAS HAIG,
G.C.B., G.C.V.O., K.C.I.E., I.S.C.
Commander-in-Chief British Armies in France.

General Headquarters,
November 7th, 1916.

ADJUTANT GENERAL'S BRANCH.

1923—Courts-Martial

(i.) No. 67882 Private E. Young, 25th Canadian Battalion was tried by Field General Court-Martial on the following charge :—

"When on Active Service, deserting His Majesty's Service."

The accused was ordered to report to his Company in the trenches. He did not do so, absented himself, and was arrested 18 days later.

The sentence of the Court was "To suffer death by being shot." The sentence was duly carried out at 6.25 a.m. on 29th October 1916.

(ii.) No. 9970 Private A. Jefferies, 6th Battalion Somerset Light Infantry was tried by Field General Court-Martial on the following charge :—

"When on Active Service, attempting to desert His Majesty's Service."

The accused absented himself from his Company while in reserve trenches and was arrested two days later at a base port, where he stated that he was proceeding on leave and had lost his leave warrant.

The accused was found guilty of desertion and sentenced "To suffer death by being shot." The sentence was duly carried out at 6.10 a.m. on 1st November 1916.

(iii.) No. 2974 Private B. McGeehan, 1/8th (Irish) Battalion King's Liverpool Regiment was tried by Field General Court-Martial on the following charge :—

"When on Active Service deserting His Majesty's Service."

The accused absented himself from his battalion just before it moved into the trenches, and was arrested a fortnight later at a place fifty miles distant.

The sentence of the Court was "To suffer death by being shot." The sentence was duly carried out at 6.18 a.m. on 2nd November 1916.

(iv.) No. 17538 Private H. MacDonald, 12th Battalion West Yorkshire Regiment, was tried by Field General Court-Martial on the following charge :—

"When on Active Service deserting His Majesty's Service."

The accused after having reported sick and having been marked "medicine and duty," absented himself from his unit and was arrested a month later at a Base port.

The sentence of the Court was "To suffer death by being shot." The sentence was duly carried out at 6.33 a.m. on 4th November 1916.

Haig's General Routine Order announcing the execution of Private Bernard McGeehan, Liverpool Irish, who had been convicted of desertion. Details of the execution of soldiers were read out on parades to 'encourage the others'. *TNA WO95/26, Adjutant General's Branch, General Routine Orders, 7 November 1916. Thanks to The National Archives for their kind permission to reproduce this image.*

McGeehan's testimony failed to impress the court and he was found guilty of desertion and sentenced to death without an appeal for mercy. After McGeehan had been found guilty, the officers from the Liverpool Irish who had known Private McGeehan submitted their written opinions. Lieutenant Daniel McCabe, originally from Londonderry, had known McGeehan before the war as they had both lived in the city. He stated that he had known McGeehan, who had at one time been employed at Londonderry Post Office. Lieutenant McCabe (who had enlisted as a private soldier) then met McGeehan after they had both enlisted in the Liverpool Irish. The final line in Lieutenant McCabe's statement, while highly unflattering, perhaps did not go far enough to save McGeehan: 'There was nothing about him at any time, except that he was inclined to be rather stupid.' Lieutenant Colonel Harry Leech, acting CO of the Liverpool Irish, was damning in his assessment of McGeehan. Leech wrote that McGeehan had been sent back to the battalion as 'useless'. According to Leech, McGeehan was 'afraid in the trenches' and was 'incapable of understanding orders'. Leech concluded by saying that McGeehan was guilty of the crime and had acted deliberately, adding, 'He seems of weak intellect and is worthless as a soldier.' Brigadier-General Stockwell noted that while McGeehan's behaviour was 'good', his ability from a fighting point of view was indifferent. Stockwell commented that while discipline within the Liverpool Irish was good, in cases involving desertion it was bad. Stockwell recommended that the sentence be carried out. Private Bernard McGeehan was executed at Poperinghe at 6.16 a.m. on 2 November 1916.

While there is no doubt that both men deserted, whether they should have been executed is highly debatable. Joseph Brennan was an ill-disciplined soldier with an appalling record of offences which commenced shortly after he had enlisted. While it would be wrong to criticise the recruiting staff of the Liverpool Irish for the failure to recognise the fact that Brennan was an American rather than a Canadian as he had stated, the instructors at Blackpool had every opportunity to expel Brennan from the army during basic training.[50] Alternatively, following his FGCM, and having established that Brennan was an American citizen who had enlisted fraudulently, he should have been returned to Britain to face a civil trial. Given the aggravated nature of his deception, the cost of his training, the disruption he had caused throughout his 'service' and discredit he had brought on the battalion, he should have received a severe prison sentence. The same might be said in the case of Private Bernard McGeehan. It is evident that McGeehan was totally unsuited to military life. His officers described him as 'stupid', 'useless', 'afraid' and 'worthless as a soldier', yet McGeehan did not suddenly acquire these traits when he arrived in France.[51] In fact, McGeehan's evidence during his FGCM alleged that the abuse he suffered from his erstwhile colleagues began as soon as he enlisted. If McGeehan displayed the same lack of intelligence during training, how did this go unnoticed by the training and medical staff? The British Army's hunger for recruits and the subsequent rush to the recruiting offices in 1914 resulted in the recruitment and retention of men who were patently ill-equipped, physically or mentally, for the rigours and discipline of military life.[52]

Privates Brennan and McGeehan stood out from the other men from the Liverpool Irish who had been charged with desertion and had escaped the death penalty. Both men had not been part of the 'core' of the battalion; McGeehan was attached to the transport section of the rear echelon, while Brennan did not arrive in France until 1916. They had both spent a relatively short time at the front, which made it difficult for them to bond with the battalion and, significantly, neither came from Liverpool. Thus, both men presented themselves as ideal and convenient 'examples'. Details of executions were promulgated and read out on parades throughout the army. In their determination to portray McGeehan as a wilful deserter, the army's Routine General Order announcing details of his desertion and execution (see p.123), claiming that he had been missing for a fortnight prior to his being apprehended. The truth, as established at his FGCM, was that he had been missing for five days. Arguably, when their names were read out in front of the battalion, few men in the Liverpool Irish would have recognised them. The guilty verdicts of their respective FGCM and the subsequent executions would, in the minds of the military hierarchy, have served their purpose *pour encourager les autres*.

Throughout the war a total of sixty-two men from sixteen battalions of the King's Liverpool Regiment were sentenced to death by FGCM. Six of these men were executed, the remainder receiving prison sentences of varying lengths. As Table 4.3 shows, by far the greatest number of desertions occurred not among the territorial or Pals battalions, but from the 1st (regular) Battalion of the regiment. Out of fifteen men from the 1st Battalion who were convicted of desertion, just one man was executed. This is surprising, given the much-vaunted reputation for stern discipline evinced by regular army battalions. To compare like with like among the other territorial battalions (5th, 6th, 7th and 9th Battalions) within the regiment, the contrast is equally revealing. A total of fourteen men from these battalions were convicted of desertion yet (thankfully) none faced the firing squad. Nine men from the Liverpool Irish were found guilty of desertion, two of whom were executed. One territorial battalion is missing from these records; the 10th (Scottish) Battalion enjoyed the distinction of not having a single soldier convicted by a FGCM on a charge of desertion. While the numbers of men convicted of desertion from the 5th and 6th

Battalions are relatively low, five men from the 7th Battalion and six from the 9th were convicted. The fact that desertion was less prevalent among the Liverpool Irishmen than their counterparts in the regular 1st Battalion, and that two men from the Irish were the only soldiers from any of the Liverpool territorial battalions to be executed during the conflict, invites notions of prejudice and bias.

Table 4.3: *Total number of death sentences passed and number of executions in all battalions of the King's Liverpool Regiment 1914–1918.*

Battalion	Death Sentences	Executed
1	15	1
3	1	0
4	6	1
1/5	1	0
6	2	0
7	5	0
2/7	1	0
1/8	9	2
2/8	2	0
9	6	0
11	3	0
12	2	1
17	2	1
18	1	0
19	1	0
20	5	0
Total	62	6

Source: Compiled from Gerard Oram, *Death Sentences passed by military courts of the British Army 1914–1924.*

In his study of the influence of race and eugenics in the application of the death penalty in the British Army, Gerard Oram devotes a chapter to what he calls 'The Irish Question'.[53] Having examined statistics for the numbers of executions in five regular divisions, which contained both Irish and non-Irish regiments, Oram concluded that death sentences were more common among Irish battalions than their English counterparts. While stating that no evidence exists to suggest that Irish soldiers were explicitly singled out for execution, Oram postulates the view that nineteenth-century racial notions of Celtic inferiority, anti-Catholicism and questions concerning the reliability of Irish soldiers had lingered on into the twentieth century and that these might explain the propensity of FGCMs in awarding the death penalty to Irish soldiers.[54] The perception of the indiscipline of Irish troops prevailed throughout and beyond the war. In April 1919, Lord Derby wrote to Lieutenant General Sir George MacDonagh about the West Lancashire Territorial Association and the formation of a post-war new Division.[55] Citing the 'obstacles' faced by the Association during the war, he informed the General that they now had 'one serious obstacle in Liverpool'. Derby's 'obstacle' was the 8th (Irish) Battalion of the Liverpool King's Liverpool Regiment. 'Taking the 8th Irish first it has been an unsatisfactory battalion throughout. Very insubordinate and slack in peacetime and not too satisfactory during the war. We were never able to get a good Commanding Officer for it and I do not believe we ever shall as long as it is known as the Irish battalion. The Irish in Liverpool are synonymous with all the lowest class.' Derby not only affronted the reputation of the officers and men of the battalion who had fought during the war. He impugned the Irish inhabitants of Liverpool, the disciplinary record of their soldiers and insulted the bravery and leadership qualities of battalion commanders such as Fagan, Leech and Heath. According to Derby, the removal of 'Irish' from the title would solve these alleged flaws, the battalion would be known 'simply as the 8th'. By doing so, and 'picking our own men', Derby claimed that he would eventually have a good battalion. The Liverpool Scottish did not escape Derby's reforming zeal. He suggested abolishing their kilts, arguing that this iconic piece of kit presented some difficulties if men were transferred between battalions. Derby acknowledged that there 'would be a certain amount of friction if the "Irish" battalion was done away with', but that the trouble had to be faced and that he was 'prepared to meet it'. Unsurprisingly, Derby urged the General to keep these matters 'strictly confidential' as he did not want 'any rumours to get out in Liverpool' until he was ready to deal with his proposals. In an otherwise excellent study of the 10th Liverpool (Scottish) and the 6th Liverpool Rifles, Helen McCartney states that an increase in the offending rates within the Rifles in 1918 was due to an influx of replacements from the Liverpool Irish.[56] According to McCartney, the rise in offending was unsurprising given that the former Liverpool Irishmen, whatever their background, came from 'this type of insubordinate tradition'. The well-earned (and undisputed) reputation of the Irish for lawlessness in the streets of Victorian Liverpool was, it seems, inherited by their heirs and went with them to France, where it stuck to them much like trench mud. It is difficult to argue with the conclusion made by the historian of the 16th (Irish) Division when he wrote: 'The uneasy amalgam of administration, sentimentality and distrust which had long characterised the military establishment's attitude towards the Catholic Irish in uniform took on an added significance during the First World War.'[57]

An examination of the Judge Advocate's records of the numbers of FGCMs relating to sixteen Regular, Territorial, New Army and Pals battalions of the King's Liverpool Regiment, reveals that the Liverpool Irish did not deserve their reputation for ill-discipline. As table 4.4 reveals, 103 men from the regular 1st Battalion appeared before FGCMs between 19 May 1915 and 21 September 1916.[58] The 4th (Extra Reserve) Battalion had fifty-five men brought before FGCMs, while the highest number of appearances from a territorial battalion came from the 7th Battalion. Within this 'military crime league table', the Liverpool Irish came a respectable joint sixth, having had twenty-five men before FGCMs. They shared the honours with the 9th Battalion, which was another territorial outfit.

Table 4.4: *Total number of offences tried by Field General Courts Martial for all battalions of the King's Liverpool Regiment 19 May 1915–21 September 1916.*

Battalion	Type	Total Number of Offences
1st	Regular	103
4th	Extra Reserve	55
5th	Territorial Force	8
6th	Territorial Force	7
7th	Territorial Force	46
8th	Territorial Force	25
9th	Territorial Force	25

10th	Territorial Force	2
11th	New Army	33
12th	New Army	28
13th	New Army	13
14th	New Army	6
17th	New Army (Pals)	3
18th	New Army (Pals)	2
19th	New Army (Pals)	11
20th	New Army (Pals)	6

Source: Compiled from TNA, WO213/4; WO213/5; WO213/6; WO213/7; WO213/8; WO213/9; WO213/10, Judge Advocate's Records, 19 May 1915–21 September 1916. These records refer to battalions on active service on the Western Front and some of these registers overlap regarding dates.

Military discipline did not cease on 11 November 1918; it reached beyond conventional military establishments and affected the maimed as well as the able-bodied. On 22 March 1919, Private John Mulcahy, a pre-war Liverpool Irish territorial, was recovering in G Ward at the 1st Western General Hospital, Fazakerly, after having his right leg amputated.[59] Perhaps fed up with being confined in a military hospital and the not unreasonable belief that he had done his bit, Private Mulcahey (despite his infirmity) left the hospital. The ward sister dutifully reported his absence and when Mulcahey failed to return, the officers of the Royal Army Medical Corps did the right thing and held a Court of Enquiry. The court concluded that Mulcahey was deficient in the following articles:

Jacket, Hospital Blue, unlined	one 18/3d
Waistcoat, Hospital, Blue	one 7/9d
Trousers, Hospital, Blue	pair 13/3d
Shirt, Cotton, Hospital	one 6/–
Pyjama Suit	one 15/–

Officers, especially senior officers, were expected to behave in a certain way. While physical courage and a paternalistic attitude towards their men were undoubtedly valuable traits in an officer, the quintessential British officer first and foremost had to be a gentleman. Non-adherence to the unwritten social code and mores of Edwardian Britain could lead to ostracism.[60] Any behaviour which questioned the integrity of an officer, or which might impugn the reputation of his regiment, was liable to have consequences. When the army hierarchy appointed Lieutenant Colonel A.H.C. Neale to command the Liverpool Irish in 1914, they believed that they had found their man. Neale, a former lieutenant in the Bedfordshire Regiment, had been 'dug out' of retirement. His immediate and rapid promotion to lieutenant colonel of the Liverpool Irish enabled Neale to act with a certain degree of autonomy. He could, for example, confirm that prospective candidates for seeking a commission were suitable and accept them into his battalion. This was the case when James Alexander Johnson, a veteran ranker of the Boer War and newspaper office manager, applied for a commission in 1914. Johnson's application was signed by Neale at Canterbury where he certified that he had known Johnson for five years.[61] Having been wounded prior to the Battle of Festubert in June 1915, Neale was invalided home, leaving Captain Johnson to assume command of the battalion along with a temporary promotion to the rank of lieutenant colonel. During their time at Whitstable, Captain Johnson agreed to assist Lieutenant Colonel Neale with his business affairs by agreeing to front four companies associated with Lieutenant Colonel Neale. Whether or not Captain Johnson felt obliged to assist Neale in his business interests, or that he had complied with Neale's request based on trust and the fact that Neale was a regular army officer and an established businessman, remains unknown. Having assumed command of the battalion when Neale was invalided, Captain, now Lieutenant Colonel, Johnson was responsible for the administration of the battalion when he noticed some discrepancies. Meanwhile, his business dealings with Lieutenant Colonel Neale began to unravel.

Matters came to head in May 1916 at the Central Criminal Court in London, when Lieutenant Colonel Johnson went on trial charged with obtaining small sums of money by false pretences.[62] The proceedings against Lieutenant Colonel Johnson had been instigated by Neale who had written to the GOC, Western Command, alleging that Johnson and others had used four companies to obtain money by false pretences.[63] Neale also alleged that he had received letters of complaint from prospective investors, and that he had spoken to Johnson about the matter while the battalion was at Bedford, and again when the battalion moved to France. During a pre-trial hearing, the

Recorder voiced his concern that the military authorities had failed to suspend Lieutenant Colonel Johnson, given the nature of the charges.[64] Decency and common sense prevailed when Lieutenant General William Campbell, Commander in Chief of the Western Command, responded to the Recorder's criticisms. Writing to the War Office, Campbell explained: 'I did not consider it fair to suspend him from his employment in case such action should prejudice his case'.[65] During the trial, Lieutenant Colonel Johnson testified under cross-examination that he had acted on behalf of Lieutenant Colonel Neale as Neale had wanted to conceal his relationship with the four companies and that he believed that this was a proper arrangement. Johnson also told the court that he had met Neale while he was on leave in October 1915 at the Grosvenor Hotel in London. The meeting was described as 'stormy', and when Johnson threatened to inform the brigadier about questions surrounding the whereabouts of kit money for 1,100 men, Neale replied, 'If you do, I'll smash you.'[66] Shortly afterwards, the jury had heard enough and stopped the case. Lieutenant Colonel Johnson was acquitted.

Military discipline within a battalion was a relatively private affair. What passed for justice was normally dispensed by its officers and NCOs, hidden within the confines of their barracks or billets. The fact that allegations of dishonesty and personal disagreements between two successive battalion commanders of the Liverpool (Irish) Battalion were exposed publicly in open court and published in the press proved embarrassing for the army in general and the battalion in particular. Lieutenant Colonel Neale never returned to the battalion; he moved to Algeria where he died, aged 57, in January in 1920. Lieutenant Col. Johnson was replaced in October 1915; his Service Record contains a series of letters to the War Office which bears testimony to his perseverance in seeking a return to active service. It is difficult to remain unsympathetic towards Johnson's plight. He may have been naive in his business dealings with Lieutenant Colonel Neale, but he was placed in an unenviable position when he inherited command of the battalion in the chaos of the trenches at Festubert in 1915. Writing to the War Office in June 1916, Lieutenant Colonel Johnson requested an interview: 'In view of the exceptional circumstances of the grave matters involved in the conduct of Lieutenant Colonel Neale to this and other transactions, I trust I may not be regarded as unduly importunate in again submitting a request for the favour of an interview.'[67] In September 1915, Major General George Harper assumed command of the 51st Highland Division. Harper, like many of his counterparts, believed that Territorial Force officers were ill-equipped to command a battalion in the field. When Johnson submitted his request for a transfer, Major

General Harper noted his application and added, 'I do not consider Lieutenant Colonel Johnson fit for the command of a battalion.'[68] Johnson also informed the War Office of the difficulties he had faced on assuming command of the Liverpool Irish in June 1915, not least because all the officers in the battalion were 'very young' and that, himself excepted, none of them had any previous war experience. He concluded his appeal by stating:

> In spite of the difficulties imposed by trench warfare, I claim that during my command I succeeded in infusing the battalion with a proper battalion spirit, and out of virtual chaos created an internal organisation that is not dependent on any one individual for its maintenance.[69]

After a period spent with the 66th Training Reserve Battalion and undergoing a command course at the Senior Officers School in March 1918, Johnson was transferred to the 13th Battalion, King's Liverpool Regiment. He died of wounds on 21 August 1918.[70]

BATTLEFRONTS: GIVENCHY, THE SOMME AND PASSCHENDAELE

The Second Action at Givenchy, 16 June 1915

Having spent the winter of 1914 and the spring of 1915 guarding railway lines and attending courses and lectures, in April 1915 the Liverpool Irish were ordered to join the 51st Highland Division at Bedford where they made some final preparations prior to embarking for France. The Liverpool Irish were accompanied by the 1/4th King's Own Royal Lancashire Regiment, 2/5th Lancashire Fusiliers, and 1/4th Loyal North Lancashire Regiment, which were to form the 154th Infantry Brigade of the 51st Highland Division. While there was little time for the Scots and Lancastrians to establish any close working and social relationships, the divisional historian of the 51st Division described how the Lancastrians were received and appreciated by the division: 'It is necessary to say, however, that they were welcomed with open arms and still less necessary to say they "played the game", and at once became an integral part and very useful part of the division.'[1] The Liverpool Irishmen's 'new' division was commanded by Major General R. Bannatine-Allason, an 'old-school' commander, who was a firm advocate of the art of delegating responsibility for training to his subordinates. The 154th Infantry Brigade was commanded by Brigadier-General Hibbert. Unfortunately, little is known as to the extent of field-training the Liverpool Irishmen were able to undertake during their time at Whitstable and Canterbury. Their responsibility for safe-guarding railways suggests that it is highly unlikely that any massed training at brigade or divisional strength took place. It is even less likely that the battalion underwent any coordinated manoeuvres involving artillery.

The remainder of the Highland Division which had over-wintered in Bedford experienced a similar array of organisational, logistical and meteorological difficulties as other territorial divisions attempting to prepare for war. Prior to the arrival of the Lancashire battalions, the weather and the agricultural nature of the countryside around Bedford conspired to frustrate the division's effort to prepare for war. The divisional historian recalled that 'movement off the roads for wheeled vehicles was difficult, in some cases impossible'.[2] Administrative difficulties persisted among the territorial battalions in 1915, since individual battalions still functioned under the old army eight-company system. The regular army had long discarded this system in favour of a more manageable four-company battalion scheme.[3] In 1914, Territorial Force battalions were still equipped with the outdated long Lee Enfield rifle and their artillery batteries operated using obsolete 15-pounders and 5-inch howitzers.[4] Such shortcomings were highlighted by the historian of the 51st Highland Division: 'most of the equipment, guns, rifles, technical stores etc., were quite out of date'.[5] Besides the lack of modern armaments, the organisational abilities of Highland Division suffered a blow when several regular adjutants and a number of instructors were taken from the division by the War Office.[6] Thus, it is unsurprising that when a staff officer of the 51st Highland Division observed the division's performance during a field day, the manoeuvres descended into farce:

> There was a Divisional field day that I attended mainly confined to the roads on account of cultivation. Neither side attacked; the brigade on one side was scattered over miles of country and advanced some two miles in four hours; while the other brigade sat in a hole and successfully escaped notice. The unprotected mountain artillery of one force were opposed by cyclists who ran away, while the infantry of the other kept well in the rear of their own field gun.[7]

As the division made its final preparations for embarkation, the lack of extensive training, modern equipment, experienced staff officers, infantry officers and NCOs in the division was acknowledged. According to the divisional historian, the 51st Highland Division went to France 'with, perhaps, some misgivings as to thorough training'.[8] The deficiencies in equipment and training did not go unnoticed by the military hierarchy in France in 1915; Haig commented that the division was 'practically untrained and very green in field duties'.[9]

The arrival of the 51st Highland Division in France in May 1915 came shortly after the Battle of Neuve Chapelle where the British experienced some success in breaching the German defences. Their arrival also coincided with the Battles of Aubers Ridge and Festubert in May 1915. These battles were designed to assist the French army who were engaged in the Battle of Artois. Following the action at Festubert and plans for further French attacks in June 1915, GHQ issued orders to the British First Army, under Douglas Haig, to support the French by carrying out a number of assaults on the left of the French army front. Haig then organised the First Army by dividing his front into three sectors: two offensive sectors and one defensive sector. The offensive sectors were allocated to British 1 Corps, comprising the 47th, 1st and 2nd Divisions; responsibility for the second offensive sector went to IV Corps containing the 51st and the Canadian 7th Divisions. The Indian Corps would be responsible for the defensive sector. The attack was planned by Lieutenant General Sir Henry Rawlinson, who issued an operational order for the attack which was to take place on 11 June; however, the attack was postponed until 15 June.[10] On 14 June 1915, Brigadier-General Hibbert issued an Operational Order detailing an attack which was to be launched at 6 p.m. the following day.[11] The order instructed IV Corps to attack German positions along the Rue D'Ouvert to the north via Chapelle St Roch. The offensive comprised three simultaneous attacks with the intention of gaining ground in the direction of Violaines. The 51st Division were to attack the northern end of Rue D'Ouvert, the 7th Division would attack the southern end, while the Canadian Division was detailed to attack the German trenches at areas marked as H2–H3; they were then to form a defensive flank. Two battalions of the 154th Brigade, the 1/4th North Lancashire and 1/6th Scottish rifles, were detailed to deliver the attack of the 51st Division. The Liverpool (Irish) Battalion were ordered to act as brigade reserve.

Having established and consolidated their battle lines over the winter of 1914, the German army had absorbed the necessary lessons on the importance of defence in depth from earlier British attacks at Neuve Chapelle. Thus, throughout the spring of 1915, the Germans set to work fortifying their front-line trenches by constructing deeper dugouts; their front-line trenches were protected by vast barbed wire entanglements, and they also established a series of strong defensive positions along their front. Prior to drawing up his plans for the proposed assault on the Rue D'Overt with Haig, Rawlinson remained unconvinced by Haig's positivity regarding the likelihood of IV Corps' success in breaching the German defences. Rawlinson's misgivings surrounding Haig's optimism and his own apprehension regarding the strength of the German defences were substantiated when he received intelligence photographs prior to the attack. Expressing his concerns in his diary, Rawlinson stated that his plans for the attack had been issued:

In the form of pious aspiration rather than anything that is likely to be actually carried into effect for we are not going to capture Rue D'Overt as easily as he appears to think. The new photos taken on the afternoon of June 12th of the enemy's trenches show that the Boches have been working like beavers and have constructed many new works which will give us trouble, they have strengthened the wire to an alarming extent and it is doubtful if we shall be able to cut it satisfactorily.[12]

The Liverpool Irish were without their commanding officer, Lieutenant Colonel A.H.C. Neale, who had been wounded by a high-explosive shell on 1 June at Richebourg, when they moved up to Le Touret on Tuesday, 15 June. They were then were ordered to remain there as Brigade Reserve.[13] The battalion was informed that the brigade was to attack later that evening and that they were to move forward at a moment's notice. Prior to the attack, the British artillery had been pounding the German lines for forty-eight hours; the bombardment intensified and was at its fiercest between 4 p.m. and 6 p.m. that evening.[14] The omens were not good on the morning of 15 June. A letter written by a platoon Sergeant of the 1/5th Seaforth Highlanders revealed that the Germans were not only aware of the impending attack, they also appeared to be in a rather confident mood. 'The Boche rose early, having apparently known our plans. In fact, some of them were heard to call across No Man's Land, "Come along Jocks; we are waiting for you". And undoubtedly, they were.'[15] That evening, the 1/4th Loyal North Lancashires and 1/6th Scottish Rifles of 154th Brigade launched their assault on the German lines. Their attack brought some success towards the western end of the German lines, after which they attempted to push on towards the German line at Rue D'Overt. Reinforcements from three companies of the 1/4th Battalion of the King's Own Lancashire Regiment were sent up to assist the attackers. Their success, such as it was, was brief. The Germans counter-attacked in the early hours of 16 June and drove the remnants of the attacking battalions back to their own lines. The attack on the northern section of the German lines by the 152nd Infantry Brigade fared no better. The 1/5th Seaforth Highlanders attacked at 6.45 p.m. straight into heavy machine gun and rifle fire. Moreover, the battalion discovered that despite the British artillery bombardment, the enemy's wire remained uncut. One survivor from the Seaforth Highlanders wrote, 'the wire was an insurmountable obstacle and the few who remained had to take cover in the nearest shell-hole until darkness allowed us to make our lines again – a sad dejected remnant of a company'.[16]

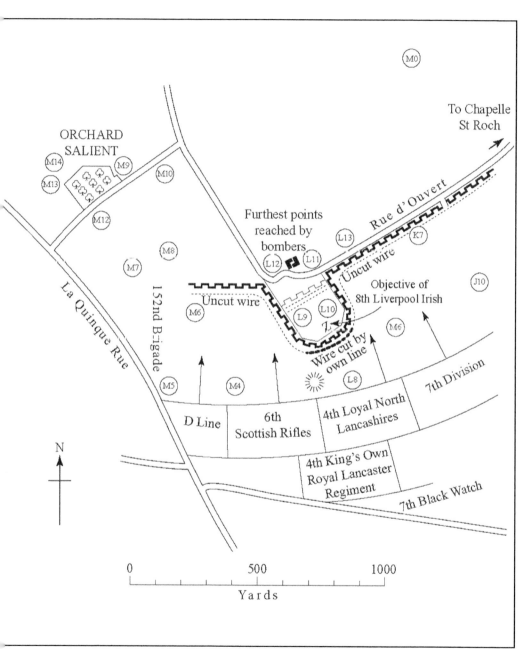

Map 3: The objective of the Liverpool Irish at Rue D'Ouvert, 16 June 1915.

The Liverpool (Irish) Battalion's struggle to get into position in the firing line was hampered by accurate German artillery fire. Captain Harold Mahon wrote that 'we had a most unhealthy journey and lost several men before we got into position'.[17] The rear areas behind the British lines also received attention from the German gunners, resulting in casualties among the battalion's non-combatants who were customarily well behind the front lines and, theoretically at least, outside the killing zones. Father Stephen Dawes, the battalion's Roman Catholic chaplain, was injured during the bombardment. A report in the *Liverpool Catholic Herald* stated that, 'A shell burst within three yards of where he was standing, and a splinter from it struck him on the forehead, rendering him unconscious.'[18] Difficulties affecting the fighting strength and readiness of the battalion were further aggravated when various companies were 'very much split', having been detailed to provide fatigue parties to collect ammunition and trench stores from the forward Royal Engineers stores en route to their assembly points.[19] At 2 a.m. on 16 June, Brigadier-General Hibbert received confirmation that the 1/4th Loyal North Lancashire and 1/6th Scottish Rifles had retired in the face of a German counter-attack. Hibbert then considered whether he should use fresh troops to throw the Germans back. He decided against a further attack that night, reasoning that while his two battalions, the 8th Liverpool Irish and the 1/7th Black Watch, had not been in the original attack, they had, however, been subjected to heavy shelling while holding the line.[20] In the fire trench with the Liverpool Irish, Captain Harold Mahon vouched for the accuracy of the German artillery, noting that the German gunners had the range 'to a nicety' from the previous day.[21] The decision about launching a further attack was made by the 51st Divisional Headquarters at noon on 16 June. Hibbert was ordered to attack the German trenches at 4.45 p.m. that evening, leaving him just a few hours to prepare his battle plans and issue orders to the commanding officers of the 8th Liverpool Irish and the 1/7th Black Watch.

Private Long, a former carter for the *Liverpool Echo*, wrote that the Germans shelled the rear areas and approach roads behind the British trenches to prevent reinforcements being brought up. 'At 2.30 we got the order to prepare for an engagement at 4 o'clock. At 3 o'clock the guns started. Then the Germans commenced to shell the trenches, and they did it well. It was terrible lying under it.'[22] Captain Ernest Murphy wrote to his brother stating that men from an adjoining regiment who had been at the front since September 1914 told him that 'they had never heard a bombardment like it'.[23] On 16 June at 3 p.m., Major Campbell Johnson (later Lieutenant Colonel), now commanding the Liverpool Irish, asked to see all officers of the battalion in the firing line where he informed them that the battalion had been ordered to make an attack on the German lines at 4.45 p.m. that evening. Captain Mahon stated that while it was a challenge to assemble the men and get them into position at very short notice, nevertheless, 'at 4.45 p.m. prompt our boys scaled the parapet'.[24] Private Long described the final minutes just prior to the attack. 'The order was passed down: "Now lads, be Irish".'[25] The Liverpool Irish had been ordered to attack the German lines at a location designated as point 'Z' (see Map 3). Brig. General Hibbert later wrote that he believed that it was 'extremely doubtful' whether the leading waves of the Liverpool Irish ever reached that point.[26] Given the ferocity of the German bombardment and lack of preparation, Captain Harold Mahon was understandably pessimistic, writing that his men had as much chance of crossing No Man's Land in the open 'as the proverbial snowball' (in hell).[27] Hibbert's report on the action praised the Irish for their determination in spite of their losses, 'Undeterred by this check, small parties of the 1/8 Liverpool R., continued most gallantly to get across. Eventually, about 7 p.m., a small number did get beyond 'Z' and began working their way up towards L10.'[28] An unnamed officer from the Liverpool Irish described the limit of his company's advance: 'We got into the German sap trench all right, but we could not get on, and I was stuck there till dusk, when I sent a message back and was ordered to return, which I did with five men and three wounded, leaving many dead.'[29]

According to Harold Mahon, wounded Liverpool Irishmen began to pour back into their own trenches within minutes of the attack. While some of the Irish managed to reach the German sap, that was as far as they could manage:

A very sad sight minutes after the first lot went over, wounded men coming back by the dozen, full of grit most of them, but many dazed and wounded so badly that they cared for little but to be carried back. I care not to recall individual cases in writing, they are to be seen but one cannot read about them.[30]

As he attempted to observe the attack from his fire trench, Mahon was unable to determine who had been killed and who had survived. Initially, he thought his friend Lieutenant Drake had been killed, only to see him being brought in with some other wounded men. Occasionally his eyes deceived him and witnessed some good fortune: 'I thought I saw a man blown to pieces and was surprised to see him run back only slightly wounded.'[31] Mahon managed to speak to Lieutenant Drake in the trench before he was taken to the Regimental Aid Post. Drake had been badly wounded but remained conscious:

'I was able to give him a drink of water and hear his "Cheeroh Mahon!" Poor lad, he died two days later. Only 20, 6.3 high and a man every inch of him, he came from Bulawayo, Rhodesia, to fight, he died well, although close to our parapet bravely leading his boys.'[32] Writing to his brother after the attack, one incident in particular stood out in Captain Ernest Murphy's memory. 'A Sergeant jumped up on the parapet of the trench and shouted, "Go on boys. It is sure death but remember we are the Irish!" Just then, he was blown to bits.'[33] By 11.15 p.m. that evening, Brigadier-General Hibbert was in no doubt that the attack had failed. He ordered the relief of the 1/7th Black Watch who had been under constant bombardment throughout the day in the fire trench and instructed the Liverpool Irish to retire to Le Touret.[34]

The casualty returns for 154th Infantry Brigade revealed that the Liverpool Irish sustained a total of 242 casualties.[35] Thirty-eight were killed, including three officers, 191 wounded, including six officers, while thirteen men, including one officer, were listed as missing in action. Officer casualties in the battalion included Captains Finegan and Brown, killed in action, Lieutenant Drake died from his wounds and Lieutenant Downes, the battalion's machine gun officer, was missing. Mahon states that he had heard that Finegan had been killed but had not seen him during the attack. Several days after the attack, Captain Brown's body was recovered by a working party of the Royal Engineers some distance out to the right of the Liverpool Irish trenches. According to Harold Mahon, Lieutenant Downes, who was with a bombing party, was reported to have been 'blown to pieces'.[36] In his report on the operations from 15 to 17 June, Brigadier-General Hibbert highlighted the actions of Lieutenant Colonel Campbell Johnson and Lieutenant Downes for their conduct during the attack by the Liverpool Irish on 16 June.[37] There had been instances of individual bravery among the ranks. Private Cuddy was awarded the Distinguished Conduct Medal for rescuing three wounded soldiers belonging to another regiment who had been lying in front of the German trenches for twelve hours. Previous attempts to rescue the men had failed when Cuddy went forward under 'heavy and sustained' rifle fire to save the men.[38] When writing his personal account of the battle, Mahon was struck by the surreal nature of his experiences: 'All this sounds strange and untrue now that I come to write it down, but it was very near and vivid when it happened.' He went on to consider whether the battle had been a defeat: 'I suppose that so far as capturing trenches was concerned it was, but we only had an hour and a half notice and it took the CO half an hour to bring the news up to the front.'[39] Mahon had been told that the attack was essentially a feint to draw German reinforcements away from a successful French attack which took place further south. Whether any of this was true, the battalion received plaudits from General French for their efforts. A cynical Mahon commented that the battalion had attempted the work of a brigade. Quoting Tennyson, he derided the exploits of the Light Brigade when compared to those of his own battalion: '"Theirs is not to reason why"; I am certain what the 600 went through was child's play to our little affair.'[40]

Private Long struggled to express the mixture of elation and grief when he and his comrades were relieved. 'We were all laughing and crying at the same time. To try and describe it is impossible. After it was over we calmed down.'[41] On the morning following the battle Lieutenant Colonel Campbell Johnson addressed the remnants of his battalion at Le Touret. Private Baker from Edge Hill recalled that emotions were still raw; even the hardened Boer War veteran Campbell Johnson strained to conceal his grief. 'This morning our Commanding Officer spoke to us, but he was too full for words and said that he was more than proud to be in command of so fine and fearless a body of Irishmen!'[42] Hibbert's reservations about launching a further attack on 16 June had been correct; unfortunately, the 51st Divisional Headquarters did not share his concerns and the Liverpool Irish were ordered into the attack.

The Liverpool Irish had arrived in France without the benefit of having undergone thorough training at brigade or divisional level. The 51st Division also lacked modern field guns and ammunition of sufficient quality and quantity which were crucial in attempting to destroy the German defences.[43] Equally important, they lacked training and experience in combined arms operations. The Liverpool (Irish) Battalion, like any other territorial battalion which had arrived in France in 1915, found themselves at the base of a very steep and painful learning curve. For the remainder of 1915, the battalion performed trench duties, trained and endured the war. In January 1916, they left the 51st Highland Division to join their own 55th West Lancashire Division. The Liverpool Irishmen had enjoyed excellent relations with the Scottish soldiers, especially with the 1/6th Scottish Rifles. Captain Mahon described how both battalions had served together from June 1915:

Since that time, the officers and men of the two regiments seemed to weld together and certainly the men, who had fought together seemed to have admiration for and confidence in each other. They gave us a good hearty Scotch send off the next day and we all hoped and still hope that we may meet again under more or less happier circumstances, for we have had both good and bad times together.[44]

Guillemont, the Somme, 8 August 1916

'The brave fight of the Liverpool Irish will always be associated with this battle.'[45]

Following the formation of the 55th Division in January 1916, Lieutenant Colonel Cochrane of the General Staff wasted no time in preparing detailed instructions for the training of the division.[46] While Cochrane was content to permit battalion commanders to frame their own training programmes, he stated that the object of training should be 'to develop the confidence of all ranks in themselves, their weapons, their comrades, and their commanders, and to imbue each officer and man with the determination to dominate the enemy, and cause him all the loss and damage possible, whether fighting him in the open or in trenches'. His memorandum included a section emphasising the importance of close-order drill, which was to be carried out daily when men were out of the trenches, and that parades should conclude with a march-past conducted by a senior officer. Weekly route marches of between six and eight miles were ordered as well as a dedicated scheme for the instruction of young officers. Specialist training was established for scouts and snipers, with a requirement that each battalion should maintain eight snipers in addition to those employed as company snipers. Bombing and machine gun schools were set up and map-reading lessons were to be provided for all ranks. Cochrane also suggested a range of topics suitable for a series of lectures, he proposed subjects such as, 'Morale, discipline, brave deeds etc.'; 'The study of men's comfort' as well as talks on first-aid and hygiene.[47] The divisional hierarchy could argue that the emphasis it had placed on training and aggression was exemplified a few months later in April 1916, when the Liverpool Irish raided the German trenches at Blaireville. The raid not only underlined the supposed aggression and fighting prowess of the Liverpool Irish, it also enhanced the reputation of the 55th Division.

By July 1916, all battalions of the division had experienced trench warfare on the Western Front for a year or more. With the exception of the divisional artillery's contribution to IV Army's bombardment on the opening day of the Somme, the remainder of the division did not take part in the initial assault on 1 July.[48] While the men were in no doubt that a major offensive was ongoing, it is debatable, however, whether any officer or man within the division was aware of the lack of progress and the true extent of British losses throughout the opening month of the campaign. The 55th Division was soon to join Haig's great offensive on the Somme where they would be tested at Guillemont. Before August 1916, individual battalions within the division had participated in previous battles while attached to other divisions. It is significant, therefore, that Guillemont marked the first action when the battalions of the 55th Division fought together as a homogenous West Lancashire unit. The fact that Guillemont had been the objective of two previous attacks during July 1916 might suggest that the battlefield topography as well as the nature and disposition of the German defences surrounding the village were well known. It is also reasonable to assume that intelligence had been gleaned from the participants of the previous attacks and that battle plans had been adjusted and improved to ensure the success of the 55th Division's attack. Ultimately, the responsibility for planning lay with the Commander-in-Chief, and General Henry Rawlinson, who commanded the IV Army. Therefore, the attack by the Liverpool Irish at Guillemont cannot be viewed in isolation; rather, it should be analysed in the wider context as forming the third component of a series of attacks made by the IV Army between 14 July and 8 August 1916.

After the failures and losses sustained during the first fortnight of the Somme campaign, Haig outlined a distinctly limited set of plans for the coming weeks: to consolidate the Longueval-Bazentin Le Petit position and make it safe from counter-attack, to establish his right flank in Ginchy and Guillemont, and to take the village of Pozières.[49] When the 55th Division moved south on 30 July 1916, they entered the line opposite an expanse of rubble which constituted the unfortunate village of Guillemont. Ominously, on the same day, General Max von Gallwitz, German commander of the Somme front, issued an order of the day to his troops:

> The enemy is expected to attack in strength during the coming days. The decisive battle of the war will be fought out on the battlefield of the Somme. It is to be made clear to all officers and men in the front line how much is at stake for the Fatherland. The utmost attention and sacrificial action is to be paid to ensuring that the enemy does not gain any more ground. His assault must be smashed before the wall of German men.[50]

Gallwitz was right in his assertion that further attacks were imminent. The following day, General Rawlinson, the IV Army commander, attended a corps commanders' conference where he instructed them to prepare for an attack against the German line at Guillemont. Following discussions with General Foch at a conference at Dury, Rawlinson agreed with the French that the villages of Guillemont and Ginchy would be attacked by the British on 19 July. However, adverse weather conditions meant that aerial observation crucial for artillery spotting could not take place on that date, and therefore the attack never materialised.[51] The weather cleared, and orders for an attack involving six divisions of IV Army were issued on 21 July, just two days before they were to deliver their assault on 23 July.[52] This undoubtedly reduced the ability of divisional staff officers, brigadiers and battalion commanders to study the ground over which they were expected to attack and, more importantly perhaps, to brief their men. To exacerbate matters, the French announced that they would not be able to attack until 24 July. Incredibly, the battle plan was complicated further by the allocation of four separate zero hours to the six attacking divisions.[53] These staggered starting times alerted the German defenders all along their line that attacks were imminent. To make the battle plan even more convoluted, the operation also incorporated a night assault; consequently and predictably, some attacking troops got lost in the maze of trenches and woods. The assault on Guillemont delivered by the 30th Division on the far right of the IV Army's attack also failed. While the division was certainly hampered by the same operational flaws which had affected the other attacking divisions, to their cost they discovered that the German system of defence in Guillemont had changed. Instead of manning their front-line trenches, the Germans had moved their machine guns and strongpoints into shell holes on the flanks. This meant that however accurate the British artillery was in bombarding the German line, it would fail to locate the enemy who were clear of their own trenches and were able to respond and adopt new defensive positions as an attack developed. To counter these new German defensive tactics, instead of a concentrated bombardment of the German trench lines, the British artillery would need to bomb the entire German front area.[54]

On 30 July, Rawlinson tried for a second time to take Guillemont; this time the attack was delivered by the 30th Division. The division's 89th Brigade comprised three battalions of the Liverpool Pals.[55] They attacked at 4.45 a.m.; dawn broke across No Man's Land revealing a thick fog which reduced visibility. The 89th Brigade attacked the German lines to the north-west, while the 90th Brigade, which included the 2nd battalion, Royal Scots Fusiliers, assaulted Guillemont village and the station. The battle did not go well for the Liverpool Pals, who faced several German counter-attacks and were forced to withdraw. The fog and mist meant that the artillery was unable to give any supporting fire to the Royal Scots, who were isolated in Guillemont village.[56] The war diarist of the 2nd Royal Scots Fusiliers noted that the attacks on both flanks had failed, and that the lack of cover in No Man's Land and heavy German machine gun fire made it impossible for the battalion to extricate itself from the village.[57] Thus, Rawlinson's second attempt to take Guillemont had failed, resulting in heavy losses for the attackers. The 89th Brigade's casualty lists included those of the Liverpool Pals, which amounted to 1,314. The 90th Brigade suffered similar losses; given their predicament in Guillemont, it is unsurprising that the heaviest toll was suffered by the 2nd Scots Fusiliers, which included 17 officers and 633 other ranks.[58]

On 2 August 1916, Haig wrote that these ongoing operations on the Somme were to be regarded as a 'wearing down battle'.[59] On the same day, he wrote to Rawlinson explaining his objectives on the Somme and the reasons behind them. Haig's priority was to bring the French forward and into line on his right flank. 'Line straightening' was critical to enable the Allied artillery to bombard the German positions. This would negate any requirement for the infantry to perform potentially costly and complicated manoeuvres during their assaults. For this to occur, the German strongpoints at Guillemont, Ginchy and Falfemont Farm had to be taken. Having stressed the importance of these positions, Haig then added the caveat that: 'These places cannot be taken, however, without due regard to economy of the means available – without careful and methodical preparation.'[60] He went on to state that 'economy' was necessary so that he would have sufficient reserves for the 'crisis of the fight' which he anticipated would occur in September 1916, and that 'preparations must be pushed on without delay'.[61] Haig, it seems, wanted Rawlinson to attack Guillemont as soon as possible, he was to accomplish this by the economic use of troops and material. Having directed Rawlinson to 'push' the preparations, Haig then stated that the attack should take place 'when commanders on the spot are satisfied that everything possible has been done to ensure success'.[62] These were hardly clear and unambiguous directions. In any event, Haig's instructions became irrelevant as Rawlinson's plan for the attack on 8 August was virtually identical to those which had failed on 14 and 30 July.

The 55th Division had arrived in the Somme area on 25 July 1916, when it relieved the 30th and 35th Divisions. Between 30 and 31 July, the divisional headquarters moved to Billon Copse, and two days later the division received its first notification that it was to prepare for an early attack. Unhelpfully, the date of the proposed attack was not forthcoming.[63] A close examination of dates, times, issue and receipt of the various external and internal Operational Orders relating to the attack on Guillemont reveal that the divisional and brigade staffs had little time to concoct a viable and detailed plan of attack. Crucially, the hurried and pressurised nature of the demands and expectations of the hierarchy meant that officers and NCOs had no time to study the terrain or familiarise themselves with the German defences. The Liverpool Irish at least made a start at familiarisation and intelligence gathering by patrolling No Man's Land in front of Guillemont. On 2 August, patrols from the Liverpool Irish reported that large numbers of German patrols were active between Guillemont and the British front lines. In response, strong fighting patrols comprising the Liverpool Irish and 1/4th King's Own Royal Lancaster's armed with 'Lewis and machine guns' intercepted and engaged the German patrols driving them back into Guillemont.[64] Three days of confusion followed. On 3 August, the division 'received instructions' that the attack on Guillemont was to take place on 7 August, but on 5 August the date was changed to 8 August.[65] At 3.45 p.m. on 6 August, XIII Corps finally issued an Operational Order to the 55th Division for the capture of Guillemont.[66] Essentially, the division was ordered to capture Guillemont and secure positions whereby the road between Guillemont and Leuze Wood and Angle Wood could be observed. The assaulting battalions had also to establish contact with the left flank of the French XX Corps and the 2nd Division, which included the 1st Battalion, King's Liverpool Regiment, on the right. The decision was made that the assault on Guillemont would be delivered by the 164th Infantry Brigade. On the evening of 7 August, Brigadier-General Edwards, commanding the 164th Infantry Brigade, issued Operational Order No. 49 which stated that the attack of Guillemont would take place the following day, 8 August. It also provided details of which battalions would be delivering the assault and their respective objectives; it did not, however, provide any indication of 'Zero' hour.[67] This Operational Order did not reach the Liverpool (Irish) Battalion until between 6 and 7 p.m. on the evening of 7 August.[68] It was at some point after this that the brigade was informed that Zero hour would be nine hours later, at 4. 20 a.m. on 8 August. With darkness falling, battalion and company commanders had just hours to organise their men, brief them, move them into position in the front-line trenches and ensure that they all had the necessary arms, equipment and stores to deliver the assault.

The objectives of the 164th Infantry Brigade was to capture the village of Guillemont and to establish itself on the eastern side of the village; Brigadier Edwards stressed that the village was to be 'captured at all costs'.[69] The 1/4th Royal Lancaster Regiment was to attack the village to the south and establish a garrison; the Liverpool Irish were tasked with attacking the northern end of Guillemont, capture it, and then construct strongpoints at designated areas. The 1/4th Loyal North Lancashire Regiment was to provide support for the attacking battalion.[70] The distance between the British and German front lines at Guillemont was 700 yards; to provide a closer 'jumping off' point for the attacking battalions, men worked day and night digging advance trenches forward into No Man's Land. The attack was preceded by an artillery bombardment which began at 9 a.m. on 7 August and continued until Zero hour.[71]

At 3.45 a.m., thirty-five minutes before Zero, the Liverpool Irish formed up outside their own trenches ready to attack. As the British artillery bombardment intensified, they began to advance and follow the barrage.[72] An hour and a half later, a message was received from Private Heaton, 'B' Company of 1st Battalion, King's Regiment, who stated that his company had been cut up and that it had retired. Minutes later, the battalion headquarters of the Liverpool Irish sent a message to 'any officer of the battalion' warning them that the attack of the '4th King's Own' (1/4th Royal Lancashire Regiment) had been held up.[73] At just after 6 a.m. reports were received that the Liverpool Irish were in the village and confirmation that the 4th Royal Lancasters had been 'hung up'. This meant that the right flank of the Liverpool Irish was exposed. Further bad news arrived at 8 a.m., after an intelligence officer had consulted with a subaltern of the 1st King's and was told that his battalion was isolated at the far side of the trucks at Guillemont station and that he believed they were now surrounded.[74] At 8.30 a.m., a message was received from a French aircraft that the French troops had reached the ravine south of the Guillemont Road and that they were in touch with the British. At the same time, Lieutenant Colonel Fagan, commanding the Liverpool Irish, reported that he had no news of his battalion except that a few wounded men had informed him that the Irish were in the village. He also reported that he had also been informed that the 1st Battalion King's Liverpool Regiment and the 4th Battalion Royal Lancaster Regiment had both 'fallen back'.[75] From then on, the narratives of the battle contained within the various War Diaries appear to concur that all subsequent reports became conflicted and confused. One report concluded that the ground over which the Liverpool Irish had attacked lay in a hollow which was full of smoke and mist when the battalion attacked. It went on to state that the Liverpool Irish got clear of their own lines and across No Man's Land without much opposition until they reached the German front line. Due to poor visibility, the battalion then veered too far to their left, and elements of the battalion were seen fighting around Guillemont station and 'traces of fighting' were discovered later at the quarry.[76] Having lost direction, the 'clearing parties' that had been detailed to clear the German trenches and dugouts after the leading waves had failed to do so, thereby leaving a number of Germans behind the Liverpool Irish.[77] On the right flank of the Liverpool Irish, the 4th Royal Lancaster Regiment encountered the German wire which proved to be a 'formidable obstacle'. The Germans waited until the battalion reached the wire and then opened fire with machine guns and rifle fire which inflicted heavy casualties. Consequently, the Liverpool Irish were isolated within the village. The 1st Battalion, King's Liverpool Regiment on their left had been cut up, while the 4th Royal Lancaster Regiment on their right had been hung up and cut up at the German wire. The failure to clear the German dug-outs after the leading waves had passed over the German front line exposed the Liverpool Irish to attacks from the rear. The battalion was isolated, surrounded and ultimately captured in the village.

Late on the evening of 8 August, Brigadier Edwards of the 164th Infantry Brigade drew up a hasty operational order in a belated attempt to reach the Liverpool Irish. His plan was that the 2/5th Lancashire Fusiliers should attack and take the German front-line trench at the quarry.[78] He stressed that the attack 'should take place as soon as possible and in any case before 2 a.m.' on 9 August. A hand-written note at the bottom of Edwards' order recorded that it was received at 1.50 a.m. The operation did not take place. The British advanced front-line trenches were extremely narrow and had been dug to provide cover for the attacking troops. When Edwards ordered his attack, these trenches were severely congested with soldiers from various battalions, either manning the trenches, or attempting to assemble for the scheduled attack which was to take place later at 4.20 a.m. on 9 August.[79]

Lieutenant Colonel Fagan's report written two days after the attack amounted to half a page. He had, after all, very little to write about since only two or three wounded survivors from his battalion had managed to return to their own trenches.[80] According to those few survivors, the battalion man-aged to reach their objectives and began to dig in, when 'The enemy then opened heavy machine gun fire on them from all sides.' Shortly after this, they were ordered to 'retire slowly' by Captain Murphy.[81] Captain Ernest Murphy's account of the events at Guillemont remained unwritten until his interview after his release from captivity following the Armistice in 1919.[82] Murphy described the confusion as the Liverpool Irish reached the village: 'Owing to the darkness and the broken nature of the village, companies became mixed up.' After crossing No Man's Land, he found some of the Liverpool Irish in an 'extended line', digging in just in front of Guillemont village. He was also informed that his senior officer, Captain Meadows, had been killed. Murphy then took charge of the men and positioned himself in the centre of the line. Concerned about the situation on the flanks, he sent two officers to the left and right flanks with instructions to try and contact the attacking battalions on both flanks. The officers failed to locate anyone, and he was informed that both flanks were exposed. The weather also proved unhelpful. Dawn was beginning to break and the area around Guillemont was enveloped with a thick mist, and visibility was worsened by the smoke from artillery barrages. Despite this, Murphy was hopeful that when the mist lifted he would be able to see the attacking battalions on his flanks. Since he had not heard any machine gun

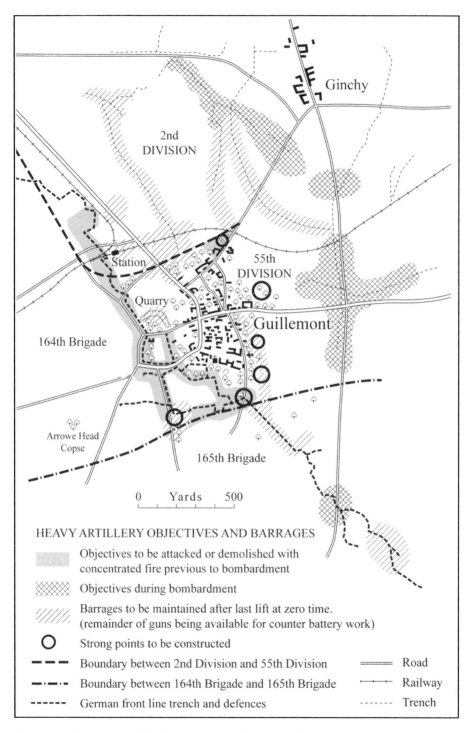

Ginchy

2nd
DIVISION

Station

55th
DIVISION

Quarry

Guillemont

164th Brigade

Arrowe Head
Copse

165th Brigade

0   Yards   500

HEAVY ARTILLERY OBJECTIVES AND BARRAGES

Objectives to be attacked or demolished with
concentrated fire previous to bombardment

Objectives during bombardment

Barrages to be maintained after last lift at zero time.
(remainder of guns being available for counter battery work)

O   Strong points to be constructed

— — —   Boundary between 2nd Division and 55th Division   ═══ Road

— · — · — Boundary between 164th Brigade and 165th Brigade   ⊢—⊢—⊢ Railway

- - - - -   German front line trench and defences   - - - - - - Trench

Map 4: Artillery map of Guillemont on the Somme indicating the dispositions of
164th and 165th Infantry Brigades on 8 August 1916.

fire on the flanks, Murphy assumed that this was a sign that 'they had been able to reach their objectives as my battalion had done'. Unfortunately, he was mistaken, and this was confirmed when a corporal reported that the Germans were in the village. He then dispatched runners to inform his battalion head-quarters of the situation in the village; however, they found it impossible to get through due to the enemy's presence in Guillemont. By now the German counter-attack was gaining ground and the Germans had managed to infil-trate the Liverpool Irishmen's right flank; they had also emerged from the ground behind the Liverpool Irish position. Captain Murphy then issued orders for the men to move towards their left flank, and to make their way along the sunken road towards the German front trench on the western side of Guillemont village. During this manoeuvre Murphy was shot in the shoul-der; 'Shortly afterwards, I rolled over, looking through the ruins of a house I saw the enemy all around, I was then taken prisoner.'[83] As the Liverpool Irish were being led away, the historian of the 55th Division described the sense of frustration and despondency in the British lines: 'the remaining survivors were captured and were marched the next day up the slope to Ginchy in full view of their comrades on the other side of the valley – powerless to help them'.[84]

At 8 a.m. on the morning of the attack, *Generalleutunant* Otto von Moser, commander of the German 27th Division, received a report of the British attack at Guillemont. He rushed to Sailly, where he was informed that the 123th and 124th Regiments had 'beaten off' the British attack.[85] Moser surveyed the scene at his German divisional headquarters which was filled with British prisoners and recorded the events in his diary. His judgemental observations and assumptions about some of the captured British soldiers are unflattering. However, he was also shrewd enough to notice from the condi-tion of some prisoners that they were from a 'fresh' division:

> There, in the grey dawn, numerous dense waves of attackers were bloodily repulsed after bitter hand to hand fighting. Already the great courtyard of the farmhouse adjoining Divisional Headquarters is full of prisoners. Including several officers. The British soldiery are a real mish mash: some of them have the faces of low criminals, obviously the scum of the population. Others, both young and old, look to be far more agreeable types. They are from a 'freshly shaved' Division: that is to say, apparently, they only moved out of rest yesterday evening to take part in the battle.[86]

When the 55th Division launched a similar attack the following day, nei-ther the British tactics, nor those of the German defenders had changed. On the morning of 9 August, Moser estimated that their haul of prisoners now totalled more than 300, which was almost certainly an underestimation. Moser praised the bravery of his troops and highlighted the actions of an Uhlan officer, Major Landbeck, serving with the infantry who managed to capture a large batch of isolated British soldiers. Moser's diary confirms British accounts of the existence of deep German dugouts and the failure of attacking troops to clear them. According to Moser, Major Landbeck had emerged from his dugout with a small garrison of men and one machine gun, he then 'linked up with an assault troop of Infantry Division 124 and forced between one hundred and two hundred British soldiers to surrender'.[87]

Writing in his personal diary after the battle, Brigadier Edwards recorded his thoughts on why the attack had failed: 'The failure of the attack was chiefly due to in the first place a too ambitious programme and in the second place to the heavy mist that prevailed when the attack was launched.'[88] Haig's failure to issue clear and unambiguous directions, his unwillingness to allow his divisions sufficient time to prepare and familiarise themselves with the terrain, and his insistence on the economic use of manpower and resources were principal factors in the failure to capture Guillemont in July and August 1916. Moreover, he might well have intervened sooner to curb Rawlinson's propensity for continuing to do the same thing in the dubious expectation that his plan would eventually deliver success. Some historians quite rightly assert that Haig had a difficult job: simultaneously running the BEF while attempting to placate his French allies and deal with the machinations of British politicians. However, Guillemont was not only strategically important, it was also a very tough nut to crack; it demanded careful planning, preparation and adequate resources. Haig and Rawlinson's failure to provide these sealed the fate of the 2nd Battalion of the Royal Scots Fusiliers and the Liverpool Pals on 30 July, the Liverpool Irish on 8 August and the attack of the Liverpool Scottish the following day. On 16 August, the RQMS of the Liverpool Scottish, refreshingly indifferent to any concerns about censorship, expressed his opinions on the high command in an angry letter to his father. His letter provides a perfect appraisal of the battles for Guillemont in July and August 1916:

The want of preparation, the vague orders, the ignorance of the objective and geography, the absurd haste, and general horrid bungling were scandalous. After two years of war it seems our higher commanders are still without common sense. In any well-regulated organisation a Divisional commander would be shot for incompetence – here another regiment is ordered to attempt the same task in the same mind-closing way.[89]

The myth that senior British officers were incompetent, aloof and uncaring has been justly debunked; yet any reasonable assessment of Haig and Rawlinson's performance during the battles for Guillemont in July and August 1916 does little to dissuade their detractors.

In the absence of reliable information regarding casualties, it was difficult for the divisional staff officers to produce accurate statistics for the total numbers of officers and men from the battalion who had been killed, wounded and missing. Brigadier Edwards' statistics were identical to those in the War Diary; no officers had been killed and just nine other ranks were listed as killed in action. One officer was reported to be wounded along with fifty-two other ranks. However, the greatest numbers were listed as missing; these included thirteen officers and 502 other ranks.[90] It took some time before more precise information about the fate of the battalion became available. Following their capture, information concerning prisoners held in Germany could be subtracted from those listed as missing and the names of the dead could be revealed. The Liverpool Irish went into action with twenty-three officers and 554 other ranks; of these, six officers had been killed, including Captain Meadows, and Lieutenants Fisher, Hope-Gordon, Levene, Sharpe and Tipping. A total of 104 other ranks had lost their lives during the battle.[91] The remainder were either wounded or captured. Ten days after the battle, Captain Harold Mahon wrote home to his mother: 'No doubt by this time news will be leaking through that the Irish have been in action. It will suffice for me to say that a finer battalion never went forward, and they fully upheld the honour of the division.'[92]

Table 5.1: *Somme battle casualties for three battalions of 55th (West Lancashire) Division, 27 July–29 September 1916.*

Officers					Other Ranks			
Battalion	Killed	Wounded	Missing	Total	Killed	Wounded	Missing	Total
1/4th (The King's Own) Royal Lancaster Regt.	9	22	1	32	74	400	76	540
1/4th Loyal North Lancashire Regt.	5	18	3	26	49	382	192	623
1/8th (Irish) King's Liverpool Regt.	3	20	13	36	88	497	569	1154

Source: LRO, FIF1/2/5, Records of the 55th (West Lancashire) Division, 1914–19, compiled from 'List of casualties 27.7.16 to 29.9.16'.

Table 5.1 contains the divisional casualty statistics for three battalions on the Somme which were compiled at the end of September. Evidently, the costs to the division and the battalions who had fought at Guillemont were enormous. The 1/4th Battalion (The King's Own) Lancaster Regiment had a total of 540 casualties. The 1/4th Loyal North Lancashire Regiment had a total of 623 casualties which included 192 men who were listed as missing. The Liverpool (Irish) Battalion's losses amounted to 88 men killed, 497 wounded, 569 missing, making a total loss of 1,154. The total casualties sustained by these three battalions between 27 July and 27 September 1916 was 2,317.

Pilckem Ridge, Passchendaele, July–August 1917

Among the extensive list of actions, battles and offensives of the Great War, arguably two battles stand out in the minds of the public: the Somme and Passchendaele. While the opening day of the Somme on 1 July 1916 has become synonymous with mindless industrial-scale slaughter, Passchendaele conjures up grotesque images of hapless soldiers being massacred in a God-forsaken quagmire north-east of Ypres in 1917. Passchendaele, perhaps more than any other battle, has agitated and divided the thoughts and opinions of military historians as well as politicians and commentators since 1918. The post-war polemics surrounding the narrative of the battle meant that Sir James Edmonds, the official British historian of the Great War, struggled to complete his *Military Operations 1917: Volume 11*, which was not published until 1948.[93] Towards the end of 1916, it was Belgium more than France which occupied the minds of British politicians, the army high command and the Royal Navy. The U-boat threat to British shipping had focused their attention on the necessity of capturing the Belgian sea ports.[94] Any offensive in Belgium would be influenced by the terrain. The high water table in Flanders meant that it was impossible to construct standard trenches; to provide cover, it was necessary to construct sandbag breastworks along the parapet. To break out of Ypres and drive towards the coast, Haig's foremost priority was to seize several important ridges which were occupied by the Germans. Haig wasted no time in ordering preparations to be made, and in November 1916 he instructed Sir Herbert Plumer, of the Second Army, to submit plans for an offensive which was to take place in 1917. Unquestionably, no British commander knew the Ypres Salient better than 'Daddy' Plumer. However, his cautious plan and modest objectives failed to match Haig's ambition to drive to the coast. Unimpressed by Plumer's scheme, which limited the initial action of the offensive to capturing the ridges at Messines and Pilckem prior to any further escalation of the operation, Haig consulted his army commanders and his staff.[95] Haig then wavered between the plans which he had received from his own GHQ staff, and those of Sir Henry Rawlinson.[96] According to Robin Prior and Trevor Wilson, Haig was content to let Plumer attack Messines ridge; however, he disliked Plumer's 'bite and hold' concept with its modest objectives in preference to the 'harroosh', or rapid advance mindset of the Fifth Army's Sir Hubert Gough.[97] Despite never having commanded a major campaign, Haig chose Gough and his Fifth Army to lead the main attack during what was to be the Third Battle of Ypres.

Haig proposed that his offensive at Ypres should be divided into two distinct phases: the first objective of the southern phase of the operation was to seize the ridge at Messines in June 1917; the second, or northern, phase would be directed against the high ground at Pilckem and Gheluvelt several weeks later towards the end of July.[98] Messines, therefore, would be a prelude to the Third Battle of Ypres. Plumer had been planning his attack on Messines since January 1917, and during this period he had ordered the excavation of twenty-one mines which were packed with a million pounds of TNT and placed beneath the German lines.[99] In contrast to the debacle which took place at Guillemont on the Somme, with its associated muddled thinking and lack of preparation, training and resources, Plumer's attack at Messines was a master class in operational planning. In the weeks prior to the attack, men trained over specially constructed models of the ground they were going to assault. For eleven days, the British artillery fired 3.5 million shells at the German lines; then at Zero hour, nineteen mines were detonated beneath the German positions.[100] If the German defenders had not suffered enough during this onslaught, 2,000 guns opened fire with a devastating bombardment on their lines.[101] Unsurprisingly, this thunderous demonstration of ferocious firepower, which was initiated before the infantry and tanks had commenced their assault, sapped the morale of the German defenders along the Messines-Wytschaete Ridge. Heinz Hagenlücke commented that, 'Even the *Reichsarchiv*' admitted that the 'moral influence of the blasting on the troops was more fatal than the actual casualties caused by it'.[102] Although delighted with the success at Messines, and with his mind still fixed on driving to the sea, Haig asked Plumer if it might be possible for his Second Army to capture the southern portion of the Gheluvelt Plateau.[103] This was important, not least because the Germans could use the plateau to bring enfilading fire onto any subsequent British attack. Haig was understandably keen to continue his offensive while the Germans were still suffering from the impact of Messines. Plumer agreed to try to assault the Gheluvelt Plateau on the condition that he was allowed three days to get his artillery into position before launching his attack.[104] Haig thought such a delay was too long and he instructed Plumer to hand over VIII and II Corps to Gough and ordered him to draw up plans for the Fifth Army to attack the Gheluvelt Plateau. Gough stated that he needed time to study the area; it took him six days to do so, providing the Germans with time to improve their defences. Having studied the ground, Gough then announced that no further attacks should take place for a further six weeks.[105]

Plumer's original request for a few days seems remarkably reasonable in comparison. Moreover, the Germans now had time to recover, reorganise and prepare for the inevitable British assault. In the weeks between the Battle of Messines in June and the initial British bombardment for the Ypres offensive in July 1917, Colonel von Lossberg, the German defence expert, toured the battle zones around Ypres. He then ordered the construction of a series of concrete strongpoints and machine gun posts. These formidable strongpoints supplemented a number of existing fortified farms dotted across the Salient.[106] Lossberg's defensive strategy depended on excellent communication between headquarters, infantry, artillery, aerodromes and the *eingreif* divisions.[107] Prior to the British assault, he managed to establish a communications network between all of these defensive elements and had them plugged into his office.[108] Two years of trench warfare had also taught the German army how to defend. At the Battle of Arras, Lossberg had improvised an elastic and flexible defence to thwart the British assault. At Ypres, however, he decreed that there should be no flexibility within the defences; rather, the front troops should remain and fight it out with the attackers until they were rescued.[109] There were several key elements to Lossberg's defensive strategy. He stressed the importance of concealment from enemy observation and the importance of vacating dugouts and strongpoints during the British bombardment. He argued that these were mantraps and that the occupants should leave them and fight in the open during the initial bombardment.[110] The second element was the necessity to launch counter-attacks as quickly as possible before the British could strengthen their lines. The theory was to invite the British further into the battle zones, engaging them all the way until they were weak from losses and short of supplies and then launching a series of counter-attacks with fresh troops.[111]

Gough's Fifth Army had amassed a total of 752 heavy and 1,422 field guns for his attack. In addition, he had additional firepower from the 300 heavy and 240 field guns of the French as well as 112 heavy and 210 field guns of the Second Army to the south.[112] The guns were supplied with over 4.2

million shells.[113] In comparison, the Germans had between 1,000 and 1,500 guns at their disposal.[114] Although outgunned, the main task of the German artillery was not directed at destroying British defences; therefore, it was more than sufficient to deal with attacking infantry. Gough's original plan was for a nine-day bombardment commencing on 18 July prior to his attack which was scheduled for 25 July. However, delays caused by moving heavy artillery into place and requests from the French led to the assault being postponed until 31 July.[115] On 24 July 1917, 164th Infantry Brigade issued instructions for the attack.[116] As part of XIX Corps, the 55th Division would be taking part in the attack with the 15th Division on its right and the 39th Division on its left. The instructions stated that the intention of the assault was to prepare for a further advance, by capturing and occupying the German positions on the Gheluvelt–Langemarck line. It also intended to establish strongpoints and obtain a footing on the Gravenstafel Spur and occupy enemy positions as far as the line at Toronto and Aviatik Farms. The operation was to be carried out in three phases: at Zero hour, the first objective required the 165th and 166th Infantry Brigades to capture and consolidate the German front-line trench system up to and including the Blue Line. The second objective would commence at Zero plus one hour and would again involve the 165th and 166th Brigades. Their objective was to capture and consolidate the German second-line trench system up to and including the Black Line. At Zero plus three hours and fifty-three minutes, the 166th Brigade would then advance to the Green Line. The third objective had two phases, the first phase would commence at Zero plus five hours and twenty minutes when the 164th Brigade would pass through the 165th and 166th Brigades on the Black Line. They would then capture and consolidate the German third trench system along the Gheluvelt–Langemarck line, up to and including the Green Line. The second phase contained directions on what action should be taken if the 164th Brigade discovered that the Germans had abandoned their positions on the Gravenstafel Switch. If this occurred, the brigade was to wait until the British artillery barrage ceased at Zero plus eight hours and twenty minutes, and then establish a line of resistance along the Gravenstafel Spur. They were also to contact the 15th Division on their left and 39th Division on their right.

Two days before the attack, motivational addresses were issued from the Divisional Commander, Major General Jeudwine, Brigadier-General Stockwell, the 164th Brigade and Lieutenant Colonel Heath, the Commanding Officer of the Liverpool Irish. Heath reminded his men of what they were fighting for; his address did not contain any high-blown references to 'King and country'. Instead, Heath offered more personal and subjective reasons for fighting, and he also appealed to their sense of identity. Heath told his battalion that they were not only fighting to defeat Prussian militarism, 'but that each one is also fighting for the freedom of mankind, for the security of his home, for the future safety of his mother, sister, sweetheart, wife, daughter and of all also that he holds dear and sacred'.[117] He concluded by appealing to their regimental loyalty, 'Let the name of the "Liverpool Irish" go down to posterity as a glorious and imperishable name.'[118] The weather in Belgium had been fine during June and most of July. However, as the divisional historian noted, 'Unfortunately, on Sunday, July 29th, a particularly heavy thunderstorm filled up the shell holes and turned roads and tracks into a morass. The succeeding days were dull and hazy, making the completion of artillery preparation particularly difficult.'[119]

Zero hour was set for 3.50 a.m. on 31 July 1917; however, the Liverpool Irish would not advance until Zero plus six hours and twenty minutes. Their task was to pass through the 165th and 166th Brigades and to 'mop up' the German defences on the left battalion front as far as Schuler Farm.[120] After the Green Line had been captured, the battalion's objectives were to consolidate the line by assisting the 1/4th North Lancashire Regiment and the 2/5th Lancashire Fusiliers. They were also responsible for the construction of small tactical outposts along the line.[121] The battalion would also have the assistance of twelve tanks from No. 16 Company of the Tanks Corps; eight tanks were detailed to take up a position in front of the leading waves of the 164th Brigade up to and beyond the Green Line.[122] Major Harry Leech, who had been with the battalion since 1914, was selected to lead the Liverpool Irish into battle. At 8.30 a.m., 164th Brigade left their 'jump off' point at Liverpool Trench and Congreve Walk. The brigade attacked on a frontage of 1,500 yards, with the 1/4th North Lancashire Regiment and the 2/5th Lancashire Fusiliers in front, while the 1/4th Royal Lancashire Regiment and the 8th Liverpool Irish were to the rear, acting in support.[123] Lieutenant Rothwell described the mood of the Liverpool Irish as they set off: 'At the appointed hour we got ready to go over the top, everybody was in the best of spirits and the men went over singing.'[124]

The narrative of Liverpool (Irish) Battalion's operation of 31 July stated that 'The "going" was very bad, numerous trenches, and other obstacles being encountered, especially in the vicinity of our own and the enemy original front lines.'[125] Apart from the bad 'going', Captain John Fitzgerald Jones, Adjutant of the Liverpool Irish wrote, 'The advance to the Black Line so far as it affected the Lan. Fus., and ourselves was almost without incident. Very few of the enemy and our own casualties were seen.' The battle intensified when the Liverpool Irish reached the Black Line. 'A perfect hell of M.G. fire was turned upon us from high ground in the vicinity of our objective.'[126] In fact, the entire battalion came under sustained and 'deadly' machine gun fire from the high ground surrounding Hindu Cott, Somme and Schuler Farm.[127] Private A. Smith, a runner with 'B' Company, was sent to the left of the battalion to get in touch with the Black Watch. He encountered a solitary Black Watch soldier who informed him his battalion had been 'wiped out'.[128] Private Gregson, also of B company, reported that they came under heavy machine gun fire about 500 yards in front of the Blue Line. His company had been advancing too quickly, and he was informed by Lieutenants Toms and Orchard that they were twelve minutes in front of their own barrage.[129] Gregson's platoon fell back about 100 yards to wait for the barrage. Having done so, they discovered 'about 5 of the enemy concealed in a large concrete dugout, apparently used as Headquarters containing maps etc'. Having started well, Private J. Evans of D Company was advancing immediately behind the 2/5th Lancashire Fusiliers and fell victim to German shellfire:

> All went well until we were about 300 yards from Bossaert Farm when a large shell burst just in front of our platoon, killing one and seriously injuring 3 others. I myself was knocked down with the concussion and partly buried with earth. As soon as I recovered from the shock, I managed to see if I could find my platoon, but not being able to see them I went forward in the direction of Border House. On the way, I met Pte. Wilson of 14 Plat. And he told me the platoon had gone on and that he was wounded, so I went on again and came across Pte. A.R. Taylor, a Lewis Gunner, of 14 Platoon who was wounded in the leg and hand. So, I dressed his wounds and left him to find his own way back.[130]

Sergeant Birtwhistle and the men of No. 6 Platoon, B Company, lost direction shortly after passing Bossaert Farm. They then came under heavy machine gun fire and took cover in shell holes. Birtwhistle's men moved off to their right and spotted a gap in the wire; while making their way through the gap, Captain Harvey Duder was killed.[131] German snipers were extremely active throughout the battle. CSM Cook, A Company, reported that as his men took cover on their way to Somme Farm, they encountered a sniper in a shell hole. Cook's men threw a grenade into the shell hole wounding the sniper, two men then charged into the hole and captured the sniper.[132] Private Cosgrove, A Company, had a similar encounter. When he reached Wurst Farm, he rushed to take cover among some bushes and trees. 'I found a sniper sitting in a tree at a distance of 80 yards and brought him down; a falling twig gave his position away.'[133]

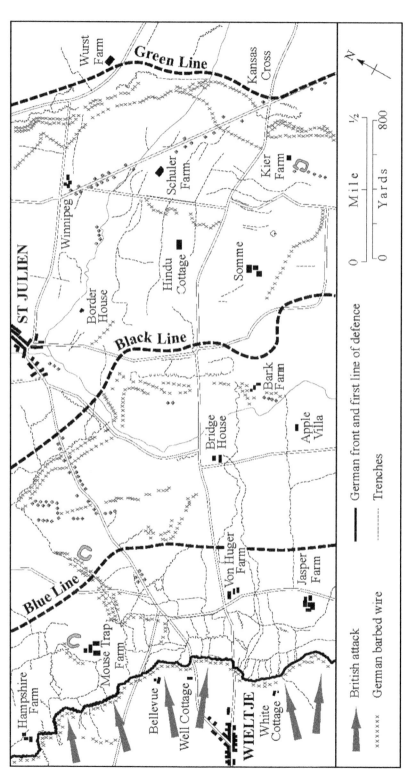

Map 5: Battle of Pilckem Ridge. Map showing the objectives of the 55th Division 31 July–2 August 1917.

To counter the German snipers, orders were shouted for Lewis Guns to open fire, Sergeant Fraser stated that he did not see or hear any Lewis Guns, adding, 'Still, I do not consider that had Lewis Guns been there they could possibly have been used, owing to his sniping being so severe.'[134] At Schuler Farm, Sergeant Fraser's doubts about machine gunners exposing themselves to enemy fire were confirmed by Lance-Corporal Morris, D Company, who reported that 'Four machine gunners were sniped through the head while firing the gun.'[135] The high casualty rate among the officers of the Liverpool Irish when the battalion was forced to pause and wait on the barrage led the author of the battalion's Narrative of Operations to conclude, 'During this pause several officers were hit by snipers concealed in a row of trees about C. 18, d. 6. 6. In spite of the fact that they wore privates' uniforms.'[136] German snipers were extremely active throughout 31 July. Given the high rate of officer casualties among the Irish, it is understandable that suspicions existed that officers were being especially targeted by German snipers. However, it is unlikely that any sniper would have been able to distinguish between an officer and a ranker if both wore identical uniforms. The battalion's narrative gives the German snipers too much credit. The harsh reality was that given the opportunity, German snipers might well have singled out officers; if they were unable to do so, they just shot at any khaki-clad British soldier who presented himself.

As mentioned earlier, the battalion did have tank support; however, their performance on the day was somewhat inconsistent. Second Lieutenant Hodson praised their actions in the area surrounding Hindu Cott:

> Here a 'tank' was doing very good work and enabled us to move forward to the machine gun emplacements … These emplacements were giving a fight. A tank came up and helped to clear this place of the enemy. The dugouts were bombed, and a number of the enemy were killed.[137]

On reaching Schuler Farm, Lieutenant Rothwell, who was left with just six survivors, began to dig in when they came under heavy machine gun fire. Having failed to identify the location of the German gunners, Rothwell decided to give whatever information he had to the tanks who were 200 yards behind his position:

> We left Sgt. Major Greenwood in charge and made a dash for the tanks. In passing, I ought to tell you that the wire at Gravenstafel Switch was very strong and hardly damaged. We got back to the tanks and found one out of action and the other making its way back to Wieltje. We managed to stop him and told him as much of the situation as possible and he promised to

help. We decided to get back to Pond Farm and make a report. On the way back, we met the Tank Observation Officer and told him the whole situation. He seemed rather lost and didn't quite know where he was.[138]

There is no doubt that 31 July had been a difficult day for the Tank Corps. The British Mark IV tank, with its sluggish speed of just 4 miles per hour, was reduced to a crawl in the muddy conditions, making them vulnerable to mechanical failure and shellfire.[139] The attack was supposed to have been supported by aircraft from the Royal Flying Corps (RFC) who were to provide contact planes which would report the precise location of the most advanced infantry sections.[140] Communication between the infantry and the aircraft was a haphazard affair; the aircraft would attract the attention of the troops by sounding a Klaxon horn and firing off white Very Lights. Meanwhile, the infantry was to fire white ground flares and use Watson Fans to indicate their position to the pilots.[141] This system might well have worked had the aircraft of the RFC been in the air above the Liverpool Irish in sufficient numbers to ensure effective communications. CSM Greenwood reported seeing a British aircraft during the action. 'One of our aeroplanes had been over at 12 noon and fired a single flare, but as I had no ground flares I could do nothing.'[142] Lieutenant Rothwell had more success when he was trying to get a message to the artillery to engage a German counter-attack near Somme Farm. Having failed to signal the artillery and then sent a runner, he managed to relay his message to a passing aircraft.[143] When the Irish reached their final objectives around Schuler and Wurst Farms, they attracted the attention of German aircraft. Private Cosgrove wrote that when his section reached Wurst Farm 'intense MG fire, artillery and aeroplane machine gun fire withered us'.[144] Second Lieutenant J.E. Fenn reported that 'enemy aeroplanes flying low were locating our positions by means of Very Lights, the result being that we were heavily shelled from the ridge on the right'.[145] Lieutenant Rothwell was 'astonished' at the appearance of four German aircraft at Schuler Farm; 'There was not one of ours in sight.'[146] According to Nick Lloyd, a combination of mist and persistent low cloud had prevented the RFC from playing a major role in the battle. While some bombing and strafing operations did proceed, the programme for offensive air patrols had to be abandoned.[147] It is obvious from the battle narratives of the Liverpool Irish that the low cloud and mist failed to keep the German pilots on the ground. The skies and weather conditions along the Pilckem Ridge on 31 July were as unforgiving for the German aviators as they were for the British, yet it was the RFC who remained at their aerodromes.

It was, perhaps, inevitable that, as men stopped to seek cover from the shelling, snipers and machine gun fire and then moved off again, some soldiers would lose direction or contact with their platoons. Sergeant Birtwhistle and fourteen of his men became disorientated; they merged with men from the Cheshire Regiment who were grateful as they were expecting a German counter-attack.[148] Private Evans, who had been concussed by an exploding shell, wandered off to find the rest of the Liverpool Irish and ended up with the Royal Sussex Regiment before finally re-joining Captain Jones and the Irish at Spree Farm.[149] The number of casualties among the Liverpool Irish grew as they advanced towards Schuler and Wurst Farms. Corporal Jones, C Company, estimated that by the time the battalion had reached Pond Farm and were about to attack a strongpoint, they had 'about a third of the battalion and what was left of the Lan. Fus.'[150] At Somme Farm, CSM Cook, A Company, reported that they had captured a battery of guns and taken many prisoners, adding, 'They surrendered without showing a fight.'[151] Cook's opposite number in D Company, CSM Greenwood, noticed that discretion was the better form of valour for the Germans at Fokker Farm, 'About 11 a.m. I noticed the Germans retiring very fast from Fokker Farm, and dugouts at D.14, a. 9. 8., in the direction of Boetleer Farm.' He noted something strange about the fleeing Germans: 'There would have been about 200 of the enemy. They were not wearing equipment.'[152] Second Lieutenant Hodson, C Company, was also aware that the German defenders lacked firepower; 'when we were attacking I do not remember seeing any of the enemy armed with a rifle and bayonet'.[153] Hodson suggested that the German defenders had been left to defend their positions 'with the bomb as these were plentiful. A number of revolvers were found in the dugouts.' Having passed Pond Farm, C Company neared their final objective where they took cover in shell holes as it was unsafe to expose themselves to German machine gun fire by trying to dig in. It was here that Corporal Jones witnessed some German ingenuity:

> We held this line for about practically an hour until ordered to cease fire by an officer on account of the enemy coming over dressed in khaki and with sandbag hats. On this ruse being discovered, the officer immediately ordered rapid fire, which continued for about seven minutes and caused heavy casualties on the enemy.[154]

The officers who had survived the attack beyond the Black Line did their best to rally what was left of a mixed force of men from the Liverpool Irish and the Lancashire Fusiliers, and lead the men to their final objectives. Major Leech and the Adjutant, Captain Jones, established a headquarters at Pond

Farm. Although, according to Jones, the signallers and runners suffered badly, and all but two of the signallers became casualties.[155] Major Harry Leech and Captain Ward went forward in an attempt to form a line between Hill 35 and Border House, while Lieutenant Best-Dunkley of the 2/5th Lancashire Fusiliers rushed forward and rallied the men at Spree Farm where he then formed a firing line. Captain Jones, Adjutant of the Liverpool Irish, described Best-Dunkley's actions as 'magnificent'.[156] Due to the large numbers of casualties sustained by both battalions, the Liverpool Irish had now merged with the 2/5th Lancashire Fusiliers in order to reach the Green Line.[157] At around 7 p.m., Jones received news that Best-Dunkley had been wounded and that he wanted to speak to him. 'I ran across and had almost arrived at his position when I was blown head over heels into a little trench and wounded in several places in the thigh. Unfortunately, both Col. Dunkley and myself were hit by our own gunners.'[158] When Captain Ward was informed that only a small number of the 2/5th Lancashire Fusiliers had reached the Green Line, he ordered B Company to move up to Wurst Farm, and D Company to occupy the Green Line at Fokker Farm.[159]

Second Lieutenant Fenn arrived on the Winnipeg–Kansas Road along with number 6 and 7 Platoons of the Liverpool Irish.[160] The combined strength of this small force was two officers and thirty men. Having established that they were 100 yards to the left of Schuler Farm, Lieutenant Orchard took charge of the operation to surround and attack Schuler Farm. They divided into three groups, with Fenn's group attacking the front of the farm. Having allowed the other two groups time to outflank the building, Fenn passed a message down to his men, 'When I blow this whistle I want every man to charge.'[161] He faced no opposition and took Schuler Farm, capturing five unarmed prisoners. While Fenn and his men were searching the farm, Lieutenants Orchard and Toms arrived and the Germans opened fire on the farm with machine gun and rifle fire. Lieutenant Orchard was fatally wounded, and Lieutenant Toms, who was also wounded, went back to report the situation to the battalion headquarters. Fenn was then joined by Captain Ward and Second Lieutenant Rothwell, who advised him to push forward to Wurst Farm and assist in consolidating the area. On his way forward, he met Captain Bodel while he was crossing the Winnipeg Road, and Bodel took command. At around 12.30 p.m., Captain Bodel attempted to get a message back by runner and carrier pigeon requesting reinforcements. Bodel had sent runners to the left to try and get in touch with the battalion on his left. They failed and Bodel then went himself, but he was also unsuccessful. The Germans opened fire with machine guns and Fenn ordered his men to return fire at visible targets only as his party were short of ammunition. 'All this time machine guns were active, and we suffered heavily. I lost all my party as a result, except Cpl. Foster.'[162] A few men from the 2/5th Lancashire Fusiliers decided to retire along the Winnipeg Road, which attracted the attention of the German machine gunners. According to Fenn, when Lieutenant Dickinson of the same battalion saw this, 'he stood up in the shell hole and shouted, "Come along lads, don't go back, but put up a fight for it", it was just as he said this that he was shot along with his runner.'[163] The Liverpool Irish were already low in numbers at Wurst Farm when Captain Bodel was killed by a shell and four men who were with him were badly wounded. At 2 p.m., the Germans counter-attacked under the cover of an artillery and machine barrage, driving Fenn and just two remaining survivors of the Liverpool Irish out of Wurst Farm.[164]

Fenn and his men joined what was left of the Irish and 2/5th Lancashire Fusiliers at Schuler Farm. As the men were digging in, Lance-Corporal Morris noticed 'three German aeroplanes firing rockets towards us'.[165] After about an hour, the Germans made a counter-attack, forcing the flanks of the Irish and Lancashire Fusiliers to collapse. They then fell back and reformed at concrete emplacements behind Schuler Farm where they established a defensive flank with Lewis and machine guns. Second Lieutenant Hodson reported, 'While we were holding the MACHINE GUN EMPLACEMENTS [sic], 3 lights were fired directly at our position. Very soon after these lights were fired, the enemy's artillery dropped shells within a few yards of where I was.'[166] The situation at Schuler Farm was becoming desperate when Major Harry Leech arrived. Reports were received that the battalion on the left of the Liverpool Irish had its right flank at Border House, some 800 yards west of Schuler Farm. Leech attempted to bend his line of defence towards Border House. He sent a few men to the left and right of the line, placing his Lewis and machine guns in the centre.[167] CSM Greenwood stated that the guns 'did fine execution amongst the enemy but we lost heavily'.[168] However, ammunition was running low and Lance-Corporal Morris recalled that men were emptying their pouches to provide more rounds for the machine guns. The Germans were now very close to the Liverpool Irish. After the attack, CSM Greenwood gave a brief description of the German *eingreif* division he had encountered on 31 July: 'The men wore steel helmets, great coats rolled, bandolier style, and a light pack on the back. A great number of snipers were used.'[169] According to Lance-Corporal Morris, during the German assault, Major Harry Leech was still trying to organise his men: 'The Boche was now very near to us; Major Leech made towards a flank where he received a wound to the head.'[170]

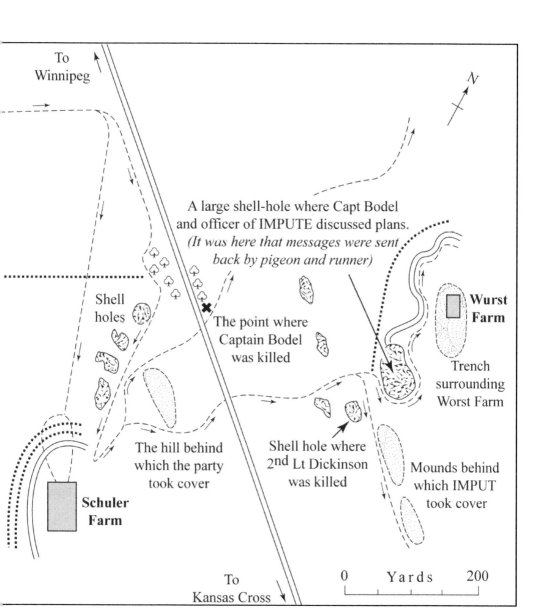

To
Winnipeg

N

A large shell-hole where Capt Bodel
and officer of IMPUTE discussed plans.
*(It was here that messages were sent
back by pigeon and runner)*

Shell
holes

✗
The point where
Captain Bodel
was killed

**Wurst
Farm**

Trench
surrounding
Worst Farm

The hill behind
which the party
took cover

Shell hole where
2nd Lt Dickinson
was killed

Mounds behind
which IMPUT
took cover

**Schuler
Farm**

To
Kansas Cross

0   Y a r d s   200

Map 6: Compiled from hand–drawn sketch detailing the topography and events around the
areas of Schuler and Wurst Farms.

Faced with relentless attacks by fresh German divisions and short of both men and ammunition, the Liverpool Irish and their comrades in the Lancashire Fusiliers withdrew to the Black Line. The survivors, Second Lieutenants Fenn and Hodson and 160 other ranks, were ordered back to the line between Strand Communication Trench and Wieltje. The battalion had fought hard and had reached their objectives, but at a great cost. Lieutenant Colonel Heath, Commanding Officer of the Liverpool Irish, congratulated his men, telling them, 'The English press is full of the gallant deeds of the lads of Lancashire.'[171] Acknowledging their losses, he continued, 'That the price of victory is at times severe is unfortunately unavoidable, and I deplore with you the loss of so many gallant friends and brave comrades.' Among those listed as missing in action was Major Harry Leech, second in command of the battalion. Having received a head wound, he was left behind when the Liverpool Irish withdrew from Schuler Farm. His friend and adjutant, Captain John Fitzgerald Jones, wrote to his Major Leech's sister two weeks after the battle. Jones informed her that he hoped and believed that Harry Leech was 'a prisoner and wounded' and that 'It would be wicked of me to hold out this hope if I did not believe it to be strictly true.' Jones wrote his four-page letter from his hospital bed at No. 7 Stationary Hospital at Boulogne. Jones held his belief that Leech was a prisoner because he had been informed that Leech's wound was not serious and that the ground where Major Leech had been lying was quickly occupied by the Germans after the Irish withdrew. He also told her of Leech's leadership qualities and his popularity among the officers and men in the battalion. 'You will know perhaps that he took the Irish into battle. It was his dearest wish and it was gratified. It was an inspiration to every officer and man in the battalion for every heart loved the "Major".' Lieutenant Colonel Heath was less optimistic when he wrote to Major Leech's sister, 'though I fear it is very unlikely that he can still be alive, I still feel that there may be just the slightest possibility of his being alive'.[172] Major Leech's father received confirmation of his son's death in a letter from Major-General Jeudwine in September 1917. Jeudwine wrote that there 'can be little doubt that he met a soldier's death on July 31st'.[173] The letter also praised Leech's affection for his battalion, 'he was,' Jeudwine wrote, 'a most gallant officer, full of courage and determination and yet most modest'. Jeudwine ended his letter by remembering his final meeting with Major Leech just before the battle. 'He was full of cheeriness and confidence and the spirit he showed cannot fail to have been a great incentive to all under him, and to have helped them to do what they did.'[174] On 6 November 1917, Private F. Jones, No. 10 Company, 164th Machine Gun Corps, who was being held as a prisoner of war at Giessen in Germany, wrote to Major Leech's mother at Sefton Park,

Liverpool. Private Jones' letter reveals what happened during Major Leech's final days in No Man's Land; it is worth quoting at length:

> I am taking advantage of my opportunity to write you. It has been my greatest sorrow that I was unable to write sooner, but when I tell you my story I hope you will forgive me. I was in the attack last July 31st and was wounded and finding myself cut off from my comrades I came across poor Major Leech lying badly wounded. I went up to him and bound him and did all in my power to save him, but I am sorry to say that his wounds were severe and prevented my plan of carrying him. We stayed out for 3 days alone thinking that help would come. On the 3rd Aug. I found myself in a German hospital in a bad condition and I was told that my comrade Major Leach was dead when we were found, and I was brought in. I have in my possession photos belonging to the Major, and a letter which I just found which prevented me from writing. My home is at 22 Bank Quay Carnarvon, N.W. Please tell mother that I am well. Write me and tell me the facts please. Hoping you are fairly well in this great hour of sorrow. Accept my greatest sympathy. Hoping to hear as early as possible.[175]

KULTUR AND CAPTIVITY

Warfare throughout history, irrespective of the righteousness or neces-sity of the cause, was (and remains) a bloody, cruel and inhumane affair. The nineteenth century witnessed the development of more deadly and destructive weaponry, yet belligerent nations failed to match the evo-lution of contemporary weapons and their capacity to kill and maim with any corresponding momentum in the provision of medical care for the wounded.[1] The corollary of the development of armaments and the neglect of the wounded on the battlefields of mid-nineteenth century Europe invoked international pressure to make war more humane. Moved by the plight of some 40,000 neglected casualties in the aftermath of the Battle of Solferino in 1859, the International Committee of the Red Cross was established at Geneva four years later in 1863.[2] The following year, the First Geneva Convention was established and was signed by sixteen states. The Convention set out the principles that medical relief should be given to the battle casualties without distinction regarding their nationality, and that medical personnel displaying the Red Cross emblem should be treated as neutrals. Further progress in the development of international humanitarian law was achieved by the updating of the Geneva Convention in 1906 and at The Hague Peace Conferences of 1899 and 1907.[3] Thus, by 1914, the nations of Europe had a series of articles which dictated how belligerent countries should treat their prisoners of war. Britain, France and Germany, who had ratified The Hague Conventions, were fully conversant with their obligations under international humanitarian law.

The radicalisation and reaction of the civilian population of the belliger-ent nations may not have been uppermost in the minds of the great men who had compiled The Hague Conventions. British propaganda had been successful in exploiting the German invasion of Belgium and the atrocities committed by its soldiers during the early months of the war. Following the first engagements with British troops at Mons, Britain's propagandists continued to cultivate Germanophobia by highlighting the mistreatment of British prisoners of war. There were, however, some unfortunate British citizens who had been visiting the Fatherland immediately before hostilities commenced. In 1913, L.M. Marshall, the minister of Princes Gate Baptist Church in Liverpool, invited five boys from his congregation to accompany him on a tour of Germany which was to depart in the summer of 1914. Having spent two years living and studying in Germany, Marshall became a convinced Germanophile: 'During this period I acquired the liveliest admiration for the higher aspects of German "Kultur" and learned to esteem the German people.'[4] Marshall had been touched by the warmth and kindness of those he met at university and in the various boarding houses where he had lodged. Shortly before the tour, three of his intended companions, who were aged 17, withdrew from the trip. Undeterred by this and news of the political upheavals in the Baltics, Marshall set off with his two 16-year-old companions on 29 July 1914. The party arrived in Germany to find the country in a state of excitement over the news of the partial mobilisation of Russian forces, but observed that there was a distinct lack of hostility towards Britain. Prior to leaving Berlin, Marshall sought advice from his friends in the city, the police and British Consular officials, who all agreed that he should carry on with his trip. The party left Berlin on 'the fatal day' of 4 August 1914.[5] For the next four months, Marshall and his companions were arrested, imprisoned, insulted and stood accused of being Russian spies. At Guesten, German officials believed that Marshall's tooth powder and sea-sickness remedy were poisons which were intended to poison the town water supply. They became victims of German bureaucracy; having satisfied one group of police and officials as to their identities and issued with passes, they were then rearrested in the next town they visited. German officials did find an incriminating document carried by one of Marshall's companions. The young man's brother had asked him to send him some picture postcards from Germany. His brother was a member of the Liverpool territorials and his address was given as the military camp in England where his battalion was attending their annual camp. This did little to convince their German captors that they were three churchmen on a tour of the Fatherland.[6]

Between periods of incarceration and detention, Marshall attended local church services; however, he gave this up after being subjected to a series of vitriolic Anglophobic diatribes from the pulpit. 'Another preacher told us that Germany was fighting against Russian despotism, French atheism and English capitalism.'[7] With the assistance of some Dutch friends and members of his own church, Marshall and his friends arrived at Folkstone four months after they had first arrived in Germany. According to Marshall, those months had not been wasted: 'My pro-Germanism vanished like mist before the rising sun.' Marshall's account of his trip to Germany was published in Liverpool in 1915. It provided English readers with an appreciation of the growth and the extent of Anglophobia in Germany during 1914. For those in Liverpool who had read Marshall's description of his incarceration and the humiliation meted out by German civilians to a non-combatant trio comprising a minister of religion and two teenage boys, it must have raised questions on the fate of British prisoners of war.

Initially, Germany had three enemy nations: Russia, France and Britain. Most of the German anger, however, was reserved for the British. Germans condemned British capitalism and accused its soldiers of being mercenaries or *geldsoldaten*.[8] In the first months of the war, German propaganda argued that Britain had also incurred the wrath of the almighty, and *Gott strafe England* (God punish England) became the slogan of choice for patriotic Germans in 1914. According to Stefan Goebel, it went beyond being a mere propaganda slogan; it was recommended as the new German salutation, replacing the usual *guten tag*.[9] The 'Hunnish' behaviour of German troops in Belgium in 1914, and Allied press reports of the various atrocities, provided British propagandists with a wealth of material to exploit the notion of German 'frightfulness' to an increasingly radicalised public. During the first months of mobile warfare, any confidence the British had in Germany adhering to the articles of The Hague Convention was misplaced. Among the many promulgations contained within the Convention regarding the treatment of prisoners of war was the ideal that prisoners were held under the power of the state which held them and not the individual soldier or corps which had captured them and, significantly, that, 'they must be humanely treated'.[10] The Convention also declared that the state which captured the men could 'utilize the labour of prisoners of war according to their rank and aptitude, officers excepted. The proviso here was that 'tasks shall not be excessive and shall have no connection with the operation of the war'.

When some wounded British soldiers were repatriated in 1915, they returned with stories of their mistreatment at German hands, and there was a public outcry. An article in the *Liverpool Echo* on 10 April 1915, under the headline '"Kultur" All the World Should Know', called for Mr Justice Younger's report on the conditions at Wittenberg prisoner-of-war camp in Germany to be made available to neutral nations. The camp had experienced an outbreak of typhus and it was alleged that their captors had withdrawn from any inter-action with the sick and dying and that the prisoners had been neglected and left to die. The report stated, 'What the prisoners found hardest to bear were the jeers with which the coffins were frequently greeted by the inhabitants of Wittenberg who stood outside the wire and who were permitted to insult the dead.'[11] A few weeks later, the same paper related Lord Kitchener's damning indictment of Germany's mistreatment of British prisoners of war.[12] In his statement to the House of Lords, Kitchener alluded to the statements made by officers and men during interviews relating to their treatment during captivity and transport to hospitals and camps and who had then escaped, been exchanged or repatriated. In 1915, a parliamentary committee was established to report on the treatment and transport of British prisoners of war from August until December 1914.[13] The statements revealed that British prisoners of war had endured a litany of cruelty, abuse and humiliation by the German army, medical staff and civilian population. Extracts from the statements of British officers and seventy-seven NCOs and men contained in the official report were later published by Keble Howard in a pamphlet entitled *The Quality of Mercy*.[14] German anger at Britain's entry into the conflict morphed into the conviction that British soldiers were fighting without a cause and were mere mercenaries. Their anger was further inflamed by rumours and propaganda that the British were using dumdum bullets to inflict more severe wounds on German soldiers.[15] Furthermore, stories that the British were using knives to mutilate captured German soldiers did nothing to assuage anti-British sentiments.[16]

State-induced mobilisation of anti-British sentiments in Germany in the autumn of 1914 had the desired effect, as captured British soldiers were to discover. Trains carrying British prisoners of war were met by crowds of angry, spitting, snarling civilians and soldiers at the various stops en route to their respective camps. At Cologne, Sergeant Gilling recalled that the crowd hurled abuse and used every available utensil to throw water and urine over the prisoners in the carriage.[17] Private Dodd stated that, to assist the crowd in directing their hostility, 'The Germans wrote "*Engländer*" outside in chalk and at every station we were jeered at.'[18] Private Arnold of the Dorset Regiment remembered that Scottish soldiers were singled out for special humiliation: 'The Scots were pulled out and called "*Fräulein*", and their kilts were lifted up.'[19] Some soldiers marvelled at the capacity and virtuosity of German women at spitting. Arriving at Torgau in 1914, Lieutenant Colonel R.C. Bond, King's Own Yorkshire Light Infantry, described being met by a crowd who seemed determined to get at the prisoners: 'There was one very old woman who distinguished herself by the violence of her denunciations and the direction of her aim … with three well-directed spits! Old German women can spit!'[20] In his examination of the statements of British prisoners of war in 1914, Keble Howard concluded that the officers and men were unanimous 'that the behaviour of the German Red Cross was so vile as to be almost incredible'.[21] Many of the prisoners claimed that Red Cross nurses refused to give them any food or water. Some spat at them, or taunted them by showing them food, coffee and water then walking off. Captain Hargreaves, Somerset Light Infantry, recounted his own experience:

> At Liege I tried personally to get the German Red Cross officials to give our wounded water. They refused. I saw some German Red Cross nurses actually bring water in cans up to our men, show it to them, and then pour it onto the platform. This also happened to me personally. At Aix-la Chapelle, there was an elaborate Red Cross dressing-station. All water and food was rigorously refused us. The German wounded on the train had their wounds dressed. This was refused us.[22]

Until the beginning of 1915, German 'frightfulness' had been an exclusively male affair – the Hun was, after all, a man. Early German propaganda and subsequent Anglophobia had obliterated gender boundaries. German women were not only radicalised; they were actively encouraged and expected to display their loathing of the enemy. Having obtained damning statements from repatriated and exchanged prisoners, the British lost little time in exploiting German cruelty. The British produced a poster by David Wilson entitled 'Red Cross or Iron Cross?', which provided a visual representation of what some of the prisoners of 1914 had endured.[23] Focusing on the condemnation of the callousness of German Red Cross nurses, the poster conveyed the sadism of the German nurses while reinforcing the moral superiority of British womanhood – 'There is no woman in Britain who would do it – There is no woman in Britain who will forget it'.

In her research into violence against prisoners of war, Heather Jones does not dispute the authenticity of the statements made by British prisoners in 1914. However, she suggests that the German Red Cross nurses were, in fact, members of the *Vaterländische Frauenvereine*, a patriotic German women's voluntary organisation which displayed emblems resembling those of Red Cross nurses. Members of this organisation were located at the major German railway stations dispensing comforts to departing troops and assisting the German wounded.[24] In the early months of the war, prisoners captured by German troops represented a physical manifestation of the success of the German army to its people and therefore provided much-valued propaganda.

The appearance of captured British soldiers also allowed non-combatants to display their patriotism by abusing the enemy whenever an opportunity to do so arose. In 1914, the German army ensured that there would be ample opportunities – literally train loads.

Table 6.1: *Strength of British Army and total numbers of British soldiers killed in action and prisoners of war, 1914, 1916 and 1918.*

Year	BEF Strength	Killed in Action	Prisoners
1914	118,000	13,009	19,915
1916	1,462,000	107,411	15,516
1918	1,202,000	80,247	107,647

Source: Calculated from *Medical Services*, pp. 122, 136, 149, 158; *Military Effort*, p. 628.

The two mobile phases of the war, August to December 1914 and the months of the *Kaiserschlacht* in the spring of 1918, provided the biggest hauls for Germany. Table 6.1 reveals the extent of the numbers of men captured from the BEF in 1914. From a total of strength of 118,000, nearly 20,000, or 16.87 per cent, became prisoners of war. During the final year of the conflict, when Britain's army had expanded to over a million men, just over 107,000 men were captured. Despite the horrors and stalemate of trench warfare and the carnage on the Somme in 1916, the total number of British prisoners for the year was comparatively low at 15,516. During the first year of the war, Germany certainly struggled to deal with the volume of prisoners and to meet its obligations under The Hague Conventions.[25] Following the debacle at Guillemont on the Somme in August 1916, Germany added practically the entire fighting battalion of the Liverpool Irish to its prisoner-of-war camps.[26]

The much-dreaded knock on the door by a telegram boy was heard all too often in the streets of Liverpool throughout the war. Notwithstanding the anguish and distress caused by official telegrams informing the recipient of the death or injury of a loved one, a message telling them that their husband, father, son or brother was 'missing' arguably brought an even greater angst. Those fortunate enough to receive a further telegram informing them that their relative had been captured and was now a prisoner of war must have felt a semblance of relief. However, any sense of relief was tempered not least due to effectiveness of British propaganda in mobilising public revulsion at Germany by exploiting the cruelties inflicted on prisoners of war. Essentially, British propaganda became something of a double-edged sword. While the exploitation of Germany's abuse of British prisoners of war for propaganda purposes was highly successful in developing Germanophobia, it unwittingly exacerbated the concerns of the families and friends of British soldiers held in Germany. Press reports, government statements and posters about the mistreatment of British prisoners of war arguably did little to assuage the concerns of the prisoners' friends and relatives that they were indeed being mistreated. As early as June 1915, the *Liverpool Echo* reported that Private Berry of the Royal Irish Rifles claimed that wounded soldiers in Munsterberg hospital were being fed 'sandstorm soup' which contained inedible chestnuts.[27] Six days after the capture of the Liverpool Irish in August 1916, the *Echo* 'special correspondent' reported that six British soldiers had been held without food or water for a week. The report also claimed that prisoners of war had been made to sit on the parapet of the trench and were used as human targets for their former comrades.[28] The discomfort and mistreatment of British prisoners of war notwithstanding, it is tempting to assume that the life chances of prisoners were enhanced since they were no longer involved in active trench warfare. Yet recent research by Mark Spoerer has revealed that during the period from October 1917 until September 1918, death rates among British prisoners of war in Germany were higher than those at the front.[29]

Within the twenty-four hours following their attack on the Somme on 8 August 1916, the Liverpool Irish prisoners were transported from the snarling battlefields around Guillemont, where everything (except cowardice or desertion) was permitted, to the unseen ground behind the German lines. Here, disoriented soldiers had entered a German-speaking other-world where, from then on, practically everything was *verboten*. The fact that the Liverpool Irish had been captured more or less en masse did not signify that they were going to remain together. Transport, capacity within the various camps, and the demands of German industry and agriculture were the deciding factors as to where the men went. For the men of the Liverpool Irish recovering from the shock of capture, the journey would be uncomfortable, and the extent of their future discomfort and their chances of survival would depend on where they were sent. In the inventory of miseries and privations endured by British prisoners of war, including the humiliation of capture, the insults of the guards and the petty Prussian camp rules, nothing was of greater magnitude for hungry men than food. According to one historian, food became the 'motif of life' in the prisoner-of-war camps of Germany.[30] Private John Burston, from

Upper Essex Street in Liverpool, was one of the Liverpool Irish captured at Guillemont in August 1916. Throughout his captivity at Dülmen and later at Wülfrath, Burston made no complaints about his treatment. While the food 'was not too bad', he complained about the quantity of his meals and stated that the prisoners 'were always hungry'.[31] Private James Slessor described the circumstances of his capture at Guillemont and the journey from Cambrai to Dülmen prison camp. Slessor wrote, 'I remained in a shell hole until dark then ventured out. I came in sight of a trench and an English Sergeant shouted to me to come in. I was much surprised to find that he was a prisoner and on our coming up to the trench I was called upon to surrender in English by one of the Germans who spoke English well.'[32] He was then plied with questions before being taken to a village behind the lines prior to being transported to a hospital at Cambrai where a kind, English-speaking nurse lent the prisoners some books. After ten days, he was transported to Dülmen prison camp. The journey was unpleasant, as the prisoners were packed into cattle trucks, each containing forty men; each truck was supplied with a loaf of bread which had to last for the journey which took a day and a half. Unlike Burston, James Slessor was unimpressed with the inferior quality of the food: 'cabbage and turnip soup and only a kind of bread which was so badly made that it was similar to putty and stuck to the knife when it was cut'. Private Henry Davies, a 29-year-old dock clerk, was wounded on 8 August 1916 on the Somme at Guillemont and lay out for two days and two nights before he was captured. He asked his captors for some water and they refused; instead, they made him walk 2 kilometres before they gave him a drink. Davies was taken to a hospital at Orhdruf where his wound was treated. He was told that an X-ray was required on his wounded arm and that this would cost him ten Marks. 'I had no money, but an English officer paid for me.'[33] Davies was then transferred to a hospital at Langensalza where he remained until February 1917. He later moved to the prisoner-of-war camp at Cassel, where the cuisine was not to his liking: 'The food was scandalous, coffee (made of burnt oats), watery soup and black bread.' The Hague Convention stated that prisoners' rations should be identical to those of the soldiers of the hostile state.[34] However, the British naval blockade of Germany had an inevitable impact on the availability of wheat in Germany and bread rationing was introduced in 1915.[35]

The much-remarked antipathy by British prisoners towards German bread was shared by the German people. *Kriegsbrot* (war bread) was born out of Germany's lack of planning for a long war combined with the impact of the British blockade which led to grain shortages, including wheat meal and fats, and meant that substitutes such as potatoes and rye meal were used to bake bread.[36] The same could be said of the 'watery' soup. Food prices in Germany had doubled between 1914 and 1916 and the German government decreed that towns with more than 10,000 inhabitants should provide soup kitchens to guarantee that civilians had one warm meal a day. By 1917, 2,207 soup kitchens had been established in 472 towns throughout Germany.[37] While Germany had agreed to adhere to the articles of The Hague Convention regarding the provision of identical rations to prisoners as those which were issued to its own soldiers, the fact that German agriculture failed to cope with the demands imposed by the conditions of war and its inability to import vital fats and proteins meant that rations would be reduced. Research by Uta Hinz revealed that the German government had taken steps to reduce prisoners' rations as early as 1915 to retain as much food as possible for its army and population and to mitigate against the effects of the British blockade.[38] Germany's primary obligations were to its army and its people, and consequently the dietary requirements for prisoners of war enshrined in The Hague Conventions became an irrelevance. In March 1915, the *Liverpool Echo* published a letter allegedly written by 'a highly-placed official of the German government'.[39] The letter purported to be a response to an unnamed correspondent who had written to the official expressing concerns over Germany's treatment of its prisoners of war. The German official was unapologetic and stated that the blame for any crisis regarding the prisoners lay with Britain and that everyone 'from the Kaiser to the gutter-boy' was against prisoner exchanges, preferring instead to keep the prisoners in Germany to suffer like the German people. He accused Britain of attempting to curry favour with neutral countries by showing them how well it treated German prisoners. They were, he wrote, 'slobbering over our Germans in England – Well, we will be honest. We will show the world we won't slobber over English prisoners. No, they shall first starve – slowly but surely.'

The daily calorific content of German soldiers' rations in August 1914 was 3,100; this fell to 2,500 by 1918.[40] The dietary situation for German civilians was much worse. By 1917, civilians were receiving just 1,000 calories per day. However, due to fluctuations in the German harvests this figure rose to 1,400 calories in the summer of 1918.[41] It is highly questionable if British prisoners of war *ever* received rations identical to those of German soldiers.[42] Likewise, it would be wholly reasonable to suggest that some prisoners did not even receive the meagre daily calorific intake of 1,000 calories allotted to German civilians. In 1914, responsibility for the welfare of British prisoners held in Germany rested with the welfare committees which had been organised by the regular army regiments of the BEF, known as Regimental Care Committees. Individual committees provided comforts, parcels and support for their respective regimental prisoners; by 1915, ninety-three of these had been established in Britain.[43] The plight of British prisoners also provoked a massive voluntary aid response from the British public. In Liverpool, the Civic Service League, Liverpool Women's War Service Bureau, the Liverpool Branch of the British Red Cross and the Liverpool Irish Comforts Fund were among the list of diverse voluntary aid groups which provided much-needed assistance to the city's prisoners of war. Difficulties arose due to a lack of coordination between the groups and the government established a central coordinating body – the Prisoners of War Help Committee (PWHC). In a letter to the *Liverpool Daily Post and Mercury* in July 1915, Sir C.P. Lucas, chairman of the PWHC, outlined the objectives of the organisation, namely to facilitate the transmission of money, comforts and 'relief in kind' and to coordinate relief.[44] Still the problems persisted, and concerns were raised about the amount of wastage and the uneven distribution of parcels whereby some men were receiving an abundance of food and comforts while others received little or none.[45] Security was also an issue and the army voiced some apprehension that the parcels might contain information that was of use to the enemy. Misgivings remained about the PWHC's lack of authority to direct and coordinate the relief effort. The combination of these criticisms culminated in the creation of the Central Prisoners of War Help Committee (CPWHC).[46] The War Office had effectively handed over power and control of the prisoner relief effort to the Red Cross to run the CPWHC, thus removing the input of many of the cherished localised prisoners' aid groups who were familiar with the needs and requirements of local soldiers. This led to a public outcry and the government intervened in 1917 to instruct the CPWHC to include representatives from local prisoners' aid organisations.

Seven weeks after the Liverpool Irish had been captured at Guillemont, T.P. O'Conner attended a concert at the Exchange Hotel in Liverpool in aid of the Liverpool Irish Prisoners of War Fund. O'Connor announced that 'The 8th's Irish Committee had sent comforts to the men of the Liverpool Irish in German prisons by the ton.'[47] He warned his audience that nothing stood between the Liverpool Irish prisoners and 'sheer starvation' except the 'generosity, memory and gratitude of their fellow citizens'. Given German bureaucracy and the fact that prisoners were continually moving between camps it is unlikely that all the men received their parcels. Private John Burston, who was imprisoned at Dülmen and Wülfrath, did not receive any parcels until February 1917, six months after being captured.[48] A day after

O'Connor's visit to Liverpool, a wounded NCO from the Liverpool Irish who was recovering at Orhdruf hospital in Germany wrote to the Liverpool Irish Comforts Fund:

> I am writing a few lines on behalf of some wounded boys of the Liverpool Irish who are now prisoners of war and in a hospital in Germany. There is about fifty of them in this hospital with myself, and I can tell you that some of your gifts would be much appreciated by the boys.[49]

In September 1915, the Civic Service League in Liverpool had 500 prisoners of war on their books. According to a local paper, 'no other local organisation can approach the volume of its kindly effort on behalf of the prisoners'.[50] In one week, the League managed to send eighty-nine parcels from its Bold Street depot and eighty-nine bales of parcels to local battalions at the front, including the Liverpool Irish. Parcels included condensed milk, soup tablets, tinned fruit, bread, biscuits, clothing, soup as well as cigarettes and tobacco. Friends and family in Liverpool could, of course, satisfy Tommy's notorious affection for nicotine by placing an order with the British American Tobacco Company. They were priced at just eight shillings for 1,000 'Wild Woodbine' cigarettes, with a 'one shilling deduction for orders going to prisoners due to no cost for postage'.[51] During the war the British Red Cross and the Order of St John worked together. Through the Central Prisoners of War Committee, they coordinated relief for British prisoners of war. Every prisoner would receive an adequate supply of food and clothing. Parcels of food, each weighing about 10 pounds, were delivered fortnightly to every prisoner who had been registered. Each emergency parcel contained:

three tins of beef,
1/4 pound of tea,
1/4 pound of cocoa,
two pounds of biscuits,
two tins of cheese or loaf goods,
one tin of dripping,
two tins of milk,
50 cigarettes.[52]

The Germans were very much in favour of the provision of Red Cross parcels for their British prisoners, not least because they provided food and clothing, thus removing some of the burden from Germany's hard-pressed resources. The same might be said of the Red Cross uniforms, which began arriving at the camps in the spring of 1915. The uniform comprised a dark blue-grey jacket, trousers and cap, and these were supplied to some of the luckier prisoners.[53] The fact that the uniforms were ideal for modification into civilian garb did not elude the Germans, who ordered the camp tailors to sew coloured bands down the legs of the trousers. For a fee, some enterprising local photographers would visit the camps and photograph individual soldiers, which became postcards for their family and friends at home.[54] What could be more reassuring for a soldier's relatives (and the British public), than photographs of British prisoners like Private Lambert of the Liverpool Irish posing in his new uniform?[55] Lambert's uniform is clean and pressed, his boots are shining, he is even sporting a shirt and tie; hardly the image of a brutalised and mistreated soldier. No images of malnourished, abused, over-worked prisoners emerged from Germany during the war.[56]

As soon as practicable after being captured, British prisoners of war were separated, officers being sent to *offizierlarger*, while NCOs and other ranks were housed in *mannschaftslager*. For logistical purposes, many of the camps were situated close to railway stations to facilitate the delivery of prisoners. The wounded were sent to hospitals, where after treatment and depending on the severity of their wounds, other ranks might qualify for return to Britain through the prisoner exchange scheme. Those who had been less seriously injured and deemed fit were sent to a prison camp. Unlike their comrades from the ranks, officers did not have to work; they were expected to pay for their food and they could also have orderlies. There was a great deal of confusion surrounding the application of the raft of international and German military laws pertaining to the treatment of prisoners of war in Germany. Whenever these two sets of law conflicted, it was the articles of international law which were violated.[57] British prisoners were subject to the German Military Law Code Book of 1872, as well as the Military Courts and the Order on Discipline. To complicate matters further, Germany had an established hierarchy of responsibility to administer the Allied prisoners of war. The Prussian War Ministry was ultimately responsible for prisoners of war; this was then delegated to twenty-five District Commanders, and then came the commandants of the prison camps.[58] Both the District Commanders and the commandants enjoyed a large degree of autonomy and, as many prisoners discovered, much depended on the personality of individual commandants. Thus, the conditions and the treatment of prisoners within the camps were due to the camp commandants.[59]

Private James Slessor Liverpool Irish who was captured at Guillemont on the Somme in August 1916 and was held at Dülmen prisoner of war camp. *Thanks to the editor of* Stand To! Th *Journal of the Western Front Association for his kind permission to reproduce this image.*

Private Lambert Liverpool Irish wearing his Red Cross uniform complete with shirt and tie and shiny boots. The German authorities were more than happy to permit some British soldiers to be photographed for propaganda purposes. Unsurprisingly, there were no photographs of starving, beaten men in rags. *Thanks to the Australian War Memorial for their kind permission to reproduce this image.*

eutenant Walter Duncan, Liverpool Irish who was captured at Guillemont on the Somme in August 1916
d escaped from an officers prisoner of war camp at Ludwigshafen-am-Rhine in Germany in February
*18. *Author's collection*

Above: Dülmen prisoner of war camp. *Author's collection.*

Below: Photo of the Liverpool Irish entering Lille in October 1918. *IWM Q9574, Thanks to the Imperial W Museum for their kind permission to reproduce this image.*

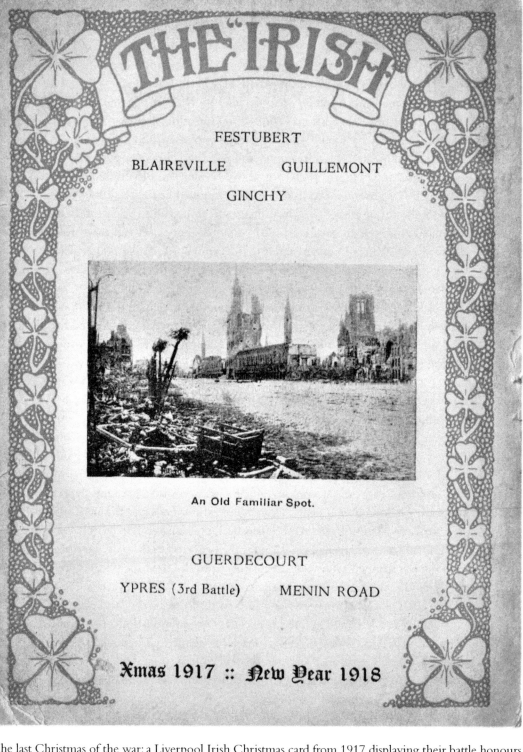

THE "IRISH"

FESTUBERT

BLAIREVILLE   GUILLEMONT

GINCHY

An Old Familiar Spot.

GUERDECOURT

YPRES (3rd Battle)   MENIN ROAD

Xmas 1917 :: New Year 1918

The last Christmas of the war: a Liverpool Irish Christmas card from 1917 displaying their battle honours around an image of the ruins of Ypres. *Author's collection*

Private John Burston had no complaints about the conditions at Dülmen camp. He described the accommodation as basic but clean, and that it remained so since two orderlies were detailed for that purpose.[60] Lieutenant Walter Duncan was moved from Cambrai to Gütersloh after being captured, which he described as being 'quite a good camp'.[61] Although Duncan did take exception to the camp interpreter, who 'gloated about the *Lusitania* and was very insulting'. He was then moved to Münden, 'an old disused oil factory which was absolutely filthy'. The *Kriegsministerium* degreed that Allied prisoners should be mixed within individual camps, the expectation being that mixed confinement would result in disagreements between the various nationalities.[62] Walter Duncan stated that Münden contained 600 Russian officers '(generally crawling with lice)', 200 French and 18 British officers. At Münden, Duncan found the Russians to be 'splendid fellows, but they varied very much'. He described the camp as not being fit for habitation, 'the sanitary arrangements were disgraceful, but there were baths which had to be paid for'. Bread was not included in the officers' rations and had to be paid for, otherwise, the rations were disgraceful. In any event, Duncan reported that 'we got our parcels fairly well' and that they were permitted to go on escorted walks on parole. In March 1917, Duncan was moved again, this time to Augustabad. The camp seems to have been a virtual paradise in comparison to the filthy factory at Münden, and Duncan was later placed in 'Lager A': a building which had been a hotel before the war. Recreational facilities included tennis courts and a football field, and a card system was in operation for walks on parole. The accommodation and sleeping arrangements were also a pleasant surprise: 'The rooms held 2–5 occupants. There were proper beds and the bed-linen was actually bed-linen.' In the winter prior to Duncan's arrival in March 1917, the commandant had given permission for the prisoners to skate on the frozen lake. This was stopped following complaints from the townspeople, compelling General von Stein to write to the commandant, who was, according to Duncan 'a decent old boy', ordering him to stop the skating and accusing him of being too lenient. Despite his excellent accommodation, an amicable commandant and the ability to stroll around the vicinity of Augustabad, Walter Duncan remained a prisoner and he was determined to escape; 'An escaping officer remembers that he is still a British officer and does all that is humanly possible to carry on the war in Germany.'[63]

Escaping was not an activity for the disorganised or the faint-hearted. As early as January 1915, the Prussian *Kriegsministerium* ordered that guards should open fire on any escapers following a single order to halt. [64] According to Walter Duncan, British officer prisoners were faced with two options: 'the alternative of settling down, and, by buying small luxuries, making himself as comfortable as the conditions in his camp will allow, giving the Boche no trouble, and not caring if his sentries are decreased. Or, he may, do what he can to carry on the war in Germany'.[65] Prior to his arrival at Augustabad, the inmates had constructed a tunnel which they had temporarily abandoned in the summer of 1916. The prisoners re-opened the tunnel again in October that year. The opening was sited beneath a disused room in the camp and ran beneath the canteen, then under a strip of ground, past the perimeter wire, under some out-buildings, eventually reaching an exit which was in an ice-house. In May 1917, seven officers escaped through the tunnel, all of whom were caught.[66] Following the escape, the Germans managed to locate and block the tunnel to prevent further use. They failed to do it properly and the British prisoners managed to re-open the tunnel by going around the obstacles placed by the Germans or by removing them. On 18 June 1917, Duncan and nine other officers escaped through the tunnel and set off on a trek through Mechlenburg towards the Dutch border. The men divided into small groups, Duncan being part of a four-man team.[67] British officers, coming from a sheltered, professional position in civilian life, may well have been able to read a map and to use a compass; they were not, however, experts in fieldcraft and living off the land. Duncan's account of his ten-day trek consisted of days lying-up in cornfields in the baking sun, being 'pestered with mosquitoes', and nights foraging for water, walking and trying to navigate in the dark while avoiding the locals. Then there was the sheer exhaustion of trying to exist on meagre rations. Duncan described one of his more enjoyable evenings when two other officers had gone off to forage, 'Meanwhile, we boiled two enamel cupfulls [*sic*] of water from the pond, murdering many tadpoles and other livestock which, when boiled, floated on the surface in swarms. Having strained these through a handkerchief, we thoroughly enjoyed our oxo.'[68] Duncan's quartet did not have to suffer for much longer. Dazed and exhausted, they were captured at the village of Benzin by three men who were convinced that Duncan's group were Russian soldiers. Their captors' suspicions were corrected when one of Duncan's group told the German men that they were British officers, and as proof he produced his service cap which he had brought with him in anticipation that just such a situation might arise.

Duncan's companions were much taller than he was, and in his unkempt, exhausted state, bent over and leaning on his stick, he looked nothing like an officer in the minds of his captors who treated the suggestion that Duncan was an officer 'as a great joke'.[69] Their arrest in Benzin also caused a stir in the village, and the local population turned out to view the prisoners at feeding time when a bucket of soup was delivered to the barn where they were being held. 'With the soup came the whole village to see "the pig-dog Englanders" being fed. Never, I suppose, had there been such excitement in the history of Benzin.'[70] Following his capture, Duncan was sent to Parchim where he was to spend the next three weeks. As punishment, he was told that he would be sent to solitary confinement for five months in line with similar sentences which had been imposed on German prisoners in England and an additional fourteen days for escaping. Fortunately, an agreement regarding reprisals was reached at The Hague in 1917, which meant that a much-relieved Lieutenant Duncan was released before his fortnight in solitary confinement was up.

All prisoners were not treated the same. On a hot summers day in July 1917 at Parchim camp, Walter Duncan witnessed a Prussian NCO making a group of Russian prisoners of war, wearing full uniform including great coats, being made to run around on the sand. He stated that he did not see this carried out with British prisoners.[71] Conversely, in his statement regarding his time at Dülmen camp, Private John Burston made no allegations of mistreatment; according to Burston, all nationalities were treated equally. Burston's *kommando* comprised ten British prisoners, the other forty being French and Russians.[72] 'A *feldwebel* was in charge, but he did not ill-treat us. There was very little sickness; if a man was sick he was allowed to see a doctor. I have no complaints to make about this place. There was no difference made in the treatment of the nationalities.' Any abuse or mistreatment of prisoners of war within the camps was dependent on the prejudices and personality of individual commandants. In some camps containing British prisoners of war, one historian observed, 'Not content with having '*Gott strafe England*' painted on the barracks, commandants did everything they could to help the Lord in punishing the English.'[73] Prisoners found ways to amuse themselves at the expense of the Germans. On his arrival at Ingolstadt camp in Bavaria in December 1917, Walter Duncan was struck by the offensive spirit which existed in the prison, where he discovered that 'there was complete unity against the Boche'.[74] The camp held over 100 French officers, thirty Russians and just twelve British officers. Being fed up with parades and forced to salute the Germans, the prisoners went on strike, which meant that German guards had to visit every room in the prison and count the prisoners. Two French officers, dressed as orderlies, removed German flags from their flag-poles, and as they could not be identified, no prisoner could be blamed. Not to be outdone, 'A British officer stole a most elaborate stop-clock for changing the sentries, a most valuable thing. He took the leather covering for boots and threw the rest in small pieces into the moat.'[75] If a civilian arrived at the camp, the prisoners stole his hat and left an envelope containing twenty Marks in its place. In December 1917, Duncan was moved yet again, this time to Ludwigshafen. Again, the prisoners went on strike after a French officer who had attempted to escape whilst en route to the tennis courts was banned from any further outings. Later, Duncan recalled a visit to the camp by General Siegal, an inspector of prisoner-of-war camps for the 2nd Bavarian Army Corps, who addressed the inhabitants in the camp. He urged the prisoners to 'behave as gentlemen', but he was 'much hooted' and there were cries of '*couchon*' (pig) and '*sale Boche*' (dirty German). 'He said he would come again.' Evidently upset by the abuse, the General did not return, so the British officers entertained themselves by bombarding him with letters reminding him of his promise and they also prepared a suitable reception for him should he ever return.

Conditions and the administration of the prisoner-of-war camps through-out Germany varied. There were very few 'good' camps. While all prisoners shared the ignominy of incarceration, officers arguably had a more comfort-able existence than their counterparts from the ranks. The major distinction between officers and men was that the officers did not have to work. Private James Slessor of the Liverpool Irish was put to work in a coal mine where he was paid one Mark (which equated to six pence) for ten days' work.[76] He regarded this as fair, given that some of his co-workers received nothing. Due to the pay and conditions in the mine, the prisoners went on strike and were duly punished by being made to parade in the open from five o'clock in the morning until noon with nothing to eat and very little clothing. It was winter and some of the men collapsed and lay where they fell before being removed 'none too-gently'.[77] Pay in the mines improved and the prisoners' wages rose to two Marks; however, the food remained poor. Some parcels from home began to arrive in the winter of 1916 and the standard of food in the camp improved, but the heavy nature of the work resulted in many of the prison-ers falling ill and being hospitalised. Slessor described how some prisoners endured harsh treatment when they were put to work cleaning out the hot chimney flues in the boiler-house at the mine. It was hot, stuffy work and the prisoners went on strike. They were then arrested and kept without food for a day by way of punishment. The foremen in the mines carried measuring sticks to gauge the amount of work which had been carried out each day. If the men failed to fulfil their allocated distance, the foremen used the sticks to beat their charges. Slessor's experiences of captivity deteriorated in the spring of 1917. He was transferred to another coal mine at Dortmund where the guards 'were very bad and everyone was punished for the least offence'.[78] He was then put to work in the blacksmith's shop where he had to use a large hammer with blistered hands. His spirits reached their nadir in 1917 after speaking to some newly arrived prisoners about how the war was progressing. 'We all began to lose heart and thought we were doomed to slavery and would never see England again. But with the parcels arriving we hoped on.'[79]

The unfortunate Private Charles Craddock of the 1st Battalion, Royal Welch Fusiliers had been captured in October 1914. The ex-miner from Birmingham had engaged in fights with German civilian workers and suffered mistreatment throughout his captivity. Early in 1917, he was at Minden camp with some men from Liverpool, including Private Cook of the King's Liverpool Regiment and Privates Crow and Foley of the Liverpool Irish. In all, some 200 British prisoners from Minden were sent to work at a coal mine. Despite being injured or sick, the *sanitäters* (paramedics) employed at the mine ignored the prisoners' appeals for medical attention, accusing them of loafing and ordering them down the mine shaft. Illness was not accepted as an excuse for any prisoner who failed to meet his quota of work and men were punished with prolonged shifts until the prescribed amount of work was completed. 'Private Cook and Private Crow of the Liverpool Irish were punished in the same way. No extra food for this; no meat at this time, grass soup and potatoes and peelings all boiled together.' The combination of heavy work, injury, mistreatment, lack of nutrition and proper medical care inevitably took its toll on the men. Craddock, who struggled through his time at the mine and was suffering from an open and 'running' leg wound, stated, 'Five died altogether while I was there. Private Foley of the Liverpool Irish was one who died.'[80] Even in death British prisoners were denied any modicum of dignity. At the end of his post-repatriation interview, Private Henry Davies insisted on making an additional comment in which he described the macabre ordeals he had experienced during funerals of British prisoners of war who had died in the camps:

> There is one thing I should like to add and that is about funerals. When any of our men died the Germans used to open up the bodies and then put them in a very thin wooden box and we had to carry them to the grave. It was beastly, as the blood used to drip out as we went along.[81]

Occasionally, the Germans provided prisoners with an opportunity to sabotage its domestic war effort. Private Henry Davies of the Liverpool Irish was hospitalised in Germany until February 1917 after which he was moved to Cassel camp in March.[82] He was put to work without having been medically examined and he attempted to explain to the Germans that he was incapable of work. As a crude incentive, the Germans warned their prisoners that anyone who refused to work would be sent to the Russian front. Davies was then sent to work on the land, installing drainage pipes to enable the inhabitants to grow corn. The work provided the prisoners with an opportunity to participate in sabotage. 'We managed to break a great many of the drain pipes before putting them in and we raked up the corn.'[83] Later, the local burgomaster told Davis that the land drainage undertaking had failed. The art of malingering came easily to British soldiers, and British soldiers excelled themselves while in enemy hands; Private Davies proved to be no exception. He managed to aggravate his wound by rubbing mustard into it. He was returned to Cassel; however, his relief was to be short-lived and he was ordered back to work within a day. This time he was sent to a salt mine. After just three hours, Davis threw down his pick, refused to work and demanded to see a doctor. He was given three days' rest before being sent to a sugar beet factory at Wabern, where he worked alongside 250 prisoners of war and 100 civilians. Henry Davies stated that he was guarded by 'boys', as every German of military age had been called up. Despite his injury and the fact that he was forced to work, Davies made no complaints about mistreatment and stated, 'The punishments at all the places I was at were the usual: confinement and dark cells.'[84]

Excluding death, there were three ways out of a German prisoner-of-war camp during the war: internment in a neutral country, by being exchanged and by escaping. Second Lieutenant Spargo sustained a severe wound to his left arm during the attack at Guillemont on 8 August 1916. After being captured, he received medical attention in a German field hospital in France where his arm was amputated; he was then transported to a German hospital at Göttingen near Hanover. Unlike most British officers in captivity, Willie Spargo had no friends or relatives in England; he was from South Africa and therefore was at a disadvantage given the length of time involved in sending and receiving letters and parcels from his home in Cape Town. Spargo wrote to the London office of his former employer, The Giant Mines of Rhodesia, asking for food and clothing to be sent from England. Unsurprisingly, given that his letters were censored by the Germans, Spargo's postcards and letters home contained no criticisms of the German medical staff: 'the Drs [*sic*] and nurses are very good to me, so cheer up and look forward to my return'.[85] Within days of his operation, Spargo wrote home expressing his hopes that he would soon be exchanged. Willie Spargo's optimism was misplaced; he soon discovered that the rules of prisoner exchanges meant that officers did not qualify for exchange. He did, however qualify for internment in Switzerland

and he was moved as an internee to Switzerland in December 1916.[86] Installed at the Palace Hotel in Mürren and away from the prying eyes of the German censor, he wrote home informing his sister of his good fortune: 'I am now out of Germany and thank heavens for it.'[87] A few weeks later, he moved to the Victoria Sanatorium in Berne to have an operation on his arm. Writing home to his mother, he asked her not to send any more food parcels as he was being well fed and well looked after in contrast to his medical experiences in German hospitals: 'This place is kept by Swiss nuns and they are so kind, how different from the German hospitals I was in.'[88] In another letter to a female friend, he blamed the Germans for the fact that he needed another operation; 'the Huns made a mess of my arm'. He also informed her that he would not be home in South Africa any time soon as 'officers do not get exchanged'.[89] His injury notwithstanding, Spargo was fortunate to have received medical attention and to have been spared the hardships, lack of food and tedium of incarceration of the prisoner-of-war camps in Germany.

Private Henry Davies, who had spent most of his time as a prisoner of war refusing to work, infecting his arm or sabotaging German agricultural schemes, was exchanged in May 1918. No doubt the Germans were glad to see the back of him. His return to England did nothing to dispel his loathing of the Germans. Back in Liverpool, Davies took exception to the contents of sympathetic letters which had been published in support of some local women who had been convicted of corresponding with the enemy. Henry Davies was clearly in no mood to forgive and forget when he wrote to the *Liverpool Echo* in August 1918:

> I was working as a prisoner of war with German civilians for a couple of years and the kind of message Germans would have in the ground for us was 'Englander swinerine' [*sic*]. No doubt your correspondents mean well, but I am convinced that while we are letting our soft hearts get the better of us, they are laughing up their sleeves. Those of us who have been in German hands have seen the kind, gentle, squareheads come out of their barracks with drawn revolvers and bayonets against defenceless men asking us to show our British pluck by singing 'Tipperary'. We are not likely to forget it. – '*Deutschland unter alles*'.[90]

The hardships endured by Lieutenant Walter Duncan during his doomed foot-slog across Germany did nothing to diminish his ardour for escaping. His 'trek' had taught him that preparation was key. He also learned that carrying a weighty, bulky rucksack was not conducive to the art of escaping. While

Duncan was at Ludwigshafen-am-Rhine, he discovered that a few French officers and one British officer had been able to escape by using the German rail system, and that they were able to do so without having been able to speak German. Duncan enrolled in a German language class which was run by a French officer who was a fluent German speaker.[91] He was taught basic German 'railway' phrases including: how to buy a ticket, how to ask which platform he should use, and how to ask if he needed to change trains. Duncan began assembling the various accoutrements necessary for his proposed journey to neutral Holland without yet knowing exactly how he was going to get out of the camp. He managed to acquire and alter a set of civilian clothes. He was already in possession of a short black coat which the Germans had somehow failed to remove after his failed escape. He made himself a waistcoat from a German blanket and altered a French orderly's overcoat which he shortened and dyed blue. To complete the ensemble, he obtained a soft felt hat which he purchased through a bribed sentry, a white shirt, a black and white tie and a pair of brown kid gloves. His escape equipment included a railway guide which had been smuggled in by a French officer, two compasses, one bought from a Russian orderly, the other having been smuggled to him in one of his parcels. He also had two maps, one of which was a detailed street plan of Aachen, and 300 German Marks. Normally, prisoner-of-war camps had their own currency due to the likelihood of German Marks being used for escape purposes. Duncan managed to obtain his Marks when he was imprisoned at Ingolstadt where camp money had ceased being used due to counterfeiting.[92] He had also put aside some escape rations: a bottle of fifty Horlick's malted milk tablets, two tins of meat lozenges, a few ounces of grape nuts and a flask of rum.

Walter Duncan's opportunity to escape came on 3 February 1918 when Major Shewan of the Royal Dublin Fusiliers, who was the last of four British officers to be exchanged from the camp, was preparing to leave. Duncan noticed that Shewan did not have a lot of luggage, whereas Duncan was in possession of a large box.[93] The usual camp routine during the exchange process was that the officer's luggage went outside the camp to the orderly room where it would be searched in his presence, sealed and then sent on to him in Holland. Duncan set about re-labelling his own box with Major Shewan's name; he also devised a locking mechanism whereby he could lock and unlock the box from inside. Two British orderlies were detailed to bring Major Shewan's luggage and leave it outside the orderly room pending the usual search. Duncan acknowledged the bravery and assistance of the orderlies, 'it was to a great extent due to the help of the senior of them that I was able to escape'.[94] The orderlies carried the box

(Duncan was by now upside down inside it) and put it onto a handcart, which was then pushed towards the orderly room. As it was outside the camp, the orderlies were under armed guard. They then placed the box on the pavement outside the orderly room and brought some of the major's other luggage inside. The sentry went with them. Prior to leaving, one of the orderlies gave Duncan's box a kick, indicating that no one else was in the area. Duncan undid his lock, got out of his box and walked around the corner attired in his splendid hand-made civilian garb.[95]

Being a Sunday, there were fewer people on the streets and Duncan decided to begin his train journey from Mannheim rather than Ludwigshafen as there was less likelihood of any soldiers from the camp being there and recognising him. He walked across a bridge over Rhine in search of the train station. His initial route was from Mannheim to Frankfurt, an overnight journey which meant that he would not be 'seen prowling about a town after midnight'.[96] He would then travel from Frankfurt to Cologne and go from there to Aachen. After some difficulty in finding the station at Mannheim, Duncan passed his first German language test at the booking office, '*Frankfurt zweiter eifach bitte*'. He received his ticket and went off to board his train. He chose a non-smoking compartment to avoid any conversations about cigarettes and matches. He had bought a book and an illustrated paper, neither of which he could read but they served their purpose in helping him to ignore everyone else on his travels. Duncan managed to conceal his lack of German by simply mumbling replies or just grunting when anyone spoke to him. It was, however, his lack of German etiquette which almost led to his undoing: 'on one occasion when I gave up my seat to a lady on a train, I ought, of course, to have offered it to her husband'.[97] Duncan arrived at his final train station at Aachen in the afternoon, but he chose not to try and leave the town in daylight and he walked around the town until he found a cinema. Once inside, he removed his compass which had been sewn into a handkerchief and was disappointed to find that despite it being luminous, he was unable to read it. He left the cinema to try and expose the compass to as much sunlight as possible. His theory worked; when night fell it functioned perfectly. At dusk, Duncan made his way to the outskirts of Aachen. He left the road and entered the fields and hid among some trees where he removed his white collar and waited until it was dark. From his position, he could see several fields and a copse in the distance leading off towards the Dutch frontier several kilometres away. Duncan began to crawl, never more than 20 yards at a time. Whatever noise he created attracted the attention of some sentries who shone a light into the fields but failed to see him. 'To make matters worse, the moon rose and lit up the fields to such an extent that if any sentry had been near I should certainly have been seen.'[98] By four o'clock in the morning, Duncan had reached a railway embankment and by examining its direction and seeing a village on the other side of the line, he was convinced that he was now in Holland. While walking along the railway lines his attention was drawn to a sign which caused him some doubt; 'In the faint light, I read what I took to be the dreaded word "*Verboten*". Later, I ascertained that the word was the Dutch "*Verboden*".'[99] He then spoke to a railway worker who confirmed that he was in Holland. The friendly Dutchman brought Duncan to his home where he gave him a meal. He was then taken to a Dutch frontier post and later to the British Consul at Rotterdam.

Walter Duncan made it home. He arrived in London on 16 February 1918 where he was received by the King four days later. After being given three months' leave, Walter Duncan joined the reserve battalion of the Liverpool Irish at Oswestry before taking up an appointment with the Home Intelligence Staff at Birmingham. He was only there for a few months before falling victim to the influenza epidemic in December 1918.[100] Private James Slessor did not get to mingle with royalty, but he recalled the joy of repatriation and the pageantry of his homecoming a few weeks after the Armistice. He returned to England aboard a converted German ship with 2,000 fellow prisoners; as the ship sailed up the Humber, Slessor was evidently delighted by the welcome:

> What a reception! There were about 2,000 on the boat and we all manned the rigging. We proceed down a double line of warships, seaplanes and airships droned overhead, and on reaching our berth, such a din from all the steam whistles. The reception from the crowds on the quay was most gratifying.[101]

There would be no fanfare or glorious welcome for Private William Aspinall of the Liverpool Irish. Even if there had been, it is doubtful whether he would have noticed or cared. Private Aspinall was repatriated to England in October 1918, just eighteen days before the Armistice. He did not go to his home in Northumberland Street; instead he was whisked off to the Royal Victoria Hospital at Netley in Hampshire as a mental patient.[102] The first event of repatriation for the former guests of the Kaiser involved military bureaucracy and lots of it. Having been cleaned, the former prisoners were given clothing, identity documents and travel warrants. Arguably, the most pleasant experience for the men was the reckoning of back pay. In their eagerness to get off on their period of leave for two months, it is unsurprising that few men opted to wait remain for two or three additional days to attend a medical board and apply for a pension. The majority accepted the £2 gratuity which acted as a disclaimer that the soldier was not suffering from any disability incurred during the war. Throughout the 1920s and 1930s, many men would come to regret this decision. During these two decades, the mortality rate for former prisoners of war was five and a half times greater than other veterans.[103] While regimental associations and Old Comrades groups flourished in the post-war years, there was little appetite for reunions among the former prisoners of war. Incarceration was neither glorious nor exciting; it was humiliating, arduous, tedious and often cruel. There were no medals won inside the German prison camps, nor were there any accounts of individual heroism in the press. Complaints about prisoner ill-treatment, work and poor food paled into insignificance compared with the slaughter on the battlefields. Besides, a new age was dawning, and Britain was attempting to improve its relationship with Germany. Pacifism and the notion that perhaps old Fritz might not have been as black as he was painted were cultivated during the 1930s. Lieutenant Walter Duncan did not live to see or read about such changes in attitudes. There is no way of knowing if he would have been persuaded by these sentiments. He did, however, record his own opinions of the Germans just before his death in 1918:

> Suffice it for me to say that, before being taken prisoner in August 1916, my experience of the character of the German was derived almost entirely of hearsay; but during eighteen months of captivity I have seen much of him with my own eyes and have lived under his rule. And now, from the somewhat vague hatred that the average Britisher had of him and his methods, I have developed a bitter loathing, which no subsequent acts or conduct of his can in one slightest degree diminish.[104]

7

HOMEFRONT

Newspaper coverage of wars from the Crimea to the Boer War throughout the nineteenth and early twentieth centuries informed and occasionally influenced British public opinion (albeit in a restricted fashion) on their country's foreign conflicts. The Great War, however, was, according to Niall Ferguson, 'the first media war'.[1] The unquestionable requirement for censorship and secrecy in wartime inevitably led to tensions between the propagandists' need to inform and bolster public opinion while simultaneously shielding them from the realities and horrors of industrial warfare. The Press Bureau, newspaper editors and their journalists colluded to ensure that no information likely to be of use to the enemy was published. Many historians of the Great War have suggested that a 'conspiracy of silence' existed during the war, whereby the public had to be shielded from the callousness of the Western Front, and therefore knew little of the realities of trench warfare.[2] The theory that the brutal realities of war were deliberately hidden from the British public has been given some credence by a famous quote made during a meeting in 1917, when Lloyd George remarked to C.P. Scott, editor of the *Manchester Guardian*, that:

> If people really knew, the war would be stopped tomorrow. But of course, they don't know and can't know. The correspondents don't write, and the censorship would not pass the truth … The thing is horrible beyond human nature to bear and I feel I can't go on with the bloody business: I would rather resign.[3]

Lloyd George, for all his faults, was speaking the truth about the 'truth' in relation to the national press. Moreover, official war correspondents at the front, such as Philip Gibbs, were both unable and unwilling to report the horrors of war. Like their national counterparts, local Liverpool newspapers did not have their journalists at the front. Therefore, they adhered to their patriotic duty and published official press reports of the military engagements and battles on the Western Front. However, complying with the Press Bureau and the government's directives did not mean that the local press abdicated its responsibility to inform their respective readerships of the experiences of local soldiers. Editors of local newspapers were fully mindful of the individual geo-graphical, social, ethnic and political communities within the city of Liverpool. Editors also understood their obligation to provide the news-hungry inhabit-ants within those communities with war articles, reports and editorials which conveyed the experiences and contribution made by individual communities in Liverpool towards the war effort. This included letters and accounts from soldiers which detailed their actions, experiences and events at the front.

The Liverpool (Irish) Battalion was just one of the many battalions which comprised the city's own King's Liverpool Regiment. Despite assuming the collective and unifying identity of the regiment, local battalions, whether reg-ular, territorial or New Army, retained their individual character and status within their respective communities in the city. Throughout the war, local newspapers acknowledged the importance of community identity and the need to inform their respective readerships in Liverpool of how their men were enduring the conflict on the Western Front. In his research on how the war was reported in Liverpool, Michael Finn dismisses the 'conspiracy of silence' theory, which argues that the brutalities of war were hidden from the public by the conspiracies of press barons and the government.[4] According to Finn, the local Liverpool press did not confine itself to reporting the major events and operations in the various theatres of the war; rather, they sought out and received unadulterated accounts of trench warfare from the men serv-ing with local battalions.[5] After the Battle of Festubert, survivors from the Liverpool Irish were eager to reassure their relatives that they were unscathed or that their injuries were not severe. They also felt compelled to relate their experiences of the battle, which were then reproduced in the local papers. In June 1915, the *Liverpool Echo* reproduced a letter from Private George Henry of the Liverpool Irish, who had written to his mother from a hospital near Norwich. Oblivious to his racist simile, he wrote:

> I found myself facing a towering Prussian. He howled for mercy, and made a feeble pass at me, but all the mercy he got was six inches of cold steel through the chest. The bodies were lying six feet deep and the groans of the dying rent the air. Deeds of heroism were performed in hundreds. One of our stretcher-bearers, a lad of eighteen, was working like a nigger while bleeding from half-a-dozen wounds:[6]

Another Liverpool territorial struggled to describe his dilemma as to whether he should have killed a wounded German. His letter, filled with short sentences, reveals how he was affected by the sights he had witnessed on the battlefield and his ordeal in trying to come to terms with what he had endured. There is nothing hidden in his graphic account:

> I found many wounded and unable to move. But the dead! The sight is in my eyes now. It was horrible. I can't describe it on paper. Heads had been smashed in and some of the poor devils had been torn literally limb from limb. In fact, every horror you could imagine that shell-fire could do, our shells had done. One wounded German as soon as he saw me, cried 'Mercy, comrade!' It's all very fine, one can't do anything to a wounded man, but what mercy do they show our men in similar circumstances?[7]

Given the need for secrecy surrounding British battle casualties, it is surprising that the *Liverpool Echo* chose to reveal the extent of the losses suffered by the Liverpool (Irish) Battalion at the Battle of Festubert in June 1915.[8] On 30 June, the paper published a full list of the battalion's casualties including the names and regimental numbers of the dead, wounded and those missing in action.[9] The sacrifice of the 8th Liverpool (Irish) Battalion at Festubert received a special mention in the *Liverpool Catholic Herald*.[10] Equating the bravery of 'an Anglo-Irish Regiment' with that of the prestigious Irish Guards, the paper went on to compare Captain Finegan's last words with those of the heroic Irish Jacobite, Patrick Sarsfield.[11] The *Herald*'s praise continued: '254 Irishmen, many of whom have never seen the land of their fathers, shed their heart's blood that day in order that the reputation for furious and incomparable valour might be preserved'.[12] In July 1915, Major Benson of the Liverpool Irish addressed a nationalist meeting in aid of comforts for the battalion. Praising the men at the front, he described 'the modest behaviour of the wives and sisters who on asking for names of the killed and wounded actually apologised for giving him trouble', adding that 'these people were not duly appreciated'.[13] A more visible representation of the physical effects of industrial warfare was the appearance of casualties. As early as August 1914, sightseers along the Mersey could observe the hospital ships as they made their way into the port of Liverpool, where the wounded would be unloaded prior to transfer to any of the forty-eight auxiliary hospitals throughout Lancashire.[14] Mrs McGuire was at New Brighton on the Wirral when she saw a grey ship bearing a 'big cross' steaming into Liverpool. Her daughter Ada wrote, 'She said she nearly wept – It seemed to bring home the pitilessness of it all.'[15] Also in 1914, William McIvor, then a 12-year-old boy, accompanied his father who was a car owner and volunteer driver, in assisting in the transport of wounded soldiers from Birkenhead railway station. 'In many cases the men had come straight from the front line. It was my first sight of casualties, serious and otherwise and my reaction of feeling utterly sickened and shocked, was, I suppose, natural.'[16] Occasionally, a shaft of light broke through the gloomy press reports. In September 1915, Corporal Connor of the Liverpool Irish was convalescing in Beckett's Park Hospital in Leeds. Connor had been a member of a bombing party at La Bassee 'when he was rendered deaf, dumb and blind by the bursting of a high-explosive shell'.[17] While in hospital, his bed had been placed near a door, the 'banging' of which caused a counter-shock and his speech and hearing were restored. The report stated that his eyesight was gradually returning. After the exploits of the Liverpool Irish at Festubert in 1915, some commentators recognised the unique qualities of the Anglo-Irish soldier. The *Liverpool Catholic Herald* parroted a theory by Professor Mahaffy of Dublin University, which extolled their characteristics, arguing that, 'the finest of our race are the children of a native Irish and an Anglo-Irish parent. Certain it is that the glorious charge of the Liverpool Irishmen may vie with the most gallant achievements of the Irish Guards and the Dublin or Munster Fusiliers. "One in name and in fame is the sea-divided Gael".'[18]

Liverpool was not only the home city of the twenty battalions which comprised the King's Liverpool Regiment; it was also home for the thousands of soldiers who had enlisted in various other regiments and branches of the army. For the fortunate few who had been granted leave, their time away from the front or their barracks provided a welcome release from the rigours of trench warfare or the pettiness and routine of camp life. Whether seeing family members, meeting old friends or just enjoying the freedom to do whatever they wanted, for the men of the BEF leave was a much-coveted experience. Despite the inevitable disciplinary consequences of being absent without leave, some Liverpool Irish soldiers were unable to resist the temptation of a few more days at home and availed themselves of the easy opportunity to unofficially extend their leave. In August 1915, Harry Boniface and his friend Alfred Halliday, of the Liverpool (Irish) Battalion, could not wait for the official award of leave and they subsequently absconded from Weeton Camp at Blackpool.[19] They were caught hiding in a goods wagon at Crewe. At their court hearing, they told the magistrate that they 'just wanted to get to Liverpool'. A month later, two more soldiers from the Liverpool Irish appeared in court at Ormskirk charged with being absentees.[20] The *Echo* reported that, 'One of the Irish stated that he got drunk with some of the "bhoys" and really did not know where he was.' The men were remanded for military escort and their police captor was awarded five shillings in respect of each of the men.

In December 1915, Private William Sweeney, 8th (Irish) Battalion, King's Liverpool Regiment appeared before Liverpool magistrates where he was sentenced to two months' imprisonment for assaulting a plainclothes police officer and a further month for breaking the officer's umbrella.[21] Sweeney, an absentee from the battalion, said, 'I lost my head, but I did not break the umbrella. It was broken through the officer giving me a blow to the head.' He had been apprehended earlier on 20 December, but he managed to break free from his military escort. Explaining the domestic reason for his actions, Sweeney told the magistrate that he intended to come to court every week and gave his reasons: 'My idea in deserting this time was to prevent the payment of the home allowance. I am not going to keep two families.' Unmoved by Sweeney's unexplained domestic circumstances, the magistrate ordered that, after Sweeney had completed his sentence in Walton jail he was to be handed over to the military authorities.

By 1915, the British army was undergoing the transition from a relatively small professional expeditionary force to a large wartime volunteer army. Public opinion had also changed; ambivalent Victorian and Edwardian attitudes towards soldiers had evaporated as the families and friends of the citizen volunteers in khaki rallied to offer their help and support. The local press also adopted a more sympathetic approach towards Tommy even when he went astray. In August 1915, the *Echo* reported on the spectacle confronting visitors to the Liverpool Police Courts, 'Every morning a considerable number of soldiers – brought there for having over stayed their leave of absence'.[22] The paper estimated that the courts were dealing with between ten and fifty absentee soldiers every day. However, the paper was keen to stress that the reasons for the soldiers' absence was not related to drunkenness. Rather, it was 'the result of an unconquerable desire to spend a few hours longer with wife and dear ones before returning to duty'. The paper also questioned the practice of granting a reward of five to fifteen shillings given to police officers for apprehending absentee soldiers, which had 'bred an undue keenness in "soldier catching"'. Having made further enquiries, the *Echo* reporter was informed that rewards were only payable to those officers who 'detected' absentees as opposed to those who merely reacted to receiving information that a soldier was absent from his unit. The paper remained unconvinced by this argument:

> There is a feeling that this offers an inducement to policemen to keep a close watch on soldiers on leave, so they can benefit financially by 'running in' any Tommy who they find has remained at home longer than the time allowed him, and some people think that rewards in such cases ought not to be given.

Describing the treatment of absentees as 'harsh', the article went on to suggest that if soldiers were left to their own devices they would return to their units of their own volition. Far from supporting the authorities in their efforts to apprehend absentees, some members of the public intervened to assist soldiers who were attempting to escape from their military escorts. In 1916, Private James Green of the Liverpool Irish was recovering from the wound he received at Festubert. Green was sent to Oswestry where he was subsequently detailed to perform military escort duty:

> While me and Hewitt were in camp, before he went to France, we used to be sent on escort duty to Liverpool to bring back deserters and absentees. There was a Sergeant, me and Hewitt, we had side arms and handcuffs and we had some exciting times when we came out of Dale Street Police Station. The prisoners were trying to escape and the crowd helping them, we used to have to handcuff them. Then it was a long journey back in the train, often the prisoners escaped and then the Sergeant would be reduced to the ranks.[23]

Pat O'Mara witnessed the impact the war was having on his own Liverpool Irish enclave in the summer of 1916. When news reached Liverpool that Lord Kitchener ('a sort of God among the slummies') had been killed, O'Mara went for an evening walk; 'The streets were pitch black, and though the *Echo* and *Express* tried to bolster the people's courage, the terrible lists of killed, wounded and missing in the papers could mean only one thing – we were getting licked.'[24] His sense of despondency failed to improve as he met friends and neighbours from his tightly knit Irish enclave:

> Had I heard of Fox's death in France that morning? No, I hadn't. I passed on. Next it was quiet Mrs Hasty, who used to share our shack in Pitt Street, drying her eyes as she came up Nelson Street. Had I heard of Mr Hasty's death in France? Willy Hasty's death – amiable Willy Hasty who had given me pennies and saved my mother many a beating? I passed on. Next it was Mrs Thomas, telling me of Peter's death. Husbands, fathers, sons, that night was awful in such revelations. Mr Fox, Mr Hasty and Peter Thomas. I could still see them as they had swirled off a short time before, looking very clumsy in their new khaki, down to Lime Street Station. Now they were dead; they would never return to the neighbourhood. Drama came in spurts like that; usually four or five neighbourhood casualties reported at the same time.[25]

Later in 1916, the citizens of Liverpool joined their countrymen in being able to see what life was like on the Western Front. In the weeks following the attack of the Liverpool Irish at Guillemont on the Somme in August 1916, the people of Liverpool were given an opportunity to see moving images (moving, in more than one sense) of the preparations and consequences of the Somme offensive which had been filmed the previous month. The film, *The Battle of the Somme*, was seen throughout the country by an estimated 20 million people; their reactions to the screenings 'ranged from shock and outrage to admiration'.[26] There is no doubt that the film was a pioneering example of war cinematography; for the first time, British audiences were able to see not only the build-up to the battle, but actual footage of the wounded and the dead. News of the film circulated around the city generating a great demand for seats in the two Lime Street cinemas, the Palais de Lux and the City Picture House, as well as the Prince of Wales Picture House in Clayton Square.[27] Far from being hidden, the families and friends of the Liverpool Irishmen were not only aware of the 'realities of war', they were confronted by them. The extensive casualty lists, soldiers' letters, the arrival of hospital ships and trains, and more poignantly perhaps, as the 'Liverpool Irish slummy' observed, the absence of husbands, fathers and brothers imparted a highly visible representation of the reality and human cost of the war. The Liverpool Irish contribution to the war inspired a correspondent to the *Echo* to suggest that the Tories and Liberals on Liverpool Council should 'sink their differences' and ask the Irish Party members of the council to select a 'suitable man' for the position of Lord Mayor of Liverpool. He concluded:

> I am sure they could find a suitable man and it would let the people of our country, not Liverpool alone, see that we have sunk our bias because we are at war. If the Irish are able to go to the front in our battlefields, why not the front in civic life?[28]

A remarkable feature of the First World War was the enormous contribution made by ordinary people towards the voluntary aid effort. The Western Front and the Home Front were inextricably linked throughout the war. The English Channel became a conduit for the vast array of letters, parcels, newspapers, soldiers, nurses and comforts, crisscrossing their way between England and France. 'Comforts' included a variety of items most of which the army did not supply, including balaclavas, knitted mittens, musical instruments and footballs. The army certainly provided food; however, the ubiquitous bully beef and hard tack biscuits challenged even the most undiscerning palates. It is therefore unsurprising that the soldiers appreciated any additional treats from home which enhanced their rations. These gifts were sent to soldiers by either family members or friends, or by one of several local voluntary aid groups in Liverpool. Newspapers, letters and gifts not only kept the men informed of life in their native city but provided tangible evidence that they were appreciated and were not forgotten.

Liverpool responded well to the numerous appeals for comforts for its soldiers, whether at the front or in captivity.[29] Civilian volunteers from St Francis Xavier Catholic Church began collecting for the Catholic Hut Flag Day in December 1914. The *Xaverian* reported, 'The Catholic Hut Flag Sunday, like so many other Sundays this year, was a rainy day. But the Children of Mary Volunteers undertook the collection and did valiantly in the pouring rain. We were sorry that their neat little baskets had such a drenching.'[30] The ethnic core of the Liverpool (Irish) Battalion hailed from the deprived working-class districts in the north end of the city. Unlike their more affluent counterparts in the prestigious 6th Rifles and Liverpool Scottish battalions, the families and friends of the Liverpool Irishmen lacked the means to send any 'luxuries' to their men at the front. In her research on the 10th Liverpool Scottish Battalion, Helen McCartney observed that the traditional role of the officers and NCOs within the battalion to provide practical assistance to their men had been negated since anything that the men required could be obtained from their middle-class families and friends at home.[31] The economic disparity and status of the battalions was acknowledged by a local paper on 2 July 1915:

> We have all read with a thrill of admiration of the gallant exploits in the field of the 8th Irish. All Liverpool is proud of the Irish lads, but we understand in the matter of parcels of 'comforts' and 'extras' they are faring much less sumptuously than other battalions at the front, such as the Rifles and the Scottish. Most of the Irish boys come from poor homes and have few well-to-do friends. That may be a good explanation of the neglect, but it is not a good reason for it. It is a reason rather for a co-operative effort to rescue the reputation of the city from the suspicion of ingratitude. There should be no Cinderella among the fighting units of the Liverpool Regiment.[32]

The Liverpool Irish community moved to rectify the situation on 21 July 1915. An executive committee was formed to provide comforts for the

'Cinderella' Liverpool (Irish) Battalion. Alderman Austin Harford presided at the inaugural meeting at the Exchange Hotel where he announced that he had received £200 in subscriptions.[33] Harford worked tirelessly throughout the war to raise funds for the Liverpool (Irish) Battalion. In August 1915, an appeal was also made by the editor of the *Xaverian* for comforts for the '8th Irish lads who are in the firing line' due to the fact that so many members of the battalion were members of the church.[34] The following month, the Liverpool Irish Ladies Committee dispatched '50,000 cigarettes, 1,000 packets of tobacco, a large quantity of matches, and considerably over half a ton of chocolates, biscuits, cake, sweets, potted meats, fish, etc'.[35] In February 1916, two signallers from the Irish wrote directly to Alderman Harford, Chairman of the Liverpool Irish Committee, expressing their gratitude for the comforts they had received. 'You can just imagine the pleasure it is to us to come out of the trenches, after enduring much hardship and necessary discomfort, to find almost invariably, selections of your gifts awaiting us for distribution.'[36] Having apologised for the battalion's recent absence from the limelight, through 'no fault of their own', the unnamed signallers asked for one gift in particular: 'To make things "tray bon" [*sic*] the signal section particularly ask for the gift of an accordion to help us in our marches and entertainments.'

In Liverpool, the Irish community busied themselves organising concerts, fetes, flag-days and special Masses to help raise funds to purchase comforts for their battalion. In September 1915, Mr Hugh Shaw and Miss Kathleen Byrne organised a garden party at Cooper's Grounds in Green Lane.[37] The band of the Liverpool (Irish) Battalion entertained the large crowds with 'patriotic airs' and the cry of 'house full' came too early for some late arrivals. All of the money collected at the party went to the Liverpool (Irish) Battalion, 'who are in need of much that would lessen the hardship of life in the trenches'. The following month, Liverpool Football Club donated £10 to provide footballs for the battalion.[38] The Liverpool (Irish) Battalion were not forgotten by the women of the Whitstable and Tankerton Branch of Queen Mary's Needlework Guild. In October 1915, the Whitstable branch included the battalion when they distributed 1,800 garments to the town's soldiers and sailors.[39] Some of the more astute members of the battalion were keen to exploit the fact that they had two sources of 'comforts'. In February 1916, Private Parkinson wrote to the local Whitstable paper asking for the gift of a football 'from such a kind and homely people'.[40] A few months later, Sergeant Garrity wrote to Mr Headicar in Whitstable asking for some socks: 'I have about a dozen men in need of them'.[41]

Occasionally, men from the reserve battalion of the Liverpool Irish based at Blackpool organised events to raise funds for the Liverpool Irish Comforts Committee. In May 1916, Major J. J. Smith, who was in temporary command of the battalion, wrote to Miss Clancy, the Honorary Secretary of the Liverpool Irish Committee, which was responsible for sending comforts to the battalion. Thanking her for the comforts and parcels which had been sent to the front, Major Smith wrote, 'I am sure you would be fully recompensed for all your trouble and hard work could you see their satisfied, happy faces when they receive their share. We sincerely appreciate all you have done for us.' The reserve battalion of the Liverpool Irish based at Blackpool also raised funds through a concert and whist drive, after which the adjutant, Captain Harvey Duder, sent £40 to the committee.[42] On Sunday, 24 September 1916, a special service was conducted in the Catholic Pro-Cathedral at Copperas Hill in the city in honour of the officers and men of the Liverpool (Irish) Battalion.[43] Local worthies, including the Protestant Lord Mayor, T.P. O'Connor, aldermen, the Belgian Consul and several officers of the Liverpool Irish including Captains Keating and Murphy, formed a procession at the Adelphi Hotel. The band of the Liverpool Irish led the parade to the cathedral which was 'taxed to its utmost holding capacity' to hear Father Bernard Vaughan praise the battalion:

> Here in Liverpool they were all proud of the 8th (Irish) Battalion, whose history went back to 1857, and whose members, when war was declared, rallied to the flag and leapt like swords from their scabbards to the King's aid.

Father Vaughan informed the congregation that the purpose of the service was to raise funds for the men of the Liverpool Irish who were serving at the front and for those who had been taken prisoner. He told them that the money was to be used to purchase 'what was euphemistically described as comforts, but what were really the bare necessities of life'.[44]

St Patrick's Day celebrations provided obvious opportunities to instigate appeals on behalf of the city's Irish soldiers. In March 1916, the *Liverpool Echo* published a poem entitled 'An "Echo" Tribute' encouraging its readership to support the Irish Flag Day:

> Will ye buy a flag of Ireland?
> Will ye buy an Irish Flag
> For the honour of St Patrick on his Day?
> Faith, I wish I'd kissed the Blarney

When I visited Killarney
Then I'd surely coax a copper from your pay,
Irishmen are in Fireland,
Where the dreary moments drag,
They're fighting German devilment to stay;
But we want ye to remember,
As ye burn your Lenten Ember
Your duty to the soldiers far away.[45]

Celtic emblems and symbols were important in reinforcing the identity of the Liverpool Irish. In March 1917, the Lord Mayor held a civic reception 'arranged with all the favourite emblems of Ireland' in honour of St Patrick and for wounded Irish soldiers in Liverpool.[47] Programmes were produced 'in green lettering on shamrock shaped leaves'. The reception was a very Irish affair; a military band played 'a selection of Irish pieces' and the Mayor's children performed an Irish jig. A few months later, Thomas Ryan, an affluent Liverpool Irish businessman and managing director of the Buxton Lime Firms, presented the Liverpool (Irish) Battalion with a 'splendid Irish wolfhound "Desmond"'.[48] Three years of appeals by the numerous civil voluntary aid organisations coupled with rising food prices inevitably affected the resources of the people of Liverpool. In November 1917, Austin Harford announced that despite appeals having been made in Liverpool over the course of a year from November 1916 to November 1917, for comforts for the Liverpool (Irish) Battalion, the amount raised was insufficient to purchase Christmas presents for the men. It was decided that a Bohemian concert would be held in the Exchange Hotel to remedy the situation.[49]

In 1917, the Lord Mayor of Liverpool, Dr Utting (later Sir John Utting), wrote to several Liverpool worthies asking for assistance in raising funds for those agencies in Liverpool who were dealing with supplies for prisoners of war to enable them to continue their work. Utting instigated an appeal to be known as The Lord Mayor's Million Shilling Fund. Sir Archibald Salvidge, boss of the Tory-Orange Liverpool Workingmen's Conservative Association, devised a plan to organise a tombola, which in turn led to the grand tombola (or lucky bag).[50] Prizes ranging from a first prize of £1 per week for life down to a week's holiday expenses for two persons were offrered, and the proceeds from the sale of tickets were devoted solely to the Prisoners of War Fund. The tickets were 2s 6d each, and the offices of the Conservative Association were besieged daily by crowds of eager applicants for tickets. No fewer than 516,840 tickets were sold, raising £61,296 for the fund. The success of the fund and the aid it provided to prisoners and their families is perhaps a happy irony given that it was the brainchild of Archibald Salvidge, the *bête noire* of the Catholic Irish in Liverpool. It is highly unlikely that the large numbers of the Liverpool (Irish) Battalion captured on the Somme in August 1916 and incarcerated in Germany would have been insulted by the source of their gifts and comforts. The fund continued its work after the Armistice to assist repatriated prisoners of war. In 1921, the fund gave £272 to widows and dependents, £1,769 towards sickness and convalescence, and paid £3,427 in maintenance costs.[51] In 1920, the fund had 176 beneficiaries; however, demand for assistance among former prisoners grew and this number rose to 545 in 1923. Despite the number of claims from the fund and widespread support of the local population, there is some evidence that events in Ireland may have influenced the actions of two female conductors employed by Liverpool Tramway.[52] In May 1918, P.J. Kelly, an Irish nationalist politician and trade union activist, investigated a case where two female members of the Municipal Employees Association in Liverpool had been dismissed for being 'pro-German' after failing to sell tickets in aid of the Prisoners of War in Enemy Countries Fund. When the women were interviewed by their manager, he asked whether they would prefer to be under German rule, and both replied 'yes'. Sam Davies has suggested that their actions were motivated by Irish nationalist sympathies.[53]

Three years of appeals by the numerous civil voluntary aid organisations coupled with rising food prices inevitably affected the resources of the people of Liverpool. The families, friends and neighbours of the men serving with Liverpool (Irish) Battalion displayed their loyalties to the British war effort and their hostility towards those whom they perceived as supporting the enemy or abdicating their obligations. The first demonstration of Liverpool Irish anti-German violence occurred in 1915. The sinking of the *Lusitania*, 'the Pride of Liverpool', by a German U-Boat on 8 May 1915 resulted in a weekend of violent Germanophobic riots in the Irish districts of the city inhabited by many of the ship's crew. Pat O'Mara had just returned home from sea. Clad in his new 'American tailored suit' he was on his way to a dance in St Martin's Hall when he heard the paper-boys yelling out the news that the *Lusitania* had been sunk.[54] Walking along Bostock Street, he noticed that nearly every house had drawn their blinds; 'All those little houses were occupied by Irish coal-trimmers, firemen and sailormen on the *Lusitania*.'[55] Yet the rioting which took place throughout various districts of the city was not initiated in, or confined to the areas of, Scotland Road and Vauxhall. Press reports on Monday, 10 May described the disturbances which had occurred during the weekend following the sinking; headlines told of 'Liverpool's Anger – German Shops Wrecked' and 'Exciting Scenes'.[56] The *Liverpool Daily Post and Mercury* claimed that the trouble had originated in Walton before spreading throughout the north end of the city. 'Saturdays trouble started in Walton Lane, Pork butchers' shops were wrecked systematically from Mile End to Rice Lane, a distance of two miles.'

Another paper described the anti-German riots in the city as 'raids', which had been on 'shops bearing Teutonic names and largely devoted to the pork business'. During the disturbances, the police had arrested sixty-seven people who were brought before the stipendiary magistrate at Dale Street police station. A few days later, a correspondent to the *Echo* described the scenes on Scotland Road:

> First, a crowd of boys rushed down Scotland Road, yelling and hooting. Everyone watched them with amusement: the whole neighbourhood in fact, was en fete. In Great Homer Street, a large crowd, the front ranks of which were children, and the leaders of which seemed to be women, were laying siege to a shop. Every few minutes a stone would go through the window and the children would sing 'Three cheers for the red white and blue'.[57]

Although the *Liverpool Catholic Herald* refused to condone the rioting, the paper claimed to appreciate the 'extenuating' circumstances which had driven those friends and relatives of the *Lusitania*'s crew, who lived in the 'Catholic portion of the city'.[58] The paper argued that the relatives of the dead crewmen 'cannot be expected to be too particular in the methods they select for securing that their indignation shall be fully appreciated'. The fact that the riots had originated in F.E. Smith's Walton constituency provided the *Catholic Herald* with the opportunity to confer a sectarian character on the rioters. The report alleged that the rioting 'overflowed into Everton and Kirkdale, two other strongholds of Toryism and Orangeism'. Amid the lurid accounts of destruction some humour managed to emerge. Having ransacked a warehouse belonging to a German provision merchant in Moor Place, the crowd armed themselves with hundreds of sheep's trotters and made off towards a German shop in Richmond Row. 'A German woman when her shop was bombarded with bricks, treated the enemy to a vigorous, and by no means ineffective, fusillade of pig's cheeks, but in the end, she was conquered by superior numbers.'[59] The looting and attacks on businesses escalated and became indiscriminate. The *Courier* described crowds 'who, in their passionate resentment against all things Teutonic, have not been able to distinguish between friends and foe'.[60] However, in the tightly knit Irish enclaves of the city, everyone knew their neighbours; moreover, they knew the shops and businesses and they knew their owners. Pat O'Mara joined the rioting mob on its rampage down Scotland Road when the crowd decided to attack suspected German businesses in other parts of the city. The mob made its way to Yaag's butchers in Great Georges Street. O'Mara knew Mr Yaag, the owner, and remembered him as 'a big wholesome fellow' whose only 'crime' was the suspicion that he had been born in Germany. For a crowd bent on extracting revenge, mere suspicion was enough. Affability and wholesomeness, or the fact that two of Mr Yaag's nephews were serving with the Liverpool (Irish) Battalion, proved inadequate grounds for leniency. O'Mara described the attack on the unsuspecting Mr Yaag and his shop: 'As we converged on the big shop, Mr Yaag, arms akimbo and thinking some urchin was fleeing from aeroplane Joe, came out, pipe in mouth and with his usual broad smile. This vanished instantly as someone kicked him in the belly and a volley of bricks went in the huge windows.'[61] Press reports on the extent of the damage caused to Yaag's shop stated that every window 'from floor to roof being smashed to atoms'.[62]

In the aftermath of the riots, a widowed Irish lady received a threatening postcard. The postcard had been sent by an anonymous, over-zealous local patriot acting on the mistaken assumption that she was a German. The widow's son, a colour Sergeant with the Liverpool Irish, sent a terse public response to the perpetrator through the letters column of the *Echo*:

> Perhaps you would permit me to denounce through your columns the absurd fanaticism of some person, who has wisely preferred to remain anonymous, and who has written an unsigned postcard to my ill and widowed mother of Irish nationality (absolutely and beyond question), with four sons serving with His Majesty's forces, to the effect that being a German, she would be served in the same manner as the pork butchers were being treated. The Germans are brave in their cruelty. There is one thing worse than that – it is to be cowardly in cruelty; and if I would dearly like to have a five-minute interview with the scoundrel who wrote the postcard I have referred to. That is denied me, and the only course open to me is to make my denunciation as public as possible.[63]

Liverpool's status as a major port and 'Gateway of the Empire' meant that the city's inhabitants were well accustomed to the sight of foreigners, sailors and otherwise, on the streets. The declaration of war had imbued the citizens of

Liverpool with a heightened need for vigilance. The destruction of Belgium and the sinking of the *Lusitania* generated an atmosphere of Germanophobia, and local authorities were understandably keen to apprehend any foreign individual who had failed to register themselves as aliens. Given the prevailing xenophobic atmosphere, predictably the Police Courts in the city were occupied in dealing with unregistered aliens. However, there was the odd moment of levity, unsurprisingly involving an Irishman. In June 1915, a local paper reported a case when an 'American' was brought before the magistrate.[64] The paper described what happened when the defendant was asked to spell his name: 'The American prisoner (with measured deliberation) M–C–G–R–I–S–K–E–N'; the magistrate obviously failed to pay attention to the spelling and asked the prisoner if he was Russian. The prisoner replied, 'Me? No, I'm an Irishman, born in Tyrone (laughter).' He then went on to inform the court that he was a naturalised American and, according to the paper, his claims were justified due to his Irish brogue and the fact that his first name was Patrick. In his defence, Patrick McGrisken told the magistrate that he had 'brought horses home for the Empire, anyhow, and having done my duty, I should like to go home again'. Having promised to register as an alien immediately, he was allowed to go free.

It is undeniable that many in the Liverpool Irish enclaves followed Redmond's brand of constitutional nationalist leadership and ratified his appeal to support the British war effort. One minor, yet significant, event which took place in Liverpool in November 1915 might provide a plausible response to the unasked question as to what the reaction might have been if the city's eligible Liverpool Irishmen had ignored or rejected the call to arms in 1914. By 1915, it became apparent that the voluntary recruiting system had failed to provide enough recruits to meet the demands of industrialised warfare. Lord Derby's National Registration Scheme (also known as the Group Scheme) was introduced in October 1915 to urge men of military age to 'attest' for military service. The scheme did not apply to Ireland; however, the *Liverpool Echo* alleged that when the registration cards were issued in England that 'it was well known at the time, there was a flight of the Irish to their native country' and that they failed to submit their registration cards when they returned to England.[65] Lord Wimbourne, Lord Lieutenant of Ireland, sent a 'personal' recruiting circular to all Irishmen of military age. While these recruiting initiatives encouraged some Irishmen to enlist, others opted for emigration to non-European destinations.

In October 1915, a total of 3,735 men of military age left the United Kingdom, of whom 990 stated that Ireland was their home country.[66] On the morning of 6 November 1915, a group of 600 Irishmen who had arrived in Liverpool en route to America made their way to the Cunard offices to collect their tickets for the voyage on board the *Saxonia*. Such an event would normally go unnoticed in Liverpool; after all, the Irish had used Liverpool as their transatlantic port of choice for more than a century. But this was wartime, and the sight of able-bodied Irishmen of military age allegedly abdicating their obligation to defend their country and families from German aggression invoked the disgust and anger of patriotic Liverpolitans. Hostile crowds gathered and surrounded the Irishmen near the Cunard offices, taunting them with shouts of '"Traitor!", "Coward!", "Germans in disguise!"'[67] The crowd then rolled sheets of paper into hard knots and pelted the would-be passengers. Individuals were singled out and questioned about their nationality, and someone shouted, 'Their motto is God save Ireland, but they won't save it themselves.' The *Echo* report denounced the passengers as 'Sinn Feinners' [*sic*] and described the sheepish behaviour of the men when they were approached by army and navy recruiting staff. Having collected their tickets, the passengers walked off in the direction of Covent Garden harried along by a 'hooting crowd'. Unfortunately, for the Irishmen, they were met by another crowd who blocked their path and forced them to perform an about-face and run the gauntlet back along the road.

The crew and stokers of the *Saxonia* met with the captain and stated that they would refuse to sail if the emigrants were permitted to board the ship. Cunard officials then announced that they would not issue tickets to any man of military age wishing to leave the country. The *Liverpool Daily Post* provided a more measured account of the incident, unlike others.[68] The *Post* stated that the hostile crowd which had confronted the 'runaways' was largely a Liverpool-Irish affair. While critical of the emigrants, the paper admitted that it did not know whom to admire the most; the stokers, or the Cunard officials, or 'the enthusiastic Liverpool Irishmen and Irishwomen who put – or tried to put their would-be absconding countrymen to the blush'. This might explain why Charles Diamond's *Liverpool Catholic Herald* modified its usually fervent defence of *all* things Irish. 'We can, of course, have no words but of condemnation for any young Irishmen who, realising what the effect of their flight would be upon the cause of Ireland, have attempted to leave the country at the present time.'[69]

The advanced Irish nationalists of 1914 still clung to the ancient rebel adage that 'England's difficulty is Ireland's opportunity'. Thus, they remained immune from any suggestion of embarrassment that they were guilty of treason. Nor were they unduly perturbed that by colluding with Germany they were vicariously aiding the German soldiers facing their own countrymen across No Man's Land on the Western Front. In the years preceding the war,

Liverpool had witnessed the expansion of many Irish nationalist and Gaelic organisations. By and large, the political allegiance of their respective memberships was grounded in constitutional nationalist doctrines espoused by the Irish Parliamentary Party. The significance of the rise of Irish nationalist groups in Liverpool had not gone unnoticed by members of the Irish Republican Brotherhood (IRB), whose revolutionary brand of nationalism advocated that physical force was necessary to secure Irish freedom. Although numerically inferior compared with their constitutional counterparts in Liverpool, IRB members attempted to infiltrate Gaelic cultural and sporting organisations in the city. Their main objective was to secure prominent positions thereby enabling them to convince others of the righteousness of a more belligerent form of nationalism. Except for the frequent sectarian Orange and Green clashes, the relationship between the Liverpool Irish nationalists and the wider populace in the city might be described as 'civil'. As a mark of respect on the death of Edward VII in 1910, the United Irish League flew the Irish flag at half mast from its building in Liverpool. Michael O'Laoghaire, an IRB member, took exception to the gesture; 'We objected to this and four of us set out to remove it. We were beaten up and did not succeed in taking down the flag.'[70]

While some Liverpool Irish nationalists had converted to the physical-force element in the city, others, like Joe Gleeson, had been born into it. 'I was born in Liverpool of Irish parents. My father was a Fenian and my uncles were Fenians.'[71] Gleeson, along with Piaras Béaslaí, joined the Gaelic League which they used as a 'recruiting ground' for the IRB. Piaras Béaslaí, born Percy Frederick Beasley, was the son of the editor of the *Catholic Times*.[72] He was educated at St Francis Xavier school in Liverpool and his family later moved to Wallasey. Beasley became fascinated with the Irish language and Celtic mythology, and after working for the *Wallasey News* he moved to Ireland in 1906. During his time in Ireland he immersed himself in Celtic culture and literature; he also Gaelicised his name and joined the IRB. When the Irish Volunteers were formed in 1913, Béaslaí was one of sixteen IRB men on its Provisional Committee. The recollections of a number of IRB veterans living in Liverpool at the time of the Volunteer split in 1914 are remarkably candid about the numbers of Liverpool Irishmen who, having rejected the atavistic revolutionary idealism of the IRB, left the Volunteers and enlisted in the fight against Germany. By the winter of 1914, IRB had been decimated. According to Joe Gleeson, just four companies remained: 'Liverpool, Bootle, Seaford and Rockferry, and there were roughly between 50 and 75 in each company'.[73] Frank Thornton provided an even lower estimate; 'after stocktaking', Thornton believed that they had just twenty-five men at Duke Street and the same in Bootle.[74]

Undaunted by lack of numbers, the remaining IRB men occupied themselves by establishing a firing range in the basement of Cahill's shop in Scotland Road. Their other activities included gun smuggling; however, things did not always go to plan:

> Joe Gleeson and myself had a box of rifles on top of a taxi on our way to Garston Docks. Then going down London Road, Liverpool, our taxi got involved with another car and hit a tram standard in the centre of the road; the usual crowds and police gathered and Joe Gleeson, as quick as lightning, hailed another taxi, tipped a policeman on the shoulder and said:'Hey, mate, give us a hand to get this box on the top of this other car, we are in a hurry to catch out boat at Garston'. Two policemen, Joe and myself tilted the box of rifles from the wrecked taxi on to the second car and off we went to Garston and safely deposited our stuff in the boat: that was sailing that night.[75]

In January 1916, Piaras Béaslaí, now installed as vice-commandant of the 1st Battalion of the Dublin brigade, visited Liverpool to deliver a cipher containing details of a shipment of German arms and ammunition bound for Ireland aboard the *Aud*.[76] However, Béaslaí was not always so surreptitious when visiting Liverpool. Frank Thornton recalled one of Béaslaí's previous visits:

> To my amazement, Pierce [*sic*] stepped off the Wallasey Ferry Boat in full Volunteer uniform. We then proceeded to walk up Water St. into Dale St., past the CID (Police Headquarters) and on to Duke St. We passed hundreds of soldiers and naval men on our way; on every occasion everybody came smartly to attention and saluted Pierce [*sic*], thinking he was wearing the uniform of one of their corps. Pierce [*sic*] delivered his lecture and we escorted him back to the ferry and he arrived safely home. Pierce Beasley [*sic*], it appears, came over every day in uniform and travelled free on boats, trains, etc., as an officer of their (British) Defence Forces.[77]

Following the death of the old Fenian leader O'Donovan Rossa in July 1915, the Irish contingent of the IRB ensured that his dead body did not touch English soil on its transit from America via the port of Liverpool. Frank Thornton and his men arranged for a Dublin Steamship boat to pull alongside the St Paul in the Mersey. The IRB men then carried the body from Prince's Landing Stage to the Nelson dock 'on Irish shoulders'.[78] The Liverpool contingent, comprising forty men, escorted the body to Dublin and paraded in the funeral cortege.[79] At the 'ticket only' interment in Glasnevin cemetery, the brotherhood had the privilege of hearing Padraig Pearse's revolutionary graveside oration when he mocked the British as fools and eulogised on the need for a blood sacrifice.[80]

The sacrifice came on Easter Monday, 24 April 1916, when approximately thirty-seven Liverpool men who had been billeted at Kimmage Camp joined their counterparts in seizing various landmarks around Dublin. As reports of the Rising reached Liverpool, the press and nationalist politicians voiced their outrage. An unfortunate journalist from the *Liverpool Echo* who planned to spend his Easter weekend on holiday in Dublin found that his trip had been somewhat curtailed.[81] He was, however, ideally placed to convey the Dubliners' reaction on the Rising to the *Echo*'s readership. 'Unmitigated censure and the strongest condemnation of this outburst of malicious folly was heard everywhere. The epithets of "fools" "blackguards", "Germans".'

The *Evening Express* reported that 'loyal Irishmen in Liverpool are most emphatic in their condemnation of the revolt in Ireland'.[82] On 2 May 1916, Austin Harford presided over a meeting of the United Irish League being held in Liverpool, where he proposed a motion, 'That this meeting of the Liverpool and District Committee of the United Irish League, speaking on behalf of the Irish Nationalists of Liverpool, Bootle, Birkenhead and South west Lancashire, places on record its strongest possible condemnation of the insane action of a small section of irresponsible Irishmen in Ireland during the last few days.' Harford did not mince his words; denouncing the Rising as a 'treacherous outrage upon Ireland and Ireland's cause,' he went on to reaffirm the UIL support for John Redmond, leader of the Irish Parliamentary Party and to invite Redmond to address a public demonstration in Liverpool, a city which was, he claimed, 'the chief stronghold of Irish Nationalism in Great Britain'.

According to Harford, the membership of Sinn Fein in Liverpool was small, insignificant, unrepresentative and irresponsible. Despite this, he was scathing about their contribution towards Irish nationalism in the city; 'These men counted for nothing in Liverpool except mischief, and that they were never able to do.' He went on to dismiss the Rising as being nothing more than a 'glorified form of Larkinism', adding that Irishmen were simply waiting for the end of the war and were looking forward to a new self-governing Ireland. Harford argued that those men who had interfered with this position 'must not think that their names would be included on the roll of Ireland's martyrs and patriots'. A few days later, the same paper published an account of how German soldiers taunted Irish soldiers about the Rising and how the Irishmen reacted. The information was supplied by Major Willie Redmond in a letter to his brother John Redmond, in which he described several notices which the Germans had put up in their trenches:

1. Irishmen! In Ireland's revolution English guns are firing on your wives
    and children. The English Military Bill has been refused. Sir Roger
    Casement is being persecuted. Throw away your arms. We will give you
    a hearty welcome.

2. We are Saxons. If you don't fire, we won't.

3. Irishmen! Heavy uproar in Ireland. English guns are firing on your
    wives and children.

According to the report, the Irish soldiers replied by singing 'Rule Britannia'
accompanied by mouth organs and melodeons.[83]

There are no references to the Rising in the War Diary of the Liverpool
Irish. The battalion was still basking in the compliments from the army's
senior commanders and the glowing press reports from home following their
spectacular raid on the German trenches one week prior to the Rising. The
historian of the 16th (Irish) Division argues that the Rising did not impact
on the division's morale or fighting abilities, but that some believed that the
Dublin rebels had stabbed them in the back.[84] Beyond the Rising, the political paths of the native Irish and Liverpool Irish diverged. At the polls, the
Liverpool Irish stayed faithful to what remained of the IPP, and they continued
to re-elect Harford and O'Connor. Just a few advanced nationalists emerged
from the Liverpool Irish enclave to play a relatively minor role in the Rising,
yet the significance of the Rising and the strategically important presence of
the clandestine Liverpool Irish republican underworld would come to the fore
during the post-war revolutionary conflicts in Ireland.

APPENDIX 1

Names of 143 members of the parish of St Francis Xavier church Everton serving with the 8th (Irish) Battalion, King's Liverpool Regiment, December 1914

R. ARMSTRONG
THOMAS BARRY
THOMAS BEDSON
FRANCIS BELL
JOHN BOOKEY
THOMAS BRENNAN
F. BROPHY
WILLIAM BRYNES
CHARLES BURNS
PETER CANAVAN
JOSEPH CAREY
WILLIAM CAREY
R. CARR
THOMAS CHURCHILL
JAMES CLARKE
THOMAS COSGROVE
JAMES COUGHLAN
THOMAS COWLE
ROBERT CRAWFORD
E. CROSSTON
E. CUDDY
THOMAS CULLEN
VALENTINE CUMMINS
H. DILLON
NICHOLAS DUFF
JOS DUGGAN
JOHN EDWARDS
THOMAS EDWARDS
J. ESTLIN
WILLIAM ESTLIN

EDWARD FITZGERALD
E. FITZSIMMONS
W. FLYNN
JAMES FOOT
THOS FOSTER
PATRICK JOS. FRENCH
MICHAEL GALLAGHER
JOHN H GALVIN
WILLIAM GRACE
THOMAS GRIFFITHS
W.M. GRIFFITHS
GEORGE HAINES
H.Y. HAINES
PETER HAINES
JOSEPH HALPIN
WILLIAM HARDEN
W HARRISON
THOMAS HELSBY
ALFRED HENNESSY
HENNESSY
ALBERT EDW HOBART
JAMES HOWE
JOSEPH HOWE
CHRISTOPHER HUGHES
JAMES HUGHES
JOHN HUGHES
THOMAS HUGHES
JOHN HUNT
INGHAM
H. JOHNSON

JOHN JOHNSON
SAMUEL JONES
EDWARD JOSEPH
THOMAS KEARNEY
JAMES KEATING
J. L. KELLY
JOHN KELLY
JOHN KELLY
LEO KELLY
M. KELLY
DANIEL KIRWAN (JUN)
DANIEL KIRWAN
JOS KRUGER
EDWARD LAFFAN
JOHN LAFFAN
PETER LAFFAN
WILLIAM LAVAN
JOHN LEDSON
FREDERICK LIMB
JOHN LIVINGSTONE
PATRICK J LONG
SIMON LYNN
FRANCIS MAGUIRE
WILLIAM MAGUIRE
A. MANLOND
W. MANLOND
J. MASON
EDW MAYLOR
WM. McANDREW
JAMES McCANN
JOHN McCANN
JOHN McCANN
RICHARD McCANN
PATRICK McCARTHY
JOHN McDERMOTT
HUGH McDONNELL
STEPHEN McGINNITY
JOHN McGREGOR
THOMAS McGUIRE
JAMES McNAMARA
THOMAS McQUILLIAM
JAMES McSHANE

G. McTIGHE
THOMAS MELIA
JAS. MELLING
J. MIDDLETON
R. MIDDLETON
W. MIDDLETON
PATRICK MOLLOY
RICHARD MORGAN
THOMAS MULCAHY
WILLIAM MURPHY
AIDEN MYTHEN
MICHAEL MYTHEN
JAMES NOLAN
THOMAS NOLAN
SAMUEL O'KEEFFE
J. PELOS
JACK PRESTON
REGINALD PRESTON
WILLIAM RAINFORD
F. REILLY
JAMES RIGBY
T. RILEY
LEWIS JOS ROBERTS
RICHARD RUDDY
THOMAS RUSH
GEORGE RUTLAND
ELIAS RYLANDS
FREDERICK SCHERGER
J. SHANNON
JOHN SHANNON
PATRICK SHANNON
F. SIMMONS
S. J. SIMMONS
WILLIAM STEEN
W. THOMPSON
GEORGE THURSTON
PATRICK TURNER
STEPHEN WALSH
H. Y. WHITE
JAS. WINTERSCALE
DANIEL WOLGER

Source: Compiled from *Xaverian* Magazine, December 1914

APPENDIX 2 ·

Details of 100 men of the 8th (Irish) Battalion, King's Liverpool Regiment. Address is Liverpool unless otherwise stated.

Key:

CQMS	Company Quarter Master Sergeant
DCM	Distinguished Conduct Medal
DOW	Died of Wounds
FGCM	Field General Court Martial
GSW	Gun Shot Wound
KIA	Killed in Action
MIA	Missing in Action
POW	Prisoner of War
RAMC	Royal Army Medical Corps
RASC	Royal Army Service Corps
V.D.	Venereal Disease

Name	Age/Rank	Number	Address	Occupation	Transferred	Casualty	Prisoner
Ashworth, William Rothwell	27 Pte	343952	Torr St.	Not known	Labour Corps 1917	No	No
Baker, Gregory	19 Pte	4572	41 Birkenhead St.	Docker	Labour Corps 28/8/17	No	No
Beardman, David Victor	21 Pte	3624	70 Beacon Lane	Warehouseman	RFA 25/6/15	No	No
Birch, Thomas Alfred	17 Pte	2007	61 Aubrey St.	Plumber	No	No	Yes 1/8/16 Dulmen
Blair, Harold	21 Pte	5350	50 Penny Lane	Iron Monger	Labour Corps 16/11/17	Debility 40% disabled	No
Blanchfield, Richard	33 Pte	4102	43 St. Anne St.	Not known	RASC 4/12/18	Yes. GSW to shoulder; 20% disabled	No
Bowker, Leonard James	20 Pte	3162	76 Edgeware St.	Driver	No	KIA 3/8/16	No

Brennan, Joseph	32Pte	4567	Coaticook, Quebec, Canada	Driver	No	Executed	Alias William E. Clark, FGCM Desertion. Executed. Pawtucket, US Citizen.
Bretherton, John	25 Pte	5419	9 Kemmel St.	Porter	No	KIA 11/1116	No
Brinnen, James	33 Pte	3452	Macdonald St.	Engine Driver	the RE 31/1/17	No	No
Brophy, Richard	22 Pte	4194	Hanover Square	Millworker	No	KIA 8/5/16	No
Brown, Joseph	25 Pte	28149	9 Anthony St.	Not known	Discharged	Ill health 16/7/15 Heart disease	No
Burgess, Walter Ernest	31 Pte	1621 & 4175	121 Field St.	Not known	the RE 17/1/17	Demobilised 16/6/18. Died 20/12/18	No
Burke, James	26 Pte	4710 & 201787	Cambridge Tce.	Labourer	Labour Corps 13/6/17	No	No
Burns, Alexander	30 Cpl.	2679	21 Duke St.	Ship's Fireman	No	DOW 26/9/16	No
Campbell, John	18 Pte	1617 & 305157	55 Kew St.	Labourer	6th King's	No	No
Carr, Thomas DCM	36 CQMS	305750	63 Clapham Road	Wheelwright	No	No	No
Carroll, Patrick	27 L/Cpl.	5479	11 Cowper Road	Bricklayer	Conscript 15/3/16	KIA 14/10/16	No
Christie, John	27 Pte	68778	4 Hardy St.	Blacksmith	MGC 17/10/16	No	No
Comish, Harry	21 Pte	2758	20 Garrick St.	Painter	No	KIA 11/9/15	No
Corbally, Bernard	19 Pte	2502	4 Rock St.	Labourer	No	KIA 2/8/16	No
Croft, John	26 Pte	4621	14 Mela St.	Dock checker	Deserted 1915; later joined RE in 1917.	No	No
Davenport, Frederick Alfred	19 Pte	5330	33 Chrysoston St.	Clerk	RE 1919	No	No
Davies, Edward	19 Pte	2949 & 305906	51 Lower Breck Rd., Anfield	Shop Assistant	No	No	Yes. 8/8/16 Minden
Doran, Patrick Daniel	18 Cpl.	87659	19 Eldon Place	Labourer	MGC 6/2/17	No	No. Irish-born Annalong, Co. Down
Duggan, Michael	23 Pte	5550	77 Phythian St.	Ship's Cook	No	KIA. Was MIA 17/9/16, but his body was found 14/11/16	No. Irish-born Kilkenny. Also sick with V.D
Dummett, William	21 Pte	4487	15 Kirkland St.	Dripping Maker	No	Died (meningitis) at Blackpool 29/12/15	No

Evans, Daniel	19 Pte	4156	Upper Milk St.	Seaman	No	Died (pneumonia) at Aldershot Hospital 8/11/16.	No
Fagan, William	17 Pte	1834	Kitchen St.	Printer	Attached to 5th King's	KIA 8/8/16.	No
Farrar, Roger	19 Pte	4151	26 Longfellow St.	Driver	No	KIA 25/12/16.	No
Finlay, William Hugh	25 Pte	5428	23 Cropper St.	Painter	Attached to 5th King's	KIA 16/8/16 at Guillemont.	No
Fitzpatrick, Joseph	21 Pte	305485	175 Commercial Road	Carter	No	GSW left thigh. Returned to Whitstable after the war.	No
Flynn, William	17 Pte	1944	Everton Road	Sawyer	No	Discharged as unfit 15/1/15.	No
Galvin, Patrick Joseph	22 Pte	30891	70 Eldon Place	Docker	MGC 15/3/17	Discharged as unfit 17/7/18.	No. Conscript
Garside, Joseph	19 Pte	3569	103 Sutton St.	Labourer	5th King's	KIA 8/8/16.	No. Released for work at Harland's Engineering Works, Manchester 14/2/16
Gill, James	28 Pte	4749	56 Richmond St.	Labourer	No	Shrapnel wounds to hip and hands. DOW Glasgow 23/10/16.	No
Gill, William	19 Pte	5333 & S/419394	4 Tancred Road	Clerk	RASC at own request 27/7/18	No.	No
Green, John	17 Pte	1697	18 Craven St., London Road	Labourer	Trench mortars 18/2/16	GSW hand 8/8/16 and GSW face 22/12/17.	No
Greenall	28 Pte	494975	84 Argos Road	Timber Labourer	Labour Corps 24/12/17	No.	No
Hall, Thomas	18 Cpl.	1731	90 Rishton St.	House Painter	No	Shrapnel wound thigh and shoulder 8/8/16.	Yes, in Germany, having been wounded 8/8/16
Halligan, Michael	19 Pte	2731	11 Croxteth Road, Bootle	Not known	No	MIA 19/7/16	No
Hannah, John	27 Pte	305055	7 Johnson St. Liverpool.	Not known	No	Discharged medically unfit 30/10/18. Chronic bronchitis.	No

Hannon, William	31 Pte	4845	7 Hardy St.	Labourer	No	Died at Blackpool 29/5/15. Chronic bronchitis	No. Irish (born Galway 28/4/84)
Harrison, William	33 Pte	4120	23 Mill Road, Everton	Labourer	No	DOW 25/9/16 GSW chest	No
Hastings, Alexander	37 CQMS	3843	251 Walton Lane	Monumental sculptor	Labour Corps 8/8/17	Discharged as unfit 16/11/18	No. Also Mentioned in Dispatches on 3/10/16 by Major Leech
Henningson, John Olaf	39 Pte	5257	4 Hardy St.	Not known	Attached 5th King's 15/7/16	KIA 11/8/16	No
Hilliary, Robert	22 Pte	307173	11 Nile St.	Clerk	No	Missing but POW 8/8/16.	Yes, 8/8/16; repatriated December 1918
Howard, Bulmer	33 Pte	4550	8 Morley Lane	Ship's scraper	No	KIA 15/5/16	No
Jenkins, James	27 Pte	2668	50C Northumberland St., Toxteth	Docker	No	DOW due to GSW to back 8/8/16	No. Grandmother's parents came from Warrenpoint, Co. Down
Jones, William Winstanley	23 Pte	2707 & 305771	89 Everton Tce.	Blacksmith's striker	17th King's	No	No. Seconded to E. Wood & Co Manchester; also served at Arcangel, Russia
Kelly, Alfred Francis	L/Cpl.	4768	70 Margaret St.	Carter	20th then 7th King's & Defence Corps.	GSW head	No
Kenny, John	21 Pte	2972	55 Oswald St.	Railway worker	No	No	No. Lewis Gunner. FGCM 22/11/18. Drunk at Lille; reduced Sgt-Pte. Also V.D
Kenny, Thomas	19 Pte	305354	61 Louis St.	Labourer	No	GSW right shoulder 70% disabled	No
King, John Francis	38 Pte	4954	12 Hardy St.	Motor driver	No	KIA 8/7/16	No. Stated he was born in Canada, but NOK at Maine, USA
Mainey, Frederick	20 Pte	4894	37 Cam St., Lodge Lane	Fishmonger	No	DOW 4/8/16	No

Name	Age/Rank	Number	Address	Occupation	Transfer/Attached	Casualty	Notes
McCarthy, Bernard	16 Pte	1858	63 Edgeware St.	Waiter	No	KIA 22/11/15	No. Aged 16 on enlisting in 1913
McGeehan, Bernard	27 Pte	2974	10 Daulby St.	Groom	No	Shot for desertion 2/11/16	Born in Co. Donegal; lived in Londonderry and Liverpool. FGCM Shot 2/11/16
McGrath, John	22 Pte	5410	45 Tichfield St.	Porter	Attached to 5th King's 15/7/16	KIA 8/8/16	No
McGuffie, Robert	22 Pte	2800 & 494272	28 Beatrice St.	Labourer	Labour Corps 14/12/17	GSW to arms and legs 10/9/16	Fraudulently enlisted in 8th Irish; originally N. Lancs. Shot and killed Pte Smith by accident
McLoughlin, William	24 Pte	2693	3 Vauxhall Road	Hairdresser	No	Wounded (slight) 15/8/15	Discharged as unfit due to deafness 1917
McNally, Edward	31 Pte	4884	31 Norfolk St.	Labourer	5th King's back to 8th 27/8/16	KIA 24/9/16	No
McNamara, Thomas	17 Pte	405299	20 Leigh St.	Labourer	RE 6/2/17	Accidently shot; GSW hand	No
Mead, Edward Stanley	19 Sgt	305288	70 Wavertree Vale	Locomotive fireman	King's African Rifles 1918	No	Awarded the Military Medal
Miller, James	28 Pte	2702	9 Opie St.	Labourer	No	GSW right thigh	Yes. Captured at Guillemont 8/8/16
Moon, William	19 Pte	2000 & 305846	3rd house Burlington St.	Ship's sealer	No	No	Yes. Captured 30/11/17; held at Dulmen
Moore, George	17 Pte	2847 & 305839	89 Burlington St.	Not known	7th King's 30/1/18	Shrapnel both legs 10/8/17; shell shock 28/11/17	Yes. Captured at Festubert 9/4/18; POW in Germany
Mulcahey, John	17 Pte	1946 & 305307	157 Upper Frederick St.	Carter	13th King's	Right leg amputated 1917	Subject of Court of Enquiry at Fazackerly Hospital for absence and theft of clothing
Mullin, Joseph	33 CQMS	4269	13 Malvern Road	Not known	Various King's Batts.	Gassed 12/5/18	No
Murray, Thomas Joseph	26 Pte	3436 & 390791	130 Stitt St.	Soda water bottler	Labour Corps 28/8/17	No	No

O'Brien, William	39 Pte	5192	11 Rock View, Old Swan	Labourer	5th King's 15/7/16	KIA 8/8/16	No
O'Connor, William John	19 L/Cpl.	5370	138 St. James St.	Labourer	Depot	No	No
Partington, George	19 Pte	4914	15 Melrose Ave.	Labourer	No	DOW 4/10/16	No. GSW buttocks 27/9/16
Patrick, Joseph	22 Pte	5245	4 Hardy St.	Not known	No	KIA 27/9/16	No
Petterson, John	23 Pte	1288	19 Elstow St.	Labourer	RAMC 1917	GSW to right arm and left leg	Pre-war territorial; re-enlisted for active service
Quirk, Owen	18 Pte	1498 & 305121	53 Great Mersey St.	Labourer	No	GSW head; posted as missing 8/8/16	No. Survived. Re-employed by Silcock's seed crushers and oil refiners in 1919
Rafferty, John	31 Pte	4068	34, Orry St.	Fireman	No	Died as result of an accident at Woking 8/10/16	No
Ravey, James	30 L/Cpl.	2724	15 Dane St.	Not known	No	KIA 15/12/16	No
Redfern, Thomas Ellis	19 Pte	4594	8 Falkland St.	Seaman	Attached 9th King's 1916	KIA 12/8/16	No
Redmond, Michael John	34 Pte	3570	7 Beaconsfield Road	Labourer	No	KIA 9/9/15	No
Rehill, Thomas	29 Cpl.	4023	26 Burnard St.	Not known	No	KIA 18/9/16	No
Rice, James	20 Pte	4431	43 Towson St.	Hairdresser	Attached 5th King's 15/7/16	DOW 9/8/16. GSW Right leg	No
Roach, John	23 Pte	1628	40 Great Mersey St.	Labourer	No	Shell shock	Yes. Dulmen captured 8/8/16
Rodden, Francis Egerton	30 Pte	3727	29 Fielding St.	Brass finisher	No	KIA 1/7/16	No. Court Martial at Canterbury; 56 days hard labour for striking a NCO
Russell, John Henry	17 Pte	305299	42 Hughes St.	Chair maker	No	Missing 8/8/16 but POW	Yes. Dulmen. Also, FGCM for desertion; death sentence commuted
Rylance, Thomas	48 Pte	2714	34 Rose Vale	Docker	Defence Corps	Discharged as unfit 30/3/16.	Father of 7 children
Scanlon, Patrick	L/Sgt	3941	5 Myrtle View	Not known	No	DOW 10/7/16.	No
Shannon, Thomas	22 L/Cpl.	2505	37 MacQueen St.	Labourer	No	KIA 8/8/16.	No

Sloey, Joseph	21 Pte	4451	19 Antonio St.	Not known	No	DOW 4/8/16. GSW abdomen	No. Mother, Margaret Murphy, Kilmore Quay, Wexford
Smith, Arthur	18 Pte	3020	38 Ceurdon St.	Carter	No	Died. Accidently shot in the head by Pte McGuffie 11/10/15	No. Court papers survive with his record. See entry for McGuffie
Somers, Lawrence	21 Pte	1913	17 Jasper St.	Point cleaner	No	KIA 26/8/15	No
Stephenson, George	19 Pte	1449	116 Robsart St.	Labourer	No	Missing 8/8/16 but POW	Yes. Dulmen. Captured 8/8/16 at Guillemont
Surson, William	19 Pte	1931	19 Fontenoy St.	Bottle washer	To 5th King's 15/7/16	KIA 8/8/16	No
Sutton, Michael	21 Pte	305174	181 Scotland Road	Tanner	7th King's 30/1/18	Wounded (slight) 8/8/16	No
Swarbrick, William	35 Pte	5190	15 Stephenson Road	Labourer	No	KIA 9/9/16	No
Tabb, William	21 Pte	393170	64 Paddington, Edge Hill	Not known	RASC 1918	Wounded in action 19/5/16	No
Traynor, William	19 Pte	1480 & 305117	13 Stitt St.	Labourer	No	Wounded 8/7/15	Yes. 8/8/16 Dulmen
Wall, Albert	17 Pte	3515	107 Venmore St.	Seaman	No	Discharged as unfit 23/1/15	No
Ward, William Henry	35 Pte	3086	209 Breckfield Road	Not known	No	Accidently drowned at La Neuville France 29/7/15	No
White, John	17 Pte	305326	158 Field St.	Carter	No	GSW head, posted as missing 8/8/16 but found	No
Williams, Isaac	19 Pte	2533	89a Fontenoy St.	Apprentice	No	Missing 8/8/16. Found wounded, GSW left leg	No

APPENDIX 3

List of prisoners of war from the 8th (Irish) Battalion, King's Liverpool Regiment captured at Guillemont and held at Dülmen Prisoner-of-war Camp, August 1916.

	Surname	Forename	Born	Number	Wounded	Address of Next of Kin.
1	Ablett	James	Liverpool	1867	No	Edge Hill, Liverpool
2	Aldred	James	Manchester	3427	No	Side Lane, Blackpool
3	Allen	John	Liverpool	2697	No	Mann St. Liverpool.
4	Allison	Walter	Liverpool	11585	No	Edge Hill Liverpool.
5	Anderton	Richard	London	8847	No	Aughton St. Preston
6	Anderson	Robert	Liverpool	2208	No	Dillmott St. Liverpool
7	Arnott	George	Blackburn	2776	No	Caunce St. Blackpool
8	Ashcroft	James	Blackpool	3001	No	Mibble Pl. Blackpool
9	Atkinson	Harold	Blackpool	3035	No	Twiss St. Liverpool
10	Auget	George	London	30926	No	Kennington, London
11	Baily	Joseph	Mitcheltown	2792	No	Mitcheltown, Co. Cork
12	Bamber	Albert E.	Longridge	25946	No	Nelson, Lancs.
13	Banks	Arthur	Liverpool	2407	No	Low Hill, Liverpool
14	Barber	Richard	Liverpool	8502	No	Salisbury St. Liverpool
15	Barends	William R.	Liverpool	12583	No	Mill St. Liverpool
16	Bennett	William H.	Liverpool	4281	No	Brick Rd. Everton
17	Berry	Michael	Liverpool	24622	No	Clubmoor, Liverpool
18	Beswick	Richard J.	Salford	27616	No	Salford, Manchester
19	Bignell	Sydney J.	West Ham	27781	No	East Ham, London
20	Birch	Thomas	Liverpool	2007	No	Aubrey St. Liverpool
21	Blackburn	John	Liverpool	4875	No	Gt. Nelson St. Liverpool
22	Blundell	Robert	Garston	13909	No	Garston, Liverpool
23	Bly	Robert	Liverpool	11589	No	Burke St. Liverpool
24	Boland	Christopher	Blackpool	2796	No	Elizabeth St. Blackpool
25	Boyle	John	Liverpool	Unknown	No	Melville Pl. Liverpool
26	Brady	Francis F.	Liverpool	33218	No	Edge Hill, Liverpool
27	Brain	Alfred	London	11827	No	Stratford, London

28	Brown	Frederick	Liverpool	11969	No	Aintree, Liverpool
29	Brown	George	Liverpool	2914	No	Rockingham St. Liverpool
30	Brown	John	Liverpool	4448	No	Everton, Liverpool
31	Brown	John	Macclesfield	3970	No	York St. Failsworth
32	Brown	Tom	Hull	3488	No	Menzies St. Aberdeen
33	Bruice	Richard	Birkenhead	25860	No	Hightown, Manchester
34	Buisere	George	Liverpool	2973	No	Edge Hill, Liverpool
35	Bullock	Herbert S.	Burnley	14011	No	Rose Hill, Burnley
36	Burrow	Alexander	Leeds	11766	No	Harehills, Leeds
37	Burston	John	Liverpool	4527	No	Essex St. Liverpool
38	Burke	Alfred J.	Liverpool	2348	No	Whiterock St. Liverpool
39	Bush	Henry	Liverpool	1768	No	Harrington St. Liverpool
40	Bushell	Charles	Wigan	28158	No	Tyldesley, Manchester
41	Butcher	John	Blackpool	3212	Left leg	High St. Blackpool
42	Butler	Joseph	Liverpool	2198	No	Wilbraham St. Liverpool
43	Butterworth	Vincent	Rochdale	28185	No	Longsight, Oldham
44	Byrne	John	Liverpool	4801	Shoulder	Greek St. Liverpool
45	Cadman	Joseph	Liverpool	25377	No	Kirkdale, Liverpool
46	Cahill	Edward	Liverpool	2420	No	Walton, Liverpool
47	Caldon	Charles	Liverpool	9589	No	Bala St. Bootle
48	Caron	Louis	Toronto	5155	No	New Hamp. USA.
49	Cassidy	Richard	Liverpool	4444	No	Edge Hill, Liverpool
50	Cattle	James	York	9768	No	Shields Rd. Newcastle.
51	Cave	Harry	Liverpool	4832	No	Gt. Howard St. Liverpool
52	Challinor	Henry	Ellesmere	3960	No	Ellesmere Port
53	Charnock	David	Wigan	23780	No	Hopwood St. Wigan
54	Clarke	Arthur	Liverpool	1526	No	Dalrymple St. Liverpool
55	Clarke	George	Liverpool	5123	No	Nursery St. Liverpool
56	Clayton	Thomas	Liverpool	5019	No	Clare St. Liverpool
57	Clements	Charles	Liverpool	13528	No	John St. Liverpool
58	Coffey	John	Liverpool	10293	No	Dingle, Liverpool
59	Coll	John	Woolton	10265	No	Anne St. Liverpool
60	Conley	Christopher	Liverpool	2336	No	Whitstable, Kent
61	Connolly	John	Oldham	27822	No	Priory St. Oldham
62	Cook	Henry	Liverpool	11435	No	Westcott Rd. Liverpool
63	Cooper	Thomas	Shrewsbury	8781	No	Shrewsbury
64	Costello	James	Liverpool	9600	Elbow	Everton, Liverpool
65	Cotham	Edward	Rainford	27480	No	Bushy Lane, Rainford
66	Courtney	John	Liverpool	2415	No	Becket St. Liverpool
67	Cousins	Samuel	Liverpool	9801	No	Edge Hill, Liverpool
68	Crompton	John	Manchester	3550	No	Blackpool
69	Cummins	John	Liverpool	31312	No	Fifth Ave. Liverpool
70	Curwen	Robert	Fylde	3530	No	Thornton le Fylde
71	Dabb	John	New Ferry	3942	No	New Ferry
72	Dacre	Stanley W.	Liverpool	27999	No	Old Swan, Liverpool
73	Davenport	Herbert	Bury	2985	No	Duckworth St. Bury

74	Davies	Edward	Liverpool	2949	No	Anfield, Liverpool
75	Davies	George	Liverpool	4245	No	Birkenhead
76	Davis	George F.	Bolton	1409	No	Bury Old Rd. Bolton
77	Devine	William J.	Liverpool	2506	No	Old Swan, Liverpool
78	Dignan	Patrick	Liverpool	3146	No	Smollett St. Liverpool
79	Disley	Robert	Lancaster	10013	No	Bolton
80	Dobson	Ellsworth	Salford	3399	No	Gt. Morton Blackpool
81	Donaghue	Thomas	Liverpool	4913	No	Wavertree, Liverpool
82	Doran	Andrew	Liverpool	4849	No	Upper Bean St. Liverpool
83	Dougherty	Henry	Liverpool	4378	No	Hopwood St. Liverpool
84	Dowe	Ernest	Chesterfield	3067	No	Talbot Rd. Blackpool
85	Doyle	Francis	Liverpool	1973	No	Tithebarn St. Liverpool
86	Doyle	Henry	Liverpool	1361	No	Whitstable, Kent
87	Draycott	Charles	Cheshire	8373	No	Steven St. Chester
88	Dunn	Edward	Montreal	4758	No	Maryville, USA.
89	Dunn	Joseph	Liverpool	2378	No	Goodall St. Liverpool
90	Dunning	George	Manchester	29866	No	James St. Manchester
91	Durkin	John	St. Asaph	12881	No	Flint St. Birkenhead
92	Eagle	Louis	Liverpool	5289	No	Scotland Rd. Liverpool
93	Eastwood	Joseph	Burnley	11635	No	Waterloo Rd. Burnley
94	Edwards	William	Ormskirk	9250	No	Blodwen St. Liverpool
95	Elliott	George H.	Staffordshire	26593	No	Bryn Gates, Wigan
96	Entwistle	Hugh	Warrington	8883	No	Darwen, Lancashire
97	Faithorn	Arthur	Liverpool	30520	No	Leyden St. Liverpool
98	Fallon	James	Liverpool	1871	No	Cottenham St. Liverpool
99	Fellows	James	Liverpool	3345	No	Red Rock St. Liverpool
100	Fern	Water	Liverpool	2372	Shoulder	Morris St. Liverpool
101	Fletcher	Robert	Liverpool	1740	No	Netherfield Rd. Liverpool
102	Fogg	Harry	Leigh	3883	No	Hurst St. Leigh
103	Forrest	Robert	Preston	2788	No	St. George's Rd. Preston
104	Forshaw	Thomas	Liverpool	Unknown	No	Horwich St. Liverpool
105	Foster	James H.	Southport	13794	No	Olive Grove, Southport
106	Fry	Thomas	Liverpool	3014	No	Index St. Liverpool
107	Francis	Albert	London	20966	No	Silverdale, Lancs.
108	Francis	Raymond	Vancouver	5265	No	San Francisco, USA
109	Frederickson	Norman	Liverpool	34681	No	Moscow Dr. Liverpool
110	Garlington	John	Darwen	39341	No	Old Lane, Darwen
111	Gates	Henry	Grafton	13081	No	Cheshunt, Herts
112	Gillett	Charles	Preston	3220	No	Durham Rd. Blackpool
113	Gilchrist	Francis	Liverpool	1593	No	Toxteth St. Liverpool
114	Gilfillan	Archibald	Liverpool	14990	No	Walton, Liverpool
115	Gorton	Thomas	Liverpool	1866	No	Colquett St. Liverpool
116	Green	Alfred	Blackburn	Unknown	No	Bank Top, Blackburn
117	Green	John	Liverpool	3996	No	Anfield, Liverpool
118	Grierson	Edward	Liverpool	1679	No	Edge Hill, Liverpool
119	Hale	Thomas	Liverpool	3708	No	Arkwright St. Liverpool

120	Halliday	Ernest	Preston	3230	No	Wilton St. Preston
121	Halpin	Charles	Blackpool	2982	No	Ward St. Blackpool
122	Halsall	James	Liverpool	4456	No	Iden St. Liverpool
123	Hanlon	John	Liverpool	11878	No	Everton, Liverpool
124	Hardman	Harold	Chester	25862	No	Edge Hill, Liverpool
125	Hardwick	Allen	Oldham	29857	No	Middleton Junction
126	Hardwick	William	Tipton	3893	No	Ellesmere Port
127	Hargreaves	Arthur	Haslingden	3204	No	Alexander Ave. Blackpool
128	Hargreaves	John	Blackpool	3691	No	Ward St. Blackpool
129	Harris	James	Liverpool	2028	No	Bond St. Liverpool
130	Harrison	James	Wigan	27801	No	Patton St. Colne
131	Hastie	Robert	Liverpool	4978	No	Simpson St. Liverpool
132	Heelis	Leonard	Liverpool	2485	No	Lydia Ann St. Liverpool
133	Hendly	George	Wolverhampton	3943	No	Ellesmere Port
134	Henry	George	Southport	4910	No	Marshide, Southport
135	Hesketh	Stanley	Liverpool	11784	No	Needham Rd. Liverpool
136	Higgins	John	Liverpool	Unknown	No	Everton, Liverpool
137	Hilliary	Robert	Limerick	4883	Ear	St. Anne's, Lancs.
138	Hoare	Patrick	Wexford	2423	No	Wavertree, Liverpool
139	Hopwood	George	Liverpool	1752	No	Low Hill, Liverpool
140	Hopwood	William	Blackpool	3666	No	Woodland Gr. Blackpool
141	Hopkins	Thomas	Liverpool	13106	No	Wavertree, Liverpool
142	Hughes	Enoch	Broughton	11301	No	North Wales
143	Hughes	James	Liverpool	27423	No	Stone St. Liverpool
144	Hughes	Stanley	Wallasey	2471	No	Egremont, Wallasey
145	Hughes	William	Birkenhead	2677	No	Seacombe, Wallasey
146	Jones	John	Liverpool	4590	No	Teulon St. Liverpool
147	Jordan	Vincent	Liverpool	8886	No	Ashfield Cott. Liverpool
148	Kavanagh	Charles	Liverpool	2282	No	Benfield St. Liverpool
149	Kearney	John	Liverpool	3156	No	Glawdy St. Liverpool
150	Keeley	Joseph	Preston	2898	No	Gt. Hanover St. Preston
151	Kerr	Robert	Liverpool	2237	No	Latham St. Liverpool
152	Kirkham	Robert	Wolverhampton	Unknown	No	Ellesmere Port
153	Knowles	Henry	Liverpool	38960	No	Woolwich
154	Knox	James	Liverpool	1517	No	Foley St. Liverpool
155	Lacey	William	Liverpool	27094	No	Edge Hill, Liverpool
156	Lambert	William	Preston	2621	No	Essex St. Preston
157	Ledwick	James	Canada	5279	No	Birch Vale, Stockport
158	Leaming	Thomas	Liverpool	10604	No	Potter St. Liverpool
159	Lewis	Edward	Liverpool	3736	No	Norbreck, BlackpoolL
160	Lifford	David	Cork	4651	No	Frederickton, Canada
161	Litt	Frederick	Liverpool	4432	No	Chirkdale St. Liverpool
162	Livingstone	Martin	Widnes	5229	No	Hornby St. Liverpool
163	Lloyd	Jonathon	Liverpool	11946	No	Toxteth Pk. Liverpool
164	Lloyd	Richard	Southport	7665	No	Russell St. Manchester
165	Loftus	William	Liverpool	11964	No	Index St. Liverpool

166	Logan	John	Liverpool	26316	No	Ascot St. Liverpool
167	Lucas	George	Manchester	27282	No	Church Road, Manchester
168	Lunt	Joseph	Liverpool	31818	No	Mann St. Liverpool
169	Lyon	James	Kendal	2764	No	Warbreck Dr. Blackpool
170	Magee	Henry	Liverpool	5166	No	Frederick St. Liverpool
171	Maher	Christopher	Liverpool	2484	No	Travers St. Liverpool
172	Manly	Daniel	Liverpool	4518	No	Pickop St. Liverpool
173	Mannerley	Thomas	Liverpool	4237	No	Stevenson St. Liverpool
174	Marshall	Adolph	Liverpool	3950	No	Fox St. Liverpool
175	Maxwell	Thomas	Blackpool	3707	No	Cocker St. Blackpool
176	McCann	James	Seacombe	2240	No	Salisbury St. Liverpool
177	McCarron	Thomas	Liverpool	4422	No	Clare St. Liverpool
178	McCarthy	George	Montreal	5253	Left leg	Randolph St. Manchester
179	McCarthy	John	Newfoundland	4497	No	Newfoundland
180	McFetridge	James	Glasgow	4601	No	Glenarm Rd. Larne.
181	McFey	Cornelius	Ormskirk	Unknown	No	Birkdale, Southport
182	McGlone	John	Liverpool	5088	No	Cabbage Hall, Liverpool
183	McLeod	William	Wigan	4653	No	Colin St. Wigan
184	McNally	James	Manchester	4308	No	Garibaldi St. Liverpool
185	Meek	James	Hebburn	8185	No	Hebburn on Tyne
186	Middleton	Joseph	Blackburn	5078	No	Bolton Rd. Blackburn
187	Miller	William	Bootle	2689	No	Regent Rd. Liverpool
188	Molley	John	Liverpool	4868	No	Gerard St. Liverpool
189	Molyneux	James	Woolton	3573	GSW	Beaconsfield Rd. Liverpool
190	Moore	Richard	Blackpool	3053	No	Kent Rd. Blackpool
191	Moorecroft	Robert	Liverpool	Unknown	No	Rupert St. Liverpool
192	Moran	James	Liverpool	5050	No	Skirving St. Liverpool
193	Morgan	Stanley	Liverpool	4881	No	Ronald St. Liverpool
194	Murphy	Patrick	Liverpool	2487	No	Adlington St. Liverpool
195	Murphy	William	Liverpool	1825	No	Melbourne St. Liverpool
196	Mylett	William	Liverpool	4343	No	Adlington St. Liverpool
197	Newly	William	Dudley	3927	No	Ellesmere Port
198	Nicholson	Frank	Lancaster	2581	No	Berry St. Preston
199	Norris	Walter	Liverpool	3791	No	Friar St. Liverpool
200	Nyland	Thomas	Wolverhampton	3938	No	Ellesmere Port
201	O'Connell	John	Liverpool	4062	No	Montague St. Liverpool
202	O'Donnell	Patrick	Droylsden	4853	No	Fairhaven, USA
203	Ogden	Matthew	Blackpool	2893	No	Grosvenor St. Blackpool
204	O'Neill	James	Blackburn	4596	No	Bedford, USA
205	Page	John	Oldham	1943	No	Horatio St. Liverpool
206	Partridge	William	Wallasey	10955	No	Seymour St. Wallasey
207	Paterson	John	Liverpool	11212	No	Kensington, Liverpool
208	Pearson	Edgar	Nelson	3446	No	Garstang Rd. Wesham, Preston
209	Price	John	Birkenhead	4898	No	Brook St. Birkenhead
210	Price	Thomas	Walsall	9569	No	Harker St. Liverpool
211	Pritchard	William	Liverpool	5250	No	Netherfield Rd. Liverpool

212	Quick	James	Millom	3126	No	Barrow in Furness
213	Quinn	Herbert	Liverpool	29493	No	Danehurst Rd. Liverpool
214	Quinn	Joseph	Liverpool	1359	No	Warren St. Liverpool
215	Quirk	Owen	Liverpool	1498	No	Gt. Mersey St. Liverpool
216	Reeves	George	Canada	Unknown	No	Mass. USA
217	Reid	Lee	Southport	Unknown	No	Southport
218	Rhodes	Reginald	Wakefield	2889	No	Durham Rd. Blackpool
219	Richardson	Albert	Liverpool	18297	No	Brisbane St. Liverpool
220	Richardson	William	Liverpool	2400	No	Bala Tce. Liverpool
221	Ridgeway	Frederick	Liverpool	1498	No	Sampson St. Liverpool
222	Roach	John	Liverpool	1628	No	Elias St. Liverpool
223	Robbins	George	Liverpool	11704	No	Fine Tce. Liverpool
224	Roberts	Richard	Liverpool	2334	No	Randal St. Liverpool
225	Roche	Edward	Limerick	4882	GSW.	None.
226	Rogers	John	Liverpool	2149	No	Low Hill, Liverpool
227	Rogers	Sydney	Liverpool	4332	No	India St. Liverpool
228	Rushton	William	Swinton	Unknown	No	Old Swan, Liverpool
229	Ryan	Patrick	Dublin	4831	No	Rose Cottage, Lancaster
230	Ryder	John	Bradford	2531	No	Mass. USA
231	Rylance	Thomas	Widnes	10770	No	Vulcan St. Garston
232	Scott	William	Liverpool	4424	No	Hunter St. Liverpool
233	Seddon	William	Liverpool	Unknown	No	Salisbury St. Liverpool
234	Sharpe	Alexander	Liverpool	2043	No	Rokeby St. Liverpool
235	Sharpe	William	Liverpool	5113	No	Liverpool
236	Shelley	Charles	Tipton	3967	No	Ellesmere Port
237	Shepherd	James	Liverpool	4738	No	Craven St. Liverpool
238	Shields	William	Liverpool	2456	No	Old Swan
239	Skelton	Arthur	Wolverhampton	9075	No	Boxton St. Liverpool
240	Smith	Harold	Blackpool	3039	No	Osbourne St. Blackpool
241	Smith	W.H.	St. Helens	29328	No	Edgeworth St. St. Helens
242	Stanton	Arthur	Leeds	4181	No	Rose Vale, Liverpool
243	Stephenson	George	Liverpool	1449	No	Netherfield Rd. Liverpool
244	Stevens	Arthur	Truro	5210	No	Portobello, Scotland
245	Sullivan	George	Liverpool	30080	No	Burscough St. Ormskirk
246	Sutcliffe	Harry	Todmorden	3025	No	Reads Rd. Blackpool
247	Swindell	James	Culcheth	27820	No	Culcheth, Warrington
248	Tait	Ernest	Liverpool	30520	No	Myrtle St. Liverpool
249	Tatham	Thomas	Blackpool	2928	No	Rakes Rd. Blackpool
250	Thomas	James	Oswestry	3946	No	New Ferry, Cheshire
251	Thomas	Israel	Liverpool	36146	No	Poulton, Wallasey
252	Thomas	William	Liverpool	4311	No	Imison St. Liverpool
253	Thompson	Arthur	Preston	3299	No	Fletcher Rd. Preston
254	Thompson	William	Poulton	3468	No	Carleton
255	Thomson	John	Liverpool	2075	No	Wordsworth St. Liverpool
256	Thomlinson	James	Liverpool	3000	No	Old Swan, Liverpool
257	Traynor	William	Liverpool	31441	No	Field St. Liverpool

258	Turner	John	Oldham	31441	No	Broadway St. Oldham
259	Vose	William	Liverpool	4985	No	Bora Pl. Liverpool
260	Walton	Frank	Liverpool	4541	No	Landseer Rd. Liverpool
261	Wainwright	William	Liverpool	11203	No	Marshall St. Liverpool
262	Wareing	Horace	Oldham	3700	No	Layton Lane, Blackpool
263	Watkins	Thomas	Liverpool	1879	No	Still St. Liverpool
264	Weaver	Thomas	Liverpool	13540	No	Crown St. Liverpool
265	Whalley	William	Lytham	2930	No	Moss Lane, Leyland
266	Whittleworth	Charles	Manchester	28089	No	Parker St. Bradford
267	Wilkinson	William	Blackpool	3642	No	Woodman Rd. Blackpool
268	Williams	Matthew	Blackpool	3044	No	Gorton St. Blackpool
269	Witt	John	Blackpool	3692	No	Alexander Rd. Blackpool
270	Woar	Henry	Preston	2584	No	Thornton St. Preston
280	Woodword	Edward	Bolton	3887	No	Shuttle St. Bolton

Source: Compiled from Registers PA 5928–PA 5940, of the Prisoners of the First World War Archives, International Committee of the Red Cross (ICRC).

BIBLIOGRAPHY

Primary Sources

MANUSCRIPTS

The National Archives, London
War Office Papers:
WO95/2887/1 War Diary, 8th (Irish) Battalion, King's Liverpool Regiment, 1 May 1915–31 Dec. 1915
WO95/2920 War Diary, 164 Infantry Brigade Headquarters, 31 Jan. 1916–31 July 1916.
WO95/2921 War Diary, 164 Infantry Brigade Headquarters, 1 Aug. 1916–29 Apr. 1919
WO95/2923/1 War Diary, 8th (Irish) Battalion, King's Liverpool Regiment, 1 Jan. 1916–31 Jan. 1918.
WO95/2983/5 War Diary, 8th (Irish) Battalion, King's Liverpool Regiment, 1 Feb. 1918–31 May 1919.
WO161/100/536, Committee on the treatment of British Prisoners of war: Interview and reports, Pte. John Burston, No. 4527, 8th (Irish) Battalion, King's Liverpool Regiment.
WO161/100/608, Committee on the treatment of British Prisoners of war: Interview and reports, Pte. Charles Craddock, No. 10219, 1st Battalion, Royal Welch Fusiliers.
WO161/100/324, Committee on the treatment of British Prisoners of war: Interview and reports, Private Henry Davis, No. 4305, 8th (Irish) Battalion, King's Liverpool Regiment.

PARLIAMENTARY PAPERS

Cd. 8984, Miscellaneous no.3, Report on the Transport of British Prisoners of War to Germany, August to December 1914 (London, 1918).

THE IMPERIAL WAR MUSEUM, LONDON

Green Papers, Docs: 15531.
Hardie Papers, Docs: 4041.
Mahon Papers, Docs: 6791.
McGuire Papers, Docs: 96/31/1.
Spargo Papers, Docs: 14181.
Edwards Papers, Docs: 78/2/1.

BIRMINGHAM LIBRARY, WOLFSON CENTRE

Sharpe Papers, Ms 1242/63/9.

LIVERPOOL CENTRAL LIBRARY
Jeudwine Papers.

ST HELENS LIBRARY
Recruiting poster.

WELLCOME LIBRARY
RAMC Collection: RAMC/276.

NATIONAL ARCHIVES OF IRELAND, DUBLIN

NATIONAL LIBRARY, DUBLIN
Ms 15188–15259, Redmond papers.

UNIVERSITY COLLEGE DUBLIN
Moynihan papers.

MILITARY HISTORY BUREAU
Witness Statements.

NEWSPAPERS: GREAT BRITAIN
Aberdeen Daily Journal
Aberdeen Weekly Journal
Blackpool Gazette
Bootle Times
Daily Mail
Daily Sketch
Express & Star
Lancashire Daily Post
Liverpool Catholic Herald
Liverpool Courier
Liverpool Daily Post and Mercury
Liverpool Echo
Liverpool Evening Express
Liverpool Mercury
London Gazette
Preston Herald
The Times
Whitstable Times and Tankerton Press

NEWSPAPERS: IRELAND
Belfast News Letter
Belfast Weekly News
Freeman's Journal
Frontier Sentinel

Irish Independent
Irish News
Irish Times
Irish Volunteer
Irish Worker
Weekly Irish Times

MAGAZINES, PERIODICALS AND JOURNALS

British Medical Journal
Contemporary Review
Cottonian
Graphic
Illustrated Sunday Herald
Irish Historical Studies
Irish Sword
Liverpolitan
Occult Review
Stand To! The Journal of the Western Front Association, No. 45.
Xavierian

CONTEMPORARY PAMPHLETS AND PUBLICATIONS

Allardyce, Mabel Desborough, *University of Aberdeen Roll of Service in the Great War 1914–1919* (Aberdeen, 1921).
Bond of Sacrifice, Volume 11, January–June 1915.
Infantry Training Manual, 1914.
Manual of Military Law (London, 1914).
Notes for Infantry Officers on Trench Warfare, 1916.
Soldiers Died in the Great War 1914–19, CD-ROM, Naval and Military Press (Heathfield, 1998).
Squalid Liverpool: By a Special Commission, Liverpool, 1883.
Statistics of the Military Effort of the British Empire during the Great War, 1914–1920 (London, 1920).

Secondary Sources

BOOKS AND ARTICLES

Akenson, Don, *An Irish History of Civilization: Volume Two* (London, 2006).
Allen, Joan, '"Keeping the faith": The Catholic press and the preservation of Celtic identity in Britain in the late nineteenth century', in Richard C. Allen and Stephen Regan (eds.), *Irelands of the Mind: Memory and identity in modern Ireland* (Cambridge, 2008).
Allen, Richard C., and Regan, Stephen (eds.), *Irelands of the Mind: Memory and identity in modern Ireland* (Cambridge, 2008).
Archer, John, E., *The Monster Evil: Policing and violence in Victorian Liverpool* (Liverpool, 2011).
Arthur, Max, *Forgotten Voices of the Great War* (London, 2003).
Arthur, Max, *When this bloody war is over: Soldiers' Songs of the First World War* (London, 2002).
Ashworth, Tony, *Trench Warfare 1914–1918: The live and let live system* (London, 2000 Pan Books edn).
Barnett, Correlli, *The Collapse of British Power* (London, 1972).

Beckett, Ian, F.W., *Britain's Part-Time Soldiers: The amateur military tradition 1558–1945* (Barnsley, 2011).

Beckett, Ian, F.W., *Riflemen Form: A study of the rifle Volunteer Movement 1859–1908* (Barnsley, 2007).

Beckett, Ian, F.W., *The Great War* (London, 2001).

Beckett, Ian, F.W., and Keith Simpson (eds.), *A Nation in Arms: The British army in the First World War* (Barnsley, 1985).

Beckett, Ian, F.W., 'The territorial force in the Great War' in Liddle, Peter, *Home Fires and Foreign Fields: British social and military experience in the First World War* (London, 1985), pp. 21–38.

Beckett, Ian, Timothy Bowman and Mark Connelly, *The British Army and The First World War* (Cambridge, 2017).

Bedborough, George, *Arms and the Clergy* (London, 1934).

Belchem, John, *Irish, Catholic and Scouse: The history of the Liverpool-Irish 1800–1939* (Liverpool, 2007).

Belchem, John, *Merseypride: Essays in Liverpool Exceptionalism* (Liverpool, 2000).

Belchem, John (ed.), *Popular Politics, Riot and Labour: Essays in Liverpool history 1790–1940* (Liverpool, 1992).

Benbough-Jackson, Mike, *Voices of the First World War: Merseyside's War* (Stroud, 2015).

Bohstedt, John, 'More than one working class: Protestant-Catholic riots in Edwardian Liverpool', in John Belchem (ed.), *Popular Politics, Riot and Labour: Essays in Liverpool history 1790–1940* (Liverpool, 1992), pp. 173–216.

Bond, Brian (ed.), *'Look to your Front': studies in The First World War* (Kent, 1999).

Bond, R. C., *Prisoners Grave and Gay* (Edinburgh, 1934).

Bourke, Joanna, *Dismembering the Male: Men's bodies, Britain and the Great War* (London, 1996).

Bourke, Joanna, *An Intimate History of Killing: Face to face killing in twentieth century warfare* (London, 2000 edn).

Bourke, Joanna, 'Shell shock, psychiatry and the Irish soldier during the First World War', in Adrian Gregory and Senia Paseta (eds.), *Ireland and the Great War* (Manchester, 2002), pp. 155–70.

Bourne, John, 'The British working man in arms', in Hugh Cecil and Peter Liddle (eds.), *Facing Armageddon* (London, 1996).

Bowman, Timothy, *Carson's Army: The Ulster Volunteer Force 1910–22* (Manchester, 2007).

Bowman, Timothy, *Irish regiments in the Great War: Discipline and morale* (Manchester, 2003).

Bowman, Timothy, 'The Irish recruiting and anti-recruiting campaigns, 1914–1918', in Bernard Taithe and Tim Thornton (eds.), *Propaganda: Political rhetoric and identity 1300–2000* (Stroud, 1999), pp. 223–38.

Bowser, Thekla, *The Story of British V.A.D. work in the Great War* (London, 1917) (London, I.W.M., reprint, 2003).

Boyce, D. George, and Roger Swift, *Problems and perspectives in Irish history since 1800* (Dublin, 1994).

Boyce, D. George, '"That third party politics should divide our tents": Nationalism, Unionism and the First World War', in Gregory and Paseta (eds.) *Ireland and the Great War: 'A War to unite us all'?* (Manchester, 2002), pp. 190–216.

Brady, L., *T.P. O'Connor and the Liverpool Irish* (London, 1983).

Braybon, Gail (ed.) *Evidence, history and the Great War: Historians and the impact of 1914–18* (Oxford, 2003).

Brewsher, F.W., *The History of the 51st Highland Division, 1914–1918* (Edinburgh, 1921).

Brown, James Scott (ed.), *The Hague Conventions and Declarations of 1899 and 1907* (Washington, D.C. and Oxford, 1915).

Brown, Malcolm, *The Imperial War Museum book of the Somme* (London, 1997).

Buckley, Suzanne, 'The failure to resolve the problem of venereal disease among the troops in Britain during World War 1' in Bond, Brian and Ian Roy (eds.), *War and society: a yearbook of military history* vol. 2 (New York, 1977), pp. 65–85.

Busteed, Mervyn, 'Little islands of Erin: Irish settlement and identity in Mid-Nineteenth century Manchester', in MacRaild Donald M. (ed.), *The Great Famine and Beyond: Irish Migrants in Britain in the Nineteenth and Twentieth Centuries* (Dublin, 2000).

Callan, Patrick, 'Recruiting for the British army in Ireland during the First World War', *Irish Sword,* xvii (1987), pp. 42–56.

Callan, Patrick, 'British recruitment in Ireland', *Revue Internationale d'Histoire Militaire*, no. 63 (1985), pp. 41–50.

Cherry, Bruce, *They Didn't Want to Die Virgins: Sex and morale in the British army on the Western Front 1914–18* (Solihull, 2016).

Chickering, Roger, *Imperial Germany and the Great War, 1914–1918* (Cambridge 3rd ed., 2014).

Coetzee, Franz and Marilyn Shevlin-Coetzee (eds.), *Authority, Identity and the Social History of the Great War* (Oxford, 1995).

Conan Doyle, Arthur, *To Arms* (London, 1914).

Cook, Tim, *At The Sharp End: Canadians fighting the Great War 1914–1916* (Toronto, 2007).

Coop, J.O. *The Story of the 55th (West Lancashire) Division* (Liverpool, 1919).

Corns, Cathryn & Hughes-Wilson, John, *Blindfold and Alone: British Military executions in the Great War* (London, 2005).

Corns, Cathryn, "Shot at dawn': Military executions in the Great War', *The RUSI Journal* , 143:1 (1998), pp. 53–55.

Corrigan, Gordon, *Mud, Blood and Poppycock* (London, 2003).

Corrigan, Gordon, *Sepoys in the Trenches: The Indian Corps on the Western Front 1914–15* (Stroud, 2006).

Cousins, Colin, *Armagh and the Great War* (Dublin, 2011).

Crozier, F.P., *A Brass Hat in No Man's Land* (London, 1930).

Davies, Sam, '"A stormy political career": P.J. Kelly and Irish Nationalist and Labour politics in Liverpool, 1891–1936', *Transactions of the Historic Society of Lancashire and Cheshire*, 148, 1999, pp. 147–90.

DeGroot, Gerald, J., *Blighty: British Society in the era of the Great War* (London, 1996).

Denman, Terence, *Ireland's Unknown Soldiers: the 16th Irish Division in the Great War* (Dublin, 1992).

Denman, Terence, 'The Irish Catholic soldier in the First World War: the 'racial environment'', *Irish Historical Studies, xxvii, No.108* (Nov. 1991).

Denvir, John, *The life story of an old rebel* (Memphis, 2010 reprint).

DeWiel, Jerome, Aan, *The Catholic Church in Ireland 1914–1918* (Dublin, 2003).

Dooley, Thomas P., *Irishmen or English Soldiers? The times and world of a southern Irish man 1876–1916 enlisting in the British army during the First World War* (Liverpool, 1996).

Duffett, Rachel, *The Stomach for Fighting: Food and the soldiers of the Great War* (Manchester, 2012).

Duncan, Walter, *How I escaped from Germany* (Liverpool, 1919).

Dungan, Myles, *They Shall Not Grow Old: Irish soldiers and the Great War* (Dublin, 1997).

Dunn, Steve, R., *Blockade: Cruiser warfare and the starvation of Germany in World War One* (Barnsley, 2016).

Edmonds, J.E., *Military Operations in France and Belgium 1915, Battles of Aubers Ridge, Festubert and Loos* (London, 1928).

Emden, Richard van, *Prisoners of the Kaiser: The last POW's of the Great War* (Barnsley, 2009).

Emsley, Clive, *Soldier, Sailor, Beggarman, Thief* (Oxford, 2013).

Englander, David and James Osborne, 'Jack, Tommy and Henry Dubb: The armed forces and the working class', *The Historical Journal, Volume 21*, 1978, pp. 593–621.

Evans, Martin and Ken Lunn (eds.), *War and Memory in the Twentieth Century* (Oxford, 1997).

Falls, Cyril, *The History of the 36th (Ulster) Division* (London, 1996 facsimile edn).

Ferguson, Niall, *The Pity of War* (London, 1998).

Fielding, Steven, *Class and Ethnicity: Irish Catholics in England, 1880–1939* (Buckingham, 1993).

Michael Finn, 'Local heroes: war news and the construction of 'community' in Britain, 1914–18', *Historical Research, vol. 83, no. 22* (August 2010).

Finn, Michael, 'The realities of war', *History Today, vol. 52* (2002).

Fitzpatrick, David, *Politics and Irish life: Provincial experiences of war and revolution* (Cork, 1998 edn).

Fitzpatrick, David, 'Militarism in Ireland, 1900–1922', in Bartlett and Jeffery (eds.), *A Military History of Ireland* (Cambridge, 1996), pp. 379–406.

Fitzpatrick, David, 'A curious middle place: The Irish in Britain 1871–1921', p. 11, in Roger Swift and Sheridan Gilley (eds.) *The Irish in Britain 1815–1939* (Maryland, 1989).

Fitzpatrick, David, 'The logic of collective sacrifice: Ireland and the British army, 1914–1918', *Historical Journal*, xxxviii (1995), pp. 1017–30.

Fitzpatrick, David (ed.), *Ireland and the First World War* (Dublin, 1988).

Haddick-Flynn, Kevin, *Orangeism: The making of a tradition* (Dublin, 1999).

Forde, Frank, 'The Liverpool Irish Volunteers', *The Irish Sword*, Vol. X, No. 39, 1971, pp. 106–23.

Forsythe, David, *The Humanitarians: The International Committee of the Red Cross* (Cambridge, 2005).

Foster, Roy, *The Irish Story: Telling tales and making it up in Ireland* (London, 2001).

Foster, Roy, *Modern Ireland 1600–1972* (London, 1989).

Foster, Roy, *Paddy and Mr Punch: Connections in Irish and English history* (Middlesex, 1993).

Fox, Sir Frank, *G.H.Q (Montreuil-sur-Mer)*, (London, 1920),

Fox, John, *Forgotten Divisions: The First World War from both sides of No Man's Land* (Wilmslow, 1994).

Fussell, Paul, *The Great War and Modern Memory* (Oxford, 2000 edn).

Garrett, Richard, *The Final Betrayal: The Armistice, 1918 and afterwards* (Southampton, 1989).

George, David Lloyd, *War Memoirs of David Lloyd George*, vol. 1 (London, 1938 Odhams edn.).

Gilbert, Martin, *First World War* (London, 1995).

Goebel, Stefan, *The Great War in Medieval Memory* (Cambridge, 2007).

Graubard, Stephen Richards, 'Military demobilization in Great Britain following the First World War', *Journal of Modern History*, vol. xix, no. 4 (1947), pp. 297–311.

Graves, Robert, *Goodbye to All That* (London, 1929).

Gregory, Adrian, *The Silence of Memory: Armistice Day 1919–1946* (Oxford, 1994).

Gregory, Adrian, 'British "War Enthusiasm" in 1914: a reassessment', in Gail Braybon, (ed.), *Evidence, History and the Great War: Historians and the impact of 1914–18* (Oxford, 2003), pp. 67–87.

Gregory, Adrian and Senia Paseta, (eds.) *Ireland and the Great War: 'A war to unite us all'?* (Manchester, 2002).

Gregson, Adrian, *From Docks and Sand: Southport and Bootle's Battalion, the King's Liverpool Regiment, in the First World War* (Solihull, 2018).

Griffith, Paddy, *Battle Tactics of the Western Front: The British Army's art of attack 1916–18* (London, 2000 edn.).

Gwynn, Denis, *The Life of John Redmond* (London, 1932).

Hagenlücke, Heinz, 'The German High Command', in Liddle, Peter, *Passchendaele in Perspective: The Third Battle of Ypres* (Barnsley, 1997), pp. 45–58.

Hinz, Uta, *Gefangen im Großen Krieg: Kriegsgefangenschaft in Deutschland 1914–1921* (Essen, 2006).

Holden, Wendy, *Shell Shock: The psychological impact of war* (London, 1998).

Holding, Steven, *Class and Ethnicity: Irish Catholics in England, 1880–1939* (Buckingham, 1993).

Holmes, Richard, *Tommy: The British soldier on the Western Front* (London, 2005).

Horne, John and Alan Kramer, (eds.), *German Atrocities 1914: A history of denial* (London, 2001).

Horne, John (ed.) *Our War: Ireland and the Great War* (Dublin, 2008).

Howard, Keble, *The Quality of Mercy: How British Prisoners of War were taken to Germany in 1914* (London, 1918).

Hughes, Clive, 'The new armies', in Ian F.W. Beckett and Keith Simpson (eds.), *A Nation in Arms: The British Army in the First World War* (Barnsley, 2004).

Irwin, Francis, S.J., *Stonyhurst War Record: A memorial of the part taken by Stonyhurst men in the Great War* (Stonyhurst, 1927).

Jackson, Alvin, *Home Rule: An Irish History 1800–2000* (Oxford, 2003).

Jackson, Daniel, M., *Popular opposition to Irish Home Rule in Edwardian Britain* (Liverpool, 2009).

Jeffery, Keith, *Ireland and the Great War* (Cambridge, 2000).

Jones, Heather, *Violence against Prisoners of War in the First World War: Britain, France and Germany, 1914–20* (Cambridge, 2011).

Kettle, T.M., *Poems and Parodies* (Dublin, 1916).

Knight, Paul, *Liverpool Territorials in the Great War* (Barnsley, 2017).

Knightly, P., *The First Casualty: The War Correspondent as Hero, Propagandist and Myth-maker from the Crimea to Vietnam* (London, 1973).

Lane, Tony, *Liverpool, gateway of empire* (London, 1987).

Lewis, David (ed.), *Remembrances of Hell: The Great War diary of Writer, Broadcaster and Naturalist Norman Ellison* (Shrewsbury, 1997).

Lewis Stempel, John, *The War Behind the Wire: The life, death and glory of British prisoners of war 1914–18* (London, 2014).

Liddle, Peter, *Passchendaele in Perspective: The Third Battle of Ypres* (Barnsley, 1997).

Liddle, Peter, *The 1916 Battle of the Somme Reconsidered* (Barnsley, 2016).

Liddle, Peter, *Home fires and foreign fields: British social and military experience in the First World War* (London, 1985).

Lloyd, Nick, *Passchendaele: A New Perspective* (London, 2017).

Marshall, L. M., *Experiences in German Gaols* (Liverpool, 1915).

Martin. F.X., (ed.), *The Irish Volunteers 1913–1915: Recollections & Documents* (Kildare, 2013 edn.).

Marwick, Arthur, *The Deluge: British Society and the First World War* (London, 1978).

Macilwee, Michael, *The Liverpool Underworld: Crime in the city 1750–1900* (Liverpool, 2011).

MacRaild, Donald, *Faith, Fraternity and Fighting: The Orange Order and Irish migrants in northern England, c. 1850–1920* (Liverpool, 2005).

MacRaild, Donald (ed.), *The Great Famine and beyond: Irish migrants in Britain in the nineteenth and twentieth centuries* (Dublin, 2000).

McCartney, Helen, B., *Citizen Soldiers: The Liverpool Territorials in the first World War* (Cambridge, 2005).

McCracken, Donal, *Forgotten Protest: Ireland and the Anglo-Boer War* (Belfast, 2003).

McDonagh, F., *The Conservative Party and Anglo-German Relations, 1905–1914* (London, 2007).

McFarland, Elaine, 'How the Irish paid their debt': Irish Catholics in Scotland and voluntary enlistment, August 1914–July 1915'. *The Scottish Historical Review*, Vol. 82, No. 214, Part 2, Oct. 2003, pp. 261–84.

McGarry, Fearghal, *The Rising Ireland: Easter 1916* (Oxford, 2011).

McGreal, Stephen, *Liverpool in the Great War* (Barnsley, 2014).

McGuire, James, K., *The King the Kaiser and Irish freedom* (New York, 1915).

McMahon, Deirdre (ed.), *The Moynihan Brothers in Peace and War 1909–1918: Their new Ireland* (Dublin, 2004).

Meleady, Dermot, *John Redmond: The National Leader* (Kildare, 2014).

Messenger, Charles, *A Call to Arms: The British army 1914–18* (London, 2005).

Middlebrook, Martin, *Your Country Needs You! Expansion of the British army infantry Division, 1914–1918* (Barnsley, 1999).

Miller, Anthony, *Poverty Deserved? Relieving the poor in Victorian Liverpool* (Birkenhead, 1988).

Miller, David, W., *Peep O'Day Boys and Defenders: Selected documents on the County Armagh disturbances 1784–96* (Belfast, 1990).

Mitchell, T.J. and G.M. Smith (eds.) *Official History of the War: Medical statistics, casualties and medical services* (London, 1930).

Mitchinson, K.W., *The Territorial Force at War, 1914–1916* (Hampshire, 2014).

Moore-Bick, Christopher, *Playing the Game: The British junior infantry officer on the Western Front 1914–18* (Solihull, 2011).

Moore, William, *The Thin Yellow Line* (London, 1974).

Moran, Lord, *The Anatomy of Courage* (London, 1945).

Morton, Desmond, *Silent Battles: Canadian Prisoners of War in Germany, 1914–1919* (Toronto, 1992).

Neal, Frank, *The Great Hunger Commemoration Service. St. Anthony's Church, Scotland Road, Liverpool, Friday 3 October 1997.* (Liverpool, 2005).

Neal, Frank, *Black '47: Britain and the Famine Irish* (London, 1998).

Neal, Frank, 'A criminal profile of the Liverpool Irish', *Transactions of the Historic Society of Lancashire and Cheshire*, 140, 1991, pp. 161–99.

Neal, Frank, *Sectarian Violence: the Liverpool experience 1819–1914: an aspect of Anglo-Irish history* (Manchester, 1988).

Nicholson, W.N., *Behind the Lines: An account of administrative staffwork in the British Army 1914–1918* (Stevenage, 1939).

Novick, Ben, *Conceiving Revolution: Irish nationalist propaganda during the First World War* (Dublin, 2001).

O Concubhair, Padraig, *'The Fenians Were Dreadful Men': The 1867 Rising* (Dublin, 2011).

O'Mara, Pat, *The Autobiography of a Liverpool Irish Slummy* (Liverpool, 2009 edn.).

O Murchadha, Ciaran, *The Great Famine: Ireland's Agony 1845–1852* (London, 2011).

Oram, Gerard, *Worthless Men: Race, eugenics and the death penalty in the British Army during the First World War* (London, 1998).

Oram, Gerard, *Death Sentences Passed by Military Courts of the British Army 1914–1924* (London, 1998).

Panyani, Panikos, 'The Lancashire anti-German riots', *Manchester Regional History Review, 2/2 (1988–89)*, pp. 3–11.

Parker, Peter, *The Old Lie: The Great War and the public-school ethos* (London, 1987).

Pennell, Catriona, *A Kingdom United: Popular responses to the outbreak of the First World War in Britain and Ireland* (Oxford, 2012).

Perry, Nicholas, *Major General Oliver Nugent and the Ulster Division 1915–1918* (Stroud, 2007).

Philpott, William, *Bloody Victory: The sacrifice on the Somme* (London, 2009).

Pooley, Colin G., 'Segregation or integration? The residential experience of the Irish in mid-Victorian Britain', in Swift, Roger and Sheridan Gilley (eds.) *The Irish in Britain 1815–1939* (Maryland, 1989).

Poynter, F.N.L. (ed.), *Medicine and Surgery in the Great War 1914–1918* (London, 1968).

Prior, Robin and Trevor Wilson, *The Somme* (London, 2005).

Prior, Robin and Trevor Wilson, *Passchendaele: The untold story* (London, 1996).

Prior, Robin and Trevor Wilson, *Command on the Western Front* (Oxford, 1992).

Proctor, Tammy, *Civilians in a World War 1914–1918* (New York, 2010).

Putkowski, Julian and Julian Sykes, *Shot at Dawn: Executions in World War One by Authority of the British Army Act* (Barnsley, 2007).

Rawson, Andrew, *The Somme Campaign* (Barnsley, 2014).

Reader, W. J., *At Duty's Call: A study in obsolete patriotism* (Manchester, 1994).

Reed, Fiona, *Medicine in the First World War Europe: Soldiers, medics, pacifists* (London, 2017).

Regulski, Christoph, *Klippfisch und Steckrüben. Die Lebensmittelversorgung der Einwohner Franfurt am Mains im Ersten Weltkrieg 1914–1918* (Frankfurt am Main, 2012).

Richardson, Matthew, 'The weapons and equipment of the British soldier at Passchendaele', in Liddle, Peter, *Passchendaele in Perspective: The Third Battle of Ypres* (Barnsley, 1997), pp. 333–48.

Robb, George, *British Culture and the First World War* (London, 2002).

Roberts, Keith, Daniel, *Liverpool Sectarianism: The rise and demise* (Liverpool, 2017).

Rothstein, Andrew, *The Soldier Strikes of 1919* (London, 1980).

Antoin-Rouzeau, Stephane, 'The French soldier in the trenches,' in Hugh Cecil and Peter Liddle (eds.), *Facing Armageddon* (London, 1996), pp. 221–29.

Ruddin, Lee, P., 'The "Firsts" World War: A history of morale of Liverpudlians as told through letters to Liverpool editors, 1915–1918', *International Journal of Regional and Local History, Vol. 9, No. 2, November 2014*, pp. 79–93.

Runaghan, Patricia, *Father Nugent's Liverpool 1849–1905* (Birkenhead, 2003).

Shannon, Kevin, *The Lion and the Rose: The 4th Battalion the King's Own Royal Lancashire Regiment 1914–1919* (Stroud, 2015).

Sheffield, G.D., *Leadership in the Trenches: Officer-men relations, morale and discipline in the British Army in the era of the First World War* (Hampshire, 2000).

Sheldon, Jack, *The German Army on the Somme, 1914–1916* (Barnsley, 2005).

Simkins, Peter, *Kitchener's Army: The raising of the new armies 1914–1916* (Barnsley, 2007 edn.).

Simmonds, Alan, G.V., *Britain and World War One* (Oxford, 2012).

Simpson, Keith, 'The Officers', in Ian F. Beckett and Keith Simpson (eds.), *A Nation in Arms* (Barnsley, 2004).

Spiers, Edward, 'The regular army in 1914', in Ian F. Beckett, and Keith Simpson (eds.), *A Nation in Arms: A study of the British army in the First World War* (Barnsley, 2004).

Spoerer, Mark, 'The Mortality of Allied Prisoners of War and Belgian Civilian Deportees in German Custody during the First World War: A Reappraisal of the effects of Forced Labour', *Population Studies, 60,2* (2006), pp. 121–36.

Steadman, Michael, *Guillemont: Somme* (Barnsley, 2012 edn.).

Steel, Nigel and Peter Hart, *Passchendaele: The sacrificial ground* (London, 2000).

Strachan, Hew, *The First World War volume 1: To arms* (Oxford, 2001).

Swift, Roger and Sheridan Gilley (eds.), *The Irish in Britain 1815–1939* (Maryland, 1989).

Threlfall, T. R., *The Story of the King's Liverpool Regiment* (London, 1916).

Till, Geoffrey, 'Passchendaele: the maritime dimension, in Peter H. Liddle (ed.) *Passchendaele in Perspective: The third Battle of Ypres* (Barnsley, 1997), pp. 73–101.

Vandiver, Frank, V., 'Field Marshall Haig at Passchendaele', in Peter Liddle (ed.) *Passchendaele in Perspective: The Third Battle of Ypres* (Barnsley, 1997), pp. 30–58.

Wainwright, David, *Liverpool Gentlemen: A history of Liverpool College* (London, 1960).

Walker, R.W. and Chris Buckland, *Citations of the Distinguished Conduct Medal, 1914–1920. 4 sections* (Uckfield, 2007).

Waller, P.J., *Democracy and Sectarianism: A political and social history of Liverpool 1868–1939* (Liverpool, 1981).

Ward, Stephen, *The War Generation* (London, 1975).

Watson, Alexander, *Enduring the Great War: Combat, morale and collapse in the German and British armies, 1914–1918* (Cambridge, 2008).

Wauchope, Piers, *Patrick Sarsfield and the Williamite War* (Dublin, 2009).

Welch, David, *Germany and Propaganda in World War I: Pacifism, Mobilization and Total War* (London, 2000).

Westlake, Ray, *The Volunteer Infantry* (London, 1992).

Wheatley, Michael, *Nationalism and the Irish Party: Provincial Ireland 1910–1916* (Oxford, 2005).

Whitehead, Ian, *Doctors in the Great War* (Barnsley, 1999).

Whitehead, Ian, 'Not a doctor's work? The role of the British regimental medical officer in the field', in Hugh Cecil and Peter Liddle (eds.), *Facing Armageddon* (London, 1996), pp. 466–74.

Williams, John, *The Home Fronts: Britain, France and Germany 1914–1918* (London, 1972).

Winter, Denis, *Death's Men: Soldiers of the Great War* (London, 1979).

Winter, Jay, *Sites of Memory, Sites of Mourning: The Great War in European cultural history* (Cambridge, 1995).

Wyrall, Everard, *The History of the King's Regiment (Liverpool)*, vols. 1–3 (London, 1928–35).

Yarnell, John, *Barbed Wire Disease: British & German Prisoners of War, 1914–19* (Stroud, 2011).

UNPUBLISHED THESES

Papworth, J.D., 'The Liverpool Irish, 1841–71', unpublished PhD, University of Liverpool, 1982.

Jones, Simon, 'Fenianism in the Liverpool Irish Rifle Volunteers', unpublished MA thesis, University of Liverpool, 1997.

ENDNOTES

Introduction

1 John Belchem, *Irish, Catholic and Scouse: The history of the Liverpool Irish, 1800–1939* (Liverpool, 2007), p.1.

2 See Tony Lane, *Liverpool, gateway of empire* (London, 1987).

3 John Belchem, *Merseypride: Essays in Liverpool exceptionalism* (Liverpool, 2006), p. 101.

4 *Report of the Register General of Births, Deaths and Marriages, for the quarter ended 30 September 1847.*

5 Don Akenson, *An Irish History of Civilization: Volume two* (London, 2006), p. 77. Unencumbered by footnotes, or any other mandatory scholarly requisites for that matter, this is a highly entertaining work. Many sacred Irish heroes have been slain and are now turning in their graves.

6 Frank Neal, *Sectarian Violence: The Liverpool Experience 1819–1914* (Liverpool, 2003), p. 1.

7 See for example, Roy Foster, *Paddy and Mr Punch: Connections in Irish and English history* (London, 1993), pp. 281–305.

8 Frank Neal, *Sectarian Violence*, pp. 89–90.

9 An address by Frank Neal, *The Great Hunger Commemoration Service. St. Anthony's church, Scotland Road, Liverpool, Friday 3 October 1997* (Liverpool, 2005), p. 4.

10 Ibid.

11 *Report of the Register General of Births, Deaths and Marriages, for the quarter ended 30 September 1847.*

12 David Fitzpatrick, 'A curious middle place: The Irish in Britain 1871–1921', in Roger Swift and Sheridan Gilley (eds.) *The Irish in Britain 1815–1939* (Maryland, 1989), pp. 11–59, p. 11.

13 Mervyn Busteed, 'Little islands of Erin: Irish settlement and identity in Mid-Nineteenth century Manchester' p. 113 in Donald M. MacRaild (ed.), *The Great Famine and Beyond: Irish Migrants in Britain in the Nineteenth and Twentieth centuries* (Dublin, 2000), pp 94–127; Roy Foster, *Modern Ireland 1600–1972* (London, 1988), p. 345.

14 John Belchem, *Irish Catholic and Scouse*, p. 13.

15 Colin G. Pooley, 'Segregation or integration? The residential experience of the Irish in mid-Victorian Britain', p. 67, in Roger Swift and Sheridan Gilley (eds.) *The Irish in Britain 1815–1939* (Maryland, 1989), pp 60–83.

16 Frank Neal, *Sectarian Violence: The Liverpool experience 1819–1914* (Manchester, 1988), p. 11.

17 Ibid., p. 10.

18 Michael Macilwee, *The Liverpool Underworld: Crime in the city 1750–1900* (Liverpool, 2011), p. 61.

19   Neal, *Sectarian Violence*, p. 109.

20   *Liverpool Mercury*, 1 Aug. 1848.

21   Steven Fielding, *Class and Ethnicity: Irish Catholics in England, 1880–1939* (Buckingham, 1993), pp. 8–9.

22   Cited in Neal, *Sectarian Violence*, pp. 114–15; *Liverpool Herald*, 17 Nov. 1855.

23   Fielding, *Class and Ethnicity*, p. 7.

24   For a full description of the groups involved and their activities, see David W. Miller, *Peep O'Day Boys and Defenders: Selected documents on the County Armagh disturbances 1784–96* (Belfast, 1990).

25   Donald MacRaild, *Faith, Fraternity and Fighting: The Orange Order and Irish migrants in northern England, c. 1850–1920* (Liverpool, 2005), pp. 36–7; P. J. Waller, *Democracy and Sectarianism: A political and social history of Liverpool 1868–1939* (Liverpool, 1981), p. 11.

26   Kevin Haddick-Flynn, *Orangeism: The making of a tradition* (Dublin, 1999), p. 205.

27   Ibid.

28   Neal, *Sectarian Violence*, p. 40.

29   Waller, *Democracy and Sectarianism*, p. 11.

30   Neal, *Sectarian Violence*, p. 40.

31   Ibid. McNeile came from a wealthy family and his father had been the Sheriff of Antrim. He graduated from Trinity College Dublin in 1810. Following his time in Liverpool, McNeile went on to serve at Chester; he finished his time in the ministry as Dean of Ripon.

32   MacRaild, *Faith, Fraternity and Fighting*, p. 48.

33   Keith Daniel Roberts, *Liverpool Sectarianism: The rise and demise* (Liverpool, 2017), p. 68.

34   Belchem, *Irish Catholic and Scouse*, p. 18.

35   Roberts, *Liverpool Sectarianism* p. 38.

36   Waller, *Democracy and Sectarianism: A political and social history of Liverpool 1868–1939* (Liverpool, 1981), pp. 24–5.

37   Ibid., pp. 23–4.

38   John Belchem (ed.), *Popular Politics, Riot and Labour: Essays in Liverpool History 1790–1940* (Liverpool, 1992), p. 13.

39   Macilwee, *The Liverpool Underworld*, pp. 59–60.

40   Frank Neal, 'A criminal profile of the Liverpool Irish,' in *Transactions of the Historic Society of Lancashire and Cheshire*, Vol. 140, 1991, pp. 161–99, p. 176.

41   Macilwee, *The Liverpool Underworld*, pp. 118–23.

42   Ian F.W. Beckett, *Riflemen Form: A study of the rifle Volunteer Movement 1859–1908* (Barnsley, 2007). See Chapter 1 for a full discussion of the protracted arguments for and against the Volunteers.

43   Ibid., p.21.

44   *Liverpool Mercury*, 8 Dec. 1859.

45   Ibid.

46   Frank Forde, 'The Liverpool Irish Volunteers', *The Irish Sword, Vol. X*, No. 39. Winter, 1971, pp. 106–23, p. 107.

47   Ibid., 20 Feb. 1846.

48   Forde, 'The Liverpool Irish Volunteers', p. 107.

49   Ibid., p. 108.

50   Belchem, *Irish, Catholic and Scouse*, p. 158.

51   Padraig O Concubhair, '*The Fenians Were Dreadful Men': The 1867 Rising* (Dublin, 2011), pp. 16–17.

52   Ibid.

53   John, E. Archer, *The Monster Evil: Policing and violence in Victorian Liverpool* (Liverpool, 2011), p. 74.

54   Belchem, *Irish, Catholic and Scouse*, p. 163.

55   Ibid.

56   *Liverpool Mercury*, 19 Sep. 1865.

57   Simon Jones, 'Fenianism in the Liverpool Irish Rifle Volunteers', unpublished MA thesis, University of Liverpool, 1997, p. 50.

58   *Liverpool Mercury*, 27 July 1868.

59   Ibid.

60   Quoted in Fearghal McGarry, *The Rising Ireland: Easter 1916* (Oxford, 2011), p. 19.

61   Neal, *Sectarian Violence*, p, 185.

62   John Belchem, *Merseypride: Essays in Liverpool exceptionalism* (Liverpool, 2000), p. 147.

63   Harry Sefton, 'The ghosts of Scotland Road', *The Liverpolitan*, July 1939; For a full account of O'Connor's political life see L. Brady, *T.P. O'Connor and the Liverpool Irish* (London, 1983).

64   Waller, *Democracy and Sectarianism*, p. 31.

65   Sefton, 'The ghosts of Scotland Road'.

66   *Liverpool Review*, 24 May 1884; Forde, 'The Liverpool Irish Volunteers', p. 108.

67   Forde, 'The Liverpool Irish Volunteers', p. 110.

68   Ibid.

69   *Liverpool Daily Post*, 21 June 1897.

70   Donal McCracken, *Forgotten Protest: Ireland and the Anglo-Boer War* (Belfast, 2003), p. 45.

71   Ibid., p. 43.

72   Forde, 'The Liverpool Irish Volunteers', p. 111.

73   *Liverpool Mercury*, 23 Jan. 1900.

74   Ibid.

75   *Liverpool Daily Post*, 17 Feb. 1900.

76   *Liverpool Catholic Herald*, 15 Sep. 1899.

77   Quoted in Belchem, *Irish, Catholic and Scouse*, p. 207; *Liverpool Catholic Herald*, 24 Nov., and 15 Dec. 1899, and 9 Feb. 1900. The much-vaunted Irish Brigade, led by Major John McBride (later husband of Maud Gone and participant in the Easter Rising, he was executed in 1916), was not large enough to be called a 'brigade'. According to Donal McCracken, estimates as to its strength vary from 140 to a highly inflated 3,000. See McCracken, *Forgotten Protest*, pp. 124–5.

78   *Liverpool Daily Post*, 28 Nov. 1900.

79   *Liverpool Mercury*, 28 Nov. 1900.

80   *Liverpool Daily Post*, 28 Nov. 1900.

81   *Liverpool Mercury*, 28 Nov. 1900. All the Liverpool Irishmen survived; they were, Sergeant McDonnell, Corporal W. Wilson, Privates Beaumont, Brophy, Carroll, Collins, McCormack and Malone; Forde, 'The Liverpool Irish Volunteers', pp. 112–13.

82   F. McDonagh, *The Conservative Party and Anglo-German Relations* (London, 2007), p. 107.

83   Peter Simkins, *Kitchener's Army: The raising of the new armies 1914–1916* (Barnsley, 2007 edn.), p.18.

84   McCartney, *Citizen Soldiers*, p. 71. Edward George Villiers Stanley, 17th Earl of Derby, born 1865, a former soldier, he was also a diplomat and racehorse owner. Served as Under Secretary of State for War under Asquith, he was promoted to Secretary of State for War under Lloyd George in December 1916.

Chapter 1: Liverpool 1914: Division, Recruitment and Unity

1   Arthur Marwick, *The Deluge: British Society and the First World War* (London, 1978), p. 26.
2   Elaine McFarland, 'How the Irish Paid Their Debt': Irish Catholics in Scotland and Voluntary Enlistment, August 1914–July 1915'. *The Scottish Historical Review*, Vol. 82, No. 214, Part 2, Oct. 2003, pp. 261–84.
3   For an extensive assessment of the anti–Home Rule campaigns in Britain see Daniel M. Jackson, *Popular opposition to Irish Home Rule in Edwardian Britain* (Liverpool, 2009). Chapter 2 discusses the opposition to Home Rule in Liverpool.
4   *Evening Express*, 30 Sep. 1912.
5   *Evening Express*, 23 Sep. 1912.
6   *The Times*, 1 Oct. 1912.
7   *Liverpool Courier*, 1 Oct. 1912.
8   *Belfast News Letter*, 1 Oct. 1912; P.J. Waller, *Democracy and Sectarianism,* p. 268.
9   *Evening Express*, 30 Sep. 1912.
10   David Fitzpatrick, 'Militarism in Ireland, 1900–1922'. In Thomas Bartlett & Keith Jeffery (eds.), *A Military History of Ireland* (Cambridge, 1996), pp. 379–406, p. 383.
11   Timothy Bowman, *Carson's Army: The Ulster Volunteer Force 1910–1922* (Manchester, 2007), p. 22.
12   *Freeman's Journal*, 26 Nov. 1913. For an in-depth account of the formation and development of the Irish Volunteers, see F.X. Martin (ed.), *The Irish Volunteers 1913–1915: Recollections & Documents* (Kildare, 2013 edn.).
13   Bureau of Military History, WS 510, Cathal Brugha Barracks, Dublin, Frank Thornton, Witness Statement, p1.
14   *Freeman's Journal*, 17 Mar. 1914.
15   *Liverpool Catholic Herald*, 28 Mar. 1914; *Freeman's Journal*, 23 Mar. 1914.
16   *Freeman's Journal*, 23 Mar. 1914.
17   *Belfast Weekly News*, 26 Mar. 1914.
18   Bowman, *Carson's Army*, p. 61.
19   *Irish Volunteer*, 28 Mar. 1914.
20   Alvin Jackson, *Home Rule: An Irish History 1800–2000* (Oxford, 2003), pp. 132–4. This figure rose to around 60,000 weapons in 1917; Bowman, *Carson's Army*, p. 179.
21   *Liverpool Echo*, 1 Aug. 1914.
22   Dermot Meleady, *John Redmond: The National Leader* (Kildare, 2014), pp. 296–7.
23   *Liverpool Echo*, 27 July 1914.
24   The UVF had landed and dispersed their weapons without incident and under the gaze of watching RIC officers. No attempt was made to stop or to apprehend the gun-runners. See, Bowman, *Carson's Army,* p. 142. Darrell Figgis, who had purchased the rifles for the INV, was present at the Howth landings and confronted the police arguing that the UVF were openly carrying rifles around in the streets of Belfast and that the INV should be permitted to do likewise in Dublin; *Liverpool Echo*, 27 July 1914.
25   *Freeman's Journal*, 1 Aug. 1914.
26   *Liverpool Courier*, 4 Aug. 1914.
27   O'Mara, *Liverpool Irish Slummy*, p. 128.
28   Ibid. 5 Aug. 1914.
29   Ibid.
30   *Belfast News-Letter*, 21 Sep. 1914; Dennis Gwynne, *Life of John Redmond* (London, 1932), p. 391.

31 Peter Simkins, *Kitchener's Army: The raising of the New Armies 1914–1916* (Barnsley, 2007), p. 14.

32 *Evening Express*, 11Sep. 1914.

33 *Liverpool Echo*, 24 Sep. 1914

34 *Liverpool Echo*, 22 Sep. 1914.

35 *Liverpool Courier*, 7 August 1914.

36 *Liverpool Echo*, 8 Sep. 1914.

37 Adrian Gregory and Senia Paseta (eds.), *Ireland and the Great War: 'A war to unite us all'?* (Manchester, 2002), p. 10.

38 *Xaverian*, Oct. 1914.

39 IWM, Docs: McGuire papers, Misses A. & R., 96/31/1, 11 Oct. 1914. It is debatable whether the children described by Ada McGuire had been deliberately mutilated by German soldiers. However, atrocities including rape and mutilation certainly occurred. See John Horne and Alan Kramer, *German Atrocities 1914: A history of denial* (Yale, 2001).

40 Keith Jeffery (ed.), *An Irish Empire* (Manchester, 1996), p. 1.

41 O'Mara, *Liverpool Irish Slummy*, p. 71.

42 John Horne and Alan Kramer, *German Atrocities* 1914, p. 80.

43 *Liverpool Catholic Herald*, 17 Mar. 1915.

44 For a discussion on Charles Diamond see Joan Allen, '" Keeping the faith": The Catholic press and the preservation of Celtic identity in Britain in the late nineteenth century', in Richard C. Allen and Stephen Regan (eds.), *Irelands of the Mind: Memory and identity in modern Ireland* (Cambridge, 2008), pp. 32–47.

45 *Liverpool Catholic Herald*, 3 Sep. 1914.

46 *Liverpool Catholic Herald*, 12 Sep. 1914. See also; T.M. Kettle, *Poems and Parodies* (Dublin, 1916).

47 Thomas Bartlett & Keith Jeffery (eds.), *A Military History of Ireland*, p. 18.

48 *Liverpool Catholic Herald*, 28 Nov. 1914.

49 Stephen Gwynne, *John Redmond's Last Years* (London, 1919), pp. 397–8.

50 *Evening Express*, 18 Sep. 1914.

51 *Liverpool Catholic Herald*, 10 Oct. 1914.

52 Dennis Gwynne, *The Life of John Redmond* (London, 1932), p. 400.

53 NLI, MS: 15/215/2/A, Redmond papers; T.P. O'Connor to Maurice Bonham Carter, 28 Dec. 1914.

54 Ibid., T.P. O'Connor to John Redmond, 27 Feb. 1914.

55 Ibid., 19 Feb. 1915.

56 Ibid., 27 Feb. 1914.

57 *Liverpool Catholic Herald*, 31 July 1915.

58 *Liverpool Echo*, 11 Sep. 1915.

59 David Fitzpatrick, 'The logic of collective sacrifice: Ireland and the British army, 1914–1918', *Historical Journal*, xxxviii (1995), pp. 1017–30.

60 *Liverpool Catholic Herald*, 10 Oct. 1914.

61 Bureau of Military History, WS 510, Cathal Brugha Barracks, Dublin, Frank Thornton, Witness Statement, p.1.

62 Figures compiled from the *Xaverian* magazine, Dec. 1915. See Appendix 1.

63 *Liverpool Catholic Herald*, 26 June 1915.

64 *Xaverian*, Sep. 1914.

65 *Liverpool Catholic Herald*, 20 Mar. 1914.

66 O'Mara, *Liverpool Irish Slummy*, p. 177.

67 *Liverpool Catholic Herald*, 20 Mar. 1915.

68   T.R. Threlfall, *The Story of the King's Liverpool Regiment* (London, 1916), pp. 169–70.

69   See Appendix 2 for the list containing service details of 100 men of the 8th (Irish) Battalion, King's Liverpool Regiment. There is a noticeable difference among these records. Some of the individual records represent a full account of a soldier's wartime record including disciplinary and medical sheets, while others barely amount to a few pages. Not all records provide information on the soldier's previous employment.

70   *Liverpool Echo*, 7 Jan. 1916.

71   *Liverpool Echo*, 15 Jan. 1916.

72   *Lancashire Daily Post*, 24 Jan. 1916.

73   *Xaverian*, Sep. 1914, p. 117.

74   Ibid.

75   Tomlinson papers. Private George Tomlinson to his family 30 Nov. 1914. I am grateful to Mr Tom Fisher and his family for granting me permission to use George's letters and other family papers.

76   *Whitstable Times and Tankerton Press*, 5 Dec. 1914; Frank Forde, 'The Liverpool Irish volunteers,' *Irish Sword*, Vol. X, No. 39, pp 106–23, Winter, 1971, p. 116.

77   IWM, Docs: 07/8/1 Diary of James Green, 8th Liverpool (Irish) Battalion, King's Liverpool Regiment (Imperial War Museum,). This is a typescript diary and precise dates are not indicated; however, Green is describing his time in Canterbury and Whitstable in the winter of 1914–15.

78   David Lewis (ed.), *Remembrances of Hell: The Great War diary of Writer, Broadcaster and Naturalist Norman Ellison* (Shrewsbury, 1997), p. 22.

79   *Whitstable Times and Tankerton Press*, 5 Dec. 1914.

80   Ibid.

81   Ibid., 16 Dec. 1914.

82   IWM, Docs: 07/8/1, Diary of James Green.

83   *Whitstable Times and Tankerton Press*, 19 Dec. 1914.

84   IWM, Docs: 07/8/1, Diary of James Green.

85   Ibid.

86   *Whitstable Times and Tankerton Press*, 2 Jan. 1914.

87   Ibid.

88   *Whitstable Times and Tankerton Press*, 2 Jan. 1914.

89   Ibid.

90   *Liverpool Echo*, 20 Jan. 1920.

91   *Whitstable Times and Tankerton Press*, 30 Jan 1915.

92   Ibid.

93   IWM, Docs: 07/8/1, Diary of James Green.

94   Ibid.

Chapter 2: Trench Life, Patrols and Raids

1   John Bourne, 'The British working man in arms', pp. 336–52, in, Hugh Cecil and Peter H. Liddle (eds.), *Facing Armageddon: The First World War experienced* (Barnsley, 1996).

2   Correlli Barnett, *The Collapse of British Power* (London, 1972), pp. 422–35.

3   Niall Ferguson, *The Pity of War* (London, 1998), p. 342.

4   IWM, Docs: 6791, Mahon Papers, May 1915, p.5.

5   IWM, Docs: 4041, Papers of Captain M. Hardie, British Army Censors Staff, Dec. 1916.

6   IWM, Docs: 15531, Green Papers, May 1915, p.3.
7   Tomlinson Papers, George Tomlinson to his sister. No date, but May 1915. I am very grateful to Mr Tom Fisher and his family for their permission to use George Tomlinson's correspondence.
8   IWM, Docs: 6791, Mahon Papers, May 1915, p.14.
9   IWM, Docs: 15531, Green Papers, May 1915, p.3.
10   Tomlinson Papers, George Tomlinson to his father, May 1915.
11   *Liverpool Echo*, 9 July 1915. Corporal Percival, 8th (Irish) Battalion, King's Liverpool Regiment to his family.
12   IWM, Docs: 15531, Green Papers, p. 5.
13   IWM, Docs: Mahon Papers, pp. 77–8.
14   Ibid., Aug. 1915, p. 45.
15   *Liverpool Echo*, 16 Oct. 1915.
16   IWM, Docs: 6791, Mahon Papers, p. 20.
17   Ibid., May 1915, p.15.
18   IWM, Docs: 15531 Green Papers, May 1915, p. 4.
19   *Liverpool Echo*, 3 Aug. 1915.
20   Ibid., 8 Nov. 1915
21   *Liverpool Daily Post*, 29 Nov. 1915.
22   *Bootle Times*, 5 Jan. 1917.
23   *Liverpool Echo*, 9 July 1915. Corporal Percival, Liverpool Irish to his family.
24   Ibid., 3 Aug. 1915.
25   IWM, Docs: 6791, Mahon Papers, Aug. 1915, p 49
26   TNA, WO95/2923/1, War Diary, 8th Liverpool (Irish) Battalion, 20 Mar. 1916.
27   IWM, Docs: 6791, Mahon Papers, Mar. 1916, p. 113. Meaning; It is dangerous leaning out.
28   F.W. Brewsher, *The History of the 51st Highland Division, 1914–1918* (Edinburgh, 1921), p. 14.
29   TNA, WO95/2887/1, War Diary, 8th Liverpool (Irish) Battalion, 29 May 1915; IWM, Docs: 6791, Mahon Papers, pp. 12–13. Mahon states that the men had been seen using the grenade as a hammer to drive tent pegs into the ground and had been warned by men in his company of the dangers involved.
30   IWM, Docs: 6791, Mahon Papers, p. 41.
31   Ibid., pp. 92–3.
32   Ibid., pp. 50–1.
33   *Liverpool Echo*, 28 Ar. 1916. 'M' and 'D' is Medicine and Duty, 'F.P.' is Field Punishment
34   IWM, Docs: 4041, Papers of Captain M. Hardie, British Army Censors Staff, Dec. 1917.
35   IWM, Docs: 6791, Mahon papers, Feb. 1916.
36   Ibid.
37   Cyril Falls, *The History of the 36th (Ulster) Division* (London, 1998 edn.), p.71.
38   Paddy Griffith, *Battle Tactics of the Western Front: The British Army's art of attack 1916–1918* (London, 1998), pp. 60–1.
39   Gordon Corrigan, *The Sepoys in the trenches: The Indian Corps on the Western Front 1914–15* (Stroud, 2006), pp. 95–122.
40   Tim Cooke, *At the Sharp End: Canadians fighting the Great War 1914–1916*, Volume One (London, 2007), pp. 291–95.
41   Joanna Bourke, *An Intimate History of Killing: Face to face killing in twentieth century warfare* (London, 2000), p. 73.
42   Harold Spender, *Contemporary Review*, Nov. 1916, p. 567.
43   F.P. Crozier, *A Brass Hat in No Man's Land* (London, 1930), p. 38.
44   *Infantry Training Manual*, 1914.

45   Joanna Bourke, *Dismembering the male: Men's bodies, Britain and the Great War* (London, 1996), pp. 42–43.

46   Ashworth, *Trench Warfare 1914–1918: The live and let live system* (London, 2000), p. 130. Ashworth defines the live and let live system as 'an arrangement whereby antagonists maximised life chances and minimised death chances'.

47   Ashworth, *Trench Warfare 1914–1918*, p. 181.

48   Cyril Falls, *The History of the 36th (Ulster) Division*, p. 72.

49   Terence Denman, *Ireland's Unknown Soldiers: The 16th (Irish) Division in the Great War* (Dublin, 1992), pp. 75–6.

50   Nicholas Perry, *Major General Oliver Nugent and the Ulster Division 1915–1918* (Stroud, 2007), p. 24.

51   PRONI, D/3835/E/2/11, Farnham-Connell Papers, Nugent to his wife, 1 Nov. 1916.

52   IWM, Docs: 6791, Mahon Papers, Nov. 1915, p. 76.

53   Ibid., p. 60.

54   F.W. Bewsher, *The History of the 51st Highland Division, 1914–1918* (Edinburgh, 1921), p. 45.

55   J.O. Coop, *The Story of the 55th (West Lancashire) Division* (Liverpool, 1919), p. 25. The Reverend J.O. Coop, was the Senior Chaplain of the 55th Division.

56   TNA, WO95/2923/1, War Diary, 8th Liverpool (Irish) Battalion, King's Liverpool Regiment, 13 May 1916.

57   *Notes for Infantry Officers on Trench Warfare* (War Office, 1916).

58   Ibid., p. 8.

59   IWM, Docs: 6791, Mahon Papers, 20 Mar. 1916, p. 109.

60   Ibid., Feb. 1916.

61   TNA, WO95/2923/1, War Diary, 8th (Irish) Battalion, King's Liverpool Regiment, 20 Mar. 1916.

62   IWM, Docs: 6791, Mahon Papers, Nov. 1915, p. 108.

63   Ibid. p. 108–9.

64   Ibid., 16/17 Apr. 1916.

65   TNA, WO95/2923/1, War Diary, 8th (Irish) Battalion, King's Liverpool Regiment, 26 May 1916.

66   *Evening Express*, 10 May 1916.

67   Ibid.

68   Ibid.

69   Philip Smith, Unpublished paper (n.d.): 'Research into the lives and H.M. Forces service history of the seventeen old boys of Hartlebury Grammar School who lost their lives in the First World War', pp. 11–13.

70   TNA, W0374/4830, Service Record of Lieutenant Edward Felix Baxter, VC, 8th (Irish) Battalion, King's Liverpool Regiment.

71   *London Gazette*, 26 Sep. 1916.

72   IWM, Docs: 6791, Mahon papers, journal entry, Apr. 1916.

73   Ibid., Mahon to his mother, 21 Apr. 1916.

74   *Liverpool Daily Post*, 5 Oct.1916.

75   While the proposed memorial was never erected in Liverpool, he is commemorated at a recently completed memorial at Blaireville, near Arras in France. The memorial is due to the efforts of Mr David Moore and an unveiling ceremony was organised by Mr Moore, when some of Lieutenant Baxter's relatives, the local Maire and other dignitaries attended. I am grateful to Mr Moore for this information and for photographs of the event. In England, a plaque commemorating the centenary of his death was unveiled at Mary Stevens Park, Stourbridge in April 2016. See *Express & Star*, 20 Apr. 2016.

76 TNA, WO95/2908, War Diary of the 55th Division, Headquarters, 'Special Order of the Day, by Major General Jeudwine', 12 July 1916.

77 TNA, WO95/2923/1, War Diary 8th (Irish) Battalion, King's Liverpool Regiment, 5–6 June 1917.

78 Ibid., 20 July 1917.

79 Ibid., 18 May 1917.

80 *Preston Herald*, 26 May 1917.

81 *Preston Herald*, 26 Jan. 1918.

82 TNA, WO95/2923/1, War Diary, 8th (Irish) Battalion, King's Liverpool Regiment, 2 Aug. 1916. This is an unusual entry for the diary in that it is written in the first person and was signed by Lt. Col. Fagan.

Chapter 3: Officers, Men and Morale

1   Gary Sheffield, *Leadership in the Trenches: Officer-men relations, morale and discipline in the British Army in the era of the First World War* (Hampshire, 2000), pp 187–9.

2   Ian Beckett, *The Great War*, p. 303.

3   Watson, *Enduring the Great War*, pp. 140–1.

4   John Bourne, 'The British working man in arms', p. 342.

5   Beckett, *The Great War*, p. 309.

6   Sheffield, *Leadership*, p. 73.

7   TNA, WO95/2908, War Diary 55th Division, Branches and Services, 'Saluting', 7 Apr. 1916.

8   Sheffield, *The Chief*, p. 143.

9   Sheffield, *Leadership*, p. 61.

10 Sir Frank Fox, *G.H.Q (Montreuil-sur-Mer)*, (London, 1920), p. 179.

11 Christopher Moore-Bick, *Playing the Game: The British junior infantry officer on the Western Front 1914–18* (Solihull, 2011), pp. 20–1; Peter Parker, *The Old Lie: The Great War and the Public-School Ethos* (London, 1987), pp. 16–17.

12 Sheffield, *Leadership*, p. 37.

13 David Wainwright, *Liverpool Gentlemen: A history of Liverpool College* (London, 1960), p. 188.

14 Ibid., p. 204.

15 Keith Simpson, 'The Officers', pp. 65–6. In Ian F. Beckett and Keith Simpson (eds.), *A Nation in Arms* (Barnsley, 2004), pp. 63–98, p. 77.

16 Holmes, *Tommy*, p. xxvi.

17 *Liverpool Echo*, 4 Oct. 1915.

18 *The Times*, 4 Dec. 1914.

19 Wolfson Centre, Birmingham Library: Ms1242/63/9, Sharpe Papers, John Sutton Sharpe to his uncle, 15 Jan. 1915.

20 TNA, WO374/63919, War Service Record of Lieutenant Smitham; Lieutenant Colonel Cooney 8th (Irish) Battalion to Col. Alexander, 5th Battalion King's Liverpool Regiment, 27 Sep. 1910.

21 TNA, WO374/38854, War Service record of Robert Pears Keating.

22 *Bond of Sacrifice*, Volume 11, January–June 1915 (London, 1915), p. 62.

23 *Bond of Sacrifice*, Volume 11, pp. 155–7.

24 Francis Irwin, S.J., *Stonyhurst War Record: A memorial of the part taken by Stonyhurst men in the Great War* (Stonyhurst, 1927), pp. 102–4. A total of 1,012 old boys from Stonyhurst served during the war, 167 of which died or were killed in action, see https://www.jesuit.org.uk. Accessed 5 Jan. 2016.

25   TNA, WO374/24281, War Service Record of Captain Herbert Finegan, 8th (Irish) Battalion, King's Liverpool Regiment. Letter from Captain Finegan's mother to the War Office listing her son's academic achievements in support for her claim to a pension.

26   *Liverpool Catholic Herald*, 26 June 1915.

27   McCartney, *Citizen Soldiers*, pp. 25–56.

28   See *London Gazette*, 5 Dec. 1914; 23 Feb. 1915; 11 Mar. 1915. Lieutenant Mountfield did not want to join the Liverpool Irish, 'that is the one Liverpool Bttn I should object to be in'. See, http://echoesofwar.blogspot.co.uk/2008/07/north-of-ypres, accessed 4 June 2016.

29   TNA, WO374/20555, War service record of Captain Harvey Duder; WO374/21190, War service record of Lieutenant Walter Duncan; WO374/9054, War service record of Lieutenant (later Lieutenant Colonel) George Brighten.

30   For an account of the award of the Military Cross to Captain Bodel and his background, see *Bootle Times*, 5 Jan. 1917; TNA, WO374/50090, War service record of Lieutenant Algernon Kenneth Hastings Neale.

31   *Bootle Times*, 10 Aug. 1917.

32   TNA, WO374/37707, War service record of James Alexander Campbell Johnson. For an obituary of Lieutenant Henry Drake, see; *Bond of Sacrifice*, Volume 11, January–June 1915, p. 133.

33   TNA, WO374/37707, Application for a commission in the war service record of James Alexander Campbell Johnson.

34   Private collection of letters relating to Harry Leech and Laurence Hutchison in possession of the author.

35   TNA, WO374/41464, War service record of Major Harry Leech. Leech's record stated that he was to be gazetted as a 2nd Lieutenant from 16 September 1914 despite his application being dated as 24 September as he had been performing duties at the camp for a week. His form also refers to his nomination to serve with the New Zealanders but that he had since withdrawn from this.

36   TNA, WO374/51472, Service record of Donal Stuart Champion D'Espinassy O'Connell O'Riordan.

37   *Graphic*, 23 Jan. 1904.

38   TNA, WO374/51472, Service record of Donal Stuart Champion D'Espinassy O'Connell O'Riordan. Director of Military Training, Sandhurst College to Mrs M. Champion, 25 Sep. 1914.

39   TNA, WO374/51472, Service record of Donal Stuart Champion D'Espinassy O'Connell O'Riordan. Application by O'Riordan for a commission in the 8th (Irish) Battalion, King's Liverpool Regiment, 24 Nov. 1914.

40   TNA, WO71/483, FGCM of Private Bernard McGeehan, see Lieutenant McCabe's witness statement. Lieutenant Daniel McCabe is commemorated on the Diamond War Memorial Londonderry; TNA, WO374/25711, war service record of James Allison Free. James Free rose to the rank of CSM and went on to win the Military Cross.

41   UCD, P57, Michael Moynihan papers. These papers contain the correspondence between Michael Moynihan, his brother John, other family members and his colleagues. He was particularly close to his brother John and the pair carried on an extensive correspondence after Michael left home to join the civil service. Throughout their correspondence, the pair debated theological, philosophical and contemporary political issues.

42   UCD, P57/109, Michael Moynihan papers, John Power to Michael Moynihan, 26 Apr.
     1916. Michael Moynihan's uncle, John Power wrote: 'I had intended to ask you to resign
     your membership of what you call the "Civil Service Rifles" and I now ask you to do so.'

43   UCD, P57, Michael Moynihan papers. For an example of Michael Moynihan's
     opinions see, P57/105, Michael Moynihan to his brother John, 23 Mar. 1914 when he
     refers to the intransigence of the Ulster Unionists and their hatred of 'the Irish', later
     referring to them as 'sneering Orange scum'.

44   TNA, WO374/49430, War service record of Lieutenant Michael Moynihan.

45   IWM, Docs: 6971, Mahon papers, copy of 'A lecture – by Lieutenant Colonel AHC
     Neale', Canterbury, 4 Dec. 1914.

46   Sheffield, *Leadership*, p. 54.

47   TNA, WO95/2923/1, War Diary, 8th (Irish) Battalion, King's Liverpool Regiment, 17 Dec.
     1917.

48   IWM, Docs: Spargo papers, Lieutenant Willie Spargo to Milly and Arthur, 16 May
     1916.

49   UCD, Moynihan Papers: P57/209, Lieutenant Michael Moynihan to his brother, 21
     Apr. 1917.

50   UCD, Moynihan Papers. P57/215, Lieutenant Michael Moynihan to his brother, 12
     Sep. 1917.

51   IWM, 78/42/1, Diary of Brigadier-General G.T.C. Edwards, 8 Oct. 1916.

52   IWM, Docs: 6791, Mahon Diary, February 1916, pp. 90–1.

53   Sheffield, *Leadership*, p. 105; Watson, *Enduring the Great War*. p. 111.

54   IWM, Docs: 15531, Green papers, p. 5

55   *Liverpool Catholic Herald*, 3 July 1915.

56   Quoted in Irwin, *Stonyhurst War Record*, p. 104.

57   IWM, Docs: 6791, Mahon papers, Private William McCleary, No. 2391, 8th (Irish)
     Battalion, King's Liverpool Regiment, to Captain Mahon's father September 1916

58   Wolfson Centre, Birmingham Library: Ms1242/63/11/1, Sharpe Papers, 'Short
     narrative of the late 2nd Lieutenant J.S. Sharpe of the 8th (Irish) Battalion King's
     Liverpool Regiment'. Letter to the relatives of Lieutenant John Sutton Sharpe from
     Captain Milne, DSO, MO of the Liverpool Irish. Undated, but 1917.

59   Birmingham Library: Ms1242/63/11/1, Sharpe Papers, Captain Milne to relatives of
     Lieutenant John Sutton Sharpe, 1917.

60   TNA, WO95/2923/1, War Diary of 8th (Irish) Battalion, King's Liverpool Regiment, 1
     Aug. 1916.

61   TNA, WO374/61572, War service record of Lieutenant John Sutton Sharp, 8th (Irish)
     Battalion, King's Liverpool Regiment.

62   TNA, WO95/2923/1, War Diary of 8th (Irish) Battalion, King's Liverpool Regiment,
     30 Jan. 1916.

63   Watson, *Enduring the Great War*, p. 65.

64   Tomlinson papers, Private George Tomlinson to his father, 16 Mar. 1916.

65   Wilson collection, newspaper cutting from the *Blackpool Gazette*, undated, but 1916.

66   Ibid.

67   IWM, Docs: Mahon papers, 6791, Diary, 17 Mar. 1916.

68   IWM, Docs: Mahon papers, 6791, Diary, 17 Mar. 1916. Had he wanted to, Harold
     Mahon could claim to be as Irish as some men serving with the battalion, as his father
     had been born in Dublin.

69   *Liverpool Catholic Herald*, 31 July 1915.

70   *Freeman's Journal*, 29 July 1915.

71   *Hansard 5 (Commons), The parliamentary debates, fifth series, House of Commons, 1909–42 (vols i–cccxciii, London, 1909–42)*, H.C. Deb. 26 July 1915, vol 73, col 1969.

72   IWM, Docs: 6791, Mahon papers, Captain Harold Mahon to his mother, 24 Apr. 1916.

73   *Liverpool Catholic Herald*, 30 Oct. 1915.

74   This is somewhat disingenuous. In October 1915, the Liverpool Irish had been at the front for five months, and during this period they had fought at Festubert and accounts of the battle. Individual casualties appeared in the *Liverpool Echo*, 30 June 1915. The Liverpool press continued to report the actions and casualties of the Liverpool Irish throughout the war.

75   TNA, WO95/2920, War diary of 164 Infantry Brigade, Bertram Cubitt, War Office to the Commander in Chief, 23 Aug. 1916.

76   LRO, 356 FIF 54/5, Records of the 55th (West Lancashire) Division, 1914–19. Major General Jeudwine on the adoption of the red rose of Lancashire as a divisional symbol.

77   Sheffield, *Leadership*, p. 95.

78   IWM, Docs: 6791, Mahon papers, 16 February 1916.

79   IWM, Docs: Brigadier-General G.T.G. Edwards papers, 30–31 Aug. 1916.

80   IWM, Docs: 6791, Mahon papers, 31 Oct. 1916.

81   IWM, Docs: 4049, Hardie papers. Papers of Captain M. Hardie, British Army Censors Staff, 'Report on Morale, lll Army', p.10, 1917.

82   IWM, Docs: 6791, Mahon papers, 13 Apr. 1916.

83   Sheffield, *Leadership*, p. 92. Research by David Englander and James Osborne revealed that in June–July 1917, 107,000 men had been without leave for eighteen months, and that more than 403,000 had not seen Blighty in twelve months; 'Jack, Tommy, and Henry Dubb: The Armed Forces and the Working Class', *The Historical Journal*, Volume 21, 1978, pp 593–621, p. 601.

84   IWM, Docs: 15531, Green papers, diary of Private James Green, undated, but 1915, pp. 5–6.

85   IWM, Docs: 6791, Mahon papers, Mahon mentions that the battalion had a few games of football at Aveluy 'which were very enjoyable', 21 Oct. 1915.

86   IWM, Docs: 6791, Mahon papers, 21 Jan. 1916.

87   TNA, WO95/2923/1, War Diary of the 8th (Irish) Battalion, King's Liverpool Regiment, 26 Mar. 1916.

88   IWM, Docs: 6791, Mahon papers, 31 Jan. 1916.

89   IWM, Docs: 6791, Mahon papers, 31 Jan. 1916.

90   McCartney, *Citizen Soldiers*, p. 81.

91   IWM, Docs: 6791, Mahon papers, 24 Feb. 1916.

92   *Liverpool Echo*, 28 Oct. 1916; Wilson Collection, newspaper cutting. The newspaper reported that Lance-Corporal Ellis had been wounded in action on three occasions and that he had been killed in action on 27 September 1916.

93   Stephane Audoin-Rouzeau, 'The French soldier in the trenches', pp. 221–9, in Hugh Cecil and Peter Liddel (eds.), *Facing Armageddon: The First World War experience* (Barnsley, 1996), p. 224; Watson, *Enduring the Great War*, p. 19.

94   IWM, Docs: 84/46/1, Captain M. Hardie, Army Censor, Report on Moral etc. [sic], 25 Aug. 1917.

95   Charles Messenger, *Call to Arms: The British Army 1914–18* (London, 2005), pp. 414–15.

96   Stephen Bull (ed.), *An Officer's Manual of the Western Front 1914–1918* (London, 2008), p. 6.

97   TNA, WO95/2923/1, War diary of the 8th (Irish) Battalion, King's Liverpool Regiment, 7 Mar. 1916.

98   Charles Messenger, *Call to Arms: The British Army 1914–18* (London, 2005), pp. 414–5.

99   Fiona Reed, *Medicine in the First World War Europe: Soldiers, Medics, Pacifists* (London, 2017), pp. 51–53.

100 T.J. Mitchell, and G.M. Smith (eds.), *Official history of the war: medical statistics, casualties and medical services* (London, 1930), pp. 87–90; Ian Beckett, *The Great War*, p. 304. Beckett argues that the British Expeditionary Force's GHQ, 'tended to use the relatively crude indices of the incidence of trench feet, shell shock and crime' as indication of the state of morale.

101 IWM, Docs: 6791, Mahon papers, Nov. 1915.

102 IWM, Docs: 6791, Mahon papers, 21 Feb. 1916.

103 IWM, Docs: 6791, Mahon papers, 24 Feb. 1916.

104 Myles Dungan, *They Shall Not Grow Old: Irish soldiers and the Great War* (Dublin, 1997), p. 82.

105 McCartney, *Citizen Soldiers*, pp. 171–6; Reed, *Medicine*, p. 143.

106 T.J. Mitchell and G.M. Smith (eds.) *Medical Services: Casualties and Medical Statistics of the Great War* (London, 1931), p. 280.

107 Messenger, *Call to Arms*, p. 396.

108 *Statistics of the Military Effort*, p. 660.

109 McCartney, *Citizen Soldiers*, p. 174.

110 LRO, 356 FIF 1/2/3, Records of the 55th (West Lancashire) Division, 1914–19, 'Summary of accidental and self-inflicted casualties since the division has been in the line, February to July 1916'.

111 TNA, WO95/2923/1, War Diary of the 8th (Irish) Battalion, King's Liverpool Regiment, 6 June 1916, 6 July 1916 and 8 July 1916.

112 IWM, Docs: 6791, Mahon papers, 26 Oct. 1915.

113 TNA, WO95/2923/1, War diary of the 8th (Irish) Battalion, King's Liverpool Regiment, 26 June 1917.

114 *Soldiers Died in the Great War*, CD-ROM, Naval and Military Press, 2011, Private Harold Potter, 306281, 8th (Irish) Battalion, King's Liverpool Regiment, CWGC, Quercamps Churchyard, France.

115 Ian Whitehead, *Doctors in the Great War* (Barnsley, 1999), p. 52.

116 Whitehead, *Doctors in the Great War*, p. 223.

117 Englander and Osborne, 'Jack, Tommy and Henry Dubb,' p. 599.

118 IWM, Docs: 6791, Mahon papers, Aug. 1915.

119 Ian Whitehead, 'Not a Doctor's Work? The role of the British regimental medical officer in the field', in Cecil and Liddel (eds.) *Facing Armageddon*, pp. 466–74, p. 471; Holmes, *Tommy*, pp. 468–71.

120 TNA, WO374/47966, Service record of Captain Joseph Ellis Milne, RAMC, 8th (Irish) Battalion, King's Liverpool Regiment.

121 Wellcome Library, RAMC Collection: RAMC/276, Scrap-book by Captain G.H. Colt, Captain Ellis Milne to Captain G.H. Holt, 27 Nov. 1915. The scrapbook also contains suggestions and details regarding the development of a stretcher for use in the trenches.

122 Wellcome Library, RAMC Collection: RAMC/276, Scrap-book by Captain G.H. Colt, Captain Ellis Milne to Captain G.H. Holt, 27 Nov. 1915.

123 *Aberdeen Weekly Journal*, 9 Mar. 1917.

124 IWM, Docs: 6791, Mahon papers, 16 Apr. 1916.

125 *Aberdeen Weekly Journal*, 9 Mar. 1917.

126 *Aberdeen Daily Journal*, 15 Mar. 1917.

127 *London Gazette*, 20 Oct. 1916.

128 *Aberdeen Weekly Journal*, 9 Mar. 1917.

129 TNA, WO95/2923/1, War diary of the 8th (Irish) Battalion, King's Liverpool Regiment, 22 Feb. 1917.

130   *Aberdeen Daily Journal*, 15 Mar. 1917.

131   *Aberdeen Daily Journal*, 6 Mar. 1917.

132   Mabel Desborough Allardyce, *University of Aberdeen Roll of Service in the Great War 1914–1919* (Aberdeen, 1921).

Chapter 4: Discipline and Leadership

1   *Manual of Military Law* (London, 1914; Reprint, 1916), p. 6.

2   K.W., Mitchinson, *The Territorial Force at War, 1914–1916* (London, 2014), p. 15.

3   Sheffield, *Leadership*, p. 11.

4   Ian Beckett, *The Great War* (London, 2007, Second edition), p. 309.

5   Sheffield, *Leadership*, pp. 68–9.

6   TNA, WO95/2923/1, War Diary of 8th (Irish) Battalion, King's Liverpool Regiment, Address by General Stockwell, 16th Infantry Brigade, 3 Aug. 1917.

7   Clive Hughes, 'The new armies', in Ian F.W. Beckett and Keith Simpson (eds.), *A Nation in Arms: The British Army in the First World War* (Barnsley, 2004), pp. 99–125, p. 109.

8   Richard Holmes, *Tommy: The British Soldier on the Western Front 1914–1918* (London, 2005), p. 556.

9   *Xaverian*, Sep. 1914.

10   Holmes, *Tommy*, pp. 556–7.

11   Clive Emsley, *Soldier, Sailor, Beggarman, Thief* (Oxford, 2013), p. 42.

12   Helen McCartney, *Citizen Soldiers: The Liverpool Territorials in the First World War* (Cambridge, 2005), p. 163–4.

13   Holmes, *Tommy*, p. 558.

14   Julian Putkowski & Julian Sykes, *Shot at Dawn: Executions in World War One by authority of the British Army Act* (Barnsley, 2007), pp. 32–3; Gerard Oram, *Worthless Men: Race, eugenics and the death penalty in the British Army during the First World War*, p. 34.

15   TNA, Service Record of Private Francis Egerton Rodden, No. 3727, 8th (Irish) Battalion, King's Liverpool Regiment. Rodden eventually rejoined the battalion in August 1915 in France where he was killed in action on 1 July 1916.

16   Putkowski & Sykes, *Shot at Dawn*, p. 13.

17   TNA, WO95/2887/1, War Diary of 8th (Irish) Battalion, King's Liverpool Regiment, 15 Nov. 1915.

18   Commanding Officers were authorised to use a great deal of discretion in allowing Company Commanders to deal with offences and cases which he, as the CO, might have been expected to hear. See *King's Regulations for the Army 1912* (reprinted with amendments up to 1 August 1914, London, 1914), p. 484. An additional punishment, Field Punishment No.2, was also available, but this was much less humiliating and gruelling affair and entailed unpleasant duties and fatigues.

19   *Manual of Military Law*, (London, 1914), 'Rules for Field Punishment', pp. 721–2. This issued guidance for the application of field punishment under Section 44 of the Army Act.

20   *Statistics of the Military Effort of the British Empire during the Great War* (London, 1922), p. 667.

21   TNA, WO95/2887/1, War Diary of 8th (Irish) Battalion, King's Liverpool Regiment, 25 Nov. 1915.

22   TNA, WO363 Soldiers' Documents, First World War 'Burnt Documents', Service record of Private James Jenkins, No. 2668, 8th (Irish) Battalion, King's Liverpool Regiment. Jenkins may have been enjoying the celebrations following the battalion's raid on the German trenches at Blaireville a few days earlier.

23   Emsley, *Soldier, Sailor, Beggarman, Thief*, p. 64.

24   Holmes, *Tommy*, pp. 358–61.

25   Emsley, *Soldier, Sailor, Beggarman, Thief*, p. 64.

26   TNA, WO32/5460, Question of abolition or retention of Field Punishment No.1.

27   *Illustrated Sunday Herald*, 29 Oct. 1916.

28   *Liverpool Echo*, 30 Oct. 1916.

29   *Liverpool Echo*, 19 Dec. 1916.

30   Cathryn Corns & John Hughes-Wilson, *Blindfold and Alone: British Military executions in the Great War* (London, 2005), pp. 440–1.

31   See William Moore, *The Thin Yellow Line* (London, 1974); Anthony Babington, *For the Sake of Example* (London, 1983); Julian Putkowski and Julian Sykes, *Shot at Dawn* (London, 1989); Gerard Oram, *Worthless Men: Race, eugenics and the death penalty in the British Army during the First World War* (London, 1998).

32   TNA, WO95/2908 War Diary 55th Division, Headquarters, Confidential Memo, 'Courts Martial', 12 June 1916.

33   Ian Beckett, Timothy Bowman and Mark Connelly, *The British Army and The First World War* (Cambridge, 2017), pp. 314–15.

34   Emsley, *Soldier, Sailor*, pp. 20–1; Cathryn Corns, "Shot at dawn': Military executions in the Great War', *The RUSI Journal*, 143:1 (1998), pp. 53–5.

35   Oram, *Death Sentences*, pp. 14–15. By comparison, just forty-six German soldiers were executed during the war. See, Watson, *Enduring the Great War*, p. 58.

36   TNA, WO213/9, Judge Advocate General's Register, 29 June 1916.

37   TNA, WO363 Soldiers' Documents, First World War 'Burnt Documents', Service record of Private John Henry Russell, No. 1921 and 305299, 8th (Irish) Battalion, King's Liverpool Regiment. Fortunately, the surviving service records for British soldiers during the Great War have now been digitised. These are available at http://www.ancestry.co.uk. Accessed, 12 June 2015.

38   TNA, WO71/483, FGCM of Private Joseph Brennan, No. 4567, 30 June 1916.

39   TNA, WO363 Soldiers' Documents, First World War, Service Record of Joseph Brennan, No. 4567, 8th (Irish) Battalion, King's Liverpool Regiment. http://www.ancestry.co.uk. Accessed, 12 June 2015.

40   TNA, WO71/483, FGCM of Private Joseph Brennan, No. 4567, 30 June 1916.

41   TNA, WO71/483, FGCM of Private Joseph Brennan, No. 4567, 30 June 1916.

42   TNA, WO363 Soldiers' Documents, First World War, Conduct Sheet within the Service Record of Joseph Brennan, No. 4567, 8th (Irish) Battalion, King's Liverpool Regiment. http://www.ancestry.co.uk. Accessed, 12 June 2015.

43   TNA, WO71/483, FGCM of Private Joseph Brennan, No. 4567, 30 June 1916.

44   TNA, WO71/483, FGCM of Private Joseph Brennan, No. 4567, 30 June 1916. Having been informed of her son's death, Mrs Clark wrote to the War Office to enquire about her entitlement to a pension. She was informed that, as her son had not made any allotments to her from his pay, that she would not be receiving any funds.

45   TNA, WO71/513, FGCM of Private Bernard McGeehan, No. 2974, 21 Oct. 1916.

46   The title of the county and city of Londonderry/Derry remains polemical. As the city has been referred to as Londonderry in the original sources, I have retained that convention throughout.

47   TNA, WO363 Soldiers' Documents, First World War, Service Record of Bernard McGeehan, No. 2974, 8th (Irish) Battalion, King's Liverpool Regiment. http://www.ancestry.co.uk. Accessed, 12 June 2015.

48   TNA, WO71/513, FGCM of Private Bernard McGeehan, No. 2974, 21 Oct. 1916.

49   TNA, WO71/513, FGCM of Private Bernard McGeehan, No. 2974, 21 Oct. 1916.

50   While the army concerned itself more with the physical health of a recruit rather than his mental capabilities, it is possible that Brennan could have been dismissed under Para 392 (iii), *King's Regulations*, 1912, in that he was 'Not likely to become an efficient soldier'.

51   A local historian of Merseyside during both world wars perhaps overstates Bernard McGeehan's intellect when he states that, 'Today, Bernard would come into the category of special needs; it is clear that he had a form of autism.' See Anthony Hogan, *Merseyside at War* (Stroud, 2014), p. 49. Notwithstanding Private McGeehan's intellectual shortcomings, he did manage to walk some 50 kilometres towards the coast and dodge the military posts on the way. TNA, WO71/513, FGCM of Private Bernard McGeehan, No. 2974, 21 Oct. 1916.

52   Watson, *Enduring the Great War*, pp.147–8.

53   Oram, *Worthless Men*, pp. 60–73.

54   Oram, *Worthless Men*, pp. 72–3.

55   LRO, DER: 17/28/3. Lord Derby to Lieutenant General Sir George MacDononagh, 18 Apr. 1919.

56   McCartney, *Citizen Soldiers*, pp. 184–5. The composition of the Liverpool Irish was much changed by 1918. Casualties sustained at Festubert, the Somme and third Ypres had all taken their toll. Figures for the Somme in August 1916 show that 13 officers and 502 other ranks were missing. See IWM, Docs: 6878, Papers of Brig. Gen. GTG Edwards, p.169. The battalion also received a draft of 290 men from the Manchester Regiment on 16 August 1916, See, TNA, WO95/2923/1, War Diary, 8th Liverpool (Irish) Battalion, 16 Aug 1916. The religious composition of the battalion had also changed by 1918, due in part to conscription. See for example, UCD, Moynihan Papers: P57–217, Lieutenant. Michael Moynihan to his brother, 26 Nov. 1917, 'We have a Catholic Chaplain with the battalion, although the actual number of Catholics is not very great.'

57   Terence Denman, 'The Irish Catholic soldier in the First World War: the "racial environment"', *Irish Historical Studies*, xxvii, No.108 (Nov.1991), pp. 352–65.

58   Given the War Office practice to reinforce battalions with men from other battalions, the introduction of conscription in 1916 and the fact that the 8th (Irish) Battalion had been captured on the Somme in August 1916, it would have been fruitless to offer comparisons beyond 1916.

59   TNA, WO363, Soldiers Documents, War Service Record of John Mulcahey, No. 1940 and 305307, 8th (Irish) Battalion, King's Liverpool Regiment, http://www.ancestry.co.uk. Accessed, 12 June 2015.

60   Sheffield, *Leadership*, p.2.

61   TNA, WO374/37707, Service record of Lieutenant Colonel James Alexander Johnson, 8th (Irish) Battalion, King's Liverpool Regiment.

62   *Globe*, 2 June 1916.

63   TNA, WO374/37707, Lieutenant Colonel Neale to GOC, Western Command, 23 August 1915. Service record of Lieutenant Colonel James Alexander Johnson, 8th (Irish) Battalion, King's Liverpool Regiment.

64   TNA, WO374/37707, see press cutting regarding the trial of Lieutenant Colonel Johnson dated 3 May 1916.

65   TNA, WO374/37707, Lieutenant General William Campbell, Commander in Chief, Western Command to the War Office, 20 May 1916.

66   *Globe*, 2 June 1916.

67   TNA, WO374/37707, Lieutenant Colonel Johnson to the War Office, 3 June 1916.

68   TNA, WO374/37707, Lieutenant. Colonel Johnson to the War Office, 12 Nov. 1916.

69   Ibid.

70   TNA, WO374/37707, 'Report of the death of an officer, Captain J.A.C. Johnson,
      8th (Irish) Battalion King's Liverpool Regiment, attached to 13th Battalion, King's
      Liverpool Regiment'.

Chapter 5: Battlefronts: Givenchy, the Somme and Passchendaele

1   F.W. Bewsher, *The History of the 51st Highland Division, 1914–1918* (Edinburgh, 1921), p. 8.

2   Bewsher, *The History of the 51st Highland Division*, p. 7.

3   Simpkins, *Kitchener's Army*, p. 18.

4   Ibid.

5   Bewsher, *The History of the 51st Highland Division*, p. 5.

6   Ibid.

7   W.N. Nicholson, *Behind the Lines: An account of administrative staff work in the British
      Army, 1914–1918* (Stevenage, 1939), pp. 46–7.

8   Bewsher, *The History of the 51st Highland Division*, p. 8.

9   J.E. Edmonds, *Military Operations, France and Belgium, 1915. Battles of Aubers Ridge,
      Festubert and Loos* (London, 1928), p. 73.

10   TNA, WO95/2844, War Diary of the 51st Division, 'Attack of the 51st Highland
      Division on the Rue D'Overt on 15th and 16th June 1915', 7 June 1915.

11   TNA, WO95/2883/1, War Diary of 154 Infantry Brigade, 'Operational Order No, 10',
      14 June 1915.

12   Robin Prior and Trevor Wilson, *Command on the Western Front: the military career of Sir
      Henry Rawlinson, 1914–18* (Oxford, 1992), p. 97.

13   TNA, WO95/2887, War Diary, 8th (Irish) Battalion, King's Liverpool Regiment, 1
      June 1915; 15 June 1915.

14   TNA, WO95/2844, War Diary 51st Headquarters, Branches and Services General
      Staff: 01/01/1915– 30/06/1916, Operation Order No. 24. By Lieut. General Sir H.S.
      Rawlinson Bt. K.C.B., C.V.O, Commanding IV Army Corps, 7 June 1915.

15   Cited in Bewsher, *The History of the 51st Highland Division*, pp. 18–19.

16   Ibid.

17   IWM, Docs: 6791, Mahon Diary, June 1915.

18   *Liverpool Catholic Herald*, 19 June 1915. Father Walter Stephen Dawes was born in
      Staffordshire and was educated at Ampleforth. During the Boer War he was appointed
      as chaplain of the Connaught Rangers. He was then sent to St Anne's church in
      Liverpool having also spent some time at St Peter's in Seel Street. Following his injury,
      Dawes did not return to the battalion.

19   TNA, WO95/2883/1, War Diary 154th Infantry Brigade, 'Report of Operations of
      154th Infantry Brigade, 15–17 June 1915', Brig. General Hibbert, 23 June 1915.

20   Ibid.

21   IWM, Docs: 6791, Mahon Diary, June 1915.

22   *Liverpool Daily Post and Mercury*, 24 June 1915.

23   Ibid.

24   IWM, Docs: 6791, Mahon Diary, June 1915.

25   *Liverpool Daily Post and Mercury*, 24 June 1915.

26   TNA, WO95/2883/1, War Diary 154th Infantry Brigade, 'Report of Operations of
      154th Infantry Brigade, 15–17 June 1915', Brig. General Hibbert, 23 June 1915.

27   IWM, Docs: 6791, Mahon Diary, June 1915.

28   TNA, WO95/2883/1, War Diary 154th Infantry Brigade, 'Report of Operations of 154th Infantry Brigade, 15–17 June 1915', Brig. General Hibbert, 23 June 1915.

29   *Liverpool Daily Post and Mercury*, 23 June 1915.

30   IWM, Docs: 6791, Mahon Diary, June 1915.

31   Ibid.

32   Ibid.

33   *Liverpool Daily Post and Mercury*, 24 June 1915.

34   TNA, WO95/2883/1, War Diary 154th Infantry Brigade, 'Report of Operations of 154th Infantry Brigade, 15–17 June 1915', Brig. General Hibbert, 23 June 1915.

35   TNA, WO95/2883/1, War Diary 154th Infantry Brigade, 'Casualty Return from 1 June 1915–30 June 1915'.

36   IWM, Docs: 6791, Mahon Diary, June 1915.

37   TNA, WO95/2883/1, War Diary 154th Infantry Brigade, 'Report of Operations of 154th Infantry Brigade, 15–17 June 1915', Brig. General Hibbert, 23 June 1915. Hibbert commended Lieutenant Colonel Campbell Johnson for 'the exercise the most commendable energy' in managing to get his battalion to launch their attack at the appointed time. Lieutenant Downes was praised for supplying the forward troops with ammunition and grenades throughout 15–16 June.

38   *Supplement to the London Gazette*, 5 Aug. 1915; R.W. Walker and Chris Buckland, *Citations of the Distinguished Conduct Medal, 1914–1920*. 4 sections (Uckfield, 2007), p. 285.

39   IWM, Docs: 6791, Mahon Diary, June 1915.

40   Ibid.

41   *Liverpool Daily Post and Mercury*, 24 June 1915.

42   Ibid.

43   Bewsher, *The History of the 51st Highland Division, 1914–1918* (Edinburgh, 1921), p. 23

44   IWM, Docs: 6791, Mahon Diary, Jan. 1916.

45   Coop, *The Story of the 55th (West Lancashire) Division*, p. 34.

46   TNA, WO95/2899 War Diary of the 55th (West Lancashire) Division, 'Memorandum on Training', 7 Jan. 1916.

47   Ibid.

48   Coop, *The Story of the 55th (West Lancashire) Division*, p. 30.

49   Gary Sheffield, *The Chief: Douglas Haig and the British Army* (London, 2011), p. 186.

50   Quoted in Jack Sheldon, *The German Army on the Somme 1914–1916* (Barnsley, 2005), p. 222.

51   Michael Steadman, *Guillemont: Somme* (Barnsley, 2012), p. 62.

52   Prior and Wilson, *Command on the Western Front*, p. 210.

53   Ibid., p. 212.

54   Robin Prior and Trevor Wilson, *Command on the Western Front*, p. 150.

55   The battalions were the 17th, 19th and 20th Battalions, King's Liverpool Regiment.

56   Steadman, *Guillemont*, pp. 69–70.

57   TNA, WO95/2340, War Diary, 2nd Battalion, Royal Scots Fusiliers, 30 July 1916.

58   Ibid., p. 70.

59   Sheffield, *The Chief*, p. 186.

60   Quoted in Prior and Wilson, *Command on the Western Front*, p. 217.

61   Sheffield, *The Chief*, p. 186.

62   Quoted in Prior and Wilson, *Command on the Western Front*, p. 217.

63   TNA, WO95/2900, War Diary of 55th Division, General Staff, 'Narrative of events including operations against Guillemont, from the 25 July to 15 August'. Aug. 1916.

64   Ibid.

65   Ibid.

66   Ibid., 'X111 Corps, Operational Order No. 37', 6 Aug. 1916 at 3.45pm.

67   TNA, WO95/2920, War diary of 164 Infantry Brigade, 'Operational Order No. 49',
     Brigadier-General G.T.G. Edwards, 7 Aug. 1916. No specific time was entered as to
     when this order was issued, except for 'pm'.

68   TNA, WO95/2923, War diary of 8th (Irish) Battalion, 'Brief summary of messages sent
     and received, 7 August and 9 August 1916'. Aug. 1916

69   TNA, WO95/2920, War diary of 164 Infantry Brigade, 'Operational Order No. 49',
     Brigadier-General G.T.G. Edwards, 7 Aug. 1916.

70   Ibid.

71   TNA, WO95/2900, War Diary of 55th Division, General Staff, 'Narrative of events
     including operations against Guillemont, from the 25 July to 15 August'. Aug. 1916.

72   TNA, WO95/2923/1, War Diary 8th (Irish) Battalion, King's Liverpool Regiment,
     'Brief summary of messages sent and received during operations 7/8/16 – 9/8/16'.
     Aug. 1916.

73   Ibid. Confusingly usually referred to as 1/4th Royal Lancaster Regiment within War
     Diaries and ephemera of the 55th Division.

74   Ibid.

75   TNA, WO95/2900, War Diary of 55th Division, General Staff, 'Narrative of events
     including operations against Guillemont, from the 25 July to 15 August'. Aug. 1916.

76   Ibid.

77   Ibid.

78   TNA, WO95/2920, War Diary of 164 Infantry Brigade, 'Operational Order No. 50',
     Brigadier-General G.T.G. Edwards, 8 Aug. 1916.

79   See WO95/2928, War Diary of 165th Infantry Brigade, report of the Commanding
     Officer of the 5th Loyal North Lancashire Regiment, Aug. 1916; WO95/2920, War
     Diary of 164 Infantry Brigade, report of Commanding Officer, 2/5th Lancashire
     Fusiliers, 12 Aug. 1916.

80   TNA, WO95/2923/1, War Diary 8th (Irish) Battalion, Kings Liverpool Regiment,
     Lieutenant Colonel E. A. Fagan, 'Account of Operations 8/9th August; 1/8th
     Liverpool Regiment'. 10 Aug. 1916.

81   Ibid.

82   TNA, WO374/49701, Service record of Captain Ernest Michael Murphy. 8th (Irish)
     Battalion, King's Liverpool Regiment, 'Statement of Captain E.M. Murphy', 6 Feb. 1919.

83   Ibid.

84   Coop, *The Story of the 55th*, p. 34

85   Quoted in Jack Sheldon, *The German Army on the Somme 1914–1916* (Barnsley, 2005),
     p. 246.

86   Ibid., p. 246.

87   Ibid.

88   IWM, Docs: 6878, Diary of Brigadier G.T.G. Edwards, 9 Aug. 1916.

89   Quoted in McCartney, *Citizen Soldiers*, p. 213; IWM, Con Shelf, R.A.S. Macfie to his
     father, 16. Aug. 1916.

90   Ibid., 31 Aug. 1916.

91   *Soldiers Died in the Great War 1914–19,* CD-ROM, Naval and Military Press. Captain
     Meadows from Wavertree had been with the battalion since 1911. His death was
     remembered by a girl in Liverpool; her message was brief and poignant 'My brave
     hero; God alone knows how much I miss him. Maggie', *Liverpool Echo*, 21 Aug. 1916.

92   IWM, Docs: 6791, Mahon papers, Mahon to his mother 18 Aug. 1916.

93   Sir J. Edmonds, *Military Operations: France & Belgium 1917* (London, 1948); Nick Lloyd, *Passchendaele: A New History* (London, 2017), p. 5.

94   Nigel Steel and Peter Hart, *Passchendaele: The sacrificial ground* (London, 2000), p. 29; Lloyd, *Passchendaele*, pp. 37; Geoffrey Till, 'Passchendaele: the maritime dimension', in Peter H. Liddle (ed.) *Passchendaele in Perspective: The third Battle of Ypres* (Barnsley, 1997), pp. 73–101, p. 83.

95   Robin Prior and Trevor Wilson, *Passchendaele: The untold story* (London, 1996), p. 46.

96   Lloyd, *Passchendaele*, p. 40.

97   Prior and Wilson, *Passchendaele*, pp. 50–1.

98   Lloyd, *Passchendaele*, pp. 41–2.

99   Prior and Wilson, *Passchendaele*, p. 57.

100   Two of the mines had failed to detonate.

101   Lloyd, *Passchendaele*, p. 53.

102   Heinz Hagenlücke, 'The German High Command', in Liddle, *Passchendaele in Perspective*, pp. 45–58, p. 50.

103   Prior and Wilson, *Passchendaele*, p. 64.

104   Frank, V. Vandiver, 'Field Marshall Haig at Passchendaele', in Liddle, *Passchendaele in Perspective*, pp. 30–44, p. 35.

105   Prior and Wilson, *Passchendaele*, p. 64.

106   Prior and Wilson, *Passchendaele*, p. 72.

107   The *eingreif* divisions were essentially counter-attacking divisions. However, as Jack Sheldon cautions, the term encapsulates more than this. Sheldon states that the term also includes a sense 'intervening decisively'. See, Sheldon, *The German Army at Passchendaele*, p. xiii.

108   Lloyd, *Passchendaele*, p. 64.

109   Prior and Wilson, *Passchendaele*, p. 72.

110   Lloyd, *Passchendaele*, p. 88.

111   Gordon Corrigan, *Mud, Blood and Poppycock* (London, 2004), p. 353.

112   Lloyd, *Passchendaele*, p. 82.

113   Ibid., p. 91.

114   Prior and Wilson, *Passchendaele*, p. 73.

115   Ibid., p. 86.

116   TNA, WO95/2920, War Diary of 164th Infantry Brigade, 'Order No. 126', 24 July 1917.

117   TNA, WO95/2923/1, War Diary of the 8th (Irish) Battalion, King's Liverpool Regiment, address by Lieutenant Colonel Heath, 29 July 1917.

118   Ibid.

119   Coop, *The Story of the 55th* (West Lancashire) Division, p. 48.

120   Ibid., 'Operational Order No. 108', 27 July 1917.

121   Ibid.

122   TNA, WO95/2920, War Diary of 164th Infantry Brigade, 'Instructions re action of tanks in forthcoming operations', 18 July 1917.

123   TNA, WO95/2921, War Diary of 164th Infantry Brigade Headquarters, 'Operations – 31 July 1917, Narrative', Aug. 1917.

124   TNA, WO95/2923/1, War Diary of the 8th (Irish) Battalion, Lieutenant Rothwell to Lieutenant Colonel Heath, 15 Aug. 1917.

125   Ibid., War Diary of the 8th (Irish) Battalion, 'Narrative of Operations 31/7/17 – 2/8/17', Aug. 1917.

126   Ibid., Captain J.F. Jones to Lieutenant Colonel Heath, undated but Aug. 1917.

127 TNA, WO95/2923/1, War Diary of the 8th (Irish) Battalion, 'Narrative of Operations 31/7/17 – 2/8/17', Aug.1917.

128 Ibid., 'Narrative of Action, 31st July/1st August 1917', Private A. Smith, No. 308250, Aug. 1917.

129 Ibid., 'Narrative of Action, 31st July/1st August 1917', Private T. Gregson, No. 7 Platoon, Aug.1917.

130 Ibid., 'Narrative of Action, 31st July/1st August 1917', Private J. Evans, No. 14 Platoon, Aug.1917.

131 Ibid., 'Narrative of Action, 31st July/1st August 1917', Sergeant Birtwhistle, No. 6 Platoon, B company, Aug. 1917.

132 Ibid., 'Narrative of Action, 31st July/1st August 1917', CSM Cook, A Company, Aug. 1917.

133 Ibid., 'Narrative of Action, 31st July/1st August 1917', Private Cosgrove, A Company, Aug. 1917.

134 Ibid., 'Narrative of Action, 31st July/1st August 1917', Sergeant Fraser, C Company, Aug. 1917.

135 Ibid., 'Narrative of Action, 31st July/1st August 1917', Lance-Corporal Morris, D Company, Aug. 1917.

136 Ibid., 'Narrative of Action, 8th (Irish) Battalion, 31st July/1st August 1917', Aug. 1917.

137 Ibid., 'Narrative of Action, 31st July/1st August 1917', Second Lieutenant Hodson, C Company, Aug. 1917.

138 Ibid., Second Lieutenant Rothwell to Lieutenant Colonel Heath, 15 Aug. 1917. Rothwell had been wounded and was writing from High Street Military Hospital, Manchester.

139 Lloyd, *Passchendaele*, p. 109.

140 TNA, WO95/2923/1, War Diary of the 8th (Irish) Battalion, 'Operational Order No. 108'. 27 July 1917.

141 Ibid. Watson Fans were pleated canvas panels measuring twelve inches in diameter. They were white on one side and dark/neutral on the reverse. They were used by attacking infantrymen in a trench to indicate their position to contact air patrols.

142 TNA, WO95/2923/1, War Diary of the 8th (Irish) Battalion, 'Narrative of Action', CSM Greenwood, Aug. 1917.

143 Ibid., Lieutenant Rothwell to Lieutenant Colonel Heath, 15 Aug. 1917.

144 Ibid., 'Narrative of Action', Private Cosgrove, Aug. 1917.

145 Ibid., 'Special report on the capture of Schuler Farm and the fighting around Wurst Farm', Aug.1917.

146 Ibid., Second Lieutenant Rothwell to Lieutenant Colonel Heath, 15 Aug. 1917.

147 Lloyd, *Passchendaele*, p. 106.

148 TNA, WO95/2923/1, War Diary of the 8th (Irish) Battalion, 'Narrative of Action', Sergeant Birtwhistle, Aug. 1917.

149 Ibid., Private Evans, Aug. 1917.

150 Ibid., Corporal Jones, C Company, Aug. 1917.

151 Ibid., CSM Cook, A Company, Aug. 1917.

152 Ibid., CSM Greenwood, D Company, Aug. 1917.

153 Ibid., Second Lieutenant Hodson, C Company, Aug. 1917.

154 Ibid., Corporal Jones, C Company, Aug. 1917.

155 Ibid., Captain Jones to Lieutenant Colonel Heath. Copy of the letter, undated but Aug. 1917.

156 Ibid.

157 Ibid., 'Narrative of Operations 31/7/17 – 2/8/17', Aug. 1917.

158   Ibid. Lieutenant Colonel Bertram Best-Dunkley died from the wounds he received during the battle and was awarded the Victoria Cross for his actions during the battle. See *London Gazette*, No. 30272, 4 Sep. 1917. He was 26 years old.

159   Ibid., 'Narrative of Operations 31/7/17 – 2/8/17', Aug. 1917.

160   Ibid., 'Special Report on Capture of Schuler Farm and fighting around Wurst Farm', Second Lieutenant Fenn, Aug.1917.

161   Ibid.

162   Ibid.

163   Ibid.

164   Ibid., 'Narrative of Operations 31/7/17–2/8/17', Aug. 1917.

165   Ibid., 'Narrative of Action', Lance-Corporal Morris, Aug. 1917.

166   Ibid., 'Narrative of Action', Second Lieutenant R.B. Hodson, Aug. 1917.

167   Ibid., 'Narrative of Action', Private T. Gregson, Aug. 1917.

168   Ibid., 'Narrative of Action', CSM Greenwood, Aug. 1917.

169   Ibid.

170   Ibid., 'Narrative of Action', Lance-Corporal Morris, Aug. 1917.

171   Ibid., 'Special Order, Lieut. Colonel E.C. Heath', 4 Aug. 1917.

172   Lieutenant Colonel Heath to Miss E. Leech, Liverpool, 12 Aug. 1917. Author's private collection.

173   Major-General Hugh Jeudwine, 55th (West Lancashire) Division to Mr Leech, Liverpool, 6 Sep. 1917. Authors' private collection.

174   Ibid.

175   TNA, WO373/41464, Record of Service, Major Harry Leech, 8th (Irish) Battalion, King's Liverpool Regiment, Private F. Jones to Major Leech's mother, 6 Nov. 1917.

Chapter 6: Kultur and Captivity

1   David Forsythe, *The Humanitarians: The International Committee of the Red Cross* (Cambridge, 2005), p. 15. The lack of medical provision for the wounded in mid-nineteenth-century Europe is demonstrated by the fact that all the major nations provided more veterinarians for horses than doctors for their wounded soldiers.

2   John Yarnall, *Barbed Wire Disease: British & German Prisoners of War, 1914–19*, p. 9.

3   See James Scott Brown (ed.), *The Hague Conventions and Declarations of 1899 and 1907* (Washington, D.C. and Oxford, 1915).

4   L.M. Marshall, *Experiences in German Gaols* (Liverpool, 1915), p.1.

5   Marshall, *Experiences*, p.4.

6   Marshall, *Experiences*, p. 10.

7   Marshall, *Experiences*, p. 42.

8   Heather Jones, *Violence against prisoners of war*, p. 57. This allegation might well have produced some ironic laughter from the British Tommy who existed on a shilling a day.

9   Stefan Goebel, *The Great War in Medieval Memory* (Cambridge, 2007), p. 146.

10   James Scott Brown (ed.), *The Hague Conventions and Declarations of 1899 and 1907* (Washington, D.C. and Oxford, 1915), pp. 108–10.

11   *Liverpool Echo*, 10 Apr. 1915.

12   *Liverpool Echo*, 28 Apr. 1915.

13   Parliamentary Papers, Cd. 8984, Miscellaneous no.3, Report on the Transport of British Prisoners of War to Germany, August to December 1914 (London, 1918). Henceforth, RTBP.

14   Keble Howard, *The Quality of Mercy: How British Prisoners of War were taken to Germany in 1914* (London, 1918).

15   Jones, *Violence*, p. 57.

16   *RTBP*, Captain Beaman, 1914, pp. 8–10.

17   *RTBP*, Sergeant Gilling, Sep. 1914, pp. 42.

18   *RTBP*, Private Dodd, Aug. 1914, p. 32.

19   *RTBP*, Private Arnold, pp. 32–3.

20   R.C. Bond, *Prisoners Grave and Gay* (Edinburgh, 1934), pp. 34–45. Quoted in John Lewis-Stempel, *The War Behind the Wire* (London, 2014), p. 69.

21   Keble Howard, *The Quality of Mercy*, p. 4.

22   *RTBP*, Captain Hargreaves, 1914, p. 12.

23   IWM, PST 2762, Poster by David Wilson, 'Red Cross or Iron Cross?', 1915.

24   Jones, *Violence*, p. 60.

25   Yarnall, *Barbed Wire*, p. 47.

26   See Appendix 3 for a list of those soldiers from the 8th (Irish) Battalion, King's Liverpool Regiment held at Dulmen Prisoner of War Camp following their capture at Guillemont.

27   *Liverpool Echo*, 29 June 1915.

28   *Liverpool Echo*, 14 Aug. 1916.

29   Mark Spoerer, 'The Mortality of Allied Prisoners of War and Belgian Civilian Deportees in German Custody during the First World War: A Reappraisal of the effects of Forced Labour', *Population Studies*, 60,2 (2006), p. 129; Jones, *Violence*, pp. 24–5.

30   Lewis-Stempel, *The War Behind the Wire*, p. 46.

31   TNA, WO161/100/536, Committee on the treatment of British Prisoners of war: Interview and reports, Pte. John Burston, No. 4527, 8th (Irish) Battalion King's Liverpool Regiment.

32   Pte James Slessor. *Stand To! The Journal of the Western Front Association*, 'A memoir by 3367 Pte. James Slessor of the Liverpool Irish (1/8 King's)', No.45, Jan. 1996, p.10. I am grateful to the editor of *Stand To!* The journal of the Western Front Association for permission to quote from this article.

33   TNA, WO161/100/324, Committee on the treatment of British Prisoners of war: Interview and reports, Private Henry Davies, No. 4305, 8th (Irish) Battalion, King's Liverpool Regiment. The interviewer noted his name as Davis, this is incorrect. According to his Medal Index card, his name and number are given as Henry Davies, No. 4305 and 306805, King's Liverpool Regiment. See TNA, WO372/5/188205.

34   James Scott Brown (ed.), *The Hague Conventions*, pp. 108–10.

35   Tammy Proctor, *Civilians in a World War 1914–1918* (New York, 2010), p. 93.

36   Steve R. Dunn, *Blockade: Cruiser warfare and the starvation of Germany in World War One* (Barnsley, 2016), pp. 119, 129. Given the lack of fuel in some camps, prisoners searching for an alternative fuel source discovered that the bread burnt very well. See Lewis-Stempel, *The War Behind the Wire*, p. 89.

37   Christoph Regulski, Klippfisch und Steckrüben. *Die Lebensmittelversorgung der Einwohner Franfurt am Mains im Ersten Weltkrieg 1914–1918* (Frankfurt am Main, 2012), p. 179.

38   Uta Hinz, *Gefangen im Großen Krieg: Kriegsgefangenschaft in Deutschland 1914–1921* (Essen, 2006), pp. 214, 246–7.

39   *Liverpool Echo*, 19 Mar 1915. Some caution is needed here, both the author of the letter and the recipient are unnamed, although the sentiments expressed in the letter tends to corroborate research by Uta Hinz.

40   Watson, *Enduring the Great War*, p. 127.
41   David Welch, *Germany and Propaganda in World War I: Pacifism, Mobilization and Total War* (London, 2000), p. 165; Roger Chickering, *Imperial Germany and the Great War, 1914–1918* (Cambridge 3rd ed., 2014), p. 165.
42   My italics, in 1915 German officials claimed that prisoners received 2,430 calories for those doing no work, while working prisoners received 2,970 calories per day. This does not tally with prisoners' accounts of their meals consisting of coffee twice a day, a portion of bread and some watery soup. See Yarnell, *Barbed Wire Disease*, p. 117.
43   One of the first such committees was established in September 1914 at Armagh, at the depot of the Royal Irish Fusiliers. See Colin Cousins, *Armagh and the Great War* (Dublin, 2011), p. 80.
44   *Liverpool Daily Post and Mercury*, 1 Jul. 1915.
45   Lewis-Stempel, *The War Behind the Wire*, p. 90.
46   Yarnall, *Barbed Wire Disease*, p. 108.
47   *Liverpool Echo*, 26 Sep 1916.
48   TNA, WO161/100/536, Committee on the treatment of British Prisoners of war: Interview and reports, Pte. John Burston, No. 4527, 8th (Irish) Battalion King's Liverpool Regiment.
49   *Liverpool Echo*, 27 Sep. 1916.
50   *Liverpool Daily Post and Echo*, 27 Sep. 1915.
51   Advert for British American Tobacco, *Liverpool Echo*, 26 Nov. 1915.
52   http://www.redcross.org.uk/Food-parcels-for-prisoners-of-war.
53   Lewis-Stempel, *The War behind the Wire*, p. 77.
54   Richard van Emden, *Prisoners of the Kaiser: The last POW's of the Great War* (Barnsley, 2009), pp. 75–6.
55   Australian War Memorial, P05901.011, Photograph of Private W. Lambert, No. 2621, at Schneidenmuhl Camp, 24 Se. 1917. Private Lambert lived at Essex Street, Preston. I am grateful to the Australian War Memorial for their kind permission to reproduce this photograph.
56   Photographs of malnourished and emaciated British prisoners of war were taken after their return to England. See for example, IWM, Q31278, Private Finch, 9th Loyal North Lancashire Regiment and IWM, Q31277, Private Veitch, 5th Yorkshire Regiment.
57   Jones, *Violence*, p. 11.
58   Lewis-Stempel, *The War Behind the Wire*, p, 70.
59   Yarnall, *Barbed Wire Disease*, p. 123;
60   TNA, WO161/100/536, Committee on the treatment of British Prisoners of war: Interview and reports, Pte. John Burston, No. 4527, 8th (Irish) Battalion King's Liverpool Regiment.
61   TNA, WO161/96/70, Committee on the treatment of British Prisoners of war: Interview and reports, Lieutenant Walter Duncan, 8th (Irish) Battalion King's Liverpool Regiment, 20 Feb. 1918; Lieutenant Walter Duncan, *How I escaped from Germany* (Liverpool, 1919), p. xxi. He had been writing an account of his escape with the intention of having it published; however, he fell victim to the influenza epidemic of 1918 and died on 19 December 1918. The book was completed and published by his family.
62   Lewis-Stempel, *The War Behind the Wire*, pp. 71–2.
63   Duncan, *How I Escaped*, p. 15.
64   Jones, *Violence*, p. 54; *RTBP*, 1918.

65   Duncan, *How I Escaped*, p. 15.
66   Duncan, *How I Escaped*, p. 21.
67   Duncan, *How I Escaped*, pp. 32–3.
68   Duncan, *How I Escaped*, p. 50.
69   Duncan, *How I Escaped*, p. 66.
70   Duncan, *How I Escaped*, p. 69.
71   TNA, WO161/96/70, Committee on the treatment of British Prisoners of war: Interview and reports, Lieutenant Walter Duncan, 8th (Irish) Battalion King's Liverpool Regiment, 20 Feb. 1918.
72   TNA, WO161/100/536, Committee on the treatment of British Prisoners of war: Interview and reports, Pte. John Burston, No. 4527, 8th (Irish) Battalion King's Liverpool Regiment.
73   Lewis-Stempel, *The War Behind the Wire*, p. 96.
74   TNA, WO161/96/70, Committee on the treatment of British Prisoners of war: Interview and reports, Lieutenant Walter Duncan, 8th (Irish) Battalion King's Liverpool Regiment, 20 Feb. 1918.
75   TNA, WO161/96/70, Committee on the treatment of British Prisoners of war: Interview and reports, Lieutenant Walter Duncan, 8th (Irish) Battalion King's Liverpool Regiment, 20 Feb. 1918.
76   Pte James Slessor. *Stand To! The Journal of the Western Front Association*, 'A memoir by 3367 Pte. James Slessor of the Liverpool Irish (1/8 King's)', No.45, Jan.. 1996, p.10.
77   Pte James Slessor. *Stand To! The Journal of the Western Front Association*, 'A memoir by 3367 Pte. James Slessor of the Liverpool Irish (1/8 King's)', No.15, Jan. 1996, p.10.
78   Pte James Slessor. *Stand To! The Journal of the Western Front Association*, 'A memoir by 3367 Pte. James Slessor of the Liverpool Irish (1/8 King's)', No.45, Jan. 1996, p.10.
79   Pte James Slessor. *Stand To! The Journal of the Western Front Association*, 'A memoir by 3367 Pte. James Slessor of the Liverpool Irish (1/8 King's)', No.45, Jan. 1996, p.10.
80   Craddock is referring to Private David Foley, No. 307021, 8th (Irish) Battalion King's Liverpool Regiment, died 10 June 1917. Pte. Foley died aged 21, he was from Mount Stewart, Cappoquin, Co. Waterford. He is buried at Cologne CWGC in southern Germany. His mother had his headstone inscribed with the words 'In loving memory of his soul sweet Jesus have mercy'.
81   TNA, WO161/100/324, Committee on the treatment of British Prisoners of war: Interview and reports, Private Henry Davies, No. 4305, 8th (Irish) Battalion, King's Liverpool Regiment.
82   TNA, WO161/100/324, Committee on the treatment of British Prisoners of war: Interview and reports, Private Henry Davies, No. 4305, 8th (Irish) Battalion, King's Liverpool Regiment. The interviewer noted his name as Davis; this is incorrect. According to his Medal Index card, his name and number are given as Henry Davies, No. 4305 and 306805, King's Liverpool Regiment. See TNA, WO372/5/188205.
83   TNA, WO161/100/324, Committee on the treatment of British Prisoners of war: Interview and reports, Private Henry Davies, No. 4305, 8th (Irish) Battalion, King's Liverpool Regiment.
84   TNA, WO161/100/324, Committee on the treatment of British Prisoners of war: Interview and reports, Private Henry Davies, No. 4305, 8th (Irish) Battalion, King's Liverpool Regiment.
85   IWM, Docs: 14181, Spargo papers, Lieutenant Willie Spargo, 8th (Irish) Battalion, King's Liverpool regiment to his mother, 29 Aug. 1916.

86   The internment of prisoners of war had been suggested by the Pope in 1915. While the French and Germans agreed to the scheme whereby partially incapacitated prisoners could be interned in Switzerland, the British objected due to the likelihood of escape. The British Foreign Office eventually overruled the War Office and Britain joined the scheme. Prisoners were regarded as being on parole and the costs of their stay were borne by their respective governments. See Yarnall, *Barbed Wire Disease*, pp. 155–59.

87   IWM, Docs: 14181, Spargo papers, Lieutenant Willie Spargo to his sister, 16 Dec.1916.

88   Ibid., Lieutenant Willie Spargo to his mother, 7 Jan.1917.

89   Ibid., Lieutenant Willie Spargo to May, 19 Jan. 1917.

90   *Liverpool Echo*, 2 Aug. 1914.

91   Duncan, *How I Escaped from Germany*, pp. 88–9.

92   Duncan, *How I Escaped from Germany*, p. 89.

93   TNA, WO161/96/70, Committee on the treatment of British Prisoners of war: Interview and reports, Lieutenant Walter Duncan, 8th (Irish) Battalion King's Liverpool Regiment, 20 Feb. 1918.

94   Duncan, *How I Escaped from Germany*, p. 90.

95   TNA, WO161/96/70, Committee on the treatment of British Prisoners of war: Interview and reports, Lieutenant Walter Duncan, 8th (Irish) Battalion King's Liverpool Regiment, 20 Feb. 1918.

96   Duncan, *How I Escaped from Germany*, p. 92.

97   TNA, WO161/96/70, Committee on the treatment of British Prisoners of war: Interview and reports, Lieutenant Walter Duncan, 8th (Irish) Battalion King's Liverpool Regiment, 20 Feb. 1918.

98   Duncan, *How I Escaped from Germany*, p. 107.

99   Ibid.

100   See the Forward in Lieutenant Walter Duncan, *How I Escaped from Germany*.

101   Pte James Slessor. *Stand To! The Journal of the Western Front Association*, 'A memoir by 3367 Pte. James Slessor of the Liverpool Irish (1/8 King's)', No.45, Jan. 1996, p.10.

102   R 51812, Prisoners of the First World War Archives, International Committee of the Red Cross (ICRC).

103   Desmond Morton, *Silent Battles: Canadian Prisoners of War in Germany, 1914–1919* (Toronto, 1992), p. 151; Lewis Stempel, *The War Behind the Wire*, p. 283.

104   Lieutenant Walter Duncan, *How I Escaped from Germany*, p. xxi.

Chapter 7: Homefront

1   Niall Ferguson, *The Pity of War* (London, 1998), p. 212.

2   Caitriona Pennell, *A Kingdom United: Popular responses to the outbreak of the First World War in Britain and Ireland* (Oxford, 2014), p. 119.

3   P. Knightly, *The First Casualty: The War Correspondent as Hero, Propagandist and Myth-maker from the Crimea to Viet*nam (London, 1973), p. 109.

4   Michael Finn, 'Local heroes: war news and the construction of 'community' in Britain, 1914 – 18', *Historical Research*, vol. 83, no. 22 (August 2010), pp. 520–38.

5   See Michael Finn, 'The realities of war', *History Today*, vol. 52 (2002), pp. 25–31.

6   *Liverpool Echo*, 28 June 1915.

7   *Liverpool Daily Post and Mercury*, 25 May 1915.

8   *Liverpool Echo*, 30 June 1915.

9   See Appendix.

10   *Liverpool Catholic Herald*, 3 July 1915.

11   Patrick Sarsfield, later 1st Earl of Lucan, was an Irish Jacobite soldier who remained loyal to James II and fought during the Williamite Wars and later on the Continent. See, Piers Wauchope, *Patrick Sarsfield and the Williamite War* (Dublin, 2009).

12   *Liverpool Catholic Herald*, 3 July 1915.

13   *Liverpool Daily Post and Mercury*, 17 July 1915.

14   *Reports by the Joint War Committee and the Joint War Finance Committee of the British Red Cross Society and the Order of St. John of Jerusalem in England on Voluntary Aid rendered to the sick and Wounded at Home and Abroad and to Prisoners of War, 1914–1919* (London, 1921), p. 640.

15   IWM, Docs: 96/31/1, McGuire papers, Ada McGuire to her sister, 28 Aug. 1914.

16   Cited in Pennell, *A Kingdom United,* p. 123.

17   *Liverpool Echo*, 29 Sep. 1915.

18   *Liverpool Catholic Herald*, 3 July 1915.

19   *Liverpool Echo*, 2 Aug. 1915.

20   *Liverpool Echo*, 20 Sep. 1915.

21   *Liverpool Echo*, 27 Dec. 1915.

22   *Liverpool Echo*, 4 Aug. 1915.

23   IWM, Docs: 15531, Green Papers, May 1916, p.6.

24   O'Mara, *Irish Slummy*, p. 174.

25   Ibid.

26   Alan G.V. Simmonds, *Britain and World War One* (Oxford, 2012), p. 243.

27   For example, see advertisements for cinemas and theatres in *Liverpool Courier*, 29 Aug. 1916. The subject of the impact of the *Battle of the Somme* film on the Liverpool public is discussed in Lee P., Ruddin, 'The "Firsts" World War: A history of morale of Liverpudlians as told through letters to Liverpool editors, 1915–1918', *International Journal of Regional and Local History*, Vol. 9, No. 2, November 2014, pp. 79–93.

28   *Liverpool Echo*, 18 Sep. 1916.

29   Stephen McGreal, *Liverpool in the Great War* (Barnsley, 2014), p. 78.

30   *Xaverian,* Dec. 1914.

31   McCartney, *Citizen Soldiers*, p. 136. To illustrate the oversupply of comforts received by some of the men, McCartney cites the case of a Sergeant who felt compelled to donate his clothing parcel to regular soldiers of a neighbouring battalion rather than to his own men who did not need it.

32   *Liverpool Daily Post and Mercury*, 2 July 1915.

33   *Liverpool Echo*, 22 July 1915.

34   *Xaverian,* Aug. 1915.

35   *Liverpool Echo*, 9 Sep. 1915.

36   *Liverpool Daily Post and Mercury*, 8 Feb. 1916.

37   *Liverpool Daily Post and Mercury*, 16 Sep. 1915.

38   *Weekly Freeman's Journal*, 2 Oct. 1915.

39   *Whitstable Times and Tankerton Press*, 2 Oct. 1915.

40   Ibid., 12 Feb. 1916.

41   Ibid., 27 May 1916.

42   *Liverpool Echo*, 24 May 1916.

43   *Liverpool Daily Post and Mercury*, 25 Sep. 1916.

44   Ibid.

45   *Liverpool Echo*, 17 Mar. 1916.

46   *Liverpool Echo*, 18 Sep. 1916.

47   *Liverpool Catholic Herald*, 24 Mar. 1917.

48   Ibid., 16 June 1917.
49   *Liverpool Daily Post and Mercury*, 27 Nov. 1917.
50   *Liverpool Courier*, 27 Apr 1920 Part LXVII (67).
51   Liverpool Record Office, M364 CMC/54, Annual accounts of the Lord Mayor's Million Shilling Fund. (Henceforth, LRO)
52   Davies, Sam, "'A stormy political career": P.J. Kelly and Irish Nationalist and Labour politics in Liverpool, 1891–1936', *Transactions of the Historic Society of Lancashire and Cheshire*, 148, 1999, pp. 147–90, pp. 164–5.
53   Ibid.
54   O'Mara, *Irish Slummy*, p. 204.
55   Ibid., p. 205.
56   *Liverpool Daily Post and Mercury*, 10 May 1915.
57   *Liverpool Echo*, 12 May 1915.
58   *Liverpool Catholic Herald*, 15 May 1915.
59   *Liverpool Catholic Herald*, 15 May 1915.
60   *Liverpool Courier*, 11 May 1915.
61   O'Mara, *Irish Slummy*, pp. 206–7.
62   *Liverpool Daily Post and Mercury*, 11 May 1915.
63   *Liverpool Echo*, 15 May 1915.
64   *Liverpool Daily Post and Mercury*, 1 June 1915.
65   *Liverpool Echo*, 6 Nov. 1915.
66   Michael Wheatley, *Nationalism and the Irish Party: Provincial Ireland 1910–1916* (Oxford, 2005), p. 231.
67   *Liverpool Echo*, 6 Nov. 1915.
68   *Liverpool Daily Post and Mercury*, 8 Nov. 1915.
69   *Liverpool Catholic Herald*, 13 Nov. 1915.
70   BMH, WS797, Statement of Michael O'Laoghaire, 9 Feb. 1953.
71   BMH, WS357, Statement of Joe Gleeson, 13 Apr. 1950.
72   NLI, Collection List No. 44: Piaras Béaslaí Papers, Biographical note compiled by Marie Coleman.
73   BMH, WS357, Statement of Joe Gleeson, 13 Apr. 1950, p.7.
74   BMH, WS510, Statement of Frank Thornton, 18 May 1951, p. 3.
75   Ibid., pp. 6–7.
76   *Irish Independent*, 24 Apr. 1952. An article written by Béaslaí describing how he delivered the cypher to Liverpool.
77   BMH, WS510, Statement of Frank Thornton, 18 May 1951, pp. 4–5.
78   Ibid., pp. 6–7.
79   *Irish Independent*, 2 Aug. 1914.
80   Foster, *Vivid Faces*, p. iv.
81   *Liverpool Echo*, 29 Apr. 1916.
82   *Evening Express*, 5 May 1916.
83   *Evening Express*, 5 May 1916.
84   Denman, *Ireland's Unknown Soldiers*, p. 144.

INDEX

Page numbers in *italics* indicate a photograph

Aachen 191, 192
absentism 114, 125, 198, 199–200
Akenson, Don 15
Allenby, General 113, 114
Ancient Order of Hibernians (AOH) 28, 29, 38
armistice 148, 193, 206
Army Act (1914) 98, 107, 109
Arras 62, 63, 155
Ashworth, Tony 60
Aspinall, Private William 193
Aubers Ridge, battle of 135
Augustabad prison camp 184, 185
Authuille 61, 97, 107
Bannatine-Allason, Major General R. 133
Baxter, Second Lieutenant Edward Felix, V.C.
    63, 64, 66–7, 68, *90, 91*
Béaslaí, Piaras (Percy Frederick Beasley) 211, 212
Beckett, Ian 72, 105, 109
Belchem, John 20
Benson, Major 197
Benzin 185–6
Best-Dunkley, Lieutenant 163
Bidwell, Captain P.S. 21
Birtwhistle, Sergeant 158, 162
Blaireville 63, 65 (map), 80, 91, 142
Blatchford, Robert 108
Bodel, Captain 55, 163, 164, 165 (map)
Boer War 24–5, 26, 74, 76, 195
Bourke, Joanna 59
Bourne, John 51, 72
Bowman, Timothy 29
Brennan, Private Joseph (aka William E. Clark)
    110, 111–15, *122*, 124, 125
Bridgewater, Major 113, 114
brigades:
    154th Infantry Brigade 79, 133, 140
    164th Infantry Brigade 94, 95, 105, 146,
    148, 149 (map), 156, 157
    165th Infantry Brigade 149, 156–7
    166th Infantry Brigade 156, 157
Britt, Sergeant 55
Brown, Lieutenant George 75
Bull, Stephen 97
Burston, Private John 174–5, 177, 184, 186
Byrne, Colonel Myles Emmet 32, 36
Cambrai prison camp 175, 184
Campbell, Lieutenant General William 131
Canning, Private 116
Carr, CQMS *118*
Carson, Sir Edward 27–8
Casement, Sir Roger 30, 214
Cassel prison camp 175
Catholic Defence Association 29
Catholic Defenders 19
Catholic Emancipation Act, 1829 18
censorship 44–5, 52, 64, 95, 151, 195
Central Prisoners of War Help Committee
    (CPWHC) 177
Chamberlin, Captain 93, 102, 103
Churchill, Winston 33
Civic Service League 177, 178
Civil Service Rifles 78, 79, *120*
Clark, William E. 113, 115, *122. See also*
    Brennan, Private Joseph
Cochrane, Lieutenant Colonel 142
Connolly, Lawrence 23
Connor, Corporal 198
Cook, CSM 158, 162
Cook, Private 96, 188
Cosgrove, Private 158, 161
court martial 98, 106
    District Court Martial 106, 107
    Field General Court Martial (FGCM) 98,
    107, 108, 109–110, 124–5, 127, 128
        Private Russell 110
        Private Joseph Brennan 111–114
        Private McGeehan 116–17
Craddock, Private Charles 188
Cuddy, Lance-Corporal E. J., 38, *87*, 140
Daley, James E. 44
Davies, Private Henry 175, 188–9, *190*
Davies, Sam 206
Derby, Lord 21, 26, 127, 209
deserters. *See* absentees
Diamond, Charles 35
Dickinson, Lieutenant 164

Divisions:
  36th Ulster Division 60
  51st Highland Division 56, 61, 79, 102, 131,
    133, 134, 141
  55th (West Lancashire) Division 62, 65
    (map), 79, 94, 99, 141, 143, 152, 159 (map)
  Scotland Division 23, 38, 39–40
Downes, Lieutenant Herbert Laidlaw *86*, 140
Drake, Lieutenant Henry Mackey 76, 80, *86*,
  139–40
Dublin Fusiliers 35, 36, 191, 198
Duder, Captain Harvey 44, 45, 76, 158, 204
Dülmen prison camp 175, 177, *182*, 184, 186
Duncan, Lieutenant Walter 71, 76, *181*, 184–6,
  187, 190–3, 194
Easter Rising 213–14
Edmonds, Sir James 153
Edwards, Brigadier-General G.T.G. 67, 79,
  94–5, 114, 146, 148, 151, 152
Evans, Private J. 158, 162
executions 108–9, *123*, 125–7
Fagan, Lieutenant Colonel Edward Arthur 71,
  91, 94, 97, 147, 148
Faulkner, Captain 21
Fenians 22, 23
Fenn, Second Lieutenant J.E. 161, 163–4, 166
Ferguson, Niall 195
Festubert, battle of 37, 38, 54–5, 79, 80, 82, *87*,
  93, 135
  reaction at home 196, 197, 198
FGCM (Field General Courts Martial). *See
  under* court martial
Field Punishment No. 1 107, 108, 111, 112,
  113, 114, 115, *122*
Fielding, Steven 18
Finegan, Captain Herbert Marion 75, 76, 80,
  86, 140, 197
Finn, Michael 196
firing squad 56, 73, 109, 113, 125
Fisher, Lieutenant 71, 100, 152
Fitzpatrick, David 28, 38
Fletcher, Private John 70–1
Flynn, Colonel D. Edgar 93
Fokker Farm 162, 163
Foley, Private 188
Forde, Frank 24
Fraser, Sergeant Samuel *119*, 160
Free, Lieutenant James Allison 77, *119*
Gaelic Athletic League 29, 211
Gallwitz, General Max von 143
Gavin, Lance-Corporal 114
George, Lloyd 195
Gheluvelt 154–5
Gheluvelt-Langemarck line 156
Ginchy 116, 143, 145, 150
Givenchy 133–41

Gleeson, Joe 211, 112
Goebel, Stefan 170
Gough, Sir Hubert 154, 155, 156
Green, Private James 46–8, 50, 52, 53, 55, 80,
  95–6, 200
Greenwood, CSM 160, 161, 162, 164
Gregson, Private 158
Griffith, Paddy 58
Guillemont 71, 81, 142–53, 154, 173, 174, 175, 201
Hagenlücke, Heinz 154
Hague Conventions 168, 170, 173, 175, 176
Haig, Sir Douglas 60, 73, 108, 135, 143, 145,
  151–2, 153–5
Haldane, W.B. 26, 32
Harford, Alderman Austin 29, 30, 38–9, 202–3,
  205, 213, 214
Hargreaves, Captain 172
Harper, Major General George 131–2
Heath, Lieutenant Colonel Edward Charles *92*,
  119, 127, 156–7, 166
Henry, Private George 196
Hibbert, Brigadier-General/General *86*, 133,
  135, 138, 139, 140, 141
Hickie, General William 60
Hindu Cott 158, 160
Hinz, Uta 176
Hodson, Second Lieutenant 160, 162, 164, 166
Home Rule 21, 27–9, 31, 34, 39
Hopkins, Gerard Manley 20
Howard, Keble 171, 172
Hutchison, Laurence 76–7
Ingolstadt prison camp 186, 191
Irish Brigade. *See* 64th (Irish) Volunteers *under*
  Volunteer Forces
Irish Guards 197, 198
Irish National Foresters 29
Irish National Volunteers (INV) 28, 29, 30,
  31–2, 38
Irish Parliamentary Party (IPP) 37, 49, 93, 211,
  213, 214
Irish Republican Brotherhood (IRB) 22, 23,
  28, 38, 211, 212
Irish Transvaal Committee 24, 25
Iron Cross 70
Jackson, Captain 100
Jeffery, Keith 34
Jenkins, Private James 107, *119*
Jeudwine, Major-General H.S. 69, 73, 94, 95,
  156, 166
Johnson, Lieutenant Colonel James Alexander
  Campbell 76, 130–2, 138, 140, 141
Jones, Captain John Fitzgerald 157, 162, 163, 166
Jones, Corporal E. *87*, 162
Jones, Heather 172
Jones, Private F. 166–7
Jones, Simon 22

Kaudy, Charles Joseph 45
Keating, Captain Richard Pears *121*, 204
Keating, Lieutenant 75
Kettle, Professor Tom 30, 35
Kitchener, Lord 36, 37, 171, 200
Knight, Sir Arnold 21
Lambert, Private 179, *180*
Landbeck, Major 151
Law, Sergeant 116
Leech, Major Harry 63, 76–7, 124, 127, 114
    at Pilckem Ridge 157, 162–3, 164, 165,
    166–7
Limrick, Captain Paul Osborne 63, 64, *89*
Liverpool Celtic Literary Society 25
Liverpool Irish Ladies Committee 203
Liverpool Protestant Association 19
Liverpool Workingmen's Conservative
    Association 27, 205–6
Lloyd, Nick 161
Logan, Newton W. 44
Long, Private 57, 138, 139, 141
Lossberg, Colonel von 155
Ludwigshafen prison camp 187, 191, 192
Lusitania 184, 206, 207, 209
MacCabe, Lieutenant Daniel 77, 80, 124
MacCartney, Helen 76, 98, 127–8, 202
MacCleary, Private William 80–1
McClelland, Sergeant 64, 66
McGeehan, Private Bernard 110, 115–16, *123*
    (execution order),124–5
McGrisken, Patrick 209
McGuire, Ada 34, 197–8
McIvor, William 197–8
McNeile, Rev. Mr Hugh 19
MacRaild, Donald 19
Mahon, Captain Harold 76, 80, *88*, 100–101,
    102, 138, 139–41, 152
    in the trenches 51–2, 53–5, 56, 57, 58
    morale and leadership 93, 94, 95, 96, 98
    patrolling and raiding 61, 62, 63, 64, 67–8
Marshall, L.M. 169–70
Meadows, Captain 58, 63, 148, 152
Messines 60, 153–5
Milne, Captain Joseph Ellis 81–2, 102–103, *120*
mobilisation 45–6
Morris, Lance-Corporal 160, 164
Moser, Generalleutunant Otto von 150, 151
Moynihan, Lieutenant Michael 77–8 79, *120*
Mulcahy, Private 129
Murphy, Captain Ernest 138, 140, 148–9, 150, 204
Murphy, Private 47, 69
Neal, Frank 16, 17, 19
Neale, Lieutenant Colonel Algernon Kenneth
    Hastings Campbell 49–50, 76, 77, 78, 80,
    130, 131, 136
Neuve Chapelle 59, 134, 135

Nichols, Signaller 55, 56
No Man's Land 53, 55, 97, 167
    Givenchy 136, 139
    Guillemont 144, 145, 146, 147, 148
    and trench raids 60, 61, 62, 63, 64, 67, 70
Nugent, Major-General Oliver 60
O'Connor, John, MP 30
O'Connor, Thomas Power 23, 93, 177–8, 204, 214
    and recruitment 27, 28–9, 30, 32–3, 34, 37, 38
O'Mara, Pat 31, 34, 39, 200, 206, 208
O'Riordan, Donal Stuart Champion
    D'Espinassy O'Connell 77
O'Rourke, Private Jim 54, *118*
OCB. *See* Officer Cadet Battalions
Officer Cadet Battalions (OCB) 78, 79
Officer Training Corps (OTC) 74, 78
Oram, Gerard 110, 126, 127
Orange Order 18, 19; Liverpool 27
Orangeism 19–20, 78, 207
Orchard, Lieutenant 158, 163
OTC. *See* Officer Training Corps
'Paddy' 18, 35–6
Parchim prison camp 186
Parsons, General Sir Lawrence 36, 37
Passchendaele 153–67
patriotism 28, 33, 34–5, 72, 101, 173, 195–6,
    203, 210
Peep O'Day boys 19
Percival, Corporal 53, 55–6
Pereira, Brigadier-General George 60
Pilckem Ridge 105, 153–67
Plumer, Sir Herbert 153–5
Pond Farm 161, 162, 163
Potter, Private Harold 101
Powell, Private 58, 62
Prior, Robin 154
prisoner-of-war camps 173, 174, 187, 189, 190,
    191. *See also specific camp names*
prisoners of war 166, 168–79, 186, 188–90,
    194, 205, 206
Rawlinson, Lieutenant General Sir Henry
    135–6, 143, 144–5, 151, 152, 154
recruitment 21, 31–3 34–5, 36–45, 46, 54, 73,
    83, 94, 104–105, 124, 125, 209–10, 211
Red Cross 168, 172, 177, 178–9
Redmond, John, MP 27, 31–3, 36, 38, 49, 93,
    209, 213
regiments:
    1/4th (King's Own) Royal Lancashire
    Regiment 116, 133, 147, 157
    1/4th (King's Own) Royal Lancaster
    Regiment 146, 147–8, 152, 153
    1/4th Loyal North Lancashire Regiment
    96, 99–100, 114, 116
        Givenchy 133, 135, 136, 138
        Guillemont 146, 152, 153

1/5th Seaforth Highlanders 136
2/5th Lancashire Fusiliers 100, 114, 133, 148
        Pilckem Ridge 157, 158, 162–3, 164, 166
1/6th Scottish Rifles 135, 136, 138, 141
6th Connaught Rangers 60
18th Manchester Regiment 81
Bedfordshire Regiment
        1st Battalion 114, 130
King's (Liverpool) Regiment
        1st Battalion 146, 147
        5th (Irish) Battalion 24–5, 26
        6th Liverpool Rifles 61, 127
        8th (Irish) Battalion 67, 75, 78, 93,
110, 127, 152, 196, 199, 204
                photographs *83, 84, 85, 87, 90, 117, 182*
                recruitment 31, 32, 37, 38, 39, 41–3
        13th Battalion 129, 132
King's Liverpool Rifles
        5th Battalion 31
        7th Battalion 31
Munster Fusiliers 198
Royal Regiment of Scotland
        1/7th Black Watch 138, 140, 158
Riley, Captain 70
Roberts, Lord 26, 74
Roberts, Private J. 110, 111
Rodden, Private Francis Egerton 106–107
Rothwell, Lieutenant 157, 160–1
Royal Army Medical Corps (RAMC) 101,
        102, 129
Royal Engineers 67, 115, 116, 138, 140
Royal Flying Corps (RFC) 161
Royal Irish Rifles 24, 59, 174
Royal Scots Fusiliers 144, 151
Rue D'Ouvert 135, 137 (map)
Russell, Private John 110–11
Ryan, Father 48–9
St Francis Xavier 38, 40
        Catholic Church 20, 33, 46, 202
        School 38, 45, 106, 211
Salvidge, Sir Archibald 27, 205, 206
Sandhurst 74, 77
Schuler Farm 157, 158, 160, 161, 162, 163, 164,
        165 (map), 166
self-inflicted wounds/injuries 44, 98–100
Sharpe, Lieutenant John Sutton 74–5, 81–2, 152
Sheffield, Gary 74, 105
Shewan, Major 191
Slessor, Private James 175, *180*, 187–8, 193
Smith, Captain 47, 48, 49
Smith, F.E., MP 27, 28, 33
Smith, Major J. J. 50, 115, 203, 203–204, 207

Smitham, Lieutenant John 75
Somme 60, 158, 201, 206
        Guillemont 142–53, 154
        Somme Farm 161, 162
South Lancashire Regiment 31, 99, 100
Spargo, Lieutenant Willie 78–9, 189–90
Spoerer, Mark 174
Spree Farm 162, 163
Stockwell, Brigadier-General 105, 124, 156
Stonyhurst College 75
Sumner, Private 107
Sweeney, Private William 199
Thompson, John 47, 55, 80
Thornton, Frank 28, 38, 211, 212
Threlfall, T.R. 40
Tomlinson, Private George 46, 52, 53, 82, *85*
Toms, Lieutenant 158, 163
training:
        Canterbury 46–7, 48, 50, 107, 133
        Weeton 111–12, 198
        Whitstable 46, 47–8, 49–50, 133, 203
trench foot 97
Ulster Volunteer Force (UVF) 28, 29–30
United Irish League (UIL) 28, 36–7, 38,
        211, 213
Utting, Sir John 205
Vaughan, Father Bernard 35, 204
Victoria Cross 67, 68, 80
Volunteer Forces
        12th Liverpool Artillery Volunteers 22, 23
        18th Lancashire Volunteers (Liverpool Irish) 24
        18th Liverpool Rifle Volunteers 75
        64th (Irish) Volunteers (Irish Brigade) 21–3,
        24, 28, 32, 36, 49
        64th Liverpool Rifle Volunteers 75
volunteers, civilian 202
Waldron, Sergeant 116
Ward, Captain 71, 163
Watkins, Private Stanley 44
Watson, Alexander 72
West Lancashire Territorial Association 26, 127
Whitehead, Lieutenant 69
Wilson, A.J.A. 103
Wilson, Trevor 154
Wimbourne, Lord 209
Wise, Pastor George 27, 28
Wittenberg prison camp 170, 171
Wülfrath prison camp 175, 177
Wurst Farm 158, 161, 162, 163, 164, 165 (map)
Yaag, Mr 208
Ypres 59, 69, 103, 116, 153, 154, 155
zero hour 144, 146, 154, 156, 157